Fodor's 2009

D0089546

SAN DIEGO

Where to Stay and Eat for All Budgets

Must-See Sights and Local Secrets

Ratings You Can Trust

Fodor's Travel Publications   New York, Toronto, London, Sydney, Auckland
www.fodors.com

FODOR'S SAN DIEGO 2009

Editor: Molly Moker

Editorial Contributor: Paul Eisenberg
Writers: Maria C. Hunt, Marlise Elizabeth Kast, Tanja Kern, Amanda Knoles, Coco Krumme, Jane Onstott, AnnaMaria Stephens, Bobbi Zane

Editorial Production: Astrid deRidder
Maps & Illustrations: David Lindroth, *cartographer*; Bob Blake and Rebecca Baer, *map editors;* William Wu, *information graphics*
Design: Fabrizio LaRocca, *creative director*; Guido Caroti, Siobhan O'Hare, *art directors*; Tina Malaney, Chie Ushio, Ann McBride, Jessica Walsh, *designers*; Melanie Marin, *senior picture editor;* Moon Sun Kim, *cover designer*
Cover Photo (SeaWorld): Wolfgang Kaehler
Production/Manufacturing: Angela L. McLean

COPYRIGHT

ISBN 978-1-4000-0703-5

ISSN 1053-5950

SPECIAL SALES

This book is available at special discounts for bulk purchases for sales promotions or premiums. Special editions, including personalized covers, excerpts of existing books, and corporate imprints, can be created in large quantities for special needs. For more information, write to Special Markets/Premium Sales, 1745 Broadway, MD 6-2, New York, New York 10019, or e-mail specialmarkets@randomhouse.com.

AN IMPORTANT TIP & AN INVITATION

Although all prices, opening times, and other details in this book are based on information supplied to us at press time, changes occur all the time in the travel world, and Fodor's cannot accept responsibility for facts that become outdated or for inadvertent errors or omissions. So **always confirm information when it matters,** especially if you're making a detour to visit a specific place. Your experiences—positive and negative—matter to us. If we have missed or misstated something, **please write to us.** We follow up on all suggestions. Contact the San Diego editor at editors@fodors.com or c/o Fodor's at 1745 Broadway, New York, NY 10019.

PRINTED IN THE UNITED STATES OF AMERICA

10 9 8 7 6 5 4 3 2 1

Be a Fodor's Correspondent

Your opinion matters. It matters to us. It matters to your fellow Fodor's travelers, too. And we'd like to hear it. In fact, we need to hear it.

When you share your experiences and opinions, you become an active member of the Fodor's community. That means we'll not only use your feedback to make our books better, but we'll publish your names and comments whenever possible. Throughout our guides, look for "Word of Mouth," excerpts of your unvarnished feedback.

Here's how you can help improve Fodor's for all of us.

Tell us when we're right. We rely on local writers to give you an insider's perspective. But our writers and staff editors—who are the best in the business—depend on you. Your positive feedback is a vote to renew our recommendations for the next edition.

Tell us when we're wrong. We're proud that we update most of our guides every year. But we're not perfect. Things change. Hotels cut services. Museums change hours. Charming cafés lose charm. If our writer didn't quite capture the essence of a place, tell us how you'd do it differently. If any of our descriptions are inaccurate or inadequate, we'll incorporate your changes in the next edition and will correct factual errors at fodors.com immediately.

Tell us what to include. You probably have had fantastic travel experiences that aren't yet in Fodor's. Why not share them with a community of like-minded travelers? Maybe you chanced upon a beach or bistro or B&B that you don't want to keep to yourself. Tell us why we should include it. And share your discoveries and experiences with everyone directly at fodors.com. Your input may lead us to add a new listing or highlight a place we cover with a "Highly Recommended" star or with our highest rating, "Fodor's Choice."

Give us your opinion instantly at our feedback center at www.fodors.com/feedback. You may also e-mail editors@fodors.com with the subject line "San Diego Editor." Or send your nominations, comments, and complaints by mail to San Diego Editor, Fodor's, 1745 Broadway, New York, NY 10019.

You and travelers like you are the heart of the Fodor's community. Make our community richer by sharing your experiences. Be a Fodor's correspondent.

Happy traveling!

Tim Jarrell, Publisher

CONTENTS

MAPS

ABOUT THIS BOOK

Our Ratings

Sometimes you find terrific travel experiences and sometimes they just find you. But usually the burden is on you to select the right combination of experiences. That's where our ratings come in.

As travelers we've all discovered a place so wonderful that its worthiness is obvious. And sometimes that place is so unique that superlatives don't do it justice: you just have to be there to know. These sights, properties, and experiences get our highest rating, **Fodor's Choice**, indicated by orange stars throughout this book.

Black stars highlight sights and properties we deem **Highly Recommended**, places that our writers, editors, and readers praise again and again for consistency and excellence.

By default, there's another category: any place we include in this book is by definition worth your time, unless we say otherwise. And we will.

Disagree with any of our choices? Care to nominate a place or suggest that we rate one more highly? Visit our feedback center at www.fodors.com/feedback.

Budget Well

Hotel and restaurant price categories from ¢ to $$$$ are defined in each chapter. For attractions, we always give standard adult admission fees; reductions are usually available for children, students, and senior citizens. Want to pay with plastic? **AE, D, DC, MC, V** following restaurant and hotel listings indicate whether American Express, Discover, Diners Club, MasterCard, and Visa are accepted.

Restaurants

Unless we state otherwise, restaurants are open for lunch and dinner daily. We mention dress only when there's a specific requirement and reservations only when they're essential or not accepted—it's always best to book ahead.

Hotels

Hotels have private bath, phone, TV, and air-conditioning and operate on the European Plan (aka EP, meaning without meals), unless we specify that they use the Continental Plan (CP, with a Continental breakfast), Breakfast Plan (BP, with a full breakfast), or Modified American Plan (MAP, with breakfast and dinner) or are all-inclusive (AI, including all meals and most activi-

ties). We always list facilities but not whether you'll be charged an extra fee to use them, so when pricing accommodations, find out what's included.

Many Listings	
★	Fodor's Choice
★	Highly recommended
⊠	Physical address
⊹	Directions
🕮	Mailing address
☎	Telephone
🖷	Fax
⊕	On the Web
✉	E-mail
🎫	Admission fee
☉	Open/closed times
Ⓜ	Metro stations
🖃	Credit cards
Hotels & Restaurants	
🏨	Hotel
🛏	Number of rooms
☖	Facilities
Ⅹ	Meal plans
✕	Restaurant
☚	Reservations
↘	Smoking
🍸	BYOB
✕🏨	Hotel with restaurant that warrants a visit
Outdoors	
🏌	Golf
⛺	Camping
Other	
℃	Family-friendly
⇨	See also
⊠	Branch address
☞	Take note

WHAT'S WHERE

BALBOA PARK	Even without the most alluring and impressive collection of museums and cultural institutions on the West Coast, and one of the world's most incredible zoos, leafy—and enormous—Balboa Park would qualify unequivocally as spectacular. It's San Diego's green lung. It's the city's arts mecca. And from this 1,200-acre patch of lush greenery, it's easy to reach all of the city's core neighborhoods of interest. You can't understand San Diego without at least a quick drive, or better yet a leisurely stroll or bike ride, through the dynamic park, which sits at the geographic heart of the city, just northeast of downtown. You could spend a couple of hours here every day for a month and never run out of museums and attractions to explore and paths to wander. In short, before turning your attention to the rest of San Diego, pay a visit here.
CORONADO	Historic Coronado, an islandlike peninsula across the bay from San Diego's waterfront, came of age as a Victorian resort community during the late 19th century, developed around the ornate Hotel Del Coronado, which to this day remains a favorite haunt of celebs, A-listers, and—well—ghosts (if you believe the stories). You reach this dignified, graceful community either via the San Diego–Coronado Bridge or the San Diego–Coronado Ferry. By ordinance, no two houses here share the same building plan. Wealthy suburbanites and the Coronado naval base, which includes the Naval Air Station North Island and the Naval Amphibious Base Coronado, also make their home here. Boutiques and restaurants line Orange Avenue, and you can catch some rays and splash in the surf at Silver Strand State Beach and Imperial Beach, which extend in a long arc to the south.
DOWNTOWN	As recently as two decades ago, downtown offered an uninviting mix of bland office towers and seedy sidewalks after sundown. Luckily, preservationists and entrepreneurs saved the day, starting with Horton Plaza, a unique six-block shopping and dining complex. Flashy restaurants, nightclubs, hotels, and boutiques have filled in all around it, and continue to do so. Now ornate old buildings blend seamlessly with sleek contemporary skyscrapers, giving a nostalgic glimpse of bygone eras but reminding everyone how far urban San Diego has come. The streets of the Gaslamp Quarter swarm year-round with locals and tourists. In 2004 Petco Park—home to baseball's Padres—scored a home run with its debut in adjacent East Village, upping the downtown ante even more.

Also notable is Seaport Village, a 14-acre waterfront shopping plaza designed to reflect the early architectural styles of California, and the Embarcadero, a sprawling and beautifully landscaped public park. Nearby, historic Little Italy has also become a desirable urban center for the young and upwardly mobile. High-rise condos and hip boutiques mix with Italian shops and eateries—listen closely and you'll hear some old-timers gossiping in their native tongue.

HARBOR & SHELTER ISLANDS AND POINT LOMA	A man-made strip of land in the bay directly across from the airport and a short drive from downtown, Harbor Island has several hotels and restaurants and makes a good base for a San Diego visit. You'll find a few more hotels and restaurants on Shelter Island, just west of Harbor Island and known for its yacht-building and sportfishing industries. From either locale, you're smack in the middle of the bay, with unsurpassed views of the downtown skyline in one direction and Coronado in the other. Standing as a buffer against the temperamental Pacific Ocean, Point Loma curves almost crescentlike along San Diego Bay and extends south into the sea. Beyond its main drags, which contain a few too many fast-food restaurants and budget motels, Point Loma contains several well-to-do neighborhoods and bayside estates (it's a favorite retirement spot for naval officers). Ocean and downtown views abound, making it a pleasant place to catch a sunset.
LA JOLLA	There may not be a more charmed setting in San Diego County than luxe, bluff-top La Jolla, which—fittingly—means "the jewel" in Spanish. Artsy and upscale, the village abounds with showcase Spanish Colonial and Mediterranean Revival homes. Posh inns, boutiques, and restaurants on or near the main thoroughfare, Prospect Street, cater to the affluent local gentry, but a surprising number of mid-range options please visitors on tighter budgets. Fortunately, the largely unspoiled scenery of its coast, coves, and verdant hillsides is still free. Although it feels like a separate entity, La Jolla is officially a section of the city of San Diego—it sits at the top of the city's string of beach neighborhoods, immediately north of Pacific Beach.
MISSION BAY & THE BEACHES	The coastal and unabashedly commercial Mission Bay area, a 15-minute drive northwest of downtown, sits between the airport and La Jolla. At its fringes are the lively

WHAT'S WHERE

	Mission Beach, Ocean Beach, and Pacific Beach communities, which are rife with surf shops, ice-cream stands, and beach bars. Just inland, Mission Bay is home to one of Southern California's leading attractions, SeaWorld, but the area also serves as a 4,600-acre aquatic park teeming with scenic coves, crystalline beaches, and plenty of great turf for boating, jet skiing, sunning, running, swimming, and fishing. Terrestrial types can jog, bike, Rollerblade, play basketball, or fly a kite on the bay's peninsulas and two main islands, Vacation Island and Fiesta Island.
MISSION VALLEY	Every city needs an area like Mission Valley, even if it lacks history and charm. This stretch of modern commercial development along the I–8 corridor contains dozens of cookie-cutter chain hotels in all price ranges, plus myriad glass-and-steel office towers, soulless condos, big-box stores, and brand-name shops at megamalls like the Fashion Valley shopping center and Westfield Mission Valley. Hotel Circle holds the bulk of the area's lodging options; football's San Diego Chargers play at nearby Qualcomm Stadium.
OLD TOWN	Although it could take the better part of a day to fully experience this tourist-driven area a few miles north of downtown, at least set aside a couple of hours to explore the remnants of San Diego's—and California's—first permanent European settlement. The former pueblo of San Diego is now preserved as a state historic park and contains several original and reconstructed buildings, along with a handful of Mexican restaurants, souvenir stands, and art galleries. The historic sites are clustered around Old Town Plaza, which you can explore easily on foot.
UPTOWN	Loosely known as Uptown (though rarely called that by locals), the trendy neighborhoods of Hillcrest, Mission Hills, North Park, and University Heights don't depend on San Diego's tourist trade for survival—all the more reason to explore them. Go a bit off the beaten path and you'll find stylish eateries, charming cafés, happening bars and clubs, and loads of niche-interest boutiques and shops. Hillcrest, the heart of the city's gay and lesbian community, caters to an upscale crowd. University Heights, especially along Park Boulevard, is a gay- and straight-friendly extension of Hillcrest, with cafés, bars, and restaurants aplenty. Mission Hills, which overlooks Old Town and the San Diego Bay, is primarily

residential, but offers stellar sightseeing for architecture fiends; look for lovingly preserved Craftsmans and some of the coolest mid-century modern homes in the county. North Park, to the east of Balboa Park, is a hip and eclectic enclave of shopping, nightlife, and art galleries. A serious community effort has revitalized the once skuzzy neighborhood.

COASTAL SAN DIEGO NORTH COUNTY	The seaside towns north of La Jolla developed separately from San Diego and from one another. Along the ocean, Del Mar contains posh golf and spa resorts, exclusive boutiques, and fancy restaurants. Small and mellow Solana Beach has evolved into a hip art and design center rife with home-furnishings shops. Head to Encinitas for its fabulous fields of flowers and gardens, but make sure to head toward the coast, too, where you'll find an authentic surf town that's home to old-timers and wishful groms (newbies in surf-speak) alike—it's about as romantically Southern Californian as you can get. Carlsbad, once known for its healing waters, now lures families to LEGOLAND California, and Oceanside shows off its harbor and Mission San Luis Rey. It's easiest to reach the area via Interstate 5, but take slower Route S21 (old U.S. 101) to get a good feel for each of the communities—you're certain to see something worth stopping for.
INTERIOR SAN DIEGO COUNTY	Inland valleys, mountains, and the vast Anza-Borrego Desert comprise more than half the land of San Diego County. Great golf, a clutch of casinos, and rural charms mark the valleys in Rancho Bernardo and Escondido. The mountains to the east, soaring to more than 6,000 feet high, offer quiet walks through pine and oak forests. Home to the San Diego Wild Animal Park, a pair of top-notch destination spas, and the Temecula wineries, inland North County feels less rushed and is less densely populated than the coastal portion of the county.
TIJUANA	From San Diego it's both easy and rewarding to venture south of the border into Mexico's Baja California peninsula. Tijuana, just 18 mi south, has grown during the past 20 years from a border town into a city of almost 1.5 million; its shops, sports events, and Mexican dining continue to attract hordes of "yanquis."

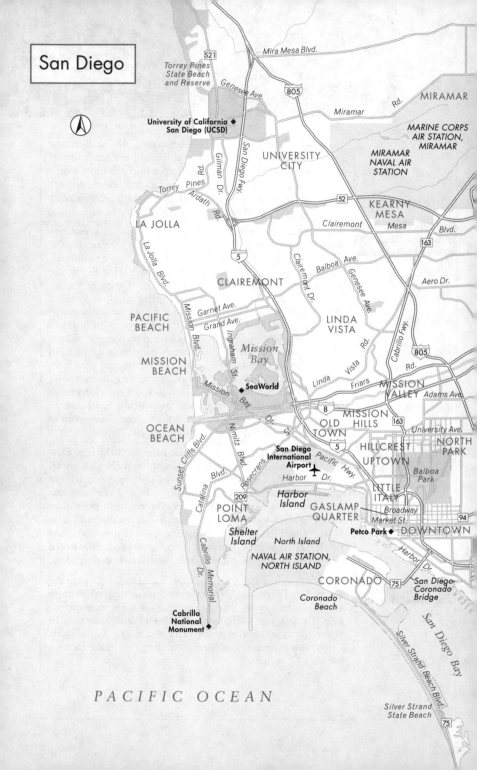

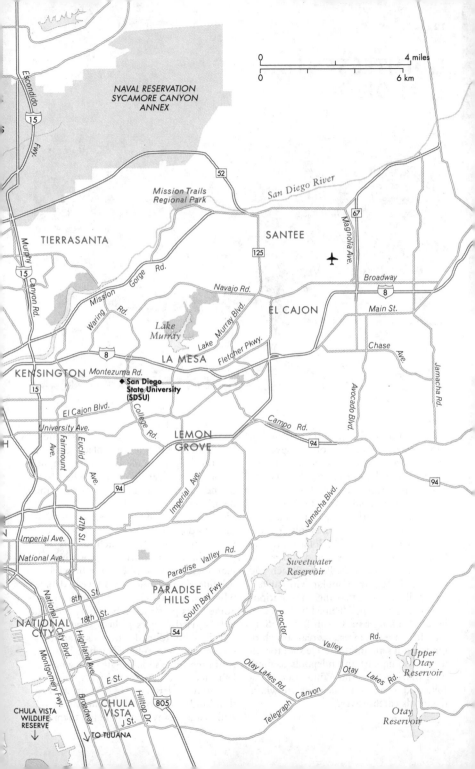

QUINTESSENTIAL SAN DIEGO

Just Beachy

Ask any non-native why they moved to San Diego, and they'll probably give you one of two answers (or both at once): the year-round gorgeous weather and the postcard-perfect beaches. Locals shrug off the high cost of living as the "sunshine tax"—a small price to pay for miles of sun-kissed shoreline. For a family-friendly outing, Coronado and La Jolla Shores are sure bets—they're clean and supervised by attentive lifeguards. Pacific Beach and Mission Beach are popular with surfers and college students—their reputations as rowdy party spots helped fuel a recent beach-drinking ban. Ocean Beach's Sunset Cliffs doesn't offer any real stretch of sand, but it's an unforgettable spot to witness crashing surf and tidepools teeming with marine life. And Windansea in La Jolla and Swami's in Encinitas are where the locals catch waves.

The Fish Taco

San Diego, one of the country's most innovative food cities, is a place to savor outstanding seafood—and you can do so on any budget. No matter what your finances, you can probably afford the definitive regional delectable, the humble fish taco. Simple storefront restaurants and even simpler open-air take-out windows and mobile taco stands dispense these treats filled traditionally with mahimahi or wahoo (but any firm white fish fillet works), and locals love to debate where to get the best and the freshest. Some folks prefer them beer-battered and lightly fried, others grilled. One ardent fan likes his topped with salsa, another swears by mayo-based white sauces. And then there's the debate over whether fish tacos are best served with coleslaw or shredded lettuce. There seem to be a thousand ways to make great fish tacos, and just as many ways to enjoy them!

San Diego's sunlit, seafront setting prompts the city's take on the Southern California lifestyle. The locals have more than a few ways to make the best of a good thing, and there's nothing stopping you from joining them.

A Picnic in the Park

Balboa Park occupies a singular place in the hearts and minds of San Diegans. Although its museums, performance spaces, playing fields, trails, and attractions (notably the San Diego Zoo) are a huge tourist draw, locals frequent the park every chance they can. We've covered its highlights throughout the book, from great rambles through the Rose and Cactus gardens to memorable tours of the museums. But perhaps the simplest way to experience Balboa Park is to flop down along a patch of grass (try entering somewhere around 6th Avenue and Laurel Street) and enjoy a picnic. In the nearby Hillcrest neighborhood, just north, you'll find plenty of spots to stock up on picnic supplies. Noshing on fine food, soaking up the Southern California sun, listening to birds chirp, and admiring lush flora— there's arguably no better way to appreciate the joys of San Diego.

A Game at the Ballpark

You don't have to be a baseball fan to respond to the infectious buzz of a San Diego Padres game at stunning Petco Park. The fun lies as much in watching the fans and enjoying the scenery as in catching the action on the field—although if the beloved Padres are taking on one of their major rivals, such as the L.A. Dodgers or San Francisco Giants, the game itself can get pretty exciting. With its Spanish Mission–style exterior and artful landscaping, Petco is more open than the typical ballpark, with ample room to stroll around and catch the game from different vantage points. The once-dreary neighborhood has blossomed since the park opened in 2004, so be sure to join the fans after the game for continued revelry at the many bars and restaurants outside. The Padres play about 80 games at Petco, the season running from early April through early October.

IF YOU LIKE

Fun in the Sun

In a city with easy access to beaches and parks and an eminently civilized climate, it would be hard not to do as the San Diegans do and venture outdoors. There's something to be said for falling asleep on powder-soft sand, but if you're looking for a little more action, there's swimming, snorkeling, diving, and deep-sea fishing trips. Rent water-sports equipment or learn how to kayak or sail. Surfing, of course, is the ultimate local pastime. If a single lesson doesn't cut it, there are a few surf camps for the truly motivated (or for parents who want to drop off their teenagers and enjoy some alone time). There's plenty more to get you outdoors away from the beach, as well. Here are a few suggestions.

Head out to the region's **inland hills**, and explore sweeping desert parks laced with hiking, mountain biking, and horseback riding trails.

Soar high above the costal scenery in a **hot-air balloon**.

Ride a bike up scenic **Route S21** from La Jolla to Oceanside—it stays close to the coast the whole way.

Break out the nine iron and spend the afternoon at one of San Diego's renowned **golf courses**—celebrated Torrey Pines is 18-hole heaven.

Hike the trails at **Tijuana Estuary in Imperial Beach**—it's one of the top spots around for observing migrant and resident waterfowl.

The Stage

San Diego makes such an outdoorsy getaway that visitors—even some residents—overlook the fact that it's a first-rate performing arts center. We don't just mean that, like all major cities, it has a fair share of theaters and music halls.

The city's most vaunted attribute is its theater scene, which draws a fair share of top-name actors. You'll find about two-dozen theaters around the area, from smaller, avant-garde spaces to major venues hosting top national touring shows. Be on the lookout for performances by the esteemed San Diego Symphony Orchestra, San Diego Opera, and San Diego Ballet.

Some venues we love:

Balboa Theatre—a dazzling octogenarian hall that reopened in 2007 after many years (and dollars' worth) of renovations—hosts local music and performing arts groups, and those just passing through in its historic confines.

It's worth visiting **Copley Symphony Hall** just to see its ornate Spanish baroque interior; the 1920s performing arts center hosts the San Diego Symphony Orchestra and touring musicians.

If you're up for unusual filmmaking, check out what's playing at the **Ken Cinema,** a superb art-house theater.

La Jolla Playhouse often presents Broadway-bound shows before they head east, and can always be counted on for first-rate acting and direction.

The **Old Globe,** the oldest professional theater in the state, occupies a handsome building in Balboa Park and hosts a world-renowned Shakespeare Festival each summer.

Bicultural History

As the site of California's earliest European settlement, San Diego occupies a special place in U.S. history. The city's well-preserved and reconstructed historic sites help you to imagine what the area was like when Spanish and Portuguese explorers and missionaries arrived, usually by sea, in the 16th and 17th centuries. San Diego was the birthplace of California, claimed for Spain by Juan Rodríguez Cabrillo in 1542. About 220 years later another Spaniard, Franciscan missionary Father Junípero Serra, established the first of 21 California missions here. And the Spanish influence didn't stop with California's admission into the Union in 1850 as America's 31st state—it's continued to support a thriving, dynamic Latin American community.

Although it doesn't date back so far, the Anglo side of U.S. history is also alive and well in San Diego, much of it revolving around the city's role as a major U.S. Navy center since the turn of the 20th century.

Here's how to enhance your understanding of San Diego's heritage:

See where explorer Juan Rodríguez Cabrillo landed in 1542 at **Cabrillo National Monument,** a 160-acre preserve perched on a bluff with fantastic views of the harbor and downtown.

Visit the beautifully preserved **Mission San Luis Rey,** in nearby Oceanside, the 18th of California's missions to be established and one of the most spectacular.

Tour the historic buildings, mostly from the 19th century and including some original adobes, preserved at **Old Town San Diego State Historic Park,** a living-history compound.

Charging It

You expect to find fancy megamalls in San Diego—it's Southern California, after all. But this city offers a far more distinctive retail experience than the mere national-chain shopping. Head for some of the more engaging neighborhoods around San Diego, from Coronado—with its blocks of chichi boutiques and galleries—to Old Town, where at Plaza del Pasado you can browse through goods reminiscent of those that might have been on offer back when Old Town San Diego *was* San Diego, and at Bazaar del Mundo Shops you can pick up arts and crafts from Mexico as well as other international goods, toys, and souvenirs. Farther afield, La Jolla has a collection of trendy designer boutiques and galleries along Prospect Street and Girard Avenue.

Here are a few of the best overall shopping destinations in metro San Diego:

Horton Plaza, in the heart of downtown, has department stores and mall shops, while the surrounding **Gaslamp Quarter** is chock-full of specialty shops and art galleries. It's also a great place to grab a bite to eat afterward. So is nearby **Little Italy,** an old fishing neighborhood that's emerged as an artsy urban hot spot with an appealing assortment of one-of-a-kind boutiques, galleries, and eateries.

Waterfront **Seaport Village** is thick with theme shops and arts-and-crafts galleries.

For a marvelous off-the-beaten-path shopping trek, head up the coast to **Solana Beach,** whose downtown **Cedros Design District** bustles with some of the hippest home-furnishings and design shops in the state.

GREAT ITINERARIES

SAN DIEGO: CULTURE MEETS THE SAND

Day 1

Start with the San Diego Zoo in Balboa Park in the morning. You could easily knock off the entire day checking out the thousands of animals, but even if you've got kids along and they're nagging you to stay, plan to end the day with at least a stroll down El Prado, an easy walk or five-minute drive south of the zoo. This is the cultural heart of San Diego, with a feast of fabulous museums set in ornate Spanish-colonial Revival buildings. Unless you're a serious museum junkie, pick whichever of the park's offerings most piques your personal interest—the choices range from photography to folk art. (With kids along, the Reuben H. Fleet Science Center may be the safest bet.) If there's time for happy hour (isn't there always?), the Prado restaurant inside Balboa Park has an outdoor patio perfect for sipping a tangy margarita.

Day 2

It's time to check out San Diego's booming and bustling downtown, beginning with a shopping scramble through Seaport Village and Horton Plaza, both of which have numerous lunch options. Next, stroll north on the Embarcadero, setting aside some time to tour the Maritime Museum or the San Diego Aircraft Carrier Museum. As early evening sets in, continue into downtown's lively Gaslamp Quarter, which pulses with hip bars, music clubs, and restaurants. If you've got kids in tow, head for the new Children's Museum near the Convention Center; with cutting-edge architecture, cool contemporary art, and loads of messy art-making activities, it's fun for the whole family.

Day 3

If you set out early enough, you might get a parking spot near La Jolla Cove. Watch the sea lions lounging on the beach at the Children's Pool and then head inland one block to Prospect Street, where you'll see the pink La Valencia hotel along with dozens of tony shops and galleries; this is also a good spot for an ocean-view lunch. Walk east on Prospect for a spin through the Museum of Contemporary Art, and then retrieve your car and head north to Torrey Pines City Park Beach and the adjacent Glider Port—this is an especially beautiful spot to watch the sun set. If you want to enjoy the weather and skip the museum, spend the afternoon at nearby La Jolla Shores, a favorite spot for sunbathing and swimming. Take note, though: During the warm summer season, you'll be sharing the water with harmless baby leopard sharks—way more exciting than scary once you get past the shock. As dinner approaches, you'll find plenty of great restaurants in La Jolla, or you might try one of the casual beach restaurants south of La Jolla, down Mission Boulevard, such as Hodad's in Ocean Beach.

Day 4

Begin with a morning visit to Cabrillo National Monument. Have lunch down near Shelter Island at one of the seafood restaurants on Scott Street, and then head over to Old Town (take Rosecrans Street north to San Diego Avenue) to see portions of San Diego's earliest history brought to life. If the daily schedule lists low tide for the afternoon, reverse the order to catch the tide pools at Cabrillo.

Day 5

Spend your final day heading into some of the communities nearby. If you're traveling with young children, visit LEGOLAND in Carlsbad or SeaWorld in Mission Bay. En route to North County stop off at Torrey Pines State Beach and Reserve. If you're not going to LEGOLAND, take Interstate 5 north to Del Mar for lunch, shopping, and sea views. A visit to Mission San Luis Rey, slightly inland from Oceanside on Route 76, will infuse some history and culture into the tour.

Alternatives:

You can make Day 2, when you're exploring downtown, more of a seafaring than a shopping experience by catching the ferry from the Broadway Pier (near Seaport Village) to Coronado. Then from Coronado's Ferry Landing Marketplace, board a bus down Orange Avenue to see the town's Victorian extravaganza, the Hotel Del Coronado. If it's whale-watching season, skip the trip to Coronado, tour the Embarcadero in the late morning, have lunch, and book an afternoon excursion boat from the Broadway Pier.

If hopping over to Mexico interests you, set aside Day 5 for a trip to Tijuana rather than an exploration of the towns north and east of San Diego. It's extremely easy to make this trip, as the border crossing is only a 15-mi drive down I–5. Easier yet, hop on the trolley. Once there, shoppers can easily pass a couple of hours exploring the garish but exuberant Avenida Revolución. Also be sure to visit Centro Cultural Tijuana (CECUT), with its Omnimax Theater and excellent exhibits on Baja California's history, flora, and fauna. For the brave-hearted, traditional bullfights at the Plaza Monumental are simultaneously violent and graceful, and quite beloved by locals.

TIPS

Watch the weather forecast prior to planning your itinerary. Try to save the downtown museums and shopping for the day with the least-promising weather. Balboa Park isn't too bad during mild rain either, as you can still tour the zoo, and the park's many museums make for pleasant rainy-day diversions. Visiting either SeaWorld or LEGOLAND are similarly prudent plans for the rare sunless day.

Sure, it's fun to dip those toes in the sand and saunter through one of the world's most incredible zoos. But don't overlook San Diego's somewhat underrated performing arts scene. It's extremely easy to add a theater performance or a concert to any of the five days described above. Some of the city's top performance venues are in Balboa Park (Day 1), Downtown (Day 2), and La Jolla (Day 3).

If you plan to tour more than a couple of museums in Balboa Park, buy the Passport to Balboa Park, which gets you into 13 attractions for just $35, or the Best of Balboa Park Combo Pass, which also gets you into the zoo (it costs $59). You can buy these at the Balboa Park Visitors Center (619/239–0512, www.balboapark.org).

Locals complain about public transportation as often as they complain about the price of fuel, but the trolleys and the Coaster are a hassle-free way to get to foot-friendly neighborhoods up and down the coast. Public transportation saves you the headache of traffic and parking, and includes free sightseeing along the way. You can head almost anywhere from the historic Santa Fe Depot downtown (don't miss the cutting-edge Museum of Contemporary Art next door to the station, either).

ON THE CALENDAR

San Diego has perfect Southern California weather that is the envy of all who live in less pleasant climes, but it still has seasons, and with them come festivals and special events. Plan well in advance if you hope to be in town for any of these celebrations.

WINTER Dec.	**Balboa Park December Nights** (☎619/239–0512 ⊕*www.balboapark.org*) draws 100,000 guests on the first Friday and Saturday of December and features carolers, holiday food, music, dance, handmade crafts, a visit from Saint Nick, a candlelight procession, and free admission to all the museums. The nighttime **Ocean Beach Parade and Tree Festival** (☎619/226–8613) takes place on Newport Avenue, generally the second weekend in December. The Ocean Beach Geriatric Surf Club tops any entry in any parade, anywhere. **Old Town Holiday in the Park** (☎619/220–5422) includes 1800s-themed candlelight tours of historic homes and other buildings in Old Town by costumed docents; reservations are recommended. The **Port of San Diego Bay Parade of Lights** (☎619/224–2240 ⊕*www.sdparadeoflights.org*) fills the harbor with lighted boats cruising in a procession that begins at Shelter Island and ends at the Coronado Ferry Landing Marketplace. The **Wild Animal Park Festival of Lights** (☎760/796–5621) includes free children's activities, Christmas caroling, live-animal presentations, and real snow.
Feb.	The **Buick Invitational** (☎619/281–4653 ⊕*www.buickinvitational.com*), a major golf event since the 1950s, attracts more than 100,000 people, including local and national celebrities, to the Torrey Pines Municipal Golf Course. **Mardi Gras in the Gaslamp Quarter** (☎619/233–5227 ⊕*www.gaslamp.org*) gets the Fat Tuesday celebration right with live music, a raucous parade, and traditional Cajun food and drink.
SPRING Feb.–Apr.	Wildflowers at **Anza-Borrego Desert State Park** (☎760/767–5311, 760/767–4684 *wildflower hotline* ⊕*www.anzaborrego.statepark.org*) are in bloom during these months. They are at their peak only for a two-week period, which var-

	ies according to winter rainfall. Phone the hotline for information.
Mar.	The **Kiwanis Ocean Beach Kite Festival** (☎619/531–1527) features a kite-making, decorating, and flying contest, plus a craft fair, food, and entertainment.
Mar. to mid-May	Tiptoe through fields of brilliantly colored ranunculuses, arranged rainbow-fashion on a hillside at **Flower Fields at Carlsbad Ranch** (☎760/431–0352 ⊕*www.theflowerfields.com*) in Carlsbad for six to eight week every spring.
Apr.	Humming along for more than 30 years, the **Adams Avenue Roots Festival** (☎619/282–7329 ⊕*www.gothere.com/adamsave*) is a free weekend festival of vintage blues, folk, jazz, country, cowboy, and international music on six outdoor stages. The **ArtWalk Festival** (☎619/615–1090 ⊕*www.artwalkinfo.com*) showcases visual and performing artists in their studios and in staged areas; self-guided tours start downtown in Little Italy. The **Del Mar National Horse Show** (☎858/792–4288 ⊕*www.sdfair.com*) at the Del Mar Fairgrounds showcases national and international championship riders and horses in western week, dressage week, and hunter–jumper week competitions. The **San Diego Crew Classic** (☎619/225–0300 ⊕*www.crewclassic.org*) brings together more than 3,000 high school, college, and masters athletes from across the United States for a rowing competition at Crown Point Shores in Mission Bay.
May	**Julian Wildflower Show** (☎760/765–1857 ⊕*www.julianca.com*) is an annual display of wildflowers gathered within a 15-mi radius of the mountain town, and usually includes desert blooms. **Old Town Fiesta Cinco de Mayo** (☎619/296–3236 ⊕*www.oldtownguide.com*), at Old Town San Diego State Historic Park, commemorates Mexico's defeat of Napoléon's cavalry during the Battle of Puebla on May 5, 1862. Besides a historic reenactment, there's plenty of food and music and dance events celebrating Latino culture.

ON THE CALENDAR

SUMMER	
June	**A Taste of the Gaslamp** (☎619/233–5227 ⊕*www.gaslamp. org*) is a weekend of gastronomy; pick up your ticket and a map of participating restaurants and go from door to door sampling the house specialties of the Gaslamp Quarter's best chefs.
	The **Temecula Valley Balloon and Wine Festival** (☎951/676–6713 ⊕*www.tvbwf.com*), a weekend event at the Lake Skinner Recreation Area in Riverside County, is a chance to taste the area's wines, ride a hot-air balloon over the vineyards in the morning, and watch an evening balloon glow.
June–July	The **San Diego County Fair** (☎858/793–5555 ⊕*www.sdfair. com*) is a classic county fair at the Del Mar Fairgrounds, with live entertainment, flower and garden shows, a carnival, livestock shows, and Fourth of July fireworks.
June–Aug.	**TGIF Jazz-in-the-Parks** (☎760/434–2904) series features free live performances at various parks in the Carlsbad area; call for a schedule.
	During the **Summer Organ Festival** (☎619/702–8138 ⊕*www. sosorgan.com*), enjoy free Monday-evening concerts under the stars at Balboa Park's Spreckels Organ Pavilion, in addition to the free year-round Sunday afternoon concerts.
June–Sept.	The **Nighttime Zoo** (☎619/234–3153 ⊕*www.sandiegozoo. org*) at the San Diego Zoo and the **Park at Dark** (☎760/796–5621 ⊕*www.wildanimalpark.com*) at the San Diego Wild Animal Park are wild ways to spend the evening, with extended evening hours and additional entertainment through the beginning of September.
	The Globe's **Summer Shakespeare Festival** (☎619/234–5623 ⊕*www.theoldglobe.org*), at the open-air Lowell Davies Festival Theatre in Balboa Park, features works of Shakespeare in repertory with other classic and contemporary plays.
July	Patriots observe the July 4th **Coronado Independence Day** (☎619/437–8788) with a 15-km run, a 5-km run/walk, a parade, U.S. Navy air–sea demonstrations, and fireworks over Glorietta Bay.
	The annual lesbian and gay **Pride Parade, Rally, and Festival** (☎619/297–7683 ⊕*www.sdpride.org*) is a weekend of entertainment in Hillcrest and Balboa Park.

		U.S. Open Sandcastle Competition (☎619/424–6663) at Imperial Beach Pier brings together sand sculptors of all ages for one of the largest castle-building events in the United States.
	July–Sept.	**Del Mar horse racing season** (☎ 858/755–1141, ⊕ *dmtc.com*) kicks off at the Thoroughbred Club in July and continues through the summer with races and special events, including free big-name concerts.
		The **San Diego Symphony Summer Pops** (☎619/235–0804 ⊕*www.sandiegosymphony.com*) series, with occasional fireworks, swings Friday and Saturday nights at Embarcadero Marina Park South.
	Aug.	The **La Jolla SummerFest** (☎858/459–3728 ⊕*www.lajolla-musicsociety.org*) chamber music festival includes concerts, lectures, master classes, and open rehearsals, mainly in La Jolla but also in downtown San Diego.
FALL Sept.		The free annual **Adams Avenue Street Fair** (☎619/282–7329 ⊕*www.gothere.com/adamsave*) attracts 50,000 jazz, blues, and rock fans to the Normal Heights neighborhood for concerts on five stages, food, games, and a carnival. The largest event of its type in Southern California, it's popular with families.
		Street Scene (☎619/236–1212 ⊕*www.street-scene.com*), a weekend urban music festival in the East Village with food, rollicks with 100 bands from around the world performing on various stages.
	Oct.	**Oktoberfest in La Mesa** (☎619/440–6161 ⊕*www.eastcountychamber.org*) is a traditional celebration featuring German sausages, Bavarian brass oompah bands, dancing, and arts and crafts.
	Nov.	**Holiday of Lights** (☎858/793–5555 ⊕*www.sdfair.com*), from Thanksgiving through New Year's Day, showcases more than 350 animated and lighted holiday displays in a drive-through setting at the Del Mar Fairgrounds.
		El Cajon's **Mother Goose Parade** (☎619/444–8712 ⊕*www.mothergooseparade.com*) is a two-hour nationally televised spectacular with 200 floats, bands, horses, and clowns. It takes place the Sunday before Thanksgiving.

WHEN TO GO

For the most part, **any time of the year is the right time** for a trip to San Diego. Have we mentioned that the weather is practically perfect? Typical days are sunny and mild, with low humidity—ideal for sightseeing and for almost any sport that does not require snow and ice. From mid-December through mid-March, awe-inspiring gray whales can be seen migrating along the coast—lucky whale-watchers can get close enough to see them frolic in the Pacific. In early spring, kaleidoscopic explosions of spring wildflowers blanket the mountainsides and desert. In fall these same mountains present one of the most impressive displays of fall color to be found in Southern California.

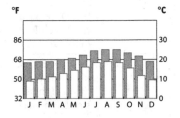

Climate

The annual high temperature averages 70°F with a low of 55°F, and the annual rainfall is usually less than 10 inches. Most of the rain occurs in January and February, but precipitation usually lasts for only part of the day or for a day or two at most.

The graph shows the average high and low temperatures for San Diego.

Exploring San Diego

WORD OF MOUTH

"I would recommend going to Old Town and getting on the Trolley tour your first day. The tour gave us a good intro to the city and the next day we went back to some of the places we wanted to spend more time at."

—Snowflake25

"My favorite place in San Diego in the summer, Petco Park. If there is a game on, you must go. It is the best place to be, sitting in the shade, in the park, watching the game, eating a hot dog, watching the crowd. Pure American fun."

—Heavens

Updated
by Marlise
Elizabeth Kast

SAN DIEGO IS A VACATIONER'S paradise, complete with idyllic year-round temperatures and 70 mi of pristine coastline. Recognized as one of the nation's leading family destinations, with SeaWorld, LEGO-LAND, and the Zoo, San Diego is equally attractive to those in search of art, culture, world-class shopping, and culinary exploration. San Diego's many neighborhoods offer diverse adventures: from the tony boutiques in La Jolla to the culinary delights in the northern suburb of Del Mar; from the authentic European charm of Little Italy to the nouveau-chic of the downtown Gaslamp Quarter, each community adds flavor and flair to San Diego's personality.

Approximately two and a half hours south of Los Angeles, San Diego County is nestled between Mexico to the south, wine country to the north, Anza-Borrego Desert State Park to the east, and the Pacific Ocean to the west. One of the city's many highlights is the 1,200-acre Balboa Park, the country's largest urban cultural park, home to 15 museums, the Globe Theater, and the San Diego Zoo. Nature abounds throughout the city: Bougainvilleas cover hillsides in La Jolla, spreading magenta blankets over whitewashed adobe walls. Downtown is a vision in purple when the jacaranda trees that line the streets bloom in spring, spreading vivid, shady canopies.

While public transportation is available, most tourists prefer to use private or rental cars to traverse the excellent freeway system that criss-crosses the county. Interstate 5 runs a direct north–south route through the coastal communities from Orange County in the north to the Mexican border. If you have time, the parallel Pacific Coast Highway offers a more leisurely route along San Diego's breathtaking coastline. Interstates 805 and 15 are the main inland arteries. Interstate 8 is the main east–west route. Routes 163, 52, and 94 serve as connectors.

A 59-mi scenic drive over much of central San Diego begins at the foot of Broadway. Signs with a white seagull on a yellow-and-blue background direct the way through the Embarcadero to Harbor and Shelter Islands, Point Loma, Cabrillo Monument, Mission Bay, Old Town, Balboa Park, Mount Soledad, and La Jolla.

Public transportation has improved a great deal in the past decade: the San Diego Trolley, which runs as far south as San Ysidro, has expanded in the north from Old Town to beyond Mission San Diego and San Diego State University. Commuter *Coaster* trains run frequently between downtown San Diego and Oceanside, with convenient stops in Del Mar, Encinitas, Carlsbad, and other charming coastal towns. In 2008 the Sprinter commuter train began operating the East–West route between Escondido and Oceanside along Highway 78. The bus system covers almost all of the county, with Fashion Valley shopping center, Old Town, and downtown as the three major bus transfer points. Old Town Trolley Tours has a hop-on, hop-off route of popular spots around the city, taking two and a half hours if you ride continuously and five hours if you plan to explore.

BALBOA PARK

1

Overlooking downtown and the Pacific Ocean, 1,200-acre Balboa Park is the cultural heart of San Diego. Ranked as one of the world's best parks by the Project for Public Spaces, it's also where you can find most of the city's museums, art galleries, the Tony Award–winning Globe Theatre, and the world-famous San Diego Zoo. Most first-time visitors see only these attractions, but the "Smithsonian of the West" is really a series of botanical gardens. Thanks to the "Mother of Balboa Park," Kate Sessions, who suggested hiring a landscape architect in 1889, gardens both cultivated and wild are an integral part of the park, featuring 350 species of trees. What Balboa Park would have looked like had she left it alone can be seen at Florida Canyon (between the main park and Morley Field, along Park Boulevard)—an arid landscape of sagebrush, cactus, and a few small trees.

TOP 5 SAN DIEGO

Balboa Park. A perfect blend of nature and culture, and the San Diego Zoo.

Coronado. Experience Sunday brunch at the historic Hotel Del Coronado.

Gaslamp Quarter. The city's nightlife headquarters is packed with restaurants, cafés, bars, clubs, and shops.

La Jolla. An upscale neighborhood where boutiques and bistros blend into emerald parks and stunning beaches.

Take Me Out to the Ballgame. Cheer on the Padres in the state-of-the-art PETCO Park.

Historic buildings dating from San Diego's 1915 Panama–California International Exposition are strung along the park's main east–west thoroughfare, El Prado, which leads from 6th Avenue eastward over the Cabrillo Bridge (formerly the Laurel Street Bridge), the park's official gateway. If you're a cinema fan, many of the buildings may be familiar—Orson Welles used exteriors of several Balboa Park buildings to represent the Xanadu estate of Charles Foster Kane in his 1941 classic, *Citizen Kane*. Prominent among them was the California Building, whose 200-foot tower, housing a 100-carillon bell that tolls the hour, is El Prado's tallest structure. Missing from the black-and-white film, however, was the magnificent blue of its tiled dome shining in the sun.

The parkland across the Cabrillo Bridge, at the west end of El Prado, is set aside for picnics and athletics. Rollerbladers zip along Balboa Drive, which leads to the highest spot in the park, Marston Point, overlooking downtown. At the green beside the bridge, ladies and gents in all-white outfits meet regularly on summer afternoons for lawn-bowling tournaments—a throwback to an earlier era.

East of Plaza de Panama, El Prado becomes a pedestrian mall and ends at a footbridge that crosses over Park Boulevard, the park's main north–south thoroughfare, to the perfectly tended Rose Garden, which has more than 2,000 rosebushes. In the adjacent Desert Garden, trails wind around prickly cacti and soft green succulents from around the

Exploring
San Diego

↑
TO NORTH
COUNTY
BEACHES

S21

Mira Mesa Blvd.

N. Torrey

Genesee Ave.

Pines Rd.

805

Miramar

Rd.

MIRAMAR

Escondido

Kearney Villa Rd.

◆ University of California
at San Diego (UCSD)

MARINE CORPS
AIR STATION,
MIRAMAR

15 Fwy.

La Jolla

Torrey

La Jolla Pkwy.

Pines Rd.

Gilman Dr.

San Diego Fwy.

Jacob Dekema Freeway

52

Clairemont

Mesa

Blvd.

163

La Jolla Blvd.

5

Clairemont

Dr.

Balboa

Ave.

Genesee Ave.

Aero Dr.

Cabrillo Fwy.

805

Murphy Canyoon Rd.

PACIFIC
BEACH

Mission Bay

Grand Ave.

LINDA
VISTA

Mission

Blvd.

Ingraham

Mission
Bay

Linda

Vista

Rd.

San Diego River

15

MISSION
BEACH

Mission Bay Dr.

◆ Sea World

Friars

Rd.

Adams Ave.

BUS
8

Old Town

8

163

University

Ave.

Fairmount

OCEAN
BEACH

Nimitz Blvd.

St.

Balboa Park

Sunset Cliffs

Blvd.

Rosecrans

Pacific

Hwy.

Catalina Blvd.

209

N. Harbor

Dr.

94

POINT
LOMA

North Island

DOWNTOWN

Cabrillo Memorial Dr.

NAVAL
AIR STATION
NORTH ISLAND

Imperial

Ave.

Harbor

Dr.

National

Ave.

CORONADO

75

8th St.

Broadway

Coronado
Beach

San

Diego

Bay

Central San Diego

Silver Strand Blvd.

CHULA VISTA
WILDLIFE
RESERVE

PACIFIC OCEAN

Silver Strand
State Beach

0 ——— 4 miles
0 ——— 6 km

world. Palm Canyon, north of the Spreckels Organ Pavilion, has more than 50 varieties of palms along a shady bridge. Pepper Grove, along Park Boulevard south of the museums, has lots of picnic tables as well as play equipment.

Parking near Balboa Park's museums is no small accomplishment, especially on sunny summer days, when the lots, which are all free, fill up quickly. If you're driving in via the Cabrillo Bridge, the first parking area you come to is off El Prado to the right, going toward Pan American Plaza. Don't despair if there are no spaces here; you'll see more lots as you continue along the same road. If you end up parking a bit far from your destination, consider the stroll back through the greenery part of the day's recreation. Alternatively, you can just park at Inspiration Point on the east side of the park, off Presidents Way. Free trams run from there to the museums every 8–10 minutes, 9:30–5:30 daily.

> A GOOD READ
>
> The size, scope, and diversity of Balboa Park's attractions are so great that it takes a few days to adequately explore everything. For an in-depth look at the park's history and hidden treasures, consult *Discover Balboa Park: A Complete Guide to America's Greatest Urban Park,* by Pamela Crooks, available at the Visitor Center in the House of Hospitality.

Numbers in the text correspond to numbers on the Balboa Park map.

SIGHTS TO SEE

❶ **Alcazar Garden.** The gardens surrounding the Alcazar Castle in Seville, Spain, inspired the landscaping here; you'll feel like royalty resting on the benches by the exquisitely tiled fountains. The flower beds are ever-changing horticultural exhibits featuring more than 6,000 annuals for a nearly perpetual bloom. Bright orange-and-yellow poppies appear in spring and deep rust and crimson chrysanthemums arrive in fall. ✉ *1439 El Prado.*

❻ **Botanical Building.** The graceful redwood-lath structure, built for the 1915 Panama-California International Exposition, now houses more than 2,000 types of tropical and subtropical plants plus changing seasonal flower displays. Ceiling-high tree ferns shade fragile orchids and feathery bamboo. There are benches beside miniature waterfalls for resting in the shade. The rectangular pond outside, filled with lotuses and water lilies that bloom in spring and fall, is popular with photographers. ✉ *1550 El Prado* ☎ *619/239–0512* ⊙ *Fri.–Wed. 10–4.*

❾ **Carousel.** Suspended an arm's-length away on this antique merry-go-round is the brass ring that could earn you an extra free ride (it's one of the few carousels in the world that continue this bonus tradition). Hand-carved in 1910, the carousel features colorful murals, big band music, and bobbing animals including zebras, giraffes, and dragons; real horsehair was used for the tails. ✉ *1889 Zoo Pl., behind zoo parking lot* ☎ *619/460–9000* ✉ *$2* ⊙ *Mid-June–Labor Day, daily 11–5:30; rest of year, weekends and school holidays 11– 4:30.*

Two Good Balboa Park Walks

It's impossible to cover all the park's museums in one day, so choose your focus before you head out. To help maximize your time, rent one of the 60-minute audio headsets that guide you on a tour of the park's history, architecture, and horticulture. If your interests run to the aesthetic, the Museum of Photographic Arts, the San Diego Museum of Art, the Mingei International Museum, and the Timken Museum of Art should be on your list. Those with a penchant for natural and cultural history shouldn't miss the San Diego Natural History Museum and the Museum of Man; visitors oriented toward space and technology should see the Reuben H. Fleet Science Center, the San Diego Air and Space Museum, and the San Diego Automotive Museum. If you're traveling with kids, the National History Museum and the Reuben H. Fleet Science Center are musts, as is catching a show at the Marie Hitchcock Puppet Theater.

For a nice walk, enter the park via Cabrillo Bridge through the West Gate. Park south of the **Alcazar Garden ①**. It's a short stretch north across El Prado to the landmark California Building, modeled on a cathedral in Mexico and now home to the **San Diego Museum of Man ②**. Look up to see busts and statues of heroes of the early days of the state carved on the facade. Next door are the **Globe Theatres ③**, which adjoin the sculpture garden of the **San Diego Museum of Art ④**, an ornate Plateresque-style structure built to resemble the 17th-century University of Salamanca in Spain.

Continuing east you'll come to the **Timken Museum of Art ⑤**, the **Botanical Building ⑥**, and the Spanish colonial–style Casa del Prado, where the San Diego Floral Association has its offices and a gift shop. At the end of the row is the **San Diego Natural History Museum ⑦**; you'll have to detour a block north to visit the **Spanish Village Art Center 8**. If you were to continue north, you would come to the **carousel 9**, the **miniature railroad 10**, and, finally, the entrance to the **San Diego Zoo 11**.

Return to the Natural History Museum and cross Fountain Plaza to reach the **Reuben H. Fleet Science Center 12**. (Beyond the parking lot to the south lies the **Centro Cultural de la Raza 13**.) You're now on the opposite side of the Prado and heading west. You'll next pass **Casa de Balboa 14**; inside are the model-railroad and photography museums and the historical society. Next door in the **House of Hospitality 15** is the Balboa Park Visitor Center, where you can buy a reduced-price pass to the museums, or dine at the Prado restaurant. Across the Plaza de Panama, the Franciscan mission–style **House of Charm 16** houses a folk art museum and a gallery for San Diego artists. Your starting point, the Alcazar Garden, is west of the House of Charm.

A second walk leads south from the Plaza de Panama, which doubles as a parking lot. The majority of the buildings along this route date from the 1935 fair, when the architecture of the Maya and native peoples of the Southwest was highlighted. The first sight you'll pass is the **Japanese Friendship Garden 17**. Next comes the ornate, crownlike **Spreckels Organ Pavilion 18**. The road forks here; veer to the left to reach the **House of Pacific Relations 19**, a Spanish mission–style cluster of cottages. Continue past the Balboa Park Club until you reach the Palisades Building, which hosts the **Marie Hitchcock Puppet Theater 20**.

Just beyond is the **San Diego Automotive Museum 21**.

The road loops back at the spaceshiplike **San Diego Air and Space Museum 22**. As you head north again, you'll notice the Starlight Bowl, an amphitheater on your right. Next comes perhaps the most impressive structure on this tour, the Federal Building, the home of the **San Diego Hall of Champions 23**. Its main entrance was modeled after the Palace of Governors in the ancient Mayan city of Uxmal, Mexico. You'll now be back at the Spreckels Organ Pavilion, having walked a little less than a mile.

TIMING

You'll want to devote an entire day to the perpetually expanding park; there are more than enough exhibits to keep you occupied for five or more hours, and you're likely to be too tired for museum-hopping when you're through.

Although some of the park's museums are open on Monday, most are open Tuesday–Sunday 10–4; in summer a number have extended hours—phone ahead to ask. On Tuesday the museums have free admission to their permanent exhibits on a rotating basis; ⇨ see What's Free When box. Free architectural, historical, or nature tours depart from the Visitor Center every Saturday at 10, while park ranger–led tours start out from the Visitor Center at 1 PM every Tuesday and Sunday. Free concerts take place Sunday afternoons at 2 PM year-round at the Spreckels Organ Pavilion, and the House of Pacific Relations hosts Sunday-afternoon folk-dance performances.

⑭ Casa de Balboa. This building on El Prado's southeast corner houses three museums: the Museum of Photographic Arts, the Museum of San Diego History, and the San Diego Model Railroad Museum. ⊠*1649 El Prado.*

⑬ Centro Cultural de la Raza. An old water tower was converted into this center for Mexican, indigenous, and Chicano arts and culture. Attractions include a gallery with rotating exhibits and a theater, as well as a collection of mural art, a fine example of which may be seen on the tower's exterior. ⊠*2004 Park Blvd.* ☎*619/235–6135* ⊕*www.centroraza.com* 🖃*Donation suggested* ⊙*Tues.–Sun. noon–4.*

❸ Globe Theatres. Even if you're not attending a play, this complex, comprising the Cassius Carter Centre Stage, the Lowell Davies Festival Theatre, and the Old Globe Theatre, is a pleasant place to relax between museum visits. Theater classics such as *The Full Monty* and *Dirty Rotten Scoundrels,* both of which later performed on Broadway, premiered on these famed stages. The theaters, done in a California version of Tudor style, sit between the sculpture garden of the San Diego Museum of Art and the California Tower. A gift shop (open one hour prior to curtain and through intermission) sells theater-related wares, including posters, cards, and brightly colored puppets. ⊠*1363 Old Globe Way* ☎*619/234–5623* ⊕*www.theoldglobe.org.*

⑯ House of Charm. This structure was rebuilt from the ground up in the mid-1990s to replicate the Franciscan mission style of the original expo building. Inside, you'll find the main branch of the Mingei International Museum of Folk Art and the San Diego Art Institute. ⊠*1439 El Prado* ⊙*Mingei Museum, Tues.–Sun. 10–4; Art Institute, Tues.–Sat. 10–4, Sun. 12–4.*

⑮ House of Hospitality. At the Balboa Park Visitors Center in this building, you can pick up schedules and route maps for the free trams that operate around the park. Audio tours are also available, as is the Best of Balboa Park Combo Pass, which affords entry to 13 museums and the zoo for $65; for $39, a seven-day pass is available for those who prefer to visit the museums without zoo entry. In addition, you can pick up a flyer that details the excellent free park tours that depart from here (or phone for a schedule). Also note the beautiful structure itself. A late 1990s rebuilding of the 1915 original, it has won awards for its painstaking attention to historical detail; 2,000 paint scrapes were taken, for example, to get the art deco colors exactly right. ⊠*1549 El Prado* ☎*619/239–0512* ⊕*www.balboapark.org* ⊙*Daily 9:30–4:30.*

⑲ House of Pacific Relations. This is not really a house but a cluster of red-tile–roof stucco cottages representing some 30 foreign countries. The word "pacific" refers to the goal of maintaining peace. The cottages, decorated with crafts and pictures, are open Sunday afternoons, when you can chat with transplanted natives and try out different ethnic foods. From the first Sunday in March through the last Sunday in October folksong and dance performances are presented on the outdoor stage around 2 PM—check the schedule at the park visitor center. Across the road from the cottages, but not affiliated with them, is the Spanish colonial–style **United Nations Building.** Inside, the United Nations Association's International Gift Shop, open daily, has reasonably priced crafts, cards, and books. ⊠ *2129 Pan American Pl.* ☎*619/234–0739* ⊕*www.sdhpr.org* ✉*Free, donations accepted* ⊙*Sun. noon–4.*

⑰ Japanese Friendship Garden. A koi pond with a cascading water wall, a 60-foot-long wisteria arbor, a tea pavilion, and a large activity center are highlights of the park's authentic Japanese garden, designed to inspire contemplation and evoke tranquillity. You can wander the various peaceful paths, meditate in the traditional stone and Zen garden, or, at times, learn such arts as origami and flower arranging at the exhibit hall. Long-term plans are to develop an additional 9 acres with more attractions, including a cherry orchard. ⊠*2215 Pan American Rd.* ☎*619/232–2721* ⊕*www.niwa.org* ✉*$4* ⊙*Tues.–Sun. 10–4.*

☾ ⑳ Marie Hitchcock Puppet Theater. One of the last of its kind, this puppet theater has been presenting shows for more than 50 years. Performances incorporate marionettes, hand puppets, rod puppets, shadow puppets, and ventriloquism, while the stories range from traditional fairy tales to folk legends and contemporary puppet plays. Pantomime, comedy, and music round out the program. Kids will be wide-eyed at the short, energy-filled productions. Adults will be overcome with nostalgia. ⊠ *2130 Pan American Rd. W* ☎*619/544–9203* ⊕*www.balboaparkpuppets.com* ✉*$5* ⊙*Showtimes mid-June–Labor Day, Wed.–Sun. 11, 1, 2:30; Sept.–mid-June, Wed.–Fri. 10 and 11:30, Sat. and Sun. 11, 1, 2:30.*

☾ ㉔ Marston House. George W. Marston (1850–1946), a San Diego pioneer and philanthropist who financed the architectural landscaping of Balboa Park—among his myriad other San Diego civic projects—lived in this 16-room home at the northwest edge of the park, now maintained by the San Diego Historical Society. Designed in 1905 by San Diego architects Irving Gill and William Hebbard, it's a classic example of the American Arts and Crafts style, which emphasizes simplicity and functionality of form. Furnishings include pieces by Tiffany, Roycroft, and Gustav Stickley. On the 5-acre grounds is a lovely English Romantic garden, as interpreted in California. Hour-long docent tours—the only way to see the house—illuminate many aspects of San Diego history in which the Marstons played a part. ⊠*3525 7th Ave.* ☎*619/298–3142* ✉*$5* ⊙ *June –Labor Day, daily 10–4:30; Labor Day–June, daily 11–3; tours on the hour Fri.–Sun.*

☾ ⑯ Mingei International Museum. All ages will enjoy the Mingei's colorful and creative exhibits of folk art, featuring toys, pottery, textiles, costumes, and curios from around the globe. Traveling and permanent exhibits in the high-ceiling, light-filled museum include everything from antique American carousel horses to the latest in Japanese ceramics. The name "Mingei" comes from the Japanese words *min,* meaning "all people," and *gei,* meaning "art." Thus, the museum's name describes what you'll find under its roof: "art of all people." The gift shop has a great selection of Navajo, Hopi, and Huichol Indian artwork. ⊠*House*

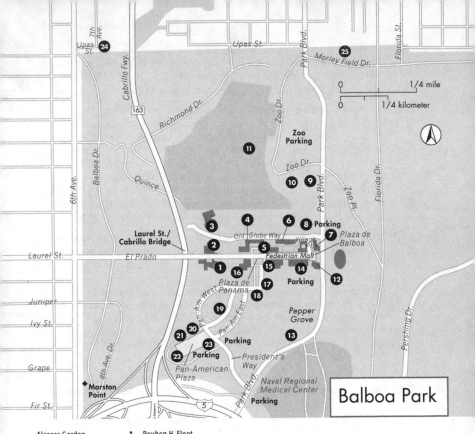

Balboa Park

1

of Charm, 1439 El Prado ☎*619/239–0003* ⊕*www.mingei.org* ✉*$7* ⊙*Tues.–Sun. 10–4.*

☺ ➓ **Miniature Railroad.** Adjacent to the zoo parking lot and across from the carousel, a pint-size 48-passenger train runs a ½-mi loop through 4 tree-filled acres of the park. The engine of this rare 1948 model train is a 1/5-scale version of a General Motors F-3 locomotive, and is one of only 50 left in the world. ✉*2885 Zoo Pl.* ☎*619/231–1515 Ext. 4051* ✉*$2* ⊙*June–Aug., daily 11–6:30; Sept.–May, weekends and school holidays 11–4:30.*

☺ ㉕ **Morley Field Sports Complex.** In addition to the 2-mi fitness course and ball diamonds, the park's athletic center has a flying-disc golf course where players toss their Frisbees over canyons and treetops to reach the challenging "holes"—wire baskets hung from metal poles. Morley Field also has a public pool, a velodrome, an archery range, playgrounds, and boccie, badminton, and tennis courts. The complex is at the northeast corner of Balboa Park, across Park Boulevard and Florida Canyon. ✉*2221 Morley Field Dr.* ☎*619/692–4919* ⊕*www. morleyfield.com.*

★ ⑭ **Museum of Photographic Arts.** World-renowned photographers such as Ansel Adams, Imogen Cunningham, Henri Cartier-Bresson, and Edward Weston are represented in the permanent collection, which includes everything from 19th-century daguerreotypes to contemporary photojournalism prints and Russian Constructivist images (many by Alexander Rodchenko). The 28,000-square-foot facility has a state-of-the-art theater for screening cinema classics as well as a learning center. On Thursday nights the museum is occasionally open for movie screenings and jazz recitals. This cultural gem is among the very best photography museums in the United States. ✉*Casa de Balboa, 1649 El Prado* ☎*619/238–7559* ⊕*www.mopa.org* ✉*$6 museum* ⊙*Daily 10–5; Memorial Day–Labor Day open until 9 Thurs.*

⑭ **Museum of San Diego History.** The San Diego Historical Society maintains its research library in the basement of the Casa de Balboa and organizes shows on the first floor. Permanent and rotating exhibits, which are often more lively than you might expect, survey local urban history after 1850, when California entered the Union. A 100-seat theater hosts public lectures, workshops, and educational programs, and a gift shop carries a good selection of books on local history as well as reproductions of old posters and other historical collectibles. ✉*Casa de Balboa, 1649 El Prado* ☎*619/232–6203* ⊕*www.sandiegohistory. org* ✉*$5* ⊙*Daily 10–5.*

☺ ⑫ **Reuben H. Fleet Science Center.** The Fleet Center's clever interactive exhib-
Fodor's Choice its are artfully educational. You can reconfigure your face to have two
★ left sides, or, by replaying an instant video clip, watch yourself coming and going at different speeds. The IMAX Dome Theater, the world's first, screens exhilarating nature and science films. A 23-passenger motion simulator ride takes you on a journey into exciting realms. The Nierman Challenger Learning Center—a realistic mock mission-control and futuristic space station—is a big hit. ✉*1875 El Prado*

☎619/238–1233 ⊕*www.rhfleet.org* ✉*Gallery exhibits $8, gallery exhibits and IMAX film $12.50* ⊙*Daily 9:30; closing hrs vary from 5 to 9, call ahead.*

★ ☾ ㉒ **San Diego Air and Space Museum.** By day, the streamlined edifice looks like any other structure in the park; at night, outlined in blue neon, the round building appears—appropriately enough—to be a landed UFO. Every available inch of space in the rotunda is filled with exhibits about aviation and aerospace pioneers, including examples of enemy planes from the world wars. All in all, there are 68 full-size aircraft on the floor and literally hanging from the rafters, and interactive exhibits that kids love (such as the DC-3 cockpit display where they can pretend to fly). In addition to exhibits from the dawn of flight to the jet age, the museum also displays a growing number of space-age exhibits, including the actual Apollo 9 space capsule. A collection of real and replicated aircraft fills the central courtyard, and a behind-the-scenes tour on Monday, Wednesday, and Friday allows you to watch volunteers restoring aircraft or creating replicas. ✉*2001 Pan American Plaza* ☎619/234–8291 ⊕*www.sandiegoairandspace.org* ✉*$15, restoration tour $5 extra* ⊙*Daily 10–4:30, until 5:30 Memorial Day–Labor Day.*

⑯ **SDAI: Museum of The Living Artist.** Outside juries decide which works created by members of the Art Institute will be displayed in rotating shows, which change every four to six weeks. Painting, sculpture, mixed media, digital art, and photography are represented—everything except crafts, reserved for the excellent small gift shop. The David Fleet Young Artists Gallery shows art created by students at area schools. ✉*House of Charm, 1439 El Prado* ☎619/236–0011 ⊕*www.sandiego-art.org* ✉*$3* ⊙*Tues.–Sat. 10–4, Sun. noon–4.*

㉑ **San Diego Automotive Museum.** Even if you don't know a choke from a chassis, you're bound to admire the sleek designs of the autos in this impressive museum. The core collection comprises vintage motorcycles and cars, ranging from an 1886 Benz to a DeLorean, as well as a series of rotating exhibits from collections around the world. There's an ongoing automobile restoration program, and the museum sponsors many outdoor automotive events. Call to find out about any rallies, races, or shows that might be scheduled. ✉*2080 Pan American Plaza* ☎619/231–2886 ⊕*www.sdautomuseum.org* ✉*$8* ⊙*Daily 10–5, last admission at 4:30.*

☾ ㉓ **San Diego Hall of Champions.** In a 70,000-square-foot building, this museum celebrates local jock heroes—such as baseball great Ted Williams and basketball star Bill Walton—via a vast collection of memorabilia, uniforms, paintings, photographs, and computer and video displays. An amusing bloopers film is screened at the Sports Theater. The Center Court activity area hosts changing programs—everything from a Chargers minitraining camp to interactive bobsled races. In keeping with the progressive nature of the San Diego sports community, there are also exhibits of such extreme sports as skateboarding, surfing, and street luge. ✉*Federal Bldg., 2131 Pan American Plaza* ☎619/234–2544 ⊕*www.sdhoc.com* ✉*$8* ⊙*Daily 10–4:30.*

⊙ ⑭ **San Diego Model Railroad Museum.** At 27,000 square feet, this is the largest indoor operating railroad museum in the world. The four main displays, built and maintained by local model railroad clubs, represent California railroads in "miniature," with the track laid on scale models of actual San Diego County terrain. The Cabrillo & Southwestern layout is in O scale, 1/48 actual size; two others are in HO scale, 1/87 actual size; and the fourth, Pacific Desert Lines, is in N scale, 1/160 actual size. When these impressive exhibits are in operation, you can hear the sounds of chugging engines, screeching brakes, and shrill whistles. A Toy Train Gallery contains an interactive Lionel exhibit that includes a camera car hooked up to a TV set showing an engineer's-eye view of the layout. Children under 15 get in free with an adult. ✉ *Casa de Balboa, 1649 El Prado* ☎ *619/696–0199* ⊕ *www.sdmrm.org* 🏷 *$6* ⊙ *Tues.–Fri. 11–4, weekends 11–5.*

★ ❹ **San Diego Museum of Art.** Known primarily for its Spanish baroque and Renaissance paintings, including works by El Greco, Goya, Rubens, and van Ruisdael, San Diego's most comprehensive art museum also has strong holdings of South Asian art, Indian miniatures, and contemporary California paintings. An outdoor Sculpture Court and Garden exhibits both traditional and modern pieces. The IMAGE (Interactive Multimedia Art Gallery Explorer) system allows you to call up the highlights of the museum's collection on a computer screen and custom-design a tour, call up historical information on the works and artists, and print color reproductions. The museum's goal is to "connect people to art and art to people," so its exhibits tend to have broad appeal, and if traveling shows from other cities come to town, you can expect to see them here. Lectures, concerts, and film events are also on the roster. Free docent tours are offered throughout the day. ✉ *1450 El Prado* ☎ *619/232–7931* ⊕ *www.sdmart.org* 🏷 *$10* ⊙ *Tues.–Sun. 10–6; Memorial Day–Labor Day until 9 Thurs.*

▌ **NEED A BREAK?** Take a respite from museum-hopping with a cup of coffee or a glass of California chardonnay in the San Diego Museum of Art's **Waters Café** (☎ *619/237–0675*), in the outdoor sanctuary of the Museum's Sculpture Court and Garden. The café serves a selection of vegetarian dishes as well as gourmet sandwiches and salads. Handmade burgers are grilled to perfection.

⊙ ❷ **San Diego Museum of Man.** If the facade of this building—the landmark California Building—looks familiar, it's because filmmaker Orson Welles used it and its dramatic tower as the principal features of the Xanadu estate in his 1941 classic, *Citizen Kane.* Inside, exhibits at this highly respected anthropological museum focus on Southwestern, Mexican, and South American cultures. Carved monuments from the Mayan city of Quirigua in Guatemala, cast from the originals in 1914, are particularly impressive. Exhibits might include examples of intricate beadwork from across the Americas, the history of Egyptian mummies, or the lifestyles of the Kumeyaay peoples who inhabited San Diego before Europeans arrived. Among the museum's more recent additions is the hands-on Children's

What's Free When

While beachcombing, sunbathing, and strolling along the beach will always be San Diego's most popular free activities, there are many other options for those days when you want to shake the sand out of your shoes and see another side of the city. The downtown location of the Museum of Contemporary Art is free every day except Wednesday, when it's closed. The La Jolla location is free the third Tuesday of each month. Old Town State Historic Park is free at all times, as are many of the museums within its boundaries. The most options for freebies can be found in Balboa Park, both on a weekly basis and at special times of the year. You can pick up a free garden tour map at the Visitor's Center and use that to explore the dozens of gardens covering the park's 1,200 acres, but you aren't limited to just that. The San Diego Zoo is free for kids under 12 the whole month of October, and everyone gets in free on the first Monday in October to celebrate Founder's Day. The December Nights festival on the first Friday and Saturday of that month includes free admission (and later hours) to most of the Balboa Park museums. The outdoor events during the festival make it something not to miss. The free concerts at the Spreckels Organ Pavilion take place Sunday afternoons at 2 PM year-round and on Monday evenings in summer. Also at the Speckels Organ Pavilion, the Twilight in the Park Summer Concert Series offers various performances Tuesday, Wednesday, and Thursday from 6:15 to 7:15. From July 8 to August 26, the San Diego Museum of Art hosts "Screen on the Green," an outdoor film festival presented in conjunction with the museum's summer exhibition. Films begin at dusk on Balboa Park's East Lawn. The Timken Museum of Art is always free. The Centro Cultural de la Raza and Veterans Memorial Center are free, but a donation is requested at each. The best deal is the Free Tuesdays in the Park, a rotating schedule of free admission to most all of Balboa Park's museums. Call ahead, as some museums are free to San Diego residents only.

First Tuesday:

Natural History Museum

Reuben H. Fleet Science Center

San Diego Model Railroad Museum

Second Tuesday:

Museum of Photographic Arts

Museum of San Diego History

Veterans Museum

Third Tuesday:

Japanese Friendship Garden

Mingei International Museum

San Diego Art Institute

San Diego Museum of Art

San Diego Museum of Man

Fourth Tuesday:

House of Pacific Relations International Cottages

San Diego Air and Space Museum

San Diego Automotive Museum

San Diego Hall of Champions

Discovery Center. ⊠*California Bldg., 1350 El Prado* ☎*619/239–2001* ⊕*www.museumofman.org* ⊒*$8* ⊗*Daily 10–4:30.*

★ ☾ **❼** **San Diego Natural History Museum.** There are 7.5 million fossils, dinosaur models, and even live reptiles and other specimens under this roof. Favorite exhibits include the Foucault pendulum, suspended on a 43-foot cable and designed to demonstrate the Earth's rotation; a full-size gray-whale skeleton; and *Ocean Oasis,* the world's first large-format film about Baja California and the Sea of Cortéz. Highlighted are regional environment exhibits and educational films at the museum's giant-screen theater. Traveling exhibits make a stop here, and the museum also sponsors community events. Call ahead for information on films, lectures, and free guided nature walks. ⊠*1788 El Prado* ☎*619/232–3821* ⊕*www.sdnhm.org* ⊒*$9* ⊗*Daily 10–5.*

☾ **⓫** **San Diego Zoo.** Balboa Park's—and perhaps the city's—most famous
Fodor's Choice attraction is its 100-acre zoo. Nearly 4,000 animals of some 800 diverse
★ species roam in hospitable, expertly crafted habitats that replicate natural environments as closely as possible. The flora in the zoo, including many rare species, is even more costly than the fauna. Walkways wind over bridges and past waterfalls ringed with tropical ferns; elephants in a sandy plateau roam so close you're tempted to pet them.

Exploring the zoo fully requires the stamina of a healthy hiker, but open-air double-decker buses that run throughout the day let you zip through three-quarters of the exhibits on a guided 35- to 40-minute, 3-mi tour. There are also express buses, used for quick transportation, that make five stops around the grounds and include some narration. The Skyfari Aerial Tram, which soars 170 feet above the ground, gives a good overview of the zoo's layout and, on clear days, a panorama of the park, downtown San Diego, the bay, and the ocean, far past the San Diego–Coronado Bridge. ■TIP➔**Unless you come early, expect to wait for the regular bus, and especially for the top tier—the line can take more than 45 minutes; if you come at midday on a weekend or school holiday, you'll be doing the in-line shuffle for a while.**

In any case, the zoo is at its best when you wander its paths, such as the one that climbs through the huge, enclosed **Scripps Aviary,** where brightly colored tropical birds swoop between branches just inches from your face, and into the neighboring **Gorilla Tropics,** one of the zoo's bioclimatic zone exhibits, where animals live in enclosed environments modeled on their native habitats. The zones look and sound natural, thanks in part to modern technology: the sounds of the tropical rain forest emerge from a 144-speaker sound system that plays CDs recorded in Africa.

The zoo's simulated Asian rain forest, **Tiger River,** has 10 exhibits with more than 35 species of animals. The mist-shrouded trails winding down a canyon into Tiger River are bordered by fragrant jasmine, ginger lilies, and orchids, giving you the feeling of descending into an Asian jungle. Tigers, Malayan tapirs, and Argus pheasants wander among the exotic trees and plants. **Ituri Forest**—a 4-acre African rain forest at the base of Tiger River—lets you glimpse huge but surprisingly graceful hippos frolicking underwater, and buffalo cavorting with monkeys on dry land. In **Sun Bear Forest** playful beasts constantly claw apart the trees and shrubs that serve as a natural playground for climbing, jumping, and general merrymaking. At the popular **Polar Bear Plunge,** where you can watch the featured animals take a chilly dive, Siberian reindeer, white foxes, and other Arctic creatures are separated from their predatory neighbors by a series of camouflaged moats. The lush, tropical environment at **Absolutely Apes,** where orangutans and siamangs climb, swing, and generally live almost as they would in the wild, is lined with 110-foot-long and 12-foot-high viewing windows that offer a unique opportunity to view these endangered apes close up.

The San Diego Zoo houses the largest number of koalas outside Australia, and they remain major crowd pleasers even though they are overshadowed by the pandas, and especially the baby pandas that result from the work of the zoo's department of Conservation and Research for Endangered Species.

For a hands-on experience there's the **Children's Zoo,** where goats and sheep beg to be petted. There is one viewer-friendly nursery where you may see various baby animals bottle-feed and sleep peacefully in large baby cribs. Children can see entertaining creatures of all sorts nearby at the Wegeforth National Park Sea Lion Show in Wegeforth Bowl and at the Wild Ones Show in Hunte Amphitheater, both put on daily.

Joan B. Kroc's **Monkey Trails and Forest Tales** spans three acres representing African and Asian forests. This is the largest and most elaborate animal habitat in the zoo's history. You can follow an elevated trail at treetop level and trek paths on the forest floor, observing some of nature's most unusual and threatened animals and birds, including African mandrills, Asia's clouded leopard, the rare pygmy hippopotamus, Visayan warty pigs from the Philippines, weaver birds that build the most elaborate nests of any species, not to mention flora such as endangered mahogany trees, rare, exotic orchids, and insect-eating plants.

Set to debut in Spring 2009, the zoo's newest exhibit, Elephant Odyssey, highlights animals of the past, present, and future. The 7-acre habitat features relatives of animal species that dotted the Southern California landscape over 10,000 years ago, such as elephants, lions, and wild horses.

The zoo rents strollers, wheelchairs, and cameras; it also has a first-aid office, a lost and found, and an ATM. It's best to avert your eyes from the two main gift shops until the end of your visit; you can spend a half day just poking through the wonderful animal-related posters, crafts, dishes, clothing, and toys. There is one guilt-alleviating fact if you buy too much: some of the profits of your purchases go to zoo programs. Audio tours, behind-the-scenes tours, walking tours, tours in Spanish, and tours for people with hearing or vision impairments are available; inquire at the entrance. Lastly, when you've finished here, you haven't seen it all until you've seen the San Diego Wild Animal Park, the zoo's 1,800-acre extension to the north at Escondido. ✉ *2920 Zoo Dr.*

"Panda-monium"

The San Diego Zoo currently has more giant pandas than any other zoo in the United States, and is the only zoo in North America to have had four successful panda births. The zoo's first success was Hua Mei, born in 1999 and the first giant panda cub born in the United States to survive to adulthood. Hua Mei's mother, Bai Yun, then had a second cub, a male, Mei Sheng, in August 2003. Two years later, in August 2005, Bai Yun and Gao Gao, her mate, became the parents of the cute-ster Su Lin, a female. In August 2007 Bai Yun gave birth to her fourth cub, Zhen Zhen, which appropriately means "precious." The female cub was just four ounces at birth, about the size of a stick of butter! When fully grown, Zhen Zhen will weigh between 220 and 330 pounds.

Hua Mei and Mei Sheng (who left in November 2007) now live in China, but Su Lin, Zhen Zhen, and their parents are generally available for viewing from 9 to 4:15 each day at the Giant Panda Research Station. All pandas in the U.S. are on loan from China, and even babies born here pass to China's control after their third birthday. By the time of your visit, China may have decided that Su Lin should come home or be sent elsewhere.

After Hua Mei was returned to China in 2004, she became a mother herself, to a set of twins born in September 2004, then to a second set of twins in August 2005—truly blessed events considering there are presumed to be only 1,500 pandas still remaining in the wild. Expect lines at the panda exhibit to be long, so arrive early.

☎619/234–3153, 888/697–2632 *Giant panda hotline* ⊕*www.sand-iegozoo.org* 🎟*$24.50 includes zoo, Children's Zoo, and animal shows; $34 includes above, plus guided bus tour, unlimited express bus rides, and round-trip Skyfari Aerial Tram rides; zoo free for children under 12 in Oct.; $60 pass good for admission to zoo and San Diego Wild Animal Park within 5 days* 🚪*AE, D, MC, V* ⊘*July–Sept., daily 9–9; Sept.–May, daily 9–4; Children's Zoo and Skyfari ride generally close 1 hr earlier.*

NEED A BREAK? If you want to eat among strolling peacocks—who will try to cadge your food—consider the **Flamingo Café**, inside the main entrance, serving sandwiches, salads, and light meals. Of the zoo's indoor restaurants, the best is **Albert's**, part of a three-tier dining complex near Gorilla Tropics. Grilled fish, homemade pizza, and fresh pasta are among the offerings, and this is the only place where wine and beer are served.

⑧ Spanish Village Art Center. More than 50 local artists, including glass-blowers, enamel workers, wood-carvers, sculptors, painters, jewelers, and photographers rent space in these 35 red-tile–roof studio-galleries that were set up for the 1935–36 exposition in the style of an old Spanish village, and they give demonstrations of their work on a rotating basis. Spanish Village is in fact a great source for one-of-a-kind, truly memorable gifts. ✉*1770 Village Pl.* ☎*619/233–9050* ⊕*www.span-ishvillageart.com* 🎟*Free* ⊘*Daily 11–4.*

⑱ Spreckels Organ Pavilion. The 2,000-seat pavilion, dedicated in 1915 by sugar magnates John D. and Adolph B. Spreckels, holds the 4,530-pipe Spreckels Organ, the largest outdoor pipe organ in the world. You can hear this impressive instrument at one of the year-round, free, 2 PM Sunday concerts, regularly performed by civic organist Carol Williams—a highlight of a visit to Balboa Park. On Monday evenings in summer, internationally renowned organists play dramatic background music to silent films. At Christmastime the park's Christmas tree and life-size Nativity display turn the pavilion into a seasonal wonderland. ✉*2211 Pan American Rd.* ☎*619/702–8138* ⊕*www.sosorgan.com.*

⑤ Timken Museum of Art. Somewhat out of place in the architectural scheme of the park, this modern structure is made of travertine imported from Italy. The small museum is a true jewel box, housing works by major European and American artists as well as a superb collection of Russian icons. ✉*1500 El Prado* ☎*619/239–5548* ⊕*www.timkenmuseum.org* 🎟*Free* ⊘*Tues.–Sat. 10–4:30, Sun. 1:30–4:30.*

CORONADO

Although it's actually an isthmus, easily reached from the mainland if you head north from Imperial Beach, Coronado has always seemed like an island and is often referred to as such. Located just 15 mi east of downtown San Diego, Coronado was a small sandbar until the late 1900's and was named after Mexico's Coronados Islands.

As if freeze-framed in the 1950s, Coronado's quaint appeal is captured in its old-fashioned storefronts, well-manicured gardens, and charming Ferry Landing Marketplace. Many of today's residents live in grand Victorian homes handed down for generations. Naval Air Station North Island was established in 1911 on Coronado's north end, across from Point Loma, and was the site of Charles Lindbergh's departure on the transcontinental flight that preceded his famous solo flight across the Atlantic. Coronado's long relationship with the U.S. Navy and its desirable real estate have made it an enclave for military personnel; it's said to have more retired admirals per capita than anywhere else in the United States.

The streets of Coronado are wide, quiet, and friendly, with lots of neighborhood parks where young families mingle with the area's many senior citizens. Grand old homes face the waterfront and the Coronado Municipal Golf Course, under the bridge at the north end of Glorietta Bay; it's the site of the annual July 4 fireworks display. Community celebrations and concerts take place in Spreckels Park on Orange Avenue.

Coronado is accessible via the arching blue 2.2-mi-long San Diego–Coronado Bay Bridge, which handles some 68,000 cars each day. The view of the harbor, downtown, and the island is breathtaking, day and night. Until the bridge was completed in 1969, visitors and residents relied on the Coronado Ferry, which today has become quite popular with bicyclists, who shuttle their bikes across the harbor and ride Coronado's wide, flat boulevards for hours. You can board the ferry, operated by **San Diego Harbor Excursion** (☎ *619/234–4111, 800/442–7847* ⊕ *www.sdhe.com*), at the Broadway Pier on the Embarcadero in downtown San Diego; you'll arrive at the Ferry Landing Marketplace in Coronado. Boats depart every hour on the hour from the Embarcadero and every hour on the half hour from Coronado, daily 9–9 from San Diego (9–10 Friday and Saturday), 9:30–9:30 from Coronado (9:30–10:30 Friday and Saturday); the fare is $3 each way, 50¢ extra for bicycles. Buy tickets at the Broadway Pier or the Ferry Landing Marketplace. In addition to nightly dinner cruises and seasonal whale-watching tours, San Diego Harbor Excursion also offers water-taxi service weekdays 2 PM–10 PM, and weekends 11 AM–11 PM. Later hours can be arranged. The taxi can run between any two points in San Diego Bay. The fare is $7 per person. Call ☎ 619/235–8294 to book.

San Diego's Metropolitan Transit System runs a shuttle bus, No. 904, around Coronado; you can pick it up where you disembark the ferry and ride it out as far as Silver Strand State Beach. Buses start leaving from the ferry landing at 10:30 AM and run once an hour on the half hour until 6:30 PM. Bus No. 901 runs daily between the Gaslamp Quarter and Coronado.

Numbers in the text correspond to numbers on the Central San Diego map.

A GOOD TOUR

Coronado is easy to navigate without a car. When you leave the ferry, you can explore the shops at the **Ferry Landing Marketplace** ❶ and from there rent a bicycle or catch the shuttle bus that runs down **Orange Avenue** ❷, Coronado's main street. Get off the bus at 10th Street and Orange to pick up a map at the Coronado Visitor Center, in the lobby of the **Coronado Museum of History and Art** ❸, and then keep strolling along the boutique-filled promenade until you reach the **Hotel Del Coronado** ❹ at the end of Orange Avenue. Right across the street from the Del is the **Glorietta Bay Inn** ❺, another of the island's outstanding early structures. If you've brought your swimsuit, you might continue on to **Silver Strand State Beach** ❻—just past the Hotel Del, Orange Avenue turns into Silver Strand Boulevard, which soon resumes its original across-the-bridge role as Route 75.

TIMING A leisurely stroll through Coronado takes at least an hour, more if you stop to shop or walk along the family-friendly beaches. Rest assured that a day spent here is time well spent, and many locals regard a Coronado visit as a quick and pleasant vacation. If you're a history buff, you might want to visit on Tuesday, Thursday, or Saturday, when you can combine the tour of the historic homes that departs from the Glorietta Bay Inn at 11 AM with a visit to the Coronado Museum of History and Art, open daily. Whenever you come, if you're not staying overnight, remember to get back to the dock in time to catch the final ferry out at 9:30 (10:30 on weekends).

SIGHTS TO SEE

❸ **Coronado Museum of History and Art.** The neoclassical First Bank of Commerce building, constructed in 1910, holds the headquarters and archives of the Coronado Historical Association, a museum, the Coronado Visitor Center, the Coronado Museum Store, and Tent City Restaurant. The collection celebrates Coronado's history with photographs and displays of its formative events and major sights. Two galleries have permanent displays, while a third hosts traveling exhibits; all offer interactive activities for children and adults. For information on the town's historic houses, pick up a copy of the inexpensive *Promenade Through the Past: A Brief History of Coronado and its Architectural Wonders* at the museum gift shop. The book traces a 60-minute walking tour of the architecturally and historically significant buildings that surround the area. The tour departs from the museum lobby on Wednesday at 2 PM and Friday at 10:30 AM and costs $10. ✉ *1100 Orange Ave.* ☎ *619/435–7242* ⊕ *www.coronadohistory.org* 💳 *Donations accepted* ⊗ *Weekdays 9–5, Sat.–Sun. 10–5.*

★ ☾ **①** **Ferry Landing Marketplace.** This collection of shops at the ferry landing is on a smaller—and generally less interesting—scale than Seaport Village, but you do get a great view of the downtown San Diego skyline. Located along the San Diego Bay, the little shops and restaurants resemble the gingerbread domes of the Hotel Del Coronado. If you want to rent a bike or in-line skates, stop in at **Bikes and Beyond** (✉ *1201 1st St. #122* ☎*619/435–7180*). ✉*1201 1st St., at B Ave.,* ☎*619/435–8895.*

⑤ **Glorietta Bay Inn.** The former residence of John Spreckels, the original owner of North Island and the property on which the Hotel Del Coronado stands, is now a popular hotel. On Tuesday, Thursday, and Saturday mornings at 11 it's the departure point for a fun and informative 1½-hour walking tour of a few of the area's 86 officially designated historic homes. It includes—from the outside only—some spectacular mansions and the Meade House, where L. Frank Baum, author of *The Wizard of Oz,* wrote additional Oz stories. ✉*1630 Glorietta Blvd.* ☎*619/435–3101, 619/435–5993 tour information* ☎*$12 for historical tour.*

④ **Hotel Del Coronado.** One of San Diego's best-known sites, the hotel has

Fodor'sChoice been a National Historic Landmark since 1977. It has a colorful his-

★ tory, integrally connected with that of Coronado itself. The Del, as natives call it, was the brainchild of financiers Elisha Spurr Babcock Jr. and H.L. Story, who saw the potential of Coronado's virgin beaches and its view of San Diego's emerging harbor. The hotel opened in 1888, just 11 months after construction began.

The Del's distinctive red-tile roofs and Victorian gingerbread architecture have served as a set for many movies, political meetings, and extravagant social happenings. It's speculated that the Duke of Windsor may have first met Wallis Simpson here. Eleven presidents have been guests of The Del, and the film *Some Like It Hot*—starring Marilyn Monroe, Jack Lemmon, and Tony Curtis—used the hotel as a backdrop.

Broad steps lead up to the main, balconied lobby, which is adorned with grand oak pillars and ceiling and opens out onto a central courtyard and gazebo. To the right is the cavernous **Crown Room,** whose arched ceiling of notched sugar pine was constructed without nails. A lavish Sunday brunch is served here from 9:30–2. During the holidays, the hotel hosts Skating by the Sea an outdoor beachfront ice-skating rink open to the public.

The patio surrounding the swimming pool is a great place to sit back and imagine what the bathers looked like during the 1920s, when the hotel rocked with good times. To its right, the Windsor Lawn provides a green oasis between the hotel and the beach. To the pool's left are the seven-story Ocean Towers accommodations, built in the 1970s. The History Gallery displays photos from the Del's early days, and books elaborating on its history and that of Kate Morgan, the hotel's resident ghost, are sold along with logo apparel and gifts in the hotel's 15-plus shops. In early 2008 the Del unveiled $150 million in luxury enhancements, including 78 new cottages and villas, a signature restaurant, a wine room, and a spa. The resort recently published a new book titled *Building the Dream: The Design and Construction of the Hotel del Coronado.*

Tours of the Del are available Tuesday at 10:30 and Friday–Sunday at 2. Reservations are required through the **Coronado Visitor Center** (☎619/437–8788 ⊕*www.coronadovisitorscenter.com*). ⊠*1500 Orange Ave.* ☎*619/435–6611* ⊕*www.hoteldel.com.*

② **Orange Avenue.** Coronado's business district and its village-like heart, this is surely one of the most charming spots in Southern California. Slow-paced and very "local" (the city fights against chain stores), it's a blast from the past, although entirely up-to-date in other respects. The military presence—Coronado is home to the U.S. Navy Sea, Air and Land (SEAL) forces—is reflected in shops selling military gear and places like McP's Irish Pub, the unofficial SEALs headquarters and a family-friendly stop for a good, all-American meal. Many clothing boutiques, home-furnishings stores, and upscale restaurants cater to visitors with deep pockets, but you can buy plumbing supplies, too, or get a genuine military haircut at Crown Barbers. The warm sun in winter truly makes Coronado seem like paradise on earth. The **Coronado Visitor Center** (⊠*1100 Orange Ave.* ☎*619/437–8788* ⊕*www.coronado-visitorscenter.com*) is open weekdays 9–5, Saturday 10–5, and Sunday 10–5 year-round.

NEED A BREAK? There's an abundance of places to find a caffeine fix on Orange Avenue between 8th Street and the Hotel Del. At the hip, mini-bistro **Cafe 1134** (⊠*1134 Orange Ave.* ☎*619/437–1134*) you can get a good curried tuna sandwich on French bread to accompany your espresso. Peruse the latest art magazine while sipping a latte at the sidewalk café of **Bay Books** (⊠*1029 Orange Ave.* ☎*619/435–0070*), San Diego's largest independent bookstore. For a deliciously sweet pick-me-up, check out the rich ice cream, frozen yogurt, and sorbet made fresh daily on the premises of **Mootime Creamery** (⊠*1015 Orange Ave.* ☎*619/435–2422*). Just look for the statue of Elvis on the sidewalk in front.

⑥ **Silver Strand State Beach.** The stretch of sand that runs along Silver Strand Boulevard from the Hotel Del Coronado to Imperial Beach is a perfect family gathering spot, with restrooms and lifeguards. The shallow shoreline and minimal crowds also make it a popular spot for kitesurfing. Don't be surprised if you see groups exercising in military style along the beach; this is a training area for the U.S. Navy's SEAL teams. Across from the beach are the Coronado Cays, an exclusive community popular with yacht owners and celebrities, and the Loews Coronado Bay Resort.

EN ROUTE San Diego's Mexican-American community is centered in Barrio Logan, under the San Diego–Coronado Bridge on the downtown side. **Chicano Park**, spread along National Avenue from Dewey to Crosby streets, is the barrio's recreational hub. It's worth taking a short detour to see the huge murals of Mexican history painted on the bridge supports at National Avenue and Dewey Street; they're among the best examples of folk art in the city.

DOWNTOWN

Downtown is San Diego's Lazarus. Written off as moribund by the 1970s, downtown is now one of the city's prime draws. The turn-around began in the late 1970s with the revitalization of the Gaslamp Quarter Historic District and massive redevelopment that gave rise to the Horton Plaza shopping center and the San Diego Convention Center. Although many consider downtown to be the 16½ block **Gaslamp Quarter,** it's actually comprised of eight neighborhoods, also including East Village, Little Italy, and Embarcadero.

Considered the liveliest of the bunch, Gaslamp's Fourth and Fifth Avenues are riddled with trendy nightclubs, swanky lounge bars, chic restaurants, and boisterous sports pubs, something of a French Quarter West (but without Bourbon Street's less savory distractions). Nearby, the most ambitious of the downtown projects is **East Village,** encompassing 130 blocks between the railroad tracks up to J Street, and from 6th Avenue east to around 10th Street. Sparking the rebirth of this former warehouse district was the 2004 construction of the San Diego Padres' baseball stadium, PETCO Park. As the city's largest downtown neighborhood, East Village is continually broadening its boundaries with its urban design of redbrick cafés, spacious galleries, roof-top bars, sleek hotels, and warehouse restaurants.

Holding true to its European roots is the charming neighborhood of **Little Italy,** inhabited by native Italians and talented artists. After an afternoon of gelati and espressos in this village enclave you may just forget that you're in Southern California. Running along the San Diego harbor is downtown's **Embarcadero,** home to the USS Midway, the Maritime Museum, and Seaport Village, with 50-plus shops, 17 restaurants, and outdoor entertainment. The Martin Luther King Jr. Promenade project put 14 acres of greenery, a pedestrian walkway, and artwork along Harbor Drive from Seaport Village to the San Diego Convention Center.

Downtown's natural attributes were easily evident to its original booster, wealthy San Francisco businessman William Heath Davis, who along with several business partners attempted the first settlement by the Bay in 1850. When Alonzo Horton arrived in San Diego in 1867, he bought 960 acres for $4,265 and gave away the land to those who would build churches. Today the William Heath Davis Historic House Museum celebrates the lives of these two San Diego pioneers.

There are reasonably priced ($4–$7 per day) parking lots along Harbor Drive, Pacific Highway, and lower Broadway and Market Street. Most restaurants offer valet parking at night, but beware of fees of $15 and up.

Numbers in the text correspond to numbers on the Central San Diego map.

EAST VILLAGE

Sprawling over 350 acres and 130 blocks, East Village is one neighborhood that cannot be contained. Slated exclusively for downtown development, this booming enclave was once branded as San Diego's gritty warehouse district, complete with packing plants, cheap hotels, and industrial fish companies. In the mid-eighties a handful of artists started buying up affordable property for loft and studio conversions. It was the 2004 opening of PETCO Park, however, that triggered the unfathomable metamorphosis. Other businesses including art galleries, music venues, and funky cafés are sprouting up on virtually every corner, while still holding true to the warehouse flavor of the past. Fortunately, the "industrially warm" vibe for which East Village is known has only been enhanced by its eclectic residents. Due to its growing popularity, East Village is now the home of San Diego's September Street Scene, the largest music festival in California.

SIGHTS TO SEE

❼ PETCO Park. Opened in 2004, PETCO Park is a state-of-the-art Major League ballpark and home to the San Diego Padres. In 2007 the park also started hosting the Rugby Union USA Sevens. Built at a cost of $450 million, the stadium features a 30- x 53-foot LED video board and 744 televisions, and is strategically designed to give fans a view of San Diego Bay, the skyline, and Balboa Park. Reflecting San Diego's beauty, the stadium is painted in shades of Indian sandstone to evoke the area's cliffs and beaches; the 42,000 seats are dark blue, reminiscent of the ocean, and the exposed steel is painted white to reflect the sails of harbor boats on the bay. A main draw of PETCO is the family-friendly lawn-like berm, "Park at the Park," where fans can view the game for a $5 fee. ✉ *100 Park Blvd.* ☎ *619/795–5000* ⊕ *www.padres.com.*

❽ Western Metal Supply Co Building. Initially scheduled for demolition to make room for PETCO Park, this historic site has been incorporated into the ballpark and supports the left field foul pole, 334 feet from home plate. Great care was taken to retain the historic nature of the building's exterior despite the extensive interior renovations. Constructed in 1909, the four-story structure originally manufactured wagon wheels and war supplies, and today holds the Padres' Team Store, the Padres' Hall of Fame Bar and Grill, and rooftop seating. ✉ *215 7th Ave.* ☎ *619/266–0555* ⊕ *www.westernmetalsupplyco.com.*

EMBARCADERO

The bustle of Embarcadero comes less these days from the activities of fishing folk than from the throngs of tourists, but this waterfront walkway—comprised of Seaport Village and the San Diego Convention Center—remains the nautical soul of the city. There are several seafood

TWO GOOD DOWNTOWN WALKS

Most people do a lot of parking-lot hopping when visiting downtown, but for the energetic, two distinct areas can be explored on foot.

To stay near the water, start a walk on the **Embarcadero** at the foot of Ash Street on Harbor Drive, where the *Berkeley*, headquarters of the **Maritime Museum** ⑬, is moored. A cement pathway runs south from the *Star of India*, one of the museum's sailing ships, along the waterfront to the pastel B Street Pier, but if you're traveling with firehouse fans, detour inland four blocks on Ash and north two blocks to the **Firehouse Museum** ⑳, at the corner of Cedar and Columbia in **Little Italy**. For true Italian culture, continue one block east on Cedar, where locals gather to play bocce ball at Amici Park. Otherwise, another two blocks south on Harbor Drive brings you to the foot of Broadway and the Broadway Pier, where you can catch harbor excursion boats and the ferry to Coronado. Approximately one block south of Broadway is the Navy Pier, home of the **San Diego Aircraft Carrier Museum** ⑪. Take Broadway inland two long blocks to Kettner Boulevard to reach the **Transit Center** ⑭—where you can board the trolley to Tijuana. Across the street you'll find the downtown branch of the **Museum of Contemporary Art, San Diego** ⑮. (If you've detoured to the Firehouse Museum, take Kettner Boulevard south to the Transit Center.) Return to Harbor Drive and continue south past Tuna Harbor to **Seaport Village** ⑨.

A tour of the working heart of downtown can begin at the corner of 1st Avenue and Broadway, near Spreckels Theater, a grand old stage that presents pop concerts and touring plays. Two blocks east and across the street sits the historic **U. S. Grant Hotel** ⑲. If you cross Broadway, you'll be able to enter **Horton Plaza** ⑱, San Diego's favorite retail playland. Fourth Avenue, the eastern boundary of Horton Plaza, doubles as the western boundary of the 16-block **Gaslamp Quarter Historic District**. Head south to Island Avenue and 4th Avenue to the **William Heath Davis House** ⑰, where you can get a touring map of the district.

TIMING

The above walks take about an hour each, although there's enough to do in downtown San Diego to keep you busy for at least two days. Although it is relatively easy to explore downtown on foot, alternative modes of transportation are available, including horse-drawn carriages, pedicabs, the San Diego Trolley, and GoCars (three-wheel cars equipped with a GPS-guided audio tour). Most of downtown's attractions are open daily, but the Museum of Contemporary Art is closed on Tuesday, and the Firehouse Museum is only open Thursday through Sunday. If you want to take a guided tour of the Gaslamp Quarter Historic District, plan to visit on a Saturday. A boat trip on the harbor, or at least a hop over to Coronado on the ferry, is a must at any time of year. From December through March, when the gray whales migrate between the Pacific Northwest and southern Baja, you should definitely consider booking a whale-watching excursion from the Broadway Pier.

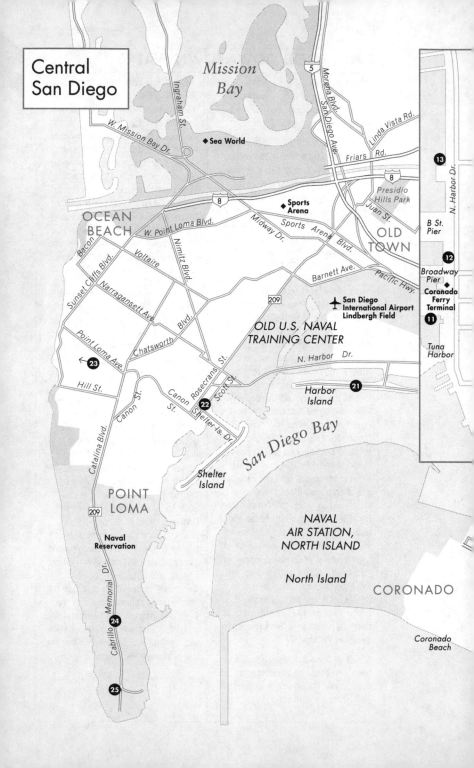

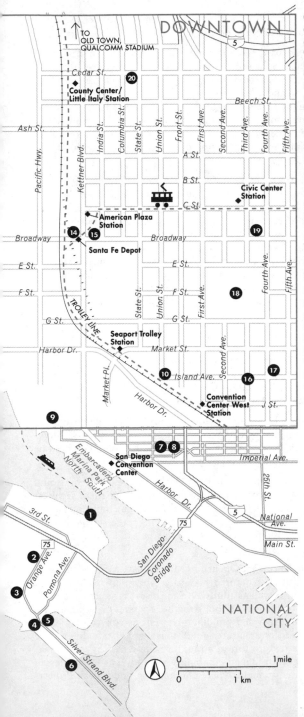

DOWNTOWN

TO OLD TOWN, QUALCOMM STADIUM

Cedar St.

County Center/
Little Italy Station

Beech St.

Ash St.

Pacific Hwy.

Kettner Blvd.

India St.

Columbia St.

State St.

Union St.

Front St.

First Ave.

Second Ave.

Third Ave.

Fourth Ave.

Fifth Ave.

A St.

B St.

C St.

Civic Center
Station

American Plaza
Station

Broadway

Broadway

Santa Fe Depot

E St.

E St.

F St.

F St.

State St.

Union St.

F St.

First Ave.

Fourth Ave.

Fifth Ave.

TROLLEY LINE

G St.

G St.

Harbor Dr.

Seaport Trolley
Station

Market St.

Second Ave.

Market Pl.

Harbor Dr.

Island Ave.

Convention
Center West
Station

J St.

Embarcadero
Marina Park
North South

San Diego
Convention
Center

3rd St.

Harbor Dr.

Imperial Ave.

25th St.

National
Ave.

Main St.

Orange Ave.

Pomona Ave.

San Diego-
Coronado
Bridge

NATIONAL
CITY

Silver Strand Blvd.

0   1 mile
0   1 km

1

restaurants here, as well as sea vessels of every variety—cruise ships, ferries, tour boats, and Navy destroyers.

On the north end of the Embarcadero at Ash Street you'll find the **Maritime Museum**. South of it, the **B Street Pier** is used by ships from major cruise lines—San Diego has become a major cruise-ship port, both a port of call and a departure point. Tickets for harbor tours and whale-watching trips are sold at the foot of **Broadway Pier**. The terminal for the Coronado Ferry lies just beyond, between Broadway Pier and B Street Pier. One block south of Broadway Pier at Tidelands Park is Military Heritage Art, a collection of works that commemorate the service of the U.S military.

Lining the pedestrian promenade between the Cruise Ship Terminal and Hawthorn Street are thirty "urban trees" sculpted by local artists. Docked at the Navy pier is the decommissioned USS *Midway*, now the home of the San Diego Aircraft Carrier Museum. **Tuna Harbor,** at the foot of G Street, was once the hub of one of San Diego's earliest and most successful industries, commercial tuna fishing. The industry has moved far away to the western Pacific, so these days there are more pleasure boats than tuna boats tied up at the G Street Pier. The pleasant Tuna Harbor Park offers a great view of boating on the bay and across to any aircraft carriers docked at the North Island naval base.

The next bit of seafront greenery is a few blocks south at **Embarcadero Marina Park North,** an 8-acre extension into the harbor from the center of Seaport Village. It's usually full of kite fliers, in-line skaters, and picnickers. Seasonal celebrations, including San Diego's Parade of Lights, the Port of San Diego Big Balloon Parade, the Sea and Air Parade, and the Big Bay July 4 Celebration, are held here and at the similar **Embarcadero Marina Park South.**

Providing a unique shopping experience, **Seaport Village** covers 14-acres of waterfront retail stores, restaurants, and cafés. Even window-shoppers are treated to a pleasant experience with 4 mi of cobblestone paths, trickling fountains, and beautiful gardens.

The **San Diego Convention Center,** on Harbor Drive between 1st and 6th avenues, is a waterfront landmark designed by Canadian architect Arthur Erickson. The backdrop of blue sky and sea complements the building's nautical lines. The center often holds trade shows that are open to the public, and tours of the building are available.

SIGHTS TO SEE

Ⓒ ⑩ **Children's Museum San Diego.** Opened in May 2008, CMSD blends con-
Fodor'sChoice temporary art with unstructured play to create an environment that
★ appeals to children as well as adults. As San Diego's largest green build-
ing project, the 50,000-square-foot structure operates on solar energy, is constructed from recycled building materials, is convection-cooled by an elevator shaft, and features an Organics-to-Go café. Interactive exhibits include a texture forest, a rain house powered by child-oper-ated bicycles, a graffiti-tagged climbing wall, and Tent City accessed through illuminated tunnels, where children can build forts. Projects

1

at the hands-on Wet Studio change monthly, and encourage visitors to work with clay or even use real cars as a canvas on which to paint. The adjoining one-acre park features outdoor reading circles and is conveniently located across from the Convention Center trolley stop. ⊠*200 W. Island Ave.* ☎ *619/233–8792* ⊕*www.childrensmuseumsd. org* ⊠*$10* ⊙*Thurs.–Tues. 9–4.*

⑫ **International Visitor Information Center.** One of the two visitor information centers operated by the San Diego Convention and Visitors Bureau (the other is in La Jolla), this is the best resource for information on the city. The staff members and volunteers who run the center speak many languages and dispense information on hotels, restaurants, and tourist attractions, including those in Tijuana, and provide discount coupons for many. Stop by when visiting the Embarcadero, since it's just across from Broadway Pier. ⊠*10401/3 W. Broadway, at Harbor Dr.* ☎*619/236–1212* ⊕*www.sandiego.org* ⊙*June–Sept., daily 9–5; Oct.–May, daily 9–4.*

⊙ ⑬ **Maritime Museum.** A must for anyone with an interest in nautical history,
FodorśChoice this collection of six restored and replica ships affords a fascinating
★ glimpse of San Diego during its heyday as a commercial seaport. The museum's headquarters are the *Berkeley,* an 1898 ferryboat moored at the foot of Ash Street. The steam-driven ship, which served the Southern Pacific Railroad in San Francisco until 1958, played its most important role during the great earthquake of 1906, when it saved thousands of people from the fires that had engulfed San Francisco. Its ornate carved-wood paneling, stained-glass windows, and plate-glass mirrors have been restored, and its main deck serves as a floating museum, with permanent exhibits on West Coast maritime history and complementary rotating exhibits.

If you crave more than a dockside experience, you can take to the water in the museum's other sailing ship, the Californian, a replica of a 19th-century revenue cutter that patrolled the shores of California. Designated the state's official tall ship, it can be boarded for a variety of half- and full-day sails (weather permitting) on weekends. (Typically, weekday cruises are reserved for schoolchildren.) Tickets may be purchased online or at the museum on the day of sail. Full-day sails leave at 10 AM and half-day sails leave between 1 and 4 PM. They're most popular on sunny days, when it's recommended to show up at least one hour ahead of desired departure. ⊠*1492 N. Harbor Dr.* ☎*619/234–9153* ⊕*www.sdmaritime.org* ⊠*$14 includes entry to all ships except the Californian* ⊙*9–8, until 9* PM *in summer.*

⑮ **Museum of Contemporary Art, San Diego.** The downtown branch of the city's modern art museum has assumed a personality of its own. Its postmodern, cutting-edge exhibitions are perfectly complemented by the steel-and-glass transportation complex of which it is a part. Four small galleries in the two-story building host rotating shows, some from the permanent collection in the older La Jolla branch, others loaned from far-flung international museums. A new downtown expansion opened nearby in January 2007, featuring an education room for hands-on interactive art activites. ■**TIP→If you get the chance, stop by TNT (Thursday Night Thing), an eclectic series of free events held at 7 pm the first Thursday of each month. Happenings include live bands, DJ lessons, films, or interpretive artists.** ✉*1001 Kettner Blvd.* ☎*619/234–1001* ⊕*www.mcasd.org* ✉ *$10; Ages 25 and under are free* ☉ *Mon.–Fri. 11–5, Thur. until 7. Closed Tues.*

⓮ **Transit Center.** The Mission–style **Santa Fe Depot,** which replaced the original 1887 station on this site when it opened in 1915 for the Panama–California International Exposition, serves Amtrak and Coaster passengers. A booth here has bus schedules, maps, and tourist brochures. Formerly an easily spotted area landmark, the graceful, tiledome depot is now overshadowed by **1 America Plaza,** the 34-story office tower across the street. At the base of this skyscraper, designed by architect Helmut Jahn, is a center linking the city's train, trolley, and bus systems. The building's signature crescent-shaped, glass-and-steel canopy arches out over the trolley tracks. The Greyhound bus station (120 W. Broadway) is a few blocks away. ✉*Broadway and Kettner Blvd.*

⓫ **San Diego Aircraft Carrier Museum.** After 47 years of worldwide service, the retired USS *Midway* began a new tour of duty on the south side of the Navy pier in 2004. Launched just after the end of World War II, the 1,001-foot-long ship was the largest in the world for the first 10 years of its existence. Now it serves as the most visible landmark on the north Embarcadero and as a floating interactive museum—an appropriate addition to the town that is the home of one-third of the Pacific fleet and the birthplace of naval aviation. Start on the hangar deck, where an F-14 Tomcat jet fighter is just one of several aircraft displayed. Through passageways and up and down ladderwells, you'll get to see how the *Midway's* 4,500 crew members lived and worked on this "city at sea." While the entire tour is impressive, you'll find yourself saying "wow" when you step out onto the 4-acre flight deck—not only the best place to get an idea of the ship's scale, but also one of the most interesting vantage points for a view of the bay and the city skyline. The museum also includes changing displays of aircraft, a flight simulator, and interactive exhibits focusing on naval aviation. There is a café and a gift shop. This is a wildly popular stop, and in its first sixth months the museum exceeded its projected visitor count for the entire year. ✉*910 N. Harbor Dr.* ☎*619/544–9600* ⊕*www.midway.org* ✉*$17* ☉*Daily 10–5.*

☝ ⓽ **Seaport Village.** On a prime stretch of waterfront that spreads out across 14 acres connecting the harbor with hotel towers and the convention center, the three bustling shopping plazas of Seaport Village are designed to reflect the New England clapboard and Spanish mission architectural styles of early California. A ¼-mi boardwalk that runs along the bay and 4 mi of paths lead to specialty shops—everything from a kite store and swing emporium to a shop devoted to hot sauces—as well as snack bars and restaurants, many with harbor views; there are about 75 in all. Seaport Village's shops are open daily 10 to 9 (10 to 10 in summer); a few eateries open early for breakfast, and

1

many have extended nighttime hours, especially in summer. (It must be noted that most of the eateries here serve only passable or even mediocre fare, charging prices that rival or exceed those of the city's better restaurants.) Live music can be heard daily from 12 to 4 at the main food court. Additional free concerts take place every Sunday from 1 to 4 at the East Plaza Gazebo of Seasport Village. If you happen to visit San Diego during the first weekend in December, be sure to check out Deck the Palms. The family event features a tropically transformed Seasport Village, complete with sand sculptures, decorated palm trees, and a surfing Santa.

The **Seaport Village Carousel** has 54 animals—lots of horses plus a giraffe, dragon, elephant, dog, and others—hand-carved and hand-painted by Charles Looff in 1895. (This is a replacement for Seaport Village's previous historic carousel, also a Looff, which was sold to a private collector in 2004.) Tickets are $2. Strolling clowns, balloon sculptors, mimes, musicians, and magicians are also on hand throughout the village to entertain kids. ⊠ *849 W. Harbor Dr.* ☎*619/235–4014, 619/235–4013 events hotline, 619/239–1228 carousel information* ⊕*www.seaportvillage.com.*

NEED A BREAK? **Upstart Crow & Co.** (⊠*835 W. Harbor Dr. #C, Seaport Village, Central Plaza* ☎*619/232–4855*), a combination bookstore and coffeehouse, serves good cappuccino and espresso with pastries and cakes.

GASLAMP QUARTER HISTORIC DISTRICT

Fodor'sChoice ★ When the move for downtown redevelopment gained momentum in the 1970s, there was talk of bulldozing the Gaslamp's Victorian-style buildings and starting from scratch. (The district has the largest collection of Commercial Victorian-style buildings in the country.) History buffs, developers, architects, and artists formed the Gaslamp Quarter Council, however, and gathered funds from the government and private benefactors to clean up and preserve the quarter, restoring the finest old buildings and attracting businesses and the public back to its heart. Their efforts have paid off. Former flophouses have become choice office buildings, and the area is filled with hundreds of trendy shops, restaurants, and nightclubs.

The majority of the quarter's landmark buildings are on 4th and 5th avenues, between Island Avenue and Broadway. If you don't have much time, stroll down 5th Avenue, where highlights include the **Louis Bank of Commerce Building** (No. 835), the **Old City Hall Building** (No. 664), the **Nesmith-Greeley Building** (No. 825), and the **Yuma Building** (No. 631). The Romanesque Revival **Keating Hotel** was designed by the same firm that created the famous Hotel Del Coronado. At the corner of 4th Avenue and F Street, peer into the Hard Rock Cafe, which occupies a restored turn-of-the-20th-century tavern with a 12-foot mahogany bar and a spectacular stained-glass domed ceiling.

The section of G Street between 6th and 9th avenues has become a haven for galleries; stop in one of them to pick up a map of the downtown arts district. Just to the north, on E and F streets from 6th to 12th avenues, the evolving Urban Art Trail has added pizzazz to drab city thoroughfares by transforming such things as trash cans and traffic controller boxes into canvases. During baseball season, the streets flood with Padres fans, and festivals, such as Mardi Gras in February, ShamROCK on St. Patrick's Day, Jazz Fest in May, and Monster Bash in October, bring in partygoers. To miss the Gaslamp Quarter would be to miss San Diego's most exciting neighborhood.

SIGHTS TO SEE

⓰ Horton Grand Hotel. This Victorian hotel was created in the mid-1980s by joining together two historic hotels, the Brooklyn Kahle Saddlery Hotel and the Grand Horton Hotel, built in the boom days of the 1880s; Wyatt Earp stayed at the Brooklyn Kahle Saddlery Hotel while he was in town speculating on real estate ventures and opening gambling halls. The two hotels were not originally located at this address; they were once about four blocks away, but were dismantled and reconstructed to make way for Horton Plaza. A small Chinese Museum behind the lobby serves as a tribute to the surrounding Chinatown district, a collection of modest structures that once housed Chinese laborers and their families. ✉*311 Island Ave.* ☎*619/544–1886*

⓲ Horton Plaza. This downtown shopping, dining, and entertainment mecca fronts Broadway and G Street from 1st to 4th avenues and covers more than six city blocks. Designed by Jon Jerde and completed in 1985, Horton Plaza is far from what one would imagine a shopping center—or city center—to be. A collage of colorful tile work, banners waving in the air, and modern sculptures, Horton Plaza rises in uneven, staggered levels to six floors; great views of downtown from the harbor to Balboa Park and beyond can be had here.

Macy's and Nordstrom department stores anchor the plaza, and an eclectic assortment of more than 130 clothing, sporting-goods, jewelry, book, and gift shops flank them. Other attractions include the country's largest Sam Goody music store, a movie complex, restaurants, and a long row of take-out ethnic food shops and dining patios on the uppermost tier—and the respected San Diego Repertory Theatre below ground level. In 2008 the **Balboa Theater**, contiguous with the shopping center, reopened its doors after a $26.5 million renovation. The historic 1920's theater seats 1,500 and offers live arts and cultural performances throughout the week.

The mall has a multilevel parking garage; even so, lines to find a space can be long. Entering the parking structure on G Street rather than 4th Avenue generally means less traffic and more parking space. Parking validation is complimentary whether you spend a bundle or just window-shop. Validation machines throughout the center allow for three hours' free parking; after that it's $6 per hour. If you use this notoriously confusing fruit-and-vegetable–themed garage, be sure to remember at which produce level you've left your car. If you're staying downtown, the Old Town Trolley Tour will drop you directly in front of Horton Plaza. ✉*324 Horton Plaza* ☎*619/238–1596* ⊕*www. westfield.com/hortonplaza* ⊙*Mon.–Fri. 10–9, Sat. 10–8, Sun. 11–7.*

⑲ U.S. Grant Hotel. Far more formal than most other hotels in San Diego and complete with a $57 million renovation in 2006, the doyenne of downtown lodgings has a marble lobby, gleaming chandeliers, attentive doormen, and other touches that hark back to the more gracious era when it was built (1910). Funded in part by the son of the president for whom it was named, the hotel was extremely opulent from the beginning; 350 of its 437 rooms had private baths, highly unusual for that time. Through the years it became noted for its famous guests—U.S. presidents from Woodrow Wilson to George Bush (the elder) have stayed here. As San Diego's only Four Diamond/Four Star Hotel, the U.S. Grant recently discovered marble floors and alabaster railings that had been covered for more than 70 years. Additional upgrades include "Sleeping with Art," $10,000 headboards painted by Frenchman Yves Clement. Taking up a city block—it's bounded by 3rd and 4th avenues, C Street, and Broadway—the hotel occupies the site of San Diego's first hotel, constructed by Alonzo Horton in 1870. ✉ *326 Broadway* ☏ *619/232–3121.*

> **GONE TO THE DOGS**
>
> In 2007 two life-sized dog statues took center stage in San Diego's downtown park next to the William Heath Davis House on the corner of 4th and Island avenues. Dedicated to San Diego's official town dog, "Bum," the bronze statue shares a prominent place alongside "Greyfriars Bobby," the official dog of Edinburgh, Scotland. When the citizens of Edinburgh discovered that, like them, San Diego had an official town dog, they presented a Greyfriars Bobby replica. In 2008, a replica of Bum was installed in Edinburgh, symbolizing the friendship between the sister cities.

■ NEED A BREAK? Fifth Avenue between F and G streets is lined with restaurants, many with outdoor patios. Hip coffeehouses have also sprung up. Try **Café LuLu's** (✉ *419 F St.* ☏ *619/238–0114*) signature raspberry mocha or a sweet, chilled blended coffee. Sunday evenings, Middle Eastern performers entertain with fire and sword dancing, as the scent of incense fills the air.

⑰ William Heath Davis House. The oldest wooden house in San Diego houses the Gaslamp Quarter Historical Foundation, the district's curator. Before Alonzo Horton came to town, Davis, a prominent San Franciscan had made an unsuccessful attempt to develop the waterfront area. In 1850 he had this prefab saltbox-style house shipped around Cape Horn and assembled in San Diego (it originally stood at State and Market streets). Audio-guided ($10) and brochure-guided ($5) museum tours are available during museum hours. Regularly scheduled two-hour walking tours of the historic district leave from the house on Saturday at 11 and cost $10. The museum also provides detailed self-guided tour maps of the district for free. ✉ *410 Island Ave., at 4th Ave.* ☏ *619/233–4692* ⊙ *Tues.–Sat. 10–6, Sun. 10–3.*

LITTLE ITALY

From the first glimpse of the traditional red-and-white checked table-cloths to the wafting aroma of fresh pressed espresso, all of your senses will tell you that you are entering Little Italy, even before the arching neon sign comes into view. Unlike many tourist-driven theme communities, this neighborhood is authentic to its roots, from the Italian-speaking residents to the genuine imported delicacies. In the 1920s, Little Italy was a thriving business and residential community populated by over 6,000 Italian families who managed fishing boats. With the decline of the tuna industry and the development of Interstate 5, the town suffered financial decline from the loss of 35% of its land area. Today the main thoroughfare—from India Street to Kettner Boulevard—has been restored with lively cafés, gelato bars, bakeries, and restaurants. As if transplanted directly from a European village, Little Italy is marked by charming subtleties like the Catholic church bell that rings on the half hour, and **Amici Park,** where Italians gather daily to play boccie. Nearly every restaurant offers patio seating and live music throughout the week. Embracing the true Italian lifestyle, many of the locals can be heard passionately conversing with flamboyant gestures outside the corner deli.

Gaining recognition as an art district, Little Italy hosts the annual Art Walk in April and the Annual Festa in October. Adding color to the streets is October Chalk La Strada, a classic street-painting exhibit where artists create impressive renderings with chalk. Prized works are commissioned as murals to be featured on the sides of buildings in Little Italy. Art lovers can browse through photography shops, art-supply stores, gallery showrooms, and the adorable Fir Street cottages. This string of brightly colored boutiques sells designer clothing, jewelry, and accessories.

Although Little Italy continues to blossom, community leaders have managed to stave the influx of fast food chains that could diminish the area's unique flavor. Little Italy's most recent development is the Porto Vista Hotel & Suites, with 193 rooms and a rooftop lounge overlooking the city. Reflecting the quaintness of the neighborhood are the more established hotels like Little Italy Inn or the Mediterranean-style La Pensione, with a courtyard and bistro.

SIGHTS TO SEE

🐚 ⑳ **Firehouse Museum.** Fire-fighting artifacts of all sorts fill this converted fire station, which at one time also served as the repair shop for all of San Diego's fire-fighting equipment. Three large rooms contain everything from 19th-century horse- and hand-drawn fire engines to 20th-century motorized trucks, the latest dating from 1942. Extinguishers, helmets, and other memorabilia from all over the world are also on display. Ages 12 and under are free. ✉*1572 Columbia St.* ☏*619/232–3473* ⊕*www.thesdfirehousemuseum.org* 🎟*$3* ⊗*Thur. and Fri. 10–2, weekends 10–4.*

HARBOR & SHELTER ISLANDS
AND POINT LOMA

1

The populated outcroppings that jut into the bay just west of downtown and the airport demonstrate the potential of human collaboration with nature. Point Loma, Mother Nature's contribution to San Diego's attractions, has always protected the center city from the Pacific's tides and waves. It's shared by military installations, funky motels and fast-food shacks, stately family homes, huge estates, and private marinas packed with sailboats and yachts. Famous for sport fishing, it is also popular for tide-pooling, with plenty of tiny pools formed in eroded rock pockets. Starfish, sea anemones, and hermit crabs cluster here when the tide is in.

In 1950 San Diego's port director thought there should be some use for the sand and mud the Works Project Administration dredged up during the course of deepening a ship channel in the 1930s and '40s. He decided it might be a good idea to raise the shoal that lay off the eastern shore of Point Loma above sea level, landscape it, and add a 2,000-foot causeway to make it accessible. His hunch paid off. Shelter Island—actually a peninsula—now supports towering mature palms, a cluster of resorts, restaurants, and side-by-side marinas. It's the center of San Diego's yacht-building industry, and boats in every stage of construction are visible in the yacht yards. A long sidewalk runs from the landscaped lawns of the San Diego Yacht Club (tucked down Anchorage Street off Shelter Island Drive) past boat brokerages to the hotels and marinas that line the inner shore, facing Point Loma. On the bay side, fishermen launch their boats or simply stand on shore and cast. Families relax at picnic tables along the grass, where there are fire rings and permanent barbecue grills. Within walking distance is the huge Friendship Bell, given to San Diegans by the people of Yokohama, Japan, in 1960.

Following the success of nearby Shelter Island, the U.S. Navy decided to use the residue that resulted from digging berths deep enough to accommodate aircraft carriers to build another recreational island. Thus in 1961 some 12 million cubic yards of sand and mud dredged from the bay were deposited adjacent to San Diego International Airport and became the 1½-mi-long peninsula known as Harbor Island. Restaurants and high-rise hotels now line its inner shore. The bay shore has pathways, gardens, and picnic spots for sightseeing or working off the calories from the various indoor or outdoor food fests held here. On the west point, Tom Ham's Lighthouse restaurant has a U.S. Coast Guard–approved beacon shining from its tower.

Numbers in the text correspond to numbers on the Central San Diego map.

A GOOD TOUR

Take Catalina Boulevard all the way south to the tip of Point Loma to reach **Cabrillo National Monument** ㉕. North of the monument, as you head back into the neighborhoods of Point Loma, you'll see the white headstones of **Fort Rosecrans National Cemetery** ㉔. Continue north on Catalina Boulevard to Hill Street and turn left to reach the dramatic **Sunset Cliffs** ㉓, at the western side of Point Loma near Ocean Beach. Park to tour the dramatic cliff tops and the boiling seas below, but be cautious, because the cliffs can be unstable. Signs generally warn you where not to go.

Return to Catalina Boulevard and backtrack south for a few blocks to find Canon Street, which leads toward the peninsula's eastern (bay) side. Almost at the shore you'll see **Scott Street** ㉒, Point Loma's main commercial drag. Scott Street is bisected by Shelter Island Drive, which leads to Shelter Island. For another example of what can be done with tons of material dredged from a bay, go back up Shelter Island Drive, turn right on Rosecrans Street, and make another right on North Harbor Drive to reach Harbor Island.

TIMING   If you're interested in seeing the tide pools at Cabrillo National Monument, call ahead or check the weather page of the *Union-Tribune* to find out when low tide will occur. Scott Street, with its Point Loma Seafoods, is a good place to find yourself at lunchtime, and Sunset Cliffs Park is where you might want to be when the daylight starts to wane. This drive takes about an hour if you stop briefly at each sight, but you'll want to devote at least an hour to Cabrillo National Monument.

SIGHTS TO SEE

★ ☾ ㉕ **Cabrillo National Monument.** This 160-acre preserve marks the site of the first European visit to San Diego, made by 16th-century explorer Juan Rodríguez Cabrillo. Cabrillo landed at this spot, which he called San Miguel, on September 15, 1542. Today the site, with its rugged cliffs and shores and outstanding overlooks, is one of the most frequently visited of all the national monuments.

The **visitor center** presents films and lectures about Cabrillo's voyage, the sea-level tide pools, and migrating gray whales. The center has an excellent shop with books about nature, history, San Diego, and the sea; requisite souvenirs are also for sale. Restrooms and water fountains are plentiful along the paths that climb to the monument's various viewing points, but, except for a few vending machines at the visitor center, there's no food. Exploring the grounds consumes time and calories; bring a picnic and rest on a bench overlooking the sailboats.

A **statue of Cabrillo** overlooks downtown from a windy promontory, where people gather to admire the stunning panorama over the bay, from the snowcapped San Bernardino Mountains, 130 mi north, to the hills surrounding Tijuana to the south. The stone figure standing on the bluff looks rugged and dashing, but he is a creation of an artist's imagination—no portraits of Cabrillo are known to exist.

The moderately steep **Bayside Trail**, 2½ mi round-trip, winds through coastal sage scrub, curving under the cliff-top lookouts and taking you ever closer to the bay-front scenery. You cannot reach the beach from this trail, and must stick to the path to protect the cliffs from erosion and yourself from thorny plants and snakes—including rattlers. You'll see prickly pear cactus and yucca, black-eyed Susans, fragrant sage, and maybe a lizard, rabbit, or a hummingbird. The climb back is long but gradual, leading up to the old lighthouse.

Old Point Loma Lighthouse's oil lamp was first lit on November 15, 1855. The light, sitting in a brass-and-iron caging above a white wooden house, shone through a state-of-the-art, French-made Third Order Fresnel lens and was visible from the sea for 25 mi. Unfortunately, it was too high above the cliffs to guide navigators trapped in Southern California's thick offshore fog and low clouds. In 1891 a new lighthouse was built 400 feet below. The old lighthouse, restored to its 1880s appearance, is open to visitors. The U.S. Coast Guard still uses the newer lighthouse and a mighty foghorn to guide boaters through the narrow channel leading into the bay. On the edge of the hill near the old lighthouse sits a refurbished radio room from World War I. It contains displays of U.S. harbor defenses at Point Loma used during World War II. An exhibit in the Assistant Keepers Quarters next door tells the story of the Old Lighthouse, the daily lives of the keepers, how lighthouses work, and the role they played in the development of early maritime commerce along the West Coast.

The western and southern cliffs of Cabrillo National Monument are prime whale-watching territory. A sheltered **viewing station** has wayside exhibits describing the great gray whales' yearly migration from Baja California to the Bering and Chukchi seas near Alaska. High-powered telescopes help you focus on the whales' water spouts. Whales are visible on clear days from late December through early March, with the highest concentration in January and February.

Catching sight of the whales can be a highlight of a San Diego visit, and park rangers can help you spot them during the annual Intertidal Life Festival, held in the latter part of January, when interpretive programs, films, speakers, a puppet show, and entertainment are provided. Note that when the whales return north in the spring, they are too far out in the ocean to be seen from the monument.

THE NOMADIC STATUE

The original Cabrillo statue was sculpted by Portugal's Alvaro DeBree for the 1939 World Fair in San Francisco, but it never arrived. Instead, California's Governor awarded it to the city of Oakland where it remained in a private garage until 1949. Learning of this, a San Diego state senator had it shipped to San Diego, placed first at the Old Point Loma Lighthouse, then later moved to the Visitor's Center in 1965 where it began to deteriorate. In 1988 the Portuguese government shipped a replacement limestone statue.

More accessible sea creatures can be seen in the **tide pools** at the foot of the monument's western cliffs. Drive north from the visitor center to Cabrillo Road on the left, which winds down to the Coast Guard station and the shore. When the tide is low you can walk on the rocks around saltwater pools filled with starfish, crabs, anemones, octopuses, and hundreds of other sea creatures and plants. Exercise caution on the slippery rocks. ⊠ *1800 Cabrillo Memorial Dr., Point Loma* ☎ *619/557–5450* ⊕ *www.nps.gov/cabr* ☞ *$5 per car, $3 per person entering on foot or by bicycle, entrance pass allows unlimited admissions for 1 wk from date of purchase; free for Golden Age and Golden Access passport and holders of Cabrillo National Monument Pass and National Parks Pass* ⊗ *Park daily 9–5.*

㉔ Fort Rosecrans National Cemetery. In 1934, 8 acres of the 1,000 set aside for a military reserve in 1852 were designated as a burial site. About 93,000 people are now interred here; it's impressive to see the rows upon rows of white headstones that overlook both sides of Point Loma just north of the Cabrillo National Monument. Some of those laid to rest at this place were killed in battles that predate California's statehood; the graves of the 17 soldiers and one civilian who died in the 1874 Battle of San Pasqual between troops from Mexico and the United States are marked by a large bronze plaque. Perhaps the most impressive structure in the cemetery is the 75-foot granite obelisk called the Bennington Monument, which commemorates the 66 crew members who died in a boiler explosion and fire on board the USS *Bennington* in 1905. The cemetery, visited by many veterans, is still used for burials. ⊠ *Rte. 209, Point Loma* ☎ *619/553–2084* ⊗ *Daily 7:30–5.*

㉒ Scott Street. Running along Point Loma's waterfront from Shelter Island to the old Naval Training Center on Harbor Drive, this thoroughfare is lined with deep-sea fishing charters and whale-watching boats. It's a good spot to watch fishermen (and women) haul marlin, tuna, and puny mackerel off their boats.

NEED A BREAK? The freshest and tastiest fish to be found along Point Loma's shores—some would say anywhere in San Diego—comes from **Point Loma Seafoods** (⊠ *2805 Emerson St., Point Loma* ☎ *619/223–1109*), behind the Vagabond Inn. There's a fish market selling raw catch of the day for customers to take home and prepare themselves, but there's also an adjacent take-out counter selling prepared hot or cold foods—seafood cocktails and salads, ceviche, crab and shrimp sandwiches made with freshly baked sourdough bread—for takeout and to be consumed on the premises. There's outdoor and indoor seating (no waiter service), and you can expect crowds throughout the year. Park a few blocks away if you're coming on the weekend; the adjoining lot suffers from extreme gridlock.

㉑ Across from the western end of Harbor Island, at the mainland's **Spanish Landing Park,** a bronze plaque marks the arrival in 1769 of a party from Spain that headed north from San Diego to conquer California. The group combined the crews of two ships, the *San Carlos* and the

San Antonio, and a contingent that came overland from Baja California. As part of a beautification program, the city has begun installing whimsical if sometimes monumental artworks in this park, which is less visited than many city parks and therefore a quiet enclave in which to spend a peaceful hour or two. If you're the hardy type, you can walk from here to the Embarcadero, and then into the heart of downtown. ⊠ *Harbour Island*

㉓ Sunset Cliffs. As the name suggests, the 60-foot-high bluffs on the western side of Point Loma south of Ocean Beach are a perfect place to watch the sun descend over the sea. To view the tide pools along the shore, use the staircase off Sunset Cliffs Boulevard at the foot of Ladera Street.

The dramatic coastline here seems to have been carved out of ancient rock. The impact of the waves is very clear: each year more sections of the cliffs are posted with caution signs. Don't ignore these warnings—it's easy to lose your footing and slip in the crumbling sandstone, and the surf can be extremely rough. Small coves and beaches dot the coastline and are popular with surfers drawn to the pounding waves, and neighborhood locals who name and claim their special spots. The homes along the boulevard—pink stucco mansions beside shingled Cape Cod–style cottages—are fine examples of Southern California luxury. ⊠ *Sunset Cliffs Blvd., Point Loma.*

LA JOLLA

La Jollans have long considered their village to be the Monte Carlo of California, and with good cause. Its coastline curves into natural coves backed by verdant hillsides covered with homes worth millions. Although La Jolla is a neighborhood of the city of San Diego, it has its own postal zone and a coveted sense of class; the ultra-rich from around the globe own second homes here—the seaside zone between the neighborhood's bustling downtown and the cliffs above the Pacific has a distinctly European flavor—and old-monied residents maintain friendships with the visiting film stars and royalty who frequent the area's exclusive luxury hotels and private clubs. Development and construction have radically altered the once serene and private character of the village, but it has gained a cosmopolitan air that makes it a popular vacation resort.

The Native Americans called the site La Hoya, meaning "the cave," referring to the grottoes that dot the shoreline. The Spaniards changed the name to La Jolla (same pronunciation as La Hoya), "the jewel," and its residents have cherished the name and its allusions ever since.

To reach La Jolla from I–5, if you're traveling north, take the La Jolla Parkway (formerly known as Ardath Road) exit, which veers into Torrey Pines Road, and turn right onto Prospect Street. If you're heading south, get off at the La Jolla Village Drive exit, which also leads into Torrey Pines Road. Traffic is often congested in this popular area, which is dotted with four-way stop signs and clogged with drivers dropping off passengers and/or trolling for a parking spot. Drive carefully and be prepared to stop frequently when you get into the village.

For those who enjoy meandering, the best way to approach La Jolla from the south is to drive on Mission Boulevard through Mission and Pacific beaches, past the crowds of in-line skaters, bicyclists, and sunbathers. The clutter and congestion ease up as the street becomes La Jolla Boulevard. Road signs along La Jolla Boulevard and Camino de la Costa direct drivers and bicyclists past homes designed by respected architects such as Irving Gill. As you approach the village, La Jolla Boulevard turns into Prospect Street.

Prospect Street and Girard Avenue, the village's main drags, are lined with expensive shops and office buildings. Through the years the shopping and dining district has spread to Pearl and other side streets. La Jolla's nightlife sometimes seems a bit somnolent, although there are some lively bars that cater primarily to the younger crowd. Their elders dine at any of several fine restaurants and then may stop by the Whaling Bar at the lovely old La Valencia hotel for a Whaler, a nightcap of sweet liqueurs, cream, and ice cream. It's a good drink, but watch out—it packs an unexpected punch.

Numbers in the text correspond to numbers on the La Jolla map.

A GOOD TOUR

At the intersection of La Jolla Boulevard and Nautilus Street, turn toward the sea to reach **Windansea Beach** ❶, one of the best surfing spots in town. **Mount Soledad** ❷, about 1½ mi east on Nautilus Street, is La Jolla's highest spot. In the village itself you'll find the town's cultural center, the **Museum of Contemporary Art, San Diego** ❸, on the less trafficked southern end of Prospect. A bit farther north, at the intersection of Prospect Street and Girard Avenue, sits the pretty-in-pink hotel **La Valencia** ❹, looking out onto the village's great natural attraction, **La Jolla Cove** ❺, which can be accessed from Coast Boulevard, one block to the west. Past the far northern point of the cove, a trail leads down to **La Jolla Caves** ❻.

The beaches along La Jolla Shores Drive north of the caves are some of the finest in the San Diego area, with long stretches allotted to surfers or swimmers. Nearby is the campus of the Scripps Institution of Oceanography. The institution's **Birch Aquarium at Scripps** ❼ is inland a bit, off Torrey Pines Road.

La Jolla Shores Drive eventually curves onto Torrey Pines Road, off which you'll soon glimpse the world-famous **Salk Institute** ❽, designed by Louis I. Kahn. The road that leads to the institute ends at the cliffs used as the **Torrey Pines Glider Port** ❾. The hard-to-reach stretch of sand at the foot of the cliffs is officially named Torrey Pines City Park Beach, but locals call it **Black's Beach** ❿ because the distinguished Black family, members of whom still reside in La Jolla, once owned a vast estate high above it. At the intersection of Torrey Pines Road and Genesee Avenue you'll come to the northern entrance of the huge campus of the **University of California at San Diego** ⑪ and, a bit farther north, to the stretch of wilderness that marks the end of what most locals consider San Diego proper, **Torrey Pines State Reserve** ⑫.

TIMING   This tour makes for a leisurely day, although it can be driven in a couple of hours, including stops to take in the views and explore the village of La Jolla (though not to hit any of the beaches—or even a fraction of all the pricey boutiques).

SIGHTS TO SEE

🐣 ⑦ **Birch Aquarium at Scripps.** The largest oceanographic exhibit in the United States, maintained by the Scripps Institution of Oceanography, sits at the end of a signposted drive leading off North Torrey Pines Road. More than 60 tanks are filled with colorful saltwater fish, and a 70,000-gallon tank simulates a La Jolla kelp forest. Besides the fish themselves, attractions include a gallery based on the institution's ocean-related research, and interactive educational exhibits on climate change and global warming. ✉ *2300 Expedition Way* ☎ *858/534–3474* ⊕ *www.aquarium.ucsd.edu* 💲 *$11, parking free for 3 hrs* ◷ *Daily 9–5, last ticket sold at 4:30.*

⑩ **Black's Beach.** Formally known as Torrey Pines City Park Beach, this secluded stretch of sand is considered one of the most beautiful beaches in San Diego. Backed by cliffs whose colors change with the angle of the sun, Black's can be accessed from Torrey Pines State Beach to the north, or by a narrow path descending the cliffs from Torrey Pines Glider Port. The fast, punchy waves of Black's Beach make it a popular spot for experienced surfers. There are no restrooms, showers, or snack shops, although some hardy (and law-breaking) entrepreneurs lug ice chests filled with sodas and beer down the cliffs to sell to the unprepared. The paths leading down to the beach are steep, and the cliffs are unstable—pay attention to the safety signs and stick to the well-traveled trails. Black's Beach was clothing-optional for many years; although nudity is now prohibited by law, many people still shed their suits whenever the authorities are out of sight. ✉ *Accessible from Torrey Pines State Beach and La Jolla Shores.*

🐣 ⑥ **La Jolla Caves.** It's a walk of 145 sometimes slippery steps down a tunnel to Sunny Jim, the largest of the caves in La Jolla Cove and the only one reachable by land. This is a one-of-a-kind local attraction, and worth the time if you have a day or two to really enjoy La Jolla. The man-made tunnel took two years to dig, beginning in 1902; later a shop was built at its entrance. Today La Jolla Cave Store, a throwback to that early shop, is still the entrance to the cave, which was named Sunny Jim after a 1920s cartoon character. The shop sells jewelry and watercolors

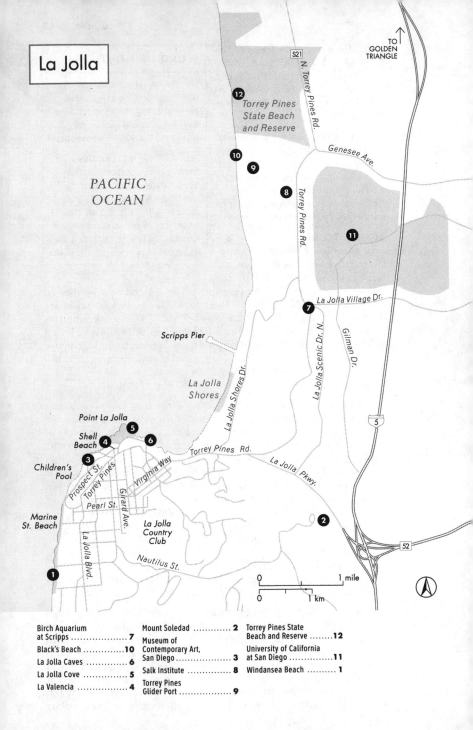

La Jolla

PACIFIC
OCEAN

TO
GOLDEN
TRIANGLE

S21

N. Torrey Pines Rd.

Torrey Pines
State Beach
and Reserve

Genesee Ave.

Torrey Pines Rd.

La Jolla Village Dr.

Gilman Dr.

La Jolla Scenic Dr. N.

Scripps Pier

La Jolla Shores Dr.

La Jolla
Shores

Point La Jolla

Shell
Beach

Children's
Pool

Prospect St.

Torrey Pines

Virginia Way

Torrey Pines Rd.

La Jolla Pkwy.

Pearl St.

Girard Ave.

Marine
St. Beach

La Jolla
Country
Club

La Jolla Blvd.

Nautilus St.

5

52

0   1 mile

0   1 km

by local artists. ✉ *1325 Cave St.* ☎*858/459–0746* ⊕*www.cavestore. com* 🏷*$4* ☉*Daily 9–5; extended summer hours.*

★ ☙ ⑤ **La Jolla Cove.** This shimmering blue inlet is what first attracted everyone to La Jolla, from Native Americans to the glitterati; it's the secret to the village's enduring cachet. You'll find the Cove—as locals always refer to it, as though it were the only one in San Diego—beyond where Girard Avenue dead-ends into Coast Boulevard, marked by towering palms that line a promenade where people strolling in designer clothes are as common as Frisbee throwers.

Smaller beaches appear and disappear with the tides, which carve small coves in cliffs covered with ice plants. Pathways lead down to the beaches. Keep an eye on the tide to avoid getting trapped once the waves come in. A long layer of sandstone stretching out above the waves provides a perfect sunset-watching spot. Be careful, these rocks can get slippery.

An underwater preserve at the north end of La Jolla Cove makes the adjoining beach the most popular one in the area. On summer days, when water visibility reaches up to 20 feet, the small beach is covered with blankets, towels, and umbrellas, and the lawns at the top of the stairs leading down to the cove are staked out by groups of scuba divers, complete with wet suits and tanks. The **Children's Pool,** at the south end of the park, has a curving beach protected by a seawall from strong currents and waves. Since the pool and its beach have become home to an ever-growing colony of Harbor seals, it's seldom utilized by swimmers, especially due to the questionable levels of bacteria. It is however the best place on the coast to view these engaging creatures. If you want to take a dip, it is best to head just north of Children's Pool to the pristine waters of La Jolla Cove. ■**TIP→ Make sure to walk through Ellen Browning Scripps Park, past the groves of twisted junipers to the cliff's edge. Perhaps one of the open-air shelters overlooking the sea will be unoccupied, and you can spread your picnic out on a table and enjoy the scenery.** ⊹*From Torrey Pines Road, turn right on Prospect, then right on Coast Blvd. The park is located at the bottom of the hill* ☎*619/235–1169* ⊕*www.sandiego.gov/park* ☉*4* AM–*8* PM.

④ **La Valencia.** The Mediterranean–style La Valencia, operating as a luxury hotel since 1926, has long been a gathering spot for Hollywood celebrities; in the 1940s Gregory Peck would invite friends to the hotel's Whaling Bar to try to persuade them to participate in one of his favorite projects, the La Jolla Playhouse, now one of the city's leading cultural institutions. Today the hotel's grand lobby, with floor-to-ceiling windows overlooking La Jolla Cove, is a popular wedding spot, and the Whaling Bar has the air of a private club for the town's monied families. ✉*1132 Prospect St.* ☎*858/454–0771 or 800/451–0772* ⊕*www. lavalencia.com.*

② **Mount Soledad.** La Jolla's highest spot can be reached by taking Nautilus Street to La Jolla Scenic Drive South, and then turning left. Proceed a few blocks to the park, where parking is plentiful and the views are astounding, unless the day is hazy, as it can be along the coast. The top of the mountain is an excellent vantage point from which to get a sense of San Diego's geography: looking down from here you can see the coast from the county's northern border to the south far beyond downtown. ✉ *6905 La Jolla Scenic Dr. S.*

★ ❸ **Museum of Contemporary Art, San Diego.** The oldest section of La Jolla's branch of San Diego's modern art museum was originally a residence, designed by Irving Gill for philanthropist Ellen Browning Scripps in 1916. In the mid-1990s the compound was updated and expanded by architect Robert Venturi and his colleagues at Venturi, Scott Brown and Associates, who respected Gill's original geometric structure and clean, Mission-style lines while adding their own distinctive touches. The result is a striking contemporary building that looks as though it's always been here.

The light-filled Axline Court serves as the museum's entrance and does triple duty as reception area, exhibition hall, and forum for special events, including the glittering Night In Monte Carlo gala each September, attended by the town's most fashionable folk. Inside, the museum's artwork gets major competition from the setting: you can look out from the top of a grand stairway onto a landscaped garden that contains permanent and temporary sculpture exhibits as well as rare 100-year-old California plant specimens and, beyond that, to the Pacific Ocean.

California artists figure prominently in the museum's permanent collection of post-1950s art, but the museum also includes examples of every major art movement since that time—works by Andy Warhol, Robert Rauschenberg, Frank Stella, Joseph Cornell, and Jenny Holzer, to name a few. Important pieces by artists from San Diego and Tijuana were acquired in the 1990s. The museum also gets major visiting shows. The Museum Café serves soups, salads, and sandwiches as well as drinks. ✉ *700 Prospect St.* ☎ *858/454–3541* ⊕ *www.mcasd.org* ✉ *$10, free every Thurs. 5–7;* ⊙ *Thurs. 11–7, Fri.–Tues. 11–5. Closed Wed.*

> ## GOLDEN TRIANGLE
>
> High-tech research-and-development companies, attracted by the proximity of the University of California at San Diego, the Scripps Institution of Oceanography, and the Salk Institute, have developed huge state-of-the-art compounds east of I–5. The area along La Jolla Village Drive and Genesee Avenue has become a proving ground for futuristic buildings, including the striking Michael Graves–designed Aventine complex and the huge, white Mormon Temple, as eye-catching as a psychedelic castle. Completed in 1993, it still startles drivers heading up the freeway.

❽ **Salk Institute.** The world-famous biological-research facility founded by polio vaccine developer Jonas Salk sits on 27 cliff-top acres. The twin structures that modernist architect Louis I. Kahn designed in the 1960s in consultation with Dr. Salk used poured concrete and other low-maintenance materials to clever effect. The thrust of the laboratory–office complex is outward toward the Pacific Ocean, an orientation that is accentuated by a foot-wide "Stream of Life" that flows through the center of a travertine marble courtyard between the buildings. Architects-to-be and building buffs enjoy the free tours of the property; call ahead to book, because the tours take place only when enough people express interest. You can, however, stroll at will through the dramatic courtyard—simultaneously monumental and eerie. ✉*10010 N. Torrey Pines Rd.* ☎*858/453–4100 Ext. 1200* ⊕*www.salk.edu* ✉*Free* ⊗*Grounds weekdays 9–5; architectural tours Mon., Wed., and Fri. at noon. Reservations required.*

9 **Torrey Pines Glider Port.** On days when the winds are just right, gliders line the cliffs, waiting for the perfect gust to carry them into the sky. Seasoned hang gliders and paragliders with a good command of the current can soar over the sea for hours, then ride the winds back to the cliffs. Less-experienced fliers sometimes land on the beach below, to the cheers and applause of the sunbathers who scoot out of the way. Tandem courses with certified instructors are also available for those who have ever wanted to try hang gliding, paragliding, or sailplane flying. If you're coming via the freeway, take the Genesee Avenue exit west from I–5 and follow the signs when you approach the coast. ✉*2800 Torrey Pines Scenic Dr.*

12 **Torrey Pines State Natural Reserve.** *Pinus torreyana,* the rarest native pine tree in the United States, enjoys a 1,700-acre sanctuary at the northern edge of La Jolla. About 6,000 of these unusual trees, some as tall as 60 feet, grow on the cliffs here. The park is one of only two places in the world (the other is Santa Rosa Island, off Santa Barbara) where the Torrey pine grows naturally. The reserve has several hiking trails leading to the cliffs, 300 feet above the ocean; trail maps are available at the park station. Wildflowers grow profusely in spring, and the ocean panoramas are always spectacular. When in this upper part of the park, respect the various restrictions. Not permitted: picnicking, smoking, leaving the trails, dogs, alcohol, or collecting plant specimens.

You can unwrap your sandwiches, however, at Torrey Pines State Beach, just below the reserve. When the tide is out, it's possible to walk south all the way past the lifeguard towers to Black's Beach over rocky promontories carved by the waves (avoid the bluffs, however; they're unstable). **Los Peñasquitos Lagoon** at the north end of the reserve is one of the many natural estuaries that flow inland between Del Mar and Oceanside. It's a good place to watch shorebirds. Volunteers lead guided nature walks at 10 and 2 on most weekends. ✉*N. Torrey Pines Rd.* ✛ *exit off I–5 onto Carmel Valley Rd. going west, then turn left (south) on Old Hwy. 101* ☎*858/755–8219* ✉*Parking $8* ⊗*Daily 8–dusk.*

11 **University of California at San Diego.** The campus of one of the country's most prestigious research universities spreads over 1,200 acres of coastal canyons and eucalyptus groves, where students and faculty jog, bike, and Rollerblade to class. If you're interested in contemporary art, check out the Stuart Collection of Sculpture—15 thought-provoking, site-specific works by artists such as Nam June Paik, William

Wegman, Niki de St. Phalle, Jenny Holzer, and others arrayed around the campus. UCSD's Price Center has a well-stocked, two-level bookstore—the largest in San Diego—and a good coffeehouse, Espresso Roma. Look for the postmodern Geisel Library (named for longtime La Jolla residents Theodor "Dr. Seuss" Geisel and his wife, Audrey), which resembles an upside-down triangle. For campus culture, political views, vegan dishes, and live music, head to the Che Café located in building 161, painted in bright murals. Bring quarters for the parking meters, or folding cash for the parking structures, since free parking is only available on weekends. ✛ *Exit I–5 onto La Jolla Village Dr. going west; take Gilman Dr. off-ramp to right and continue on to information kiosk at campus entrance on Gilman Dr.* ☎*858/534–4414 campus tour information* ⊙*90-min campus tours Sun. at 2 from South Gilman Information Pavilion; reserve before 3 Fri.*

❶ **Windansea Beach.** Named for a hotel that burned down in the late 1940s, Windansea Beach has increasingly gained notoriety due to its association with surfers. Fans of pop satirist Tom Wolfe may recall *The Pump House Gang,* which pokes fun at the Southern California surfing culture. Wolfe drew many of his barbs from observations he made at Windansea, the surfing beach west of La Jolla Boulevard near Nautilus Street. The classic reef break here forms an unusual A-frame wave, making it one of the most popular (and crowded) surf spots in San Diego County. Just below the parking lot is a palm-covered surf shack, constructed in 1946 and named a historical landmark in 1998. ⊠*La Jolla.*

▌ NEED A BREAK? | A breakfast of the excellent buttery croissants or brioches at the **French Pastry Shop** (⊠ *5550 La Jolla Blvd.* ☎*858/454–9094*) is good preparation for time at Windansea Beach.

MISSION BAY, BEACHES & SEAWORLD

Mission Bay Park is San Diego's monument to sports and fitness. This 4,600-acre aquatic park has 27 mi of shoreline including 19 of sandy beach. Playgrounds and picnic areas abound on the beach and low grassy hills. On weekday evenings joggers, bikers, and skaters take over. In the daytime, swimmers, water-skiers, anglers, and boaters—some in single-person kayaks, others in crowded powerboats—vie for space in the water. The San Diego Crew Classic, which takes place in late March or April, fills this area of the bay with teams from all over the country. One Mission Bay caveat: swimmers should note signs warning about water pollution; on occasions when heavy rains or other events cause pollution, swimming is strongly discouraged.

North of Belmont Park to Pacific Beach, Mission Boulevard runs along a two block–wide strip embraced by the Pacific Ocean on the west and the bay on the east. Called Mission Beach, it's a famous and lively funzone for families and young people both; if it isn't party time at the moment, it will be five minutes from now. The pathways in this area are lined with vacation homes, many for rent by the week or month.

Those fortunate enough to live here year-round have the bay as their front yard, with wide sandy beaches, volleyball courts, and—less of an advantage—an endless stream of sightseers on the sidewalk.

North of Mission Beach is the college-packed party town of Pacific Beach, or "PB" as locals call it. The laid-back vibe of this surfer's mecca draws in free-spirited locals who roam the streets on skateboards and beach cruisers, in the local uniform of board shorts, bikinis, baseball caps, and beanies. Lining the main strip of Grand and Garnet Avenues are tattoo parlors, smoke shops, vintage stores, and coffee houses. The energy level peaks during happy hour, when PB's cluster of nightclubs, bars, and 150 restaurants open their doors to those ready to party.

South of Mission Beach is the more chilled-out, hippy-esque town of Ocean Beach, commonly referred to as "OB." The main thoroughfare of this funky neighborhood is dotted with dive bars, coffee houses, surf shops, and 1960s diners. Bursting with character, OB is a magnet for everyone from surfers and musicians to children and artists. Newport Avenue, generally known for its boisterous bars, is also home to San Diego's largest antiques district.

Numbers in the text correspond to numbers on the Mission Bay map.

A GOOD TOUR

If you're coming from I–5, the **San Diego Visitor Information Center ❶** is just about at the end of the Clairemont Drive–East Mission Bay Drive exit (you'll see the prominent sign). At the point where East Mission Bay Drive turns into Sea World Drive, drive west and if you wish, detour left to **Fiesta Island ❷**, popular with jet-skiers and speedboat racers. Continue around the curve to the west to reach **SeaWorld San Diego ❸**, the area's best-known attraction.

You'll next come to Ingraham Street, the central north–south drag through the bay. If you take it north, you'll shortly spot Vacation Road, which leads into the focal point of this part of the bay, the waterskiing hub of **Vacation Isle ❹**. At Ingraham, Sea World Drive turns into Sunset Cliffs Boulevard and intersects with West Mission Bay Drive. Veer left toward Sunset Cliffs Boulevard, over the bridge, toward Ocean Beach. Turn right at West Point Loma Boulevard until you reach **Ocean Beach Dog Beach ❿**. The family-friendly beaches that line this area are ideal for fishing, surfing, and exploring the many tide pools. At the dead end, turn left onto Brighton and right at Abbott to reach **Ocean Beach Pier ❾**. Just before the Pier, turn left onto Newport Avenue, OB's main drag. The old school atmosphere of this surfer town will make you feel like you've entered an endless summer. For a beachfront stroll and spectacular ocean views, detour right on Bacon Street and right on Del Monte until you reach **Sunset Cliffs ⓫**. To complete the OB loop, turn left on Bacon, right on Newport, and left at Sunset Cliffs.

Take Ingraham Street over the bridge and head north past Baleen Resort. Continue on Ingraham Street before going left on Garnet Avenue, the epicenter of Pacific Beach. If you're into surfing, be sure to check out the waves at Crystal Pier, the ending point of Garnet Avenue. Turn left onto Mission Boulevard to enter Mission Beach. Continue past the local dive bars and retail shops until you reach Santa Clara on your left. Ample parking is available here at the **Mission Bay Aquatic Center** ❽. Courses and equipment are available for surfing, sailing, rowing, and windsurfing. Launching from this parking area is the well-paved, peaceful Bayside Walk and Bike Path; the picnic tables, grassy area, and waterfront view make this an ideal family spot. For a more lively contrast, cross the street to reach the Mission Beach Boardwalk, a classic boardwalk popular with young, hip surfers. Exit left onto Mission Boulevard to reach Belmont Park, which includes an amusement park, Wave House, and the Giant Dipper wooden roller coaster.

If you continue east on West Mission Bay Drive, just after it leaves Mission Boulevard you'll come to the Bahia Resort Hotel, where you can catch the ***Bahia Belle*** ❻ for a cruise around the bay. Ventura Cove, opposite the Bahia Hotel, is another good spot to unpack your cooler. As you continue southeast toward SeaWorld Drive, you'll pass **Hospitality Point** ❺, where there are nice, quiet places to have a picnic.

TIMING It would take less than an hour to drive this tour. You may not find a visit to SeaWorld fulfilling unless you spend at least half a day; a full day is recommended. Belmont Park is open daily, but not all its attractions are open year-round.

SIGHTS TO SEE

❻ ***Bahia Belle.*** At the dock of the Bahia Resort Hotel, on the eastern shores of West Mission Bay Drive, you can board a restored sternwheeler for a sunset cruise of the bay and party until the wee hours. There's always music, mostly jazz, rock, and blues, and on Friday and Saturday nights the music is live. You can imbibe at the *Belle*'s full bar, which opens at 9:30 PM, but many revelers like to disembark at the Bahia's sister hotel, the Catamaran Resort, and have a few rounds at the Cannibal Bar before reboarding (the boat cruises between the two hotels, which co-own it, stopping to pick up passengers every half hour). The first cruise on Sunday is devoted to kids, but most cruises get a mixed crowd of families, couples, and singles. ✉*998 W. Mission Bay Dr., Mission Bay* ☎*858/539–7779* 🎫*$6 for unlimited cruising; cruisers must be at least 21 after 9:30* PM*; free for guests of Bahia and Catamaran hotels* ⏲*Sept.–Nov. and Feb.–May, Fri. and Sat. 6:30* PM*–1* AM*, departures every hr on the ½ hr; June, Wed.–Sat. 6:30* PM*–1* AM*; July and Aug., Wed.–Sun. 6:30* PM*–1* AM*; closed Dec.–Jan.*

❼ **Belmont Park.** The once-abandoned amusement park between the bay and Mission Beach boardwalk is now a shopping, dining, and recreation complex. Twinkling lights outline the **Giant Dipper,** an antique wooden roller coaster on which screaming thrill-seekers ride more than 2,600 feet of track and 13 hills (riders must be at least 4'2"). Created in 1925 and listed on the National Register of Historic Places, this is one of the few old-time roller coasters left in the United States. The **Plunge,** an indoor swimming pool, also opened in 1925, and was the largest—60 feet by 125 feet—saltwater pool in the world at the time (it's

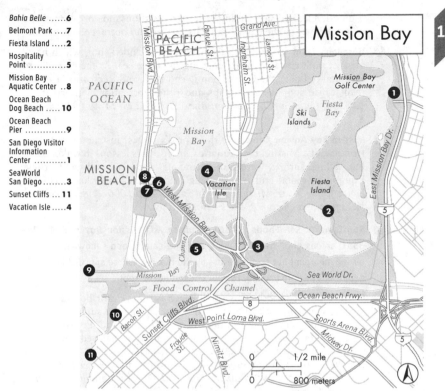

had fresh water since 1951). Johnny Weismuller and Esther Williams are among the stars who were captured swimming here on celluloid. Other Belmont Park attractions, nonvintage, include a video arcade; a submarine ride; bumper cars; a tilt-a-whirl; and an antique carousel. Belmont Park also has the most consistent wave in the county at the **Wave House,** where the FlowRider provides surfers and bodyboarders a near perfect simulated wave on which to practice their skills. The rock wall challenges both junior climbers and their elders. ⊠*3146 Mission Blvd., Mission Bay* ☎*858/488–1549, 858/228–9283 for pool* ⊕*www.belmontpark.com* ✉*$6 for roller coaster, other rides cost $2 to $5, or buy a full-day unlimited ride package $22.95 for 50" and over, $15.95 for under 50"; pool $7 for one-time entry* ⊙*Park opens at 11 daily, ride hrs vary seasonally; pool open weekdays 5:30–8* AM, *noon–1* PM, *and 2:30–8* PM *and weekends 8–4.*

❷ Fiesta Island. The most undeveloped area of Mission Bay Park, this is popular with bird-watchers (there's a large protected nesting site for the California tern at the northern tip of the island) as well as with dog owners—it's the only place in the park where pets can run free. Jet-Skiers and speedboat racers come here, too. At Christmas the island provides an excellent vantage point for viewing the bay's Parade of Lights. In July the annual Over-the-Line Tournament, a competition involving a unique local version of softball, attracts thousands of players and oglers, drawn by the teams' raunchy names and outrageous behavior.

⑤ Hospitality Point. Enjoy lunch in this pretty, secluded spot, which has a view of sailboats and yachts entering the open sea. At the entrance to Hospitality Point, the City of San Diego Park and Recreation Department office supplies area maps and other recreational information. ⊠*2500 Quivira Ct., Mission Bay* ☎*619/235–1169* ☉*Mon.–Fri. 8–5.*

⑧ Mission Bay Aquatic Center. As the world's largest instructional waterfront facility, Mission Bay Aquatic Center offers lessons in wakeboarding, sailing, surfing, waterskiing, rowing, kayaking, and windsurfing. Equipment rental and free parking are also available here. ⊠*1001 Santa Clara Place, Mission Beach* ☎*858/488–1000* ⊕*www.mission-bayaquaticcenter.com* ☉*Tues.–Sun. 8–5* PM.

NEED A BREAK?

Sportsmen's Sea Foods (⊠*1617 Quivira Rd., Mission Bay* ☎*619/224–3551*) serves good fish-and-chips, seafood salads, and sandwiches to eat on the inelegant but scenic patio—by the marina, where sportfishing boats depart daily—or to take out to your chosen picnic spot.

⑩ Ocean Beach Dog Beach. This small beach is a haven for both dogs and visitors who enjoy playing in gentle surf. During the summer months there can be as many as 100 dogs running in the sand. For those who prefer to stay clear of the canine action, there is a paved path and a grassy park across from the beach. ✛ *Head west on I–8 toward The Beaches. Turn left onto Sunset Cliffs Blvd, toward the town of Ocean Beach. Turn right onto Point Loma, and Dog Beach will be the first turn on the right.*

⑨ Ocean Beach Pier. This T-shaped pier is a popular fishing spot and home to the Ocean Beach Pier Café and a small tackle shop. Constructed in 1966, it is the longest pier on the West Coast and a perfect place to take in views of the harbor, ocean, and Point Loma Peninsula. Surfers flock to the waves that break just below. ⊠*1950 Abbott St., Ocean Beach.*

① San Diego Visitor Information Center. In addition to being an excellent resource for tourists—it makes hotel and motel reservations, sells tickets to several attractions at a discount, offers various maps and guides, and has a small gift shop—this privately owned information center is also a gathering spot for runners, walkers, and exercisers. For boaters it's the place to pick up a map detailing Mission Bay Park launch depths and speeds. ⊠*2688 E. Mission Bay Dr., Mission Bay* ☎*619/276–8200* ⊕*www.infosandiego.com* ☉*Mon.–Sat. 9–5, until 6 in summer, Sun. 9:30–4:30, until 5:30 in summer.*

☟ ③ SeaWorld San Diego. One of the world's largest marine-life amusement parks, SeaWorld is spread over 189 tropically landscaped bayfront acres—and it seems to be expanding into every available square inch of space with new exhibits, shows, and activities. The biggest attraction in its 40 years of existence opened on Memorial Day 2004: **Journey To Atlantis** involves a cruise on an eight-passenger "Greek fishing boat"

Fodor'sChoice
★

1

down a heart-stopping 60-foot plunge to explore a lost, sunken city. After this journey serenaded by dolphins calls, you view a 130,000-gallon pool, home to exotic Commerson's dolphins, a small black-and-white South American species known for speed and agility.

The majority of SeaWorld's exhibits are walk-through marine environments. Kids get a particular kick out of the **Shark Encounter,** where they come face-to-face with sandtiger, nurse, bonnethead, black-tipped, and white-tipped reef sharks by walking through a 57-foot clear acrylic tube that passes through the 280,000-gallon shark habitat. The hands-on **California Tide Pool** exhibit gives you a chance to get to know San Diego's indigenous marine life. At **Forbidden Reef** you can feed bat rays and go nose-to-nose with creepy moray eels. At **Rocky Point Preserve** you can view bottlenose dolphins, as well as Californian sea otters. At **Wild Arctic,** which starts out with a simulated helicopter ride to a research post at the North Pole, beluga whales, walruses, and polar bears can be viewed in areas decked out like the wrecked hulls of two 19th-century sailing ships. **Manatee Rescue** lets you watch the gentle-giant marine mammals cavorting in a 215,000-gallon tank. Various **freshwater and saltwater aquariums** hold underwater creatures from around the world. And for younger kids who need to release lots of energy, **Sesame Street Bay of Play at SeaWorld,** opened in 2008, is a hands-on fun zone that features three family-friendly Sesame Street–themed rides.

SeaWorld's highlights are its large-arena entertainments. You can get front-row seats if you arrive 30 minutes in advance, and the stadiums are large enough for everyone to get a seat in the off-season. Introduced in 2006 and starring the ever-beloved Shamu the Killer Whale, **Believe** features synchronized whales and brings down the house. Another favorite is Sesame Street presents Lights, Camera, Imagination! in 4-D, a new film that has Cookie Monster, Elmo, and other Sesame Street favorites swimming through an imaginary ocean and flying through a cinematic sky. **Clyde and Seamore's Risky Rescue,** the sea lion and otter production, also is widely popular.

Not all the shows are water-oriented. **Pets Rule!** showcases the antics of more common animals like dogs, cats, birds, and even a pig. One segment of the show actually has regular house cats climbing ladders and hanging upside down as they cross a high wire. The majority of the animals used in the show were adopted from shelters.

SEAWORLD CHECKLIST

It's a good idea to take a change of clothes with you to SeaWorld, especially if the weather is on the cool side and you sit in the first 10 rows at one of the marine shows, or ride Shipwreck Rapids; you can rent a locker to stow belongings. Hats, sunblock, and shirts with long sleeves are also recommended, since SeaWorld, like any area of sunny San Diego near a reflective body of water, is a great place to get a memorable sunburn. And remember that Sea-World concessions won't provide drink lids or straws, which endanger the animals—so bring that sippy cup if you need it.

Trainer for a Day gives you a first-hand look at how SeaWorld's trainers work, and allows you to help them with everything from food preparation to training techniques. The $545 fee may seem hefty, but it buys a once-in-a-lifetime opportunity. A less expensive treat ($36 adults, $19 children) is the **Dine With Shamu** package, which includes a buffet lunch or dinner and allows you the thrill of eating while the whales swim up to you or happily play nearby.

Shipwreck Rapids, SeaWorld of San Diego's first adventure ride, offers plenty of excitement—but you may end up getting soaked. For five minutes, nine "shipwrecked" passengers careen down a river in a raft-like inner tube, encountering a series of obstacles, including several waterfalls. There's no extra charge, making this one of SeaWorld's great bargains—expect long lines. Those who want to head to higher ground might consider the **Skytower,** a glass elevator that ascends 265 feet; the views of San Diego County are especially spectacular in early morning and late evening. The **Bayside Skyride,** a five-minute aerial tram ride that leaves from the same spot, travels across Mission Bay. Combined admission for the Skytower and the tram is $5. The fact that Anheuser-Busch is the park's parent company is evident in the presence of the beer company's signature Clydesdales, huge horses that you can visit in their "hamlet" when they're not putting on demonstrations or parading through the park.

The San Diego 3-for-1 Ticket ($109 for adults, $86 for children ages 3 to 9) offers five consecutive days of unlimited admission to SeaWorld, the San Diego Zoo, and the San Diego Wild Animal Park. This is a good idea, because if you try to get your money's worth by fitting everything in on a single day, you're likely to end up tired and cranky. Many hotels, especially those in the Mission Bay area, also offer SeaWorld specials that may include rate reductions or two days' entry for the price of one. ⊠ *500 Sea World Dr., near west end of I–8, Mission Bay* ☎ *800/257–4268* ⊕ *www.seaworld.com* ⊠ *$59 adults, $49 kids; parking $10 cars, $6 motorcycles, $15 RVs and campers; 1-hr behind-the-scenes walking tours $12 extra* ⊟ *AE, D, MC, V* ⊗ *Daily 10–dusk; extended hrs in summer.*

⓫ Sunset Cliffs. On the south end of Ocean Beach, the Sunset Cliffs area is made up of several beaches and 68 acres of walking paths carved into the jagged cliffs. A long staircase leads visitors from the top of Ladera Street down to the water. Although an ideal photo spot, Sunset Cliffs are not recommend for children due to the challenging descent, unpredictable surf, and lack of lifeguards. ⊹ *Take I–8 west until it becomes Sunset Cliffs Blvd. Continue straight into Sunset Cliffs Park, Ocean Beach.*

❹ Vacation Isle. Ingraham Street bisects this island, providing two distinct experiences for visitors. The west side is taken up by the Paradise Point Resort & Spa, but you don't have to be a guest to enjoy the hotel's lushly landscaped grounds and bay-front restaurants. The water-ski clubs congregate at **Ski Beach** on the east side of the island, where there's a parking lot as well as picnic areas and restrooms. Ski Beach is the site of the annual Thunderboat Regatta, held in September. At a pond on the south side of the island, children and young-at-heart adults take part year-round in motorized miniature boat races. ⊠ *Mission Bay.*

1

OLD TOWN

San Diego's Spanish and Mexican roots are most evident in Old Town, the area north of downtown at Juan Street, near the intersection of Interstates 5 and 8. As the first European settlement in Southern California, Old Town San Diego's first houses, of sun-dried adobe bricks arranged around a central plaza, began to appear in the 1820s; by the 1850s, after the discovery of gold drew prospectors to California from around the globe, they began to be replaced with wood-frame structures. In the 1860s, however, the advent of Alonzo Horton's New Town to the southeast stole thunder from Old Town, which began to wither. Efforts to preserve it began early in the 20th century, and when it became a state historic park in 1968 the process of restoration gained momentum.

Although Old Town was largely a 19th-century phenomenon, the pueblo's true beginnings took place much earlier and on a hill overlooking it, where soldiers from New Spain established a military outpost in May 1769 and two months later Father Junípero Serra established the first of California's missions, San Diego de Alcalá. The missionaries forced San Diego's original inhabitants, the Kumeyaay Indians—called the Diegueños by the Spaniards—to abandon their seminomadic lifestyle and live at the mission; they also expected the Indians to adopt Spanish customs and Christianity as their religion, although the Indians resisted fiercely.

In 1774 the hilltop was declared a Royal Presidio, or fortress, and the mission was moved 6 mi west to a new site along the San Diego River. The Kumeyaays, responding to the loss of more of their land, attacked and burned it in 1775. Their revolt was short-lived, however. A later assault on the presidio was less successful, and by 1800 about 1,500 Kumeyaays were living on the mission's grounds, receiving religious instruction and adapting to Spanish ways.

When Mexico gained independence from Spain in 1821, the new nation claimed Spanish lands in California and flew the Mexican flag over the presidio. The Mexican government, centered some 2,000 mi away in Monterrey, stripped the missions of their lands, and an aristocracy of landholders began to emerge. At the same time, settlers began to move down from the presidio to what is now Old Town.

A rectangular plaza was laid out along today's San Diego Avenue to serve as the settlement's center. In 1846, during the war between Mexico and the United States, a detachment of U.S. Marines raised the Stars and Stripes over the plaza for the first time. The flag was removed once or twice, but by early 1848 Mexico had surrendered California, and

CLOSE UP

California's Padre President

San Diego, the first European settlement in Southern California, was founded by Father Junípero Serra in July 1769. A member of the Franciscan order, Father Serra was part of a larger expedition chartered by King Charles III of Spain and headed by explorer Don Gaspar de Portola to travel north from Baja California and occupy the territory known then as Alta California.

When they arrived in San Diego, the Spaniards found about 20,000 Kumeyaay Indians living in a hundred or so villages along the coast and inland. The missionaries attempted to convert them to Christianity, and taught them agricultural and other skills so they could work what would become the missions' vast holdings.

Mission San Diego Alcalá, established on a hillside above what is now Mission Valley, was the first of the 21 that the Franciscans ultimately built along the coast of California. After establishing the mission and presidio in San Diego, Serra and Portola moved on, founding the Mission San Carlos Borromeo and presidio at Monterey. This was later moved to Carmel, where Father Serra settled and maintained his headquarters until his death in 1784.

Father Serra, the padre president of California, established nine missions. Besides those at San Diego and Monterey, these were: San Antonio de Padua, 1771; San Gabriel, 1771; San Luis Obispo, 1772; Dolores, 1776; San Juan Capistrano, 1776; Santa Clara, 1777; and San Buenaventura, 1782. He personally oversaw the planning, construction, and staffing of each of these, and conferred the sacraments. His work took him from Carmel to locations up and down the length of California. It's estimated that during this period he walked more than 24,000 mi in California visiting missions.

The missions comprised millions of acres and were in fact small self-sufficient cities with the church as the centerpiece. In addition to converting the Indians to Christianity and teaching them European ways, the padres managed farming, education, and industries such as candle making and tanning. San Diego is the southernmost mission, while the mission at Sonoma, San Francisco Solano, the last to be founded, in 1823, is the northernmost; each was established a day's walk—about 30 mi—from the previous one and was linked to El Camino Highway. The missions were the earliest form of lodging in the Golden State, known far and wide for the hospitality they afforded visitors.

Father Serra spent barely a year in San Diego before embarking on his journey to establish missions across California, but his presence left a lasting imprint. You can see some of the history at the Junípero Serra Museum and at Mission San Diego Alcalá. Within walking distance from Old Town, the Junípero Serra Museum at Presidio Hill displays furniture, housewares, and tools from the Native Americans, Spanish, and Mexicans through 1929. Also showcased at the museum is a historic cannon, salvaged from a sunken vessel at the bottom of San Diego Bay. You can trace the steps of Father Serra along El Camino Real by driving U.S. 101, the historic route that traverses coastal California from south to north.

—Bobbi Zane

the U.S. flag remained. San Diego became an incorporated city in 1850, with Old Town as its center.

On San Diego Avenue, the district's main drag, art galleries and expensive gift shops are interspersed with tacky curio shops, restaurants, and open-air stands selling inexpensive Mexican pottery, jewelry, and blankets. The Old Town Esplanade on San Diego Avenue between Harney and Conde streets is the best of several mall-like affairs constructed in mock Mexican-plaza style. Shops and restaurants also line Juan and Congress streets.

Access to Old Town is easy thanks to the nearby Transit Center. Ten bus lines stop here, as do the San Diego Trolley and the Coaster commuter rail line. Two large parking lots linked to the park by an underground pedestrian walkway ease some of the parking congestion, and signage leading from I–8 to the Transit Center is easy to follow.

Numbers in the text correspond to numbers on the Old Town San Diego map.

A GOOD TOUR

Because of the steep hills leading up to Heritage Park and Presidio Park, it's best to use a car to see all of Old Town's sights.

Visit the information center at Robinson-Rose House on Wallace Street, facing Old Town Plaza, to orient yourself to the various sights in **Old Town San Diego State Historic Park ❶**. When you've had enough history, cross north on the west side of the plaza to **Plaza del Pasado ❷**, where you can shop or stop for a bite to eat. Walk down San Diego Avenue, which flanks the south side of Old Town's historic plaza, east to Harney Street and the **Thomas Whaley Museum ❸**. It's best to hop in a car at this point for the next sights. Continue east 2½ blocks on San Diego Avenue beyond Arista Street to **El Campo Santo ❹** cemetery. **Heritage Park ❺** is perched on a hill above Juan Street, north of the museum and cemetery. Drive west on Juan Street and north on Taylor Street, which leads to Presidio Drive. This takes you up the hill on which **Presidio Park ❻** and the **Junípero Serra Museum ❼** sit.

TIMING It takes about two hours to walk through Old Town. Try to time your visit to coincide with the free daily tours given by costumed park staff. They depart daily at 11 AM from the Robinson-Rose House Visitor Center and take about one hour. If you go to Presidio Park, definitely drive instead of walk, and allot another hour to explore the grounds and museum.

SIGHTS TO SEE

❹ **El Campo Santo.** The old adobe-wall cemetery established in 1849 was until 1880 the burial place for many members of Old Town's founding families—as well as for some gamblers and bandits who passed through town. Antonio Garra, a chief who led an uprising of the San Luis Rey Indians, was executed at El Campo Santo in front of the open grave he had been forced to dig for himself. These days the small cemetery is a

peaceful stop for visitors to Old Town. Most of the markers give only approximations of where the people named on them are buried; some of the early settlers laid to rest at El Campo Santo really reside under San Diego Avenue. ⊠*North side of San Diego Ave. S, between Arista and Ampudia Sts.*

5 **Heritage Park.** A number of San Diego's important Victorian buildings are the focus of this 7.8-acre park, up the Juan Street hill near Harney Street. The buildings, moved here and restored by Save Our Heritage Organization, include Southern California's first synagogue, a one-room Classical Revival structure built in 1889 for Congregation Beth Israel. The most interesting of the park's six former residences might be the Sherman Gilbert House, which has a widow's walk and intricate carving on its decorative trim. It was built for real-estate dealer John Sherman in 1887 at the then-exorbitant cost of $20,000—indicating just how profitable the booming housing market could be. All the houses, some of which may seem surprisingly colorful, do in fact accurately represent the bright tones of the era. Most of the homes are now used as offices and shops, except for the 1893 Burton House which serves as a tea house, and the 1887 Bushyhead House and the adjacent 1889 Christian House, which together are doing business as the Heritage Park Inn. The climb up to the park is a little steep, but the view of the harbor is great. Only the synagogue is open to visitors. ✉*County parks office, 2455 Heritage Park Row* ☎*619/291–9784.*

🖐 **❼ Junípero Serra Museum.** The hill on which San Diego's original Spanish presidio (fortress) and California's first mission were perched is now the domain of a Spanish mission–style museum established, along with Presidio Park, by department store magnate and philanthropist George Marston in 1929 to commemorate the history of the site from the time it was occupied by the Kumeyaay Indians through its Spanish, Mexican, and American periods. Artifacts include Kumeyaay baskets, Spanish riding gear, and a painting that Father Serra would have viewed in Mission San Diego de Alcalá. The education room has hands-on stations where kids can grind acorns in *metates* (stones used for grinding grain), dig for buried artifacts with archaeology tools, or dress up in period costumes—one represents San Diego founding father Alonzo Horton. Ascend the tower to compare the view you'd have gotten before 1929 with the one you have today. The museum, now operated by the San Diego Historical Society, is at the north end of Presidio Park, near Taylor Street. ✉*2727 Presidio Dr.* ☎*619/297-3258* ⊕*www.sandiegohistory.org* 💰*$5* ⊙ *Weekdays 11–3; weekends 10–4:30.*

▮ OFF THE BEATEN PATH

Mission San Diego de Alcalá. It's hard to imagine how remote California's earliest mission once must have been; these days, it's accessible by a major freeway (I–15) and by the San Diego Trolley. Mission San Diego de Alcalá, the first of a chain of 21 missions stretching northward along the coast, was established by Father Junípero Serra on Presidio Hill in 1769 and moved to this location in 1774. There was no greater security from enemy attack here: Padre Luis Jayme, California's first Christian martyr, was clubbed to death by the Kumeyaay Indians he was trying to convert in 1775. The present church is the fifth built on the site; it was reconstructed in 1931 following the outlines of the 1813 church. It measures 150 feet long but only 35 feet wide because, without easy means of joining beams, the mission buildings were only as wide as the trees that served as their ceiling supports were tall. Father Jayme is buried in the sanctuary; a small museum named for him documents mission history and exhibits tools and artifacts from the early days. From the peaceful palm-bedecked gardens out back you can gaze at the 46-foot-high *campanario* (bell tower), the mission's most distinctive feature; one of its five bells was cast in 1822. ✉*10818 San Diego Mission Rd.* ⊕*from I–15, take Friars Rd. east and Rancho Mission Rd. south* ☎*619/283-7319* ⊕*www.missionsandiego.com* 💰*$3 donation suggested* ⊙ *Mon.–Fri. 7:30–4.*

★ **❶ Old Town San Diego State Historic Park.** The six square blocks on the site of San Diego's original pueblo are the heart of Old Town. Most of the 20 historic buildings preserved or re-created by the park cluster around **Old Town Plaza,** bounded by Wallace Street on the west, Calhoun Street on the north, Mason Street on the east, and San Diego Avenue on the south. The plaza is a pleasant place to rest, plan your tour of the park, and watch passersby. San Diego Avenue is closed to vehicle traffic here.

Some of Old Town's buildings were destroyed in a fire in 1872, but after the site became a state historic park in 1968, reconstruction and restoration on the structures that remained began. Seven of the original adobes are still intact. The tour pamphlet available at Robinson-Rose House gives details about all the historic houses on the plaza and in its vicinity; a few of the more interesting ones are noted below. Several reconstructed buildings serve as restaurants or as shops purveying wares reminiscent of those that might have been available in the original Old Town; Racine & Laramie, a painstakingly reproduced version of San Diego's first (1868) cigar store, is especially interesting. The noncommercial houses are open daily 10–5; none charges admission, though donations are appreciated.

The **Robinson-Rose House** (☎ *619/220–5422*), on Wallace Street facing Old Town Plaza, was the original commercial center of Old San Diego, housing railroad offices, law offices, and the first newspaper press. Built in 1853 but in ruins at the end of the 19th century, it has been reconstructed and now serves as the park's visitor center and administrative headquarters. It contains a model of Old Town as it looked in 1872, as well as various historic exhibits. Just behind the Robinson-Rose House is a replica of the Victorian-era Silvas-McCoy house, originally built in 1869.

On Mason Street, at the corner of Calhoun Street, is the **Cosmopolitan Restaurant/Casa de Bandini,** once one of the prettiest haciendas in San Diego. Built in 1829 by a Peruvian, Juan Bandini, the house served as Old Town's social center during Mexican rule. Albert Seeley, a stage-coach entrepreneur, purchased the home in 1869, built a second story, and turned it into the Cosmopolitan Hotel, a way station for travelers on the daylong trip south from Los Angeles. It later served as a store and a factory and, now, as the Cosmopolitan restaurant.

Seeley Stable (✉ *2630 Calhoun St.*), next door to the Cosmopolitan building, became San Diego's stagecoach stop in 1867, and was the transportation hub of Old Town until near the turn of the century, when trains became the favored mode of travel. The stable houses a collection of horse-drawn vehicles, some so elaborate that you can see where the term "carriage trade" came from. Also inside are Western memorabilia, including an exhibit on the California *vaquero,* the original American cowboy, and a collection of Native American artifacts.

The **Casa de Estudillo** (✉ *4001 Mason St.*) was built on Mason Street in 1827 by the commander of the San Diego Presidio, José Maria Estudillo. The largest and most elaborate of the original adobe homes, it was occupied by members of the Estudillo family until 1887. It was purchased and restored in 1910 by sugar magnate and developer John D. Spreckels, who advertised it in bold lettering on the side as "Ramona's Marriage Place." Despite meticulous attention to historical detail in the restoration, Spreckels's claim that the small chapel in the house was the site of the wedding in Helen Hunt Jackson's popular novel *Ramona* had no basis; that didn't stop people from coming to see it, however.

1

The **San Diego Union Museum** (⊠ *Twigg St. and San Diego Ave.*) is in a New England–style, wood-frame house prefabricated in the eastern United States and shipped around Cape Horn in 1851. The building has been restored to replicate the newspaper's offices of 1868, when the first edition of the *San Diego Union* was printed.

Also worth exploring in the plaza area are the free **Dental Museum, Mason Street School, Wells Fargo History Museum, First San Diego Courthouse, Casa de Machado y Silvas Commercial Restaurant Museum,** and the **Casa de Machado Y Stewart.** Ask at the visitor center (⊠ *4002 Wallace St.* ☏ *619/220–5422* ⊕ *www.parks.ca.gov*) for locations.

NEED A BREAK

Located directly across from Old Town's Historic Park, O'Hungry's (⊠ *2547 San Diego Ave.* ☏ *619/298–0133*) offers sensational soups, hearty sandwiches, and refreshing beers-by-the yard. The massive brews come in special serving glasses with their own wooden stands. On those hot summer days there's no better way to escape the heat and still catch all the Old Town action.

❷ **Plaza del Pasado.** North of San Diego's Old Town Plaza lies the area's unofficial center, built to represent a colonial Mexican square and until recently known as Bazaar del Mundo. In mid-2005, this collection of shops and restaurants around a central courtyard formerly in blossom with magenta bougainvillea, scarlet hibiscus, and other flowers in season, was transferred to new management and remodeled to what it might have looked like in the early California days, from 1821 to 1872, complete with shops stocked with items reminiscent of that era. Nine shops are open, and there are also three restaurants, including Casa de Reyes, serving Mexican food. The transformation of this area is not popular with the San Diegans, however, who loved shopping, drinking margaritas, and listening to live mariachi music in their old bursting-with-color bazaar, even if it was not an authentic representation of Old San Diego. They lament that the color-free Plaza del Pasado (Place of the Past) is all too accurate a representation of the arid San Diego of yore. Expect further changes. ⊠ *2754 Calhoun St.* ☏ *619/297–3100* ⊕ *www.plazadelpasado.com* ☽ *Shops daily Jan.–Mar. 10–6; Apr.–Dec. 10–10.*

❻ **Presidio Park.** The hillsides of the 40-acre green space overlooking Old Town from the north end of Taylor Street are popular with picnickers, and many couples have taken their wedding vows on the park's long stretches of lawn, some of the greenest in San Diego. You may encounter enthusiasts of the sport of grass-skiing, gliding over the grass and down the hills on their wheeled-model skis. It's a nice walk from Old Town to the summit if you're in good shape and wearing the right shoes—it should take about half an hour. You can also drive to the top of the park via Presidio Drive, off Taylor Street.

If you do decide to walk, look in at the Presidio Hills Golf Course on Mason Street. It has an unusual clubhouse that incorporates the ruins of Casa de Carrillo, the town's oldest adobe, constructed in 1820. At the end of Mason Street, veer left on Jackson Street to reach the **Presidio Ruins,** where adobe walls and a bastion have been built above the foundations of the original fortress and chapel. Archaeology students from San Diego State University who excavated the area have marked off the early chapel outlines, although they reburied the artifacts they uncovered in order to protect them. Also on-site are the 28-foot-high Serra Cross, built

> **AMERICA'S MOST HAUNTED**
>
> Built on a former gallows site in 1856, the Whaley House is one of 30 houses designated by the Department of Commerce to be haunted. Legend has it that the house is inhabited by seven spirits, making it the "most haunted house in America."

in 1913 out of brick tiles found in the ruins, and a bronze statue of Father Serra. Before you do much poking around here, however, it's a good idea to get some historical perspective at the Junípero Serra Museum, just to the east. Take Presidio Drive southeast of the museum and you'll come to the site of Fort Stockton, built to protect Old Town and abandoned by the United States in 1848. Plaques and statues also commemorate the Mormon Battalion, which enlisted here to fight in the battle against Mexico. ⊠ *1 block north of Old Town.*

❸ **Thomas Whaley Museum.** Thomas Whaley was a New York entrepreneur who came to California during the gold rush. He wanted to provide his East Coast wife with all the comforts of home, so in 1857 he had Southern California's first two-story brick structure built, making it the oldest double-story brick building on the West Coast. The house, which served as the county courthouse and government seat during the 1870s, stands in strong contrast to the Spanish-style adobe residences that surround the nearby historic plaza and marks an early stage of San Diego's "Americanization." A garden out back includes many varieties of Old Garden roses from before 1867, when roses were first hybridized. The place is perhaps most famed, however, for the ghosts that are said to inhabit it. ⊠ *2476 San Diego Ave.* ☎ *619/297–7511* ⊕ *www.whaleyhouse.org* 🎫 *$6 before 5, $10 after 5.* ☉ *Sept.–May, Mon.–Tues. 10–5, Thurs.–Sun. 10–10; June–Aug. 10–10 daily.*

UPTOWN

Unconventional among San Diego's neighborhoods, Uptown encompasses the three unique communities of Hillcrest, North Park, and University Heights, all pedestrian-friendly. In addition to its cultural diversity, Uptown is embraced for its urban boldness, retro style, upscale eateries, and artistic flair. The self-contained residential-commercial Uptown District, on University and 8th avenues, was built to resemble an inner-city neighborhood, with shops and restaurants within easy walking distance of high-priced town houses. To the northeast, Adams Avenue, reached via Park Boulevard heading north off Washington Street, has many antiques stores. Adams Avenue leads east

1

into Kensington, a handsome old neighborhood that overlooks Mission Valley.

Northwest of Balboa Park, **Hillcrest** is San Diego's center for the gay community and artists of all types. As "San Fran South," Hillcrest is one of the city's most interesting neighborhoods. University, 4th, and 5th avenues are filled with cafés, a superb collection of restaurants (including many outstanding ethnic eateries), and boutiques (among which are several indie bookstores selling new and used books along 5th below University). A haven for the fashionably bold, Hillcrest is sprinkled with thrift stores, clothing boutiques, and funky costume shops. The neighborhood hosts the annual LGBT Pride Event every July, which draws upwards of 150,000 visitors to the streets. It also hosts Cityfest, a street festival held every August, with live bands, food booths, and beer gardens.

North Park, named for its location north of Balboa Park, is centered at the intersection of University and 30th. Unique among the three communities, it has a thriving business district, essentially a "downtown" of its own. Despite the constant renovations upgrading the neighborhood, care has been taken to maintain North Park's 1950s atmosphere by retaining the original architectural facades. High-end condominiums and local merchants are often cleverly disguised behind historic signage from barber shops, bowling alleys, and theater marquees of a bygone era. This self-sufficient community offers everything from single-family homes and apartments to nightclubs and shopping.

Sandwiched between Hillcrest and North Park, **University Heights** has some of the characteristics of both enclaves, and consequently less of a unique flavor. It is home to the Diversionary Theatre, which specializes in productions with a predominately gay and lesbian theme. During the summer, University's Trolley Barn Park hosts free summer concerts for families.

A GOOD TOUR

Although Uptown is sprawling, it is relatively easy to navigate each of the neighborhood communities. For a brief walking tour through North Park, begin at the corner of Ray Street and University Avenue. As the home of several small galleries, this one-block stretch between University and North Park Way comes alive on the second Saturday of each month for the "Ray at Night" art festival. Turn right onto North Park Way and another right onto 30th Street, where the French Quarter–style building of Urban Solace offers live jazz and bluegrass while you enjoy a weekend brunch. Head north on 30th until you reach University Avenue. Trace the old trolley route by turning left on University Avenue, taking note of the architectural treasures like Chito's Shoe Repair, dating back to 1939. Continue until you reach the Birch North Park Theater, built in 1929 and the home of Lyric Opera San Diego. As you retrace your steps east on 30th, stop in at Off the Record, an authentic vinyl shop that has managed to survive as a dying breed. Continue by car, traveling west on University Avenue through University Heights and Hillcrest. The cross streets of University and 5th are an excellent spot to explore the heart of Hillcrest on foot.

TIMING   The highlight of the Uptown tour is exploring the heart of Hillcrest, located at the intersection of University and Fifth avenues. Shoppers will want to begin at University and First avenues and continue 12 blocks down to Park Boulevard. This entire tour (minus the shopping), should take no more than 1½ hours.

SIGHTS TO SEE

Birch North Park Theatre. Built in 1928, this stunning period theatre seats 730 and is owned by the Lyric Opera San Diego. Considered the jewel of North Park, the theatre was reopened in October 2005 after extensive renovations. Known for its excellent acoustics, the theatre features a wide selection of concerts and productions from opera to quartets. The original lobby now serves as the entrance to the famed Hawthorn's restaurant and lounge. ✉ *2891 University Ave., North Park* ☎ *619/239–8836* ⊕ *www.birchnorthparktheatre.net.*

NEED A
BREAK

With a focus on urban community, **Claire de Lune** (✉ *2906 University Ave. North Park* ☎ *619/688–9845*), a living-room style coffeehouse, will lure you in with its velvet couches, live jazz, wooden floors, and upstairs lounge. Their mouthwatering desserts include carrot cake, chocolate éclairs, and a raspberry cheesecake. White dragon tea and tropical star are considered house-brewed favorites. For a midweek escape, drop by on Thursday for a traditional belly dance performance.

Farmer's Market. Considered San Diego's best farmer's market, this weekly bazaar offers everything from vegan fruit pies and strawberry lemonade to homemade hummus and Turkish kabobs. A wide assortment of fresh produce and flowers are delivered straight from San Diego's local farms. ✉ *3960 Normal St., between Blaine Ave. and Lincoln Ave., Hillcrest* ☎ *619/237–1632* ⊕ *www.sdfarmbureau.org* ⊗ *Sun. 9–1* PM.

Spruce Street Bridge. Constructed in 1912 by Edwin Capps, this 375-ft suspension bridge originally served as a passageway between isolated neighborhoods and trolley lines. Spanning across Kate Sessions Canyon (commonly referred to as Arroyo Canyon), today this wobbly bridge is considered one of San Diego's best-kept secrets, with its scenic and somewhat hair-raising stroll over treetops below. ✉ *Spruce St. and 1st Ave., Hillcrest.*

Where to Eat

BEST BETS FOR SAN DIEGO DINING

With hundreds of restaurants to choose from, how will you decide where to eat? We've selected our favorite restaurants by price, cuisine, and experience in the Best Bets list below. In the first column, Fodor's Choice properties represent the "best of the best" in every price category. Bon appétit!

Fodor's Choice ★

A.R. Valentien, $$$$
Bread & cie, ¢
George's California Modern, $$$
Jsix, $$
Mistral, $$$
Nine-Ten, $$$
Ortega's Mexican Bistro, $
Restaurante Romesco, $$
Taka, $
Zenbu, $$

Best By Price

¢

Bread & cie
El Zarape
Phuong Trang
Saffron Noodles & Saté

$

Barbarella
Café Chloe
Karen Krasne's Extraordinary Desserts
Michele Coulon Dessertier
Ortega's Mexican Bistro
Taka

$$

Avenue 5
Jsix
Restaurante Romesco
Royal India
Sushi Ota
Zenbu

$$$

George's California Modern
Mistral
Molly's Restaurant
Nine-Ten
Nobu
Tapenade

$$$$

A.R. Valentien
1500 Ocean
Le Fontainebleau
Quarter Kitchen

Best By Cuisine

AMERICAN

A.R. Valentien,, $$$$
Avenue 5, $$
George's California Modern, $$$
Jsix, $$
Nine-Ten, $$$

ASIAN

Red Pearl Kitchen, $
Saffron Noodles & Sate, ¢
Zenbu, $$

CAFÉS

Bread & cie, ¢
Café Chloe, $
Karen Krasne's Extraordinary Desserts, $
Michele Coulon Dessertier, $

CHINESE

China Max, $
Dumpling Inn, ¢
Emerald Chinese Seafood Restaurant, $

FRENCH

Bertrand at Mister A's, $$$
Chez Loma, $$$
Le Fontainebleau, $$$$
Tapenade, $$$

INDIAN

Monsoon, $
Royal India, $$

ITALIAN

Barbarella, $
Pizzeria Arrivederci, $

2

JAPANESE

Nobu, $$$

Sushi Ota, $$

Taka, $

MEDITERRANEAN

Dussini Mediterranean
Bistro, $$

Mistral, $$$

Restaurante
Romesco, $$

LATIN/MEXICAN

El Zarape, ¢

Isabel's Cantina, $

Ortega's Mexican
Bistro, $

SEAFOOD

El Pescador, $

Fish Market, $$

Oceanaire Seafood
Room, $$$

Tin Fish, $

Best By Experience

BEST WATER VIEWS

1500 Ocean, $$$$

Fish Market, $$

George's California
Modern, $$$

Jordan at Tower 23,
$$$

Marine Room, $$$$

Mistral, $$$

BEST BRUNCH

Barbarella, $

Bread & cie, ¢

Café Chloe, $

Jordan at Tower 23,
$$$

Nine-Ten, $$$

BEST FOR FAMILIES

Isabel's Cantina, $

Ortega's Mexican
Bistro, $

Pizzeria Arrivederci, $

Rimel's Rotisserie, $

Tartine, $

BEST OUTDOOR DINING

A.R. Valentien, $$$$

Barbarella, $

Café Chloe, $

1500 Ocean, $$$$

Osteria Romantica, $

Tapenade, $$$

TRENDY

Dish, $

Jsix, $$

Nobu, $$$

Quarter Kitchen, $$$$

Red Circle, ¢

Zenbu, $$

ROMANTIC

Betrand at
Mister A's, $$$

Chez Loma, $$$

1500 Ocean, $$$

George's California
Modern, $$$

Laurel, $$$

Mistral, $$$

WINE LISTS

A.R. Valentien, $$$$

1500 Ocean, $$$$

Laurel, $$$

Molly's Restaurant &
Bar, $$$

GOOD FOR GROUPS

Emerald Chinese
Seafood Restaurant, $

Nobu, $$$

Oceanaire Seafood
Room, $$$

Red Pearl Kitchen, $

Royal India, $$

BEST FOR BUSINESS

BiCE, $$$$

George's California
Modern, $$$

Molly's Restaurant &
Bar, $$$

Oceanaire Seafood
Room, $$$

Taka Sushi, $

Zodiac, $$

BEST HOTEL DINING

A.R. Valentien, $$$$

1500 Ocean, $$$$

Jsix, $$

Le Fontainebleau, $$$

Mistral, $$$

Nine-Ten, $$$

Updated by
Maria C. Hunt

SAN DIEGO'S STATUS AS A VACATIONER'S PARADISE and its growth into the eighth-largest city in the United States have made it a magnet for restaurateurs and chefs from around the globe. The city now takes for granted cuisines such as Cambodian, Ethiopian, Afghan, and Laotian. But a good deal of the new talent also is homegrown, and it's not unusual for local cooks to attend leading culinary academies and return home fired by the desire to remake San Diego cuisine. The county's growing corps of innovative and cutting-edge chefs (many based in the northern suburbs, see Chapter 7 for listings) includes William Bradley of Addison at the Grand Del Mar, Jeff Jackson at A.R. Valentien, and Carl Schroeder at Market Restaurant + Bar. The leading point of view is that a region this blessed with gorgeous locally grown vegetables, fruits, herbs, and seafood should make a culinary statement.

Downtown is always an obvious for great dining. The über-trendy Gaslamp Quarter delights visitors looking for not just good food, but a good (if not rowdy) time as well. Near the waterfront on the upper western edge of downtown, the gentrified Little Italy district has become a center for affordable, traditional, and contemporary Italian fare. The area offers surprises, too, such as an authentic English pub, a fine Argentine–Italian steak house, and a jazz supper club. Adjacent to the Gaslamp, diverse and trendy restaurants and cafés thrive in the East Village neighborhood, an urban-feeling area of luxury condos to the north and east of PETCO Park.

San Diego's neighboring enclaves share a sense of energy, fueled by a collective caffeine high acquired in the coffeehouses (some of which are listed in Chapter 4) that the city is known for. The uptown neighborhoods centered by Hillcrest—an urbane district with a San Francisco flavor—are marked by increasing culinary sophistication. Mission Valley, the heart of the city's shopping district, abounds with big restaurants of varying quality. And scenic La Jolla, with many of San Diego's most expensive restaurants, offers some of the best dining in the city. In Chula Vista you'll find authentic Mexican fare, while Coronado—the peninsula city across San Diego Bay—has both casual, neighborhood-style eateries and extravagant hotel dining rooms with dramatic water views. Great cooking blossoms beyond the city's official borders; to the north, Del Mar's, Solana Beach's, and Rancho Santa Fe's elegant surroundings have attracted good cuisine.

WHAT IT COSTS					
	¢	$	$$	$$$	$$$$
Restaurants	under $10	$10–$18	$19–$27	$28–$35	over $35

Prices are for a main course at dinner, excluding 7.75% tax.

CORONADO

Coronado is a picturesque community filled with neat wood-frame homes, the historic turrets of the Hotel del Coronado, and one of the most beautiful beaches in the area. Though there are exceptions, many restaurants here rely on tourist traffic, so often the cuisine is adequate but not stellar.

AMERICAN

$$$$ ✗ **1500 Ocean.** The fine dining restaurant at Hotel Del Coronado offers a memorable evening that showcases the best organic and naturally raised ingredients the Southland has to offer. Chef Brian Sinnott, who honed his technique in San Francisco, presents sublimely subtle dishes such as crisply fried squash blossoms stuffed with ricotta and basil, local rockfish in tomato shellfish broth, and duck confit with black kale and cranberry beans. The interior, at once inviting and elegant, evokes a posh cabana, while the terrace offers ocean views. An excellent international wine list and equally clever desserts and artisanal cheeses complete the experience. ✉ *Hotel Del Coronado, 1500 Orange Ave.* ☎ *619/522–8490* ▭ *AE, D, DC, MC, V* ⊘ *No lunch.*

$$$ ✗ **Sheerwater.** This casual but pricey all-day dining room is the primary restaurant at Hotel Del Coronado. A spacious, breeze-swept terrace enjoys extraordinary ocean views, while the indoor room can be on the noisy side, especially when families are present. The menu offers a local take on all-American fare, with dishes such as chili-dusted shrimp cocktail in tequila-spiked sauce, and splits the entrée list between meats and seafood offerings such as grilled salmon and sea bass. ✉ *Hotel Del Coronado, 1500 Orange Ave.* ☎ *619/435–6611* ▭ *AE, D, DC, MC, V.*

$$ ✗ **Tent City.** In the historic First Bank of Commerce building along with the Coronado Museum of History and Art, this restaurant serves an eclectic cuisine that emphasizes strong flavors and light effects, as evident in the "stacked" salad of crab, shrimp, and sliced yellow tomatoes starter. Main events include jazzed-up chicken and seafood variations. The restaurant's name memorializes the waterside summer camp that San Diego residents frequented from 1900 to 1939. The dining room is pleasant, but the sidewalk terrace beckons in fine weather. ✉ *1100 Orange Ave.* ☎ *619/435–4611* ▭ *AE, D, MC, V.*

$ ✗ **Coronado Brewing Company.** The carefully crafted beers are good by themselves, but they also make a good accompaniment to bratwurst and beer-battered onion rings, served in mountainous portions. There's indoor seating, a pair of sidewalk terraces and, best of all, a walled garden that provides a quiet haven from the bustle of Orange Avenue. Simple choices are the wisest, from the Philadelphia-style steak sandwich to wood-fired pizzas to baby back ribs basted with spicy, ginger-flavored barbecue sauce. It is a brewery, but it's still popular with families. ✉ *170 Orange Ave.* ☎ *619/437–4452* ▭ *MC, V.*

FRENCH

$$$ ✗ **Chez Loma.** This is widely considered one of the most romantic restaurants in Southern California, and it's a favorite with guests at nearby Hotel Del Coronado. Tucked away on a side street, the restaurant is

KNOW HOW

A fair number of San Diego restaurants offer "early-bird specials" before peak dining hours. There's no rule about the time for the specials, but they're generally offered between 5 and 6:30 on weekdays. Instead of calling it an early-bird special, many finer restaurants offer prix-fixe menus served early in the evening. Check the restaurants' Web sites for times and special menus.

With the boom of new apartments and condominiums in Little Italy, parking near many of its restaurants has become a problem. The Parkade, a controlled-price public parking garage at the corner of Sixth Avenue and K Street, usually has ample parking even in the evening. There's also a local San Diego Trolley stop that's less than two blocks from Little Italy's India Street restaurant row. A plus, especially for those who lunch here, is the proximity of San Diego Bay, which is just a few streets to the west. It offers a superb promenade that leads to interesting places; long walks also help with the digestion of vast plates of pasta. If you use the trolley to get to downtown and Gaslamp Quarter restaurants, you can avoid parking fees that may exceed $20 and valets who expect tips.

CHILDREN

San Diego rolls out the red carpet for everyone, including children, although some of the more formal establishments and large, expense account–oriented steakhouses probably are inappropriate venues for kids. Children's menus are neither unknown nor particularly common, but most establishments will cheerfully offer a few suggestions for the younger set if asked. Fast food is readily available in all quarters of the city. Hillcrest, while decidedly adult in nature, has the most popular "kid magnet" in town: the Corvette Diner Bar & Grill, which hosts many kiddie birthday parties thanks to a 1950s menu and decor, and servers who entertain with song and dance. Children are well received at Kearny Mesa's Convoy Street Chinese restaurants that specialize at lunch time in dim sum (myriad small dishes). Youngsters who have never tried it may be delighted by egg rolls, fried pork dumplings, and fried shrimp rolls. California-style Mexican cuisine that's usually a hit with kids is not hard to find, especially in the bustling Old Town area, where Old Town Mexican Café offers high chairs and crayons to kids. Fish tacos are a standard here, but if you're not sure what your kids will like, try a cheese quesadilla (melted cheese in a flour tortilla), chips, or rolled tacos with guacamole. Always sample the salsa before offering it to your little ones, as it's often spicy.

DRESS

San Diego restaurants have largely abandoned the battle to require stylish attire of their patrons who like to dress casually, and while "Appropriate Dress Required" signs are sometimes displayed in the entrance, this generally means nothing more than clean and reasonably neat clothing. Some "dress-up" places remain, notably the Fontainebleau Room at the Westgate Hotel and Bertrand at Mister A's. Otherwise, a "come-as-you-are" attitude generally prevails, with women in jeans and heels or a dress and men in an open-collar dress shirt and pants.

MEALTIMES

Unless otherwise noted, the restaurants listed in this guide are open daily for lunch and dinner. Lunch is typically served 11:30–2:30, and dinner service in most restaurants begins at 5:30 and ends at 10. A number of establishments serve until 11 or later on Friday and Saturday nights, and one top-quality downtown restaurant, Rainwater's on Kettner, always seats until at least 11 pm without exception.

PRICES

Meal prices in San Diego have caught up with those of other major metropolitan areas. However, increasing real estate prices and rents are reflected by more expensive entrées, especially in districts like La Jolla, the Gaslamp Quarter, and Little Italy. Some locals take advantage of the city's traditionally large portions by splitting any course they like, from appetizer to dessert. Most restaurants tolerate this, while several charge a few dollars extra for a shared plate. Diners can also find reasonably priced meals along the Convoy Street Asian restaurant row, in Ocean Beach, and in neighborhoods away from downtown. Even in the Gaslamp district, outposts of national chains offer affordable menus, although these do not feature the San Diego cuisine that the town's better chefs are currently inventing. As a rule, Mexican restaurants offer good value, and in most cases will fill you up. The old-line pizza and spaghetti houses perform a similar service, although they are not the culinary equals of the new wave of Italian restaurants.

Some restaurants listed are marked with a price range ($$–$$$, for example). This indicates one of two things: either the average cost straddles two categories or, if you order strategically, you can get out for less than most diners spend.

RESERVATIONS

Reservations are always a good idea; we mention them only when they're essential or not accepted. Book as far ahead as you can, and reconfirm as soon as you arrive. (Large parties should always call ahead to check the reservations policy.)

SMOKING

Smoking is banned in restaurants, but some permit cigarette smoking on their terraces.

SPECIALTIES

Because of its multiethnic population, you can find cuisine from nearly every part of the world in San Diego. A local specialty is the fish taco, filled with any sort of fish the restaurant chooses. Something else to look for is the local spiny lobster; when they're in season, roughly from late October to early March, restaurants serve these tasty beasts simply grilled, or lightly fried Baja California–style, or elaborately sauced and presented in the shell in good—and not so good—interpretations of lobster thermidor. In addition to Mexican fare, San Diego has three Chinese restaurants that specialize in the luxurious Hong Kong–style of cooking: Emerald Chinese Seafood, Jasmine, and China Max, on Convoy Street in the heavily commercial Kearny Mesa neighborhood.

in a former house with lots of windows, soft lighting, and an upstairs Victorian parlor where coffee and dessert are served. The more elaborate dishes among the carefully prepared French bistro menu are boeuf bourguignon, rack of lamb with balsamic marinade, and filet mignon. A specially priced early dinner menu and two choices of fixed-price menus for $38 or $45 offer more value. There's sidewalk dining and Sunday brunch, too. ⊠*1132 Loma Ave.* ☎*619/435–0661* ▭*AE, D, MC, V* ☉*No lunch.*

$ ✗**Tartine.** There's always a dish of water for canine pals on the terrace of this French inspired café a block from San Diego Bay. Famous sandwiches include ham-and-Brie slathered with grain mustard, or Gorgonzola cheese, walnuts, mache, and sliced pears. Clever salads and soups round out the daytime menu. Dinner brings a bruschetta of the day, herbed gnocchi, steamed mussels, and specials like braised pork shoulder. The stars of the menu are the house-made desserts such as lemon tart, blueberry streusel coffee cake, and chocolate layer cake. Continental breakfast commences at 6 AM, when quiche and just-baked pastries silently command "Eat me!" This may be Coronado's best bet for casual but stylish fare. ⊠*1106 1st St.* ☎*619/435–4323* ▭*MC, V.*

MEDITERRANEAN

$$ ✗**Restaurante Romesco.** Mediterranean bistro meets Baja California
Fodor$Choice ingredients in this restaurant by Javier Plascencia and family, Tijuana's
★ first family of restaurateurs. The varied menu starts with smoked marlin carpaccio with mango salsa or tomato bruschetta, continues with entrées such as lobster ravioli in brandy cream sauce and mesquite grilled duck breast, and ends with crepes in *cajeta* caramel. Romesco offers a full bar and the rare chance to taste some of the fine wines made in Baja California Norte, Mexico's premier wine country. Service can be leisurely to the point of lax; according to Mexican custom, diners must request the check when they are ready to leave. ⊠*4346 Bonita Rd., Chula Vista* ☎*619/475–8627* ▭*AE, MC, V* ☉*Closed Mon. No lunch weekends.*

SEAFOOD

$$$ ✗**Mistral.** Evocatively named after the warm wind that blows across
Fodor$Choice southern France and Italy, the new dinner-only fine-dining restaurant at
★ Loews Coronado Bay Resort features fine Mediterranean cuisine built around naturally raised meats and organic local produce. Chef Martin Batis's creative menu ranges from large Mexican sea scallops with spinach agnolotti, cumin-rubbed lamb chops with roasted garlic, and chicken roasted with tarragon from the resort's extensive herb garden. A well-edited wine list and housemade desserts like apple tarte tatin with chai ice cream complete the experience. The soft new decor plays up the sweeping views of the bay visible from every table. ⊠*Loews Coronado Bay Resort, 4000 Coronado Bay Rd.* ☎*619/424–4477* ▭*AE, DC, MC, V* ☉*Closed Mon. No lunch.*

DOWNTOWN

The dramatically restored Gaslamp Quarter offers vigorous nightlife and more than 100 restaurants, mostly running along 4th, 5th, and 6th avenues. They range from casual spots for burgers, sushi, and tacos to stylish restaurants serving fresh seafood, Italian cuisine, and aged steaks at prices that may appeal only to business travelers. Farther east near PETCO Park is the East Village's eclectic mix of independent restaurants, offering everything from French bistro fare to burgers and artisan baked bread. Just north of downtown, Little Italy offers many Italian restaurants, with a couple of surprises tossed in.

AMERICAN

$$$$ ✗ **Quarter Kitchen at The Ivy.** This spacious modern restaurant in the new $100 million Ivy Hotel is a must-see. The extravagantly priced menu ranges from steaks to Asian-inspired to fun finger food. Come for the scene, the impressive wine list, and the items meant for sharing, like the hamachi sashimi with real grated wasabi root, fried popcorn shrimp with dipping sauces, or the S'mores: buttery graham crackers layered with marshmallow and fudge. Park elsewhere; valet parking here is $20–$30, even with dinner. ✉ *600 F St., Gaslamp Quarter* ☎ *619/814–1000* ▭ *AE, D, DC, MC, V.*

$$$ ✗ **Avenue 5.** American cuisine gets a French twist at this new spot serving fine seasonal cuisine and cocktails. Partners Chef Colin MacLaggan and Nicholas Carbonne have created a clean-feeling brick-walled space with an art gallery feel. Start with his original ahi tuna sashimi with an avocado relish or a fine duck confit with Port reduction before tucking into the Sottish salmon with salsify and wild mushrooms. Desserts shine as well; the fromage blanc cheesecake is not to be missed. ✉ *2760 5th Ave., Middletown* ☎ *619/542–0394* ▭ *AE, MC, V* ⊙ *Closed Mon. No lunch Sun.*

$$$ ✗ **Molly's Restaurant.** Tucked away on the ground floor of the Marriott Marina, Molly's attracts in-the-know locals and guests with its fine California cuisine paired with an award-winning wine list. The dinner-only restaurant done in dark wood and marble makes an intimate setting for Chef Timothy Au's eggplant napoleon with prosciutto and tomato confit, Maine lobster cannelloni, and Niman Ranch pork chop with apple confit and broccoli rabe. Wine lovers will revel in sommelier Lisa Redwine's (seriously) list of boutique wines from California, Oregon, and Washington. Large-format bottles and vertical tastings are a specialty; so are wine dinners created to showcase collectors' cellars. Reservations are advised. ✉ *333 W. Harbor Dr., Downtown* ☎ *619/230–8909* ▭ *AE, D, DC, MC, V* ⊙ *No lunch.*

$$ ✗ **Anthology.** Chef Bradley Ogden helped develop the Asian-influenced American menu that plays second fiddle to the fine contemporary jazz and blues music by artists including Diane Schuur, Herb Alpert, and Stanley Clark. The modern three-level dining room features a pleasant top-floor patio and wonderful acoustics. Stick to simple choices such as the duet of blue cheese soufflés, the Caesar salad, or the tapioca pudding cooked to order. ✉ *1337 India St., Little Italy* ☎ *619/595–0300* ▭ *AE, D, MC, V.*

$$
Fodor's Choice
★

✕**Jsix.** Creative and carefully prepared seafood reigns on this menu that reflects the diverse flavors found along the West Coast from Mexico to Washington. Chef Christian Graves favors fresh, light fare, using sustainably raised seafood such as the sashimi platter served with house-made potato chips, wild bass with sunchokes and Swiss chard, and diver scallops with Beluga lentils. Cheeses, salami, and pickles made in-house also grace the menu. Non-seafood options include vegetarian butternut squash ravioli and an indulgent naturally raised beef rib-eye with lobster mashed potatoes. Desserts are made with equal care, and the bar boasts cocktails made with seasonal fruit. The eclectic decor includes blown-glass pendant lights, a wall of fezes, and a dramatically backlighted bar. ✉*616 J St., Gaslamp Quarter* ☎*619/531–8744* ▭*AE, D, DC, MC, V.*

$$

✕**Stingaree.** You wouldn't expect to find fine cuisine at a hip, three-level nightclub, but then you discover Stingaree. Chef Antonio Friscia wows with dishes like calamari, scallops, and prawns in a spicy ménage à trois; gourmet macaroni and cheese studded with bacon; local fish in a medley of veggies from Chino Farm; and Moroccan lamb with Meyer lemon couscous. Midweek (Tuesday–Thursday) brings a three-courses-for-$30 menu. Dress to impress at Stingaree, which is done in ultra-mod tones of chocolate, turquoise, and orange. Though bottle service reigns here, the spectacular wine list ranges from reasonable labels from California and France to once-in-a-lifetime bottles such as Domaine de la Romanée Conti. A generous happy hour called Six at Seven offers Kobe beef burgers or asparagus and porcini ravioli for $7 between 6 and 7 PM. On weekends the dining room rocks; buying dinner allows you to skip the long line and $20 club admission; be prepared for crowds and bouncers with attitude. ✉*454 6th Ave., Gaslamp Quarter* ☎*619/544–9500* ▭*AE, D, MC, V* ☺*No lunch.*

$

✕**Neighborhood.** There's no ketchup in the house—the young owners don't want anything to mar the flavor of their perfectly seasoned burgers topped with pickled daikon and spicy Cajun sauce or the 777 burger with tomato confit and béarnaise and piled on artisan buns. They also serve Stone Smoked Porter braised beef ribs and ricotta gnudi in sweet sage butter sauce and duck confit. Wash it down with one of the many international artisan beers such as Delirium Tremens on tap and Allagash Curio, Belgian triple ale aged in Jim Beam casks, or wines by the glass offered at this urban, energetic spot. Lunch is served from 12 to 2 daily; the restaurant reopens at 5 for dinner. ✉ *777 G St., East Village* ☎*619/446–0002* ◿*Reservations not accepted* ▭*AE, MC, V.*

¢

✕**The Waterfront.** Not a destination for children, this historic bar and eatery, which opened in the 1930s and claims to be San Diego's oldest watering hole, is an attraction for anyone in search of genuine atmosphere. The bar has supported the elbows of tuna fishermen and aviation workers in earlier eras and now attracts lawyers, construction workers, and other souls hungry for bar food such as a $7.50 bowl of really good chili, burgers that can't be beat, smoking-hot onion rings and french fries, and other great-tasting grub, including fish tacos. The Waterfront serves from early morning until 1:30 AM. ✉*2044 Kettner Blvd., Little Italy* ☎*619/232–9656* ▭*AE, D, MC, V.*

ARGENTINEAN

$$ ✗**Puerto La Boca.** Named for a waterfront neighborhood in Buenos Aires that was home to generations of newly arrived Italian immigrants, this handsome restaurant is at the gateway to an area filling up with trendy boutiques, including a Harley-Davidson showroom. Like the cooking in Buenos Aires, the menu marries the traditional Argentine love of beef—and lots of it—with traditional Italian recipes and techniques, and the results are entirely satisfying. A long list of sizable steaks is crowned by the *parrillada,* a feast of beef cuts, sausage, and chicken served on a table-top grill. The sliced tomatoes in a creamy Roquefort sauce open the meal perfectly, and if you don't want beef, try the unusual "Bombonera" pizza, which shares its name with the BA soccer stadium where the Boca Juniors play. ⊠*2060 India St., Little Italy* ☎*619/234–4900* ▭*AE, D, MC, V.*

ASIAN

$$ ✗**Red Circle.** Despite the Russian-sounding name, Red Circle offers tasty small plates inspired by the Japanese yakitori concept. Tables with low loungy seating, a dramatic bar, and metallic gold and silver touches on columns give the room a neoclassical feel. Order the $30 three-course menu or à la carte skewers filled with bacon-wrapped asparagus, soy ginger-glazed salmon, or marinated Portobello mushrooms, all served with dipping sauces. Heartier items include crispy Asian pork ribs, blackened ahi tuna, or rib-eye steak. Later in the evening, a DJ starts spinning; converting the restaurant into a nightspot. ⊠*420 E St, Gaslamp Quarter* ☎*619/234–9211* ▭*AE, MC, V.*

$ ✗**Red Pearl Kitchen.** Vivid red Venetian plaster walls, a loungy vibe, and a widely varied menu of Pan-Asian fare make Red Pearl Kitchen unique among San Diego's Asian restaurants. Chef Lincoln Williams takes diners on a culinary journey with dishes like Chinese five-spice chicken wings, duck lettuce wraps, black-pepper caramel shrimp, and Kobe beef with red curry and rice noodles designed for sharing. Pair them with one of many sakes, Asian food-loving wines, or creative cocktails like the Jade Mistress. Dishes designed for sharing make it a perfect place to bring a group. On weekends the bar and lounge are dominated by exuberant twentysomethings—and the service can become harried and offhand. ⊠*440 J St., Suite 108, Gaslamp Quarter* ☎*619/231–1100* ▭*AE, MC, V.*

BRITISH

$ ✗**Princess Pub & Grille.** Packed to the rafters during any televised British football (soccer) championship, this cheerful neighborhood place is the unofficial headquarters of transplanted Brits, Australians, and New Zealanders. The selection of imported beers and ales, most of them from the U.K., is quite impressive, and the menu complements them well with such offerings as sausage rolls, fish-and-chips, and spicy chicken curry. The oversize buffalo burgers have a loyal following. Breakfast brings eggs with bangers and baked beans. The patrons seem equally fond of conversation and darts. ⊠*1665 India St., Little Italy* ☎*619/702–3021* ▭*MC, V.*

CAFÉS

$ ✕**Karen Krasne's Extraordinary Desserts.** The sleek, newer branch of the original Karen Krasne's pastry shop near Balboa Park is a few blocks east of India Street, which is Little Italy's main drag. It's worth a trip for Paris-perfect cakes, tarts, and incredibly rich pot-de-crème desserts. In a converted commercial space that has won architectural awards and is celebrated for a "Zen-like" atmosphere, Krasne's serves unusual and delicious breakfasts, lunches, and light dinners, and specializes in luxuries such as artisanal cheeses, private-blend tea, and made-on-premises chocolates and ice creams. The panini sandwiches are creative and filling. ⊠*1430 Union St., Little Italy* ☎*619/294–7001* ▤*AE, D, MC, V.*

¢ ✕**Bread on Market.** The baguettes at this artisanal bakery near the PETCO Park baseball stadium are every bit as good as the ones you'd buy in Paris. Focaccia and other superior loaves are the building blocks for solid but pricey sandwiches, which range from Genoa salami and sweet butter to a vegan sandwich with locally grown avocado. The menu extends to a daily soup, a fruit-garnished cheese plate, and an appetizing Mediterranean salad. Snackers gravitate here for fudge-textured brownies, almond biscotti, and other irresistible sweets. During baseball season, the "take-me-out-to-the-ballgame" box lunch offers a choice of sandwich, chips, a freshly baked cookie, and a bottle of water for $10.75. ⊠*730 Market St., East Village* ☎*619/795–2730* ▤*MC, V* ☁*Closed Sun. No dinner.*

FRENCH

$$$$ ✕**Bertrand at Mister A's.** Restaurateur Bertrand Hug's sumptuous 12th-floor dining room offers serene decor, contemporary paintings, and a view that stretches to Mexico and San Diego Bay, making it perfect for a sunset cocktail. Chef Stephane Voitzwinkler creates luxurious and similarly priced seasonal dishes such as sautéd foie gras, Dover sole, and Kobe flatiron steak with béarnaise. The dessert list encompasses a galaxy of sweets. Service, led by the charming Hug, is expert and attentive. ⊠*2550 5th Ave., Middletown* ☎*619/239–1377* ⌕*Reservations essential* ▤*AE, DC, MC, V* ☁*No lunch weekends.*

$$$$ ✕**Le Fontainebleau.** On the second floor of the elegant Westgate Hotel, this restaurant is worthy of the famous château for which it is named. Normandy-born chef Fabrice Hardel writes seasonal menus, but usually offers classics like chateaubriand for two, Dover sole meunier, and French steak au poivre, dramatically flambéed at your table. Pairing the multi-course tasting menu with specially selected wines costs in excess of $100 per person, a price that seems not unreasonable when accompanied by the live harp or piano music that is a Le Fontainebleau staple. ⊠*Westgate Hotel, 1055 2nd Ave., Downtown* ☎*619/557–3655* ▤*AE, D, DC, MC, V* ☁*No lunch.*

$ ✕**Cafe Chloe.** The intersection of 9th and G is now the meeting point for San Diego's café society, thanks to the super-chic and friendly Café Chloe. Surrounded by luxury high-rises, hotels, and boutiques, the area's residents head to this pretty and Parisian spot for breakfast, lunch, and dinner. Start the day with whole-wheat pancakes and sour-cherry sauce, lunch on smoked trout and apple salad or a casserole of macaroni, pancetta, and Gorgonzola, or enjoy chicken vol-au-vent or steak frites for dinner. The fine selection of wines by the glass, imported teas, and coffee make it a lovely place to while away the afternoon. ☒*721 9th Ave., East Village* ☎*619/232–3242* ▭*AE, MC, V.*

2

GREEK

$$ ✕**Athens Market Taverna.** This cheerful eatery with an outdoor patio bustles with office workers and members of San Diego's small but active Greek community. Appetizers such as the flaming cheese dish called saganaki, hummus, and stuffed grape leaves are particularly tasty. Entrées include *arni psito* (roast leg of lamb), a very convincing rendition of eggplant moussaka, and the house Greek pasta, with garlic, onion, and cheese. The baklava (a layering of crisp phyllo pastry, nuts, and honey) or Greek rice pudding makes an excellent dessert. Athens Market Taverna and the ever-present owner Mary Pappas seem as timeless as Greece itself, and the place remains a local classic. ☒*109 W. F St., Downtown* ☎*619/234–1955* ▭*AE, D, DC, MC, V* ⊘*Closed Sunday, no lunch weekends.*

INDIAN

$$ ✕**Royal India.** Experience cuisine once reserved for royalty as brothers Sam and Jag Kambo lovingly re-create their mother's North Indian recipes. Everything from the mint chutney to the smoky tomato sauce that graces the chicken tikka Masala is made from scratch. Dining here is first-rate, whether it's the daily lunch buffet or the sumptuous dinners that include sizzling chili-lemon chicken kebabs, stuffed paneer, indulgent lamb korma, and garlic naan. Elegant but comfortable decor is highlighted by a carved antique maple bar, stunning chandeliers, and golden arches from a palace in Jodhpur. Don't miss the signature cocktails, such as Indian mojito and mango martini, or desserts, including mango mousse and rice pudding redolent of warm spices. ☒*329 Market St., Downtown* ☎*619/269–9999* ▭*AE, D, DC, MC, V.*

$ ✕**Monsoon.** An exceptionally attractive restaurant, Monsoon delights with features such as a room-centering waterfall that splashes like a cloudburst from a bower of hanging plants. Folding doors allow some tables to share the outdoor atmosphere of the terrace, but at a distance from the sidewalk. The menu offers many dishes not easily found at local Indian eateries, including a sweetly spiced mango soup, and "balti"-style lamb with tomato, garlic, ginger, and coconut. The dozens of curries and similar dishes are spiced to taste, and baked-to-order breads should not be missed. ☒*729–733 4th Ave., Gaslamp Quarter* ☎*619/234–5555* ▭*AE, D, DC, MC, V.*

IRISH

$ ✕**The Field.** A family-run pub decorated with artifacts from an Irish farm, the Field has character to spare. Both on the outdoor terrace and indoors, diners enjoy solid meals of Irish stew, corned beef and cabbage, steak with an Irish whiskey–peppercorn sauce or, best of all, a *boxty,* a lacy but substantial potato pancake served crisp and hot with such fillings as sage-flavored chicken or Irish bacon and cheese. As the evening wears on, the crowd grows younger, livelier, louder, and sometimes rowdier. A traditional Irish breakfast is served on weekends.

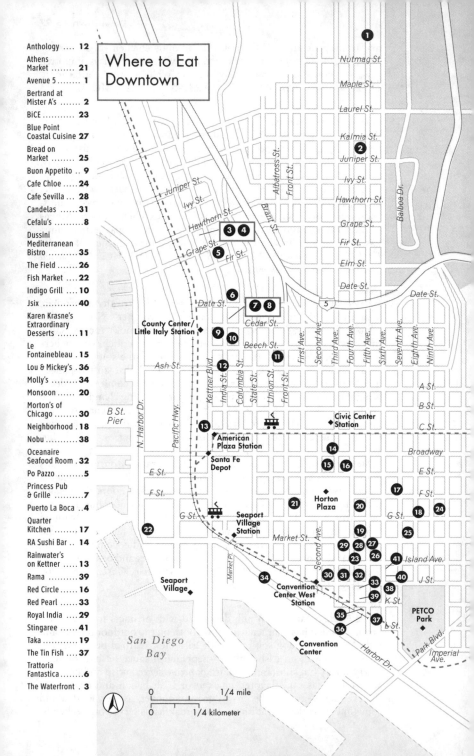

Where to Eat Downtown

✉ *544 5th Ave., Gaslamp Quarter* ☎ *619/232–9840* ☐ *AE, D, DC, MC, V.*

ITALIAN

$$$$ ✗ **BiCE.** The venerable Italian restaurant founded in 1926 brings its high-style Italian food to San Diego in a comfortable and classy space that features a cheese and charcuterie bar. Italian-born chefs create satisfying dishes including a lobster and hearts of palm salad, house-made pastas such as pappardelle in tomato-cream sauce, and tender branzino cooked in paper. Waiters in white tuxes deliver efficient and polished service. ✉ *425 Island Ave., Gaslamp Quarter* ☎ *619/239–2322* ☐ *MC, V.*

$$$ ✗ **Po Pazzo.** An eye-catching new creation from leading Little Italy restaurateurs Joe and Lisa Busalacchi, Po Pazzo earns its name, which means "a little crazy," mixing a bar with a restaurant serving modern Italian fare. A steak house with an accent, this stylish eatery offers attractive salads and thick cuts of prime beef, as well as a top-notch presentation of veal saltimbocca, and risotto in an osso buco "sauce" that defines richness. It's fun but pricey, although at lunch the Kobe beef burger with fresh-from-the-fat fries is an affordable way to enjoy the experience. ✉ *1917 India St., Little Italy* ☎ *619/238–1917* ☐ *AE, D, DC, MC, V* ⊗ *No lunch weekends.*

$$ ✗ **Buon Appetito.** This charmer serves Old World–style cooking in a casual but decidedly sophisticated environment. Choose a table on the breezy sidewalk or in an indoor room jammed with art and fellow diners. Baked eggplant *all'amalfitana*, in a mozzarella-topped tomato sauce, is a dream of a dish, and in San Diego, tomato sauce doesn't get better than this. Consider also veal with tuna sauce, branzino (sea bass) in a mushroom sauce, hearty seafood cioppino, and expert osso buco paired with affordable and varied wines. The young Italian waiters' good humor makes the experience fun. ✉ *1609 India St., Little Italy* ☎ *619/238–9880* ☐ *AE, MC, V.*

$$ ✗ **Trattoria Fantastica.** Sicilian flavors abound on the menu, which is highlighted by such offerings as a salmon salad and the pasta *palermitana*—rigatoni with spicy sausage, olives, capers, and marinara sauce. Many pastas come with cargoes of fresh seafood, and the pizzas baked in the wood-burning oven are robust and beautifully seasoned. Reserve ahead if you want to score a table in the shady courtyard, and also keep this in mind as a snack break for beautiful pastries, remarkable gelato, and freshly brewed Italian coffees. ✉ *1735 India St., Little Italy* ☎ *619/234–1735* ☐ *AE, DC, MC, V.*

¢ ✗ **Cefalu's.** A welcome budget option in an increasingly expensive, trendy neighborhood, Cefalu's serves excellent pizza by the slice until 4 PM daily, and one wedge is big enough to make a satisfying lunch. Spaghetti with meatballs or made-in-Little-Italy sausage makes a good alternative to a strong list of torpedo sandwiches (sliced sirloin with onions and peppers, anyone?), and the pizza list encompasses familiar favorites and house specialties like the "Fantasia," which is highlighted with sun-dried tomatoes and Gorgonzola cheese. ✉ *1655B India St., Little Italy* ☎ *619/236–9622* ♿ *Reservations not accepted* ☐ *MC, V.*

JAPANESE

$$$ ✕**Nobu.** This outpost of the famous Nobu Matsuhisa restaurant empire in the Hard Rock Hotel is known for inventive and fresh sushi and hot dishes created with a modern Japanese-Peruvian flair. The sexy if rather noisy room with scorched ash wood treatments and jade-green walls makes a cool space to enjoy Nobu classics like white fish tiradito with yuzu citrus and rocoto pepper, lobster in wasabi sauce, or succulent black cod with miso glaze. If you're feeling slightly adventurous, let the sushi chef's whims guide you through a delicious omakase tasting menu. ⊠*Hard Rock Hotel, 207 5th Ave., Gaslamp Quarter* ☎*619/702–3000* ▭*AE, MC, V* ☾*No lunch.*

> **ADVENTUROUS EDIBLES**
>
> If you've ever wanted to try the Japanese delicacy uni, San Diego is the place to do it. The red sea urchins found in the waters off La Jolla are considered some of the best in the world. The succulent part of the creature is actually its sex organs. Don't think about that though as fresh sea urchin melts in your mouth, leaving a slight sweet and briny taste.

$ ✕**RA Sushi Bar Restaurant.** Servers in semi-sensational T-shirts (mottos include "Pleasure yourself") challenge a young clientele to strive for sexy "attitude" in this small, intimate space carved out of a former department store. Two ultra-hip bars—one for cocktails, one for sushi, both for being seen mostly—fuel the popularity, bolstered by a dining-room menu from which you can make a meal out of the many appetizers, such as coconut shrimp tempura and scallops in spicy "dynamite" sauce. Otherwise, choose sushi combination plates, black pepper–coated filet mignon, seared ahi tuna with ginger-cilantro butter, and hearty noodle dishes. ⊠*474 Broadway, Gaslamp Quarter* ☎*619/321–0021* ▭*AE, D, DC, MC, V.*

$ ✕**Taka.** Even though it's on a prominent corner, Taka modestly lets its pristine fish imported from around the world and its creative presentations attract a crowd each night. Start with one of the sushi chef's appetizers such as monkfish liver with ponzu or slices of tender hamachi sashimi or a spicy scallop roll before diving into cooked foods such as a crisp soft-shell crab, or an East meets West–style filet mignon. This is a favorite with Japanese visitors. ⊠*555 5th Ave., Gaslamp Quarter* ☎*619/338–0555* ▭*AE, MC, V* ☾*No lunch.*

Fodor's Choice ★

MEDITERRANEAN

$$ ✕**Dussini Mediterranean Bistro.** This modern remake of a former Old Spaghetti Factory packs a lot of seating—and fun—into half the space occupied by its predecessor. The sizeable upstairs bar offers a number of pool tables, but this is a polite, family-friendly place with notably congenial servers. Splurge on the lobster macaroni and cheese or the Tuscan-braised lamb shank. ⊠*275 5th Ave., Gaslamp Quarter* ☎*619/233–4323* ▭*AE, D, DC, MC, V.*

MEXICAN

$$$ ✕**Candelas.** The scents and flavors of imaginative Mexican cuisine with a European flair permeate this handsome, romantic restaurant and nightspot in the shadow of San Diego's tallest residential towers.

2

Candles glow everywhere around the small, comfortable dining room. There isn't a burrito or taco in sight. Fine openers such as cream of black bean and beer soup, and salad of watercress with bacon and pistachios warm diners up for local lobster stuffed with mushrooms, jalapeño peppers, and aged tequila; or tequila-flamed jumbo prawns over creamy, seasoned goat cheese. The adjacent bar pours many elegant tequilas and has become a popular, often jam-packed nightspot. ✉416 3rd Ave., Downtown ☎619/702–4455 ▤AE, D, DC, MC, V ⊗No lunch weekends.

SEAFOOD

$$$$ ✗ **Blue Point Coastal Cuisine.** If there's a convention in town, Blue Point gets jammed with diverse diners who share a taste for sophisticated seafood. The menu swims with classics like crab legs and seared ahi tuna, served with internationally accented fare like the steamed mussels in a tomato saffron broth or the Blue Point stack, a gingery salad of blue crab, shrimp, and lobster claws. The small but serious oyster bar, which serves both raw and imaginatively prepared shellfish, offers a warm-up for a menu of more seafood, plus chicken and steaks for those who prefer. The wine list is impressive, and the service efficient and friendly. The airy dining room has gleaming woodwork and walls of windows looking onto 5th Avenue and Market Street, a prime corner for people-watching. ✉565 5th Ave., Gaslamp Quarter ☎619/233–6623 ▤AE, D, DC, MC, V ⊗No lunch.

$$$ ✗ **Oceanaire Seafood Room.** Engineered to recall an oceanliner from the 1940s—there are tubes of Brylcreem in the men's room, for goodness sake—Oceanaire is a bit put-on, but admirable for the long bar serving up classic cocktails, oysters, and sashimi, and a carefully prepared menu that offers up to 25 daily "fresh catches," and many specialties ranging from convincing Maryland crab cakes and oysters Rockefeller to richly stuffed California sole, a luxurious one-pound pork chop, and irresistible hash brown potatoes. Chef Brian Malarkey creates a daily menu that may include the deliciously hot, spice-fired "angry" lobster. Service is a casual thing in San Diego, which makes the professional staff here all the more notable. ✉400 J St., Gaslamp Quarter ☎619/858–2277 ▤AE, D, DC, MC, V ⊗No lunch.

$$ ✗ **Fish Market.** Fresh mesquite-grilled, steamed, and skewered fish and shellfish are the specialty at this informal restaurant. There's also an excellent little sushi bar, and the shellfish bar serves good crab cocktails and steamed clams. The view is stunning: enormous plate-glass windows look directly out onto the harbor. A more formal restaurant upstairs, Top of the Market, is expensive but worth the splurge, and is the place to find such rarities as true Dover sole. ✉750 N. Harbor Dr., Embarcadero ☎619/232–3474 Fish Market, 619/234–4867 Top of the Market ▤AE, D, DC, MC, V.

$ ✗ **The Tin Fish.** On the rare rainy day, the staff takes it easy at this eatery less than 100 yards from the PETCO Park baseball stadium (its 100-odd seats are all outdoors). Musicians entertain some evenings, making this a lively spot for dinners of grilled and fried fish and shellfish, as well as seafood burritos and tacos. The quality here routinely surpasses that at grander establishments—for instance, the bread used for

Where to Refuel Around Town

San Diego has a few homegrown chains as well as many stand-alone eateries that will amiably fill you up without demanding too much in return.

The Mission, a local mini chain open only for breakfast and lunch, has three locations: Mission Beach, North Park, and the PETCO Park district. The latter, the newest, occupies a vintage 1870 building originally known as Rosario Hall. Called the Mission SoMa (short for "South of Market Street"), it fulfills its mission as a breakfast-and-lunch destination (as at the other two, there's no service after 3 PM) with a menu that runs the gamut from banana-blackberry pancakes to a Zen breakfast complete with tofu and brown rice, to creative black-bean burritos and a smoked turkey sandwich.

If there's something for everyone at the Mission, the statement is equally true of San Diego's enormously popular **Sammy's Woodfired Pizza** chain. With convenient outlets in La Jolla, Mission Valley, and the Gaslamp Quarter, Sammy's makes friends with oversize salads, a vast selection of pizzas, entrées, and pastas, and the fun "messy sundae," which lives up to its name.

Filippi's Pizza Grotto locations (the best are on India Street in Little Italy and in Pacific Beach) please crowds with vast platters of spaghetti and meatballs, as well as very good pizzas.

Also homegrown and from the same post–World War II era as Filippi's, **Anthony's Fish Grotto** enjoys considerable renown for batter-fried fish fillets and shellfish, as well as chowders, charbroiled fish, and other simple, well-prepared offerings. Anthony's on the Embarcadero, downtown, is built over the water and often has a line at the door; the Chula Vista branch is at freeway Exit 10, minutes south of downtown.

If you can't leave San Diego without downing a fish taco, be advised that the nation-spanning **Rubio's** chain was founded here and has multiple locations.

Besides chains, keep these streets or neighborhoods in mind for refueling: funky Ocean Beach, famed for its easy-going breakfast places; Little Italy (India Street), with endless Italian options; and Hillcrest in the vicinity of the 5th Avenue–University Avenue intersection, a buffet of international cuisines. If you want Asian, Convoy Street is the place to go.

—David Nelson

sandwiches stuffed with fried oysters and the like is baked on the premises. Service hours vary with the day of the week, the weather, and whether it's baseball season or not, but generally Tin Fish is open from 11 to 8 Sunday through Thursday and until 11 PM on weekends. ✉*170 6th Ave., Gaslamp Quarter* ☎*619/238–8100* ⚓*Reservations not accepted* ▭*AE, D, MC, V.*

SOUTHWESTERN

$$ ✕**Indigo Grill.** Chef-partner Deborah Scott uses inspirations from Mexico to Alaska to infuse her contemporary Southwestern cuisine. Indigo Grill has an interior with natural wood and stone accents, and a broad terrace whose cool breezes do nothing to moderate the chilies that

heat such one-of-a-kind offerings as stacked beet salad, pecan-crusted trout, salmon roasted on a well-seasoned wooden plank, and a beautifully flavored rack of lamb. Creative desserts are often so generous in size that they can satisfy two with ease. Increasing competition in the neighborhood hasn't come near to cooling this hot spot's popularity. ⊠*1536 India St., Little Italy* ☎*619/234–6802* ▭*AE, D, DC, MC, V* ⊗*No lunch weekends.*

SPANISH

$$ ✕**Cafe Sevilla.** Increasingly a nightclub, Sevilla fills Thursday through Sunday evenings with youthful throngs who crowd the ground-floor bar for drinks, tapas, and live music. Others head to the downstairs club for classics from the Spanish kitchen and professional flamenco dancing. There isn't a quiet corner to be found. The kitchen does a respectable job with the traditional shellfish and chicken paella (there are also strictly meat and seafood versions). It also makes highly flavorful baked rabbit and roasted pork tenderloin, and a new favorite is a trio of dramatically presented *brochetas,* or skewers, of spiced shrimp, zesty Spanish sausages, and steak with mushrooms and onions. ⊠*555 4th Ave., Gaslamp Quarter* ☎*619/233–5979* ▭*AE, MC, V* ⊗*No lunch.*

STEAKHOUSES

$$$$ ✕**Morton's, The Steakhouse.** Housed in the soaring Harbor Club towers near both the San Diego Convention Center and the Gaslamp Quarter, Morton's teems with conventioneers out for a night on the town. The newly expanded Bar 12-21 offers an extensive list of original cocktails and tasty appetizers such as filet mignon sliders. For the main event, servers present the menu by wheeling up a cart laden with crimson prime steaks, behemoth lamb chops, and huge Maine lobsters that may wave their claws in alarm when they hear the prices quoted (based on the market, but always astronomical). Expect a treat, since this restaurant knows how to put on a superb spread that takes the concept of indulgence to new heights. ⊠*Harbor Club, 285 J St., Downtown* ☎*619/696–3369* ▭*AE, D, DC, MC, V* ⊗*No lunch.*

$$$ ✕**Rainwater's on Kettner.** San Diego's premier homegrown steak house also ranks as the longest-running of the pack, not least because it has the luxurious look and mood of an old-fashioned Eastern men's club. The cuisine is excellent: open with the signature black-bean soup with Madeira. Continue with the tender, expertly roasted prime rib, superb veal's liver with onions and bacon, broiled free-range chicken, fresh seafood, or the amazingly succulent pork chops, all served in vast portions with plenty of hot-from-the-oven cornsticks on the side. The prime steaks sizzle, as does the bill. The well-chosen wine list has pricey but superior selections. ⊠*1202 Kettner Blvd., Downtown* ☎*619/233–5757* ▭*AE, MC, V* ⊗*No lunch weekends.*

$$ ✕**Lou & Mickey's.** The restaurant nearest the San Diego Convention Center, this handsome, 1940s-style establishment lures with thick steaks and chops, equally meaty seafood cuts such as the unusual T-bone of Alaskan halibut, richly sauced pastas, and chicken dishes of surprising flavor and sophistication. Be extravagant by opening with a shellfish platter laden with oysters, stone crab, mussels, and lobster, then move

on to the $45-per-serving Alaskan king crab legs. If you're on a budget, visit at lunch or invest in a filling and rather tasty garlic meat loaf po' boy sandwich, which costs just $10.45, or the monumental cheeseburger served with a good pound of hot french fries. Either way, plan on finishing with an impressive wedge of key lime pie. ⊠ *224 5th Ave., Gaslamp Quarter* ☎ *619/237–4900* ⊟ *AE, DC, MC, V.*

THAI

$$ ✕ **Rama.** Gauzy draperies, murals of Thai dancers, and a rock wall flowing with water create a dreamy rain-forest effect in the back room of this excellent newcomer to the Gaslamp Quarter's booming restaurant row. One of the best Thai restaurants in San Diego, Rama combines professional service with a kitchen that understands the subtle demands of spicing the myriad dishes. The tart, pungent, spiced-to-order (as everything can be) *talay* (seafood soup—it literally means "ocean") pairs well with a crispy duck salad as a light meal for two. Dozens of curries and stir-fries take the tastebuds on exciting adventures in flavor. The front dining room is now a private club, so reservations are advised. ⊠ *327 4th Ave., Gaslamp Quarter* ☎ *619/501–8424* ⊟ *AE, D, DC, MC, V.*

HARBOR & SHELTER ISLANDS AND POINT LOMA

Point Loma has a storied history as the center of the tuna fishing industry and is developing into an area of charming neighborhood restaurants. Most restaurants here, and on Harbor and Shelter islands, are casual neighborhood spots or view restaurants that cater to tourists.

AMERICAN

$$$ ✕ **Island Prime and C Level Lounge.** This sizable eatery on the shore of Harbor Island is two restaurants in one: the extravagant, dinner-only Island Prime, and the much less formal (if by no means inexpensive) lunch-and-dinner C Level Lounge, which has a choice terrace. Both venues tempt with unrivaled views of downtown San Diego's ever-taller skyline, and in Island Prime, the expense account–ruffling menu of steaks and seafood lists most choices simply as "market price" (and when the bill arrives, it suggests that Chef Deborah Scott shops at a pretty extravagant market). Besides prime steaks, pork chops, and lamb rack, the entrées include composed dishes like the plank-roasted salmon with cucumber salsa. Lunch is the best time at C Level Lounge, which serves hearty pastas and sandwiches. Reservations are strongly suggested. ⊠ *880 Harbor Island Dr., Harbor Island* ☎ *619/298–6802* ⊟ *AE, D, DC, MC, V* ☺ *No lunch at Island Prime.*

> ### A FISH TALE
>
> From the 1930s to the early '70s, San Diego was the capitol of the American tuna fishing industry. Visit Point Loma to see the remnants of the fishing industry or stop by Whole Foods for a sample of this favorite fish canned by American Tuna, a company formed by six local fishing families who only use poles—not nets—to catch premium albacore tuna in a sustainable way.

$$ ✕**Roseville.** This comfortable new spot continues the restaurant renaissance under way in Point Loma. Native son George Riffle, who honed his skills in NYC at Picholine, has created an inviting spot for French-leaning seasonal fare. The 95-seat restaurant will feature local seafood such as spot prawns, vermilion rockfish, spiny lobster, and sand dabs along with organic produce and international wines. ⊠*1125 Rosecrans St., Point Loma* ☎*619/223–7300* ▤*AE, MC, V* ⊗ *No lunch.*

KEARNY MESA & CLAIREMONT

Though it's mostly an industrial and residential area that doesn't attract many tourists, Kearny Mesa and Clairemont offer a diversity of small independent and ethnic restaurants. Convoy Street—the commercial heart of the busy Kearny Mesa area—is the unofficial Asian Restaurant Row of San Diego, and presents a comprehensive selection of Chinese, Korean, and Vietnamese restaurants, a number of which qualify as "Best in Class."

ARGENTINEAN

$$ ✕**Pampas Argentine Grill.** Meats, mostly cut in hefty portions, grilled and served with zesty chimichurri sauce are the main thrust of the menu at this comfy steakery a few blocks east of the Convoy Street restaurant row. Choices include rib eye, filet mignon, and strip steaks, along with marinated boneless chicken and the seafood of the day. Reasonably priced and served for two or more, the "Parrillada Pampas" is a grilled-at-the-table feast of beef, spicy sausage, and sweetbreads. The spacious restaurant is gently lighted and hung with paintings that strive for the romance of the tango. There's live music on weekends. ⊠*8690 Aero Dr., Kearny Mesa* ☎*858/278–5971* ▤*AE, D, MC, V* ⊗*Closed Mon.*

CHINESE

$$ ✕**Jasmine.** This cavernous, Hong Kong–style establishment seats no fewer than 400 people; even so, there are frequently lines outside at lunchtime on weekends, when groups arrive to enjoy fragrant soups, steaming noodles, and dim sum from carts that constantly circle the room. At dinner it's a hard choice between the seafood from the wall-mounted tanks and "Peking duck two ways"—the crisp skin sandwiched in tasty buns as a first course, the meat deliciously stir-fried for a savory follow-up. A supplementary menu of "special-priced dishes" offers bargains like one-half of a roasted chicken for $7.50. It must be added that servers sometimes seem rude and abrupt. ⊠*4609 Convoy St., Kearny Mesa* ☎*858/268–0888* ▤*AE, MC, V.*

$ ✕**China Max.** This good-looking Convoy Street eatery has won hundreds of loyal fans, not only because of the quality, variety, and authenticity of the cooking, but because a value-priced late-supper menu is offered nightly from 9 to 11 PM. Dishes not to be missed include the stir-fried shrimp with lettuce "taco," country-style *mei fun* noodles, the one-of-a-kind sautéed cruller with pungent Chinese chives, and pan-fried lamb chops in black-pepper sauce. Tanks teem with seafood, all priced according to the market. The dim sum dumplings and pastries

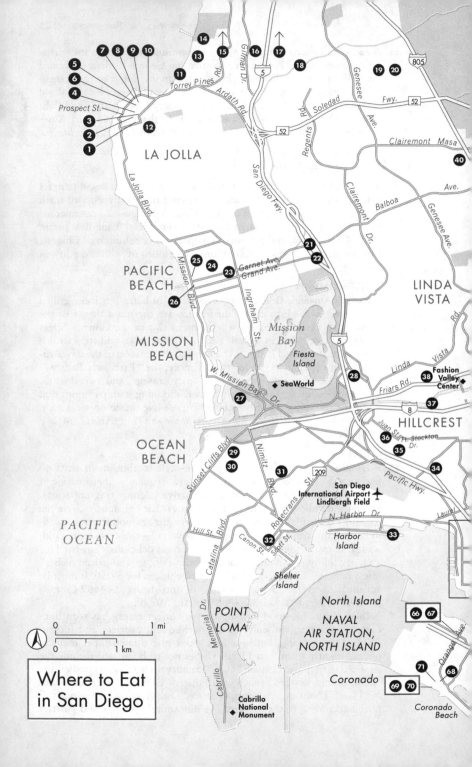

Where to Eat in San Diego

PACIFIC OCEAN

PACIFIC BEACH

MISSION BEACH

OCEAN BEACH

LA JOLLA

Prospect St.

Torrey Pines

La Jolla Blvd

Mission Blvd.

Garnet Ave.
Grand Ave.

Ingraham St.

W. Mission Bay Dr.

Mission Bay

Fiesta Island

SeaWorld

Gilman Dr.

Ardath Rd.

San Diego Fwy.

Regents Rd.

Soledad

Genesee Ave.

Clairemont Dr.

Balboa

Clairemont Mesa

Ave.

Genesee Ave.

LINDA VISTA

Linda Vista Rd.

Fashion Valley Center

Friars Rd.

HILLCREST

Juan St.
Ft. Stockton Dr.

Sunset Cliffs Blvd.

Nimitz Blvd.

Rosecrans St.

San Diego International Airport Lindbergh Field

N. Harbor Dr.

Pacific Hwy.

Laurel

Harbor Island

Catalina Blvd.

Hill St.

Canon St.

Scott St.

Shelter Island

North Island

NAVAL AIR STATION, NORTH ISLAND

Coronado

Orange Ave.

Coronado Beach

POINT LOMA

Memorial Dr.

Cabrillo

Cabrillo National Monument

0   1 mi
0   1 km

2

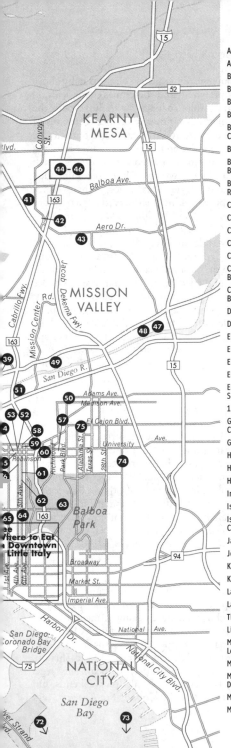

Andre's Restaurant **28**

A.R. Valentien **15**

Baja Betty's **57**

Barbarella **14**

Barolo **20**

Blue Coral **18**

Bombay Exotic
Cuisine of India **58**

Bread & Cie **55**

Buga Korean
B.B.Q. Restaurant **40**

Busalacchi's
Ristorante **61**

Cafe Japengo **17**

Caffe Bella Italia **23**

Chez Loma **71**

Chicago on a Bun **19**

China Max **44**

Coronado
Brewing Company **67**

Corvette Diner
Bar & Grill **59**

Dish **60**

Dumpling Inn **45**

El Agave **35**

El Pescador **12**

El Zarape **50**

Elijah's **16**

Emerald Chinese
Seafood Restaurant **42**

1500 Ocean **70**

George's
California Modern **9**

Gringo's **26**

Hash House A Go Go **62**

Hob Nob Hill **65**

Hodad's **30**

India Princess **52**

Isabel's Cantina **24**

Island Prime and
C Level Lounge **33**

Jasmine **46**

Jordan **25**

Kaiserhof **29**

King's Fish House. **51**

Lanna **22**

Laurel **64**

The Linkery **74**

Little Fish Market **48**

Mama's Bakery &
Lebanese Deli **75**

Marine Room **11**

Michele Coulon
Dessertier **1**

Mistral **72**

Mr. Peabody's **38**

Nine-Ten **5**

Oki Ton
Japanese Bistro **47**

Ortega's,
A Mexican Bistro **54**

Osteria Romantica **13**

Pampas
Argentine Grill **43**

Phuong Trang **41**

Pizzeria
Arrivederci **56**

The Prado **63**

Prego Ristorante **49**

Red Marlin **27**

Restaurante Romesco **73**

Ricky's Family
Restaurant **37**

Rimel's Rotisserie **3**

Roppongi **7**

Roseville **32**

Saffron Noodles
and Saté **34**

Sambuca Italian
Bistro **53**

Sheerwater **69**

Sushi on the Rock **6**

Sushi Ota **21**

Tapenade **2**

Tartine **66**

Tent City **68**

Trattoria Acqua **10**

The Venetian **31**

Whisk'n'ladle **8**

Zenbu **4**

Zocalo Grill **36**

The Zodiac **39**

served at lunch may be San Diego's best. ✉*4698 Convoy St., Kearny Mesa* ☎*858/650–3333* ▤*MC, V.*

$ ✗**Emerald Chinese Seafood Restaurant.** Emerald is sought out by those who prefer elaborate, carefully prepared, and sometimes costly seafood dishes. Even when the restaurant is full to capacity with 300 diners, the noise level is moderate and conversation flows easily between bites of the best Chinese cuisine in the area. Market-priced—and that can be high—shrimp, prawns, lobsters, clams, and fish reside in tanks until the moment of cooking. Simple preparations flavored with scallions, black beans, and ginger are among the most worthy. Other recommended dishes include beef with Singapore-style satay sauce, honey-walnut shrimp, baked chicken in five spices, Peking duck served in two savory courses, and, at lunch, the dim sum. ✉*3709 Convoy St., Kearny Mesa* ☎*858/565–6888* ▤*AE, D, DC, MC, V.*

¢   ✗**Dumpling Inn.** Modest, family-style, and wonderful, this is in some ways the most likable of Convoy Street's Asian restaurants. The tiny establishment loads its tables with bottles of aromatic and spicy condiments for the boiled, steamed, and fried dumplings that are the house specialty. These delicately flavored, hefty mouthfuls preface a meal that may continue simply, with hearty pork and pickled cabbage soup, or elaborately, with Shanghai-style braised pork shank. Ask about daily specials, such as shredded pork in plum sauce served on a sea of crispy noodles. You may bring your own wine or beer; the house serves only tea and soft drinks. ✉*4619 Convoy St., #F, Kearny Mesa* ☎*858/268–9638* ▤*MC, V* ☉*Closed Mon.*

KOREAN

$$ ✗**Buga Korean B.B.Q. Restaurant.** The cook-it-yourself fun of Korean barbecue and Japanese-style shabu-shabu focuses attention on your table's built-in cooking unit, not on the modest surroundings. Suspended exhaust-fan hoods create something of a draft when the restaurant is full of guests barbecuing sharply marinated cuts of meat and seafood. Shabu-shabu, a multicourse meal of paper-thin meats, vegetables, and noodles, is cooked in iron pots of boiling liquid that provide a final course of tasty broth. Order a combination barbecue dinner and expect a near avalanche of food. Pleasant servers explain how everything works. The restaurant is a few blocks west of the Convoy Street corridor. ✉*5580 Clairemont Mesa Blvd., Clairemont* ☎*858/560–1010* ▤*MC, V.*

VIETNAMESE

¢   ✗**Phuong Trang.** One of the most popular Vietnamese restaurants in San Diego, Phuong Trang cooks up hundreds of appetizers, soups, noodle dishes, and main courses, which can make choosing a meal a bewildering process. Waiters tend to steer you to tasty offerings like fried egg rolls, char-grilled shrimp paste wrapped around sugarcane, beef in grape leaves, and fresh spring rolls filled with pork and shrimp. Broken rice and a grilled pork chop make a satisfying meal. The large, relatively spare dining room gets packed, especially on weekends, but service is speedy, if sometimes curt. ✉*4170 Convoy St., Kearny Mesa* ☎*858/565–6750* ▤*MC, V.*

LA JOLLA

Some of the area's best restaurants are in La Jolla, offering fine California, Italian, and French cuisine, the best of which showcases San Diego's abundant local produce. Though there are many neighborhood favorites on the side streets, ocean-view restaurants along Prospect Street are very popular, so it's a good idea to plan ahead if trying to secure a table.

AMERICAN

$$$$
Fodor's Choice
★
✕**A.R. Valentien.** Known for his insistence on in-season, fresh-today produce and seafood, Chef Jeff Jackson writes menus daily for this cozy room in the luxurious, Craftsman-style Lodge at Torrey Pines. His take on food combinations is simultaneously simple and inventive, like appetizers of tuna carpaccio with fresh horseradish and crisp capers, and figs with homemade ricotta, pine nuts, and thyme. Notable main events may be pan-roasted swordfish with fresh shell beans, turnips, and mustard greens; and roasted Colorado lamb rack with green risotto and tomato preserves. A five-course tasting menu ($95 with paired wines, $65 without) explores the day's market through the eyes of a talented chef. At lunch on the outdoor terrace, consider the "Drugstore" hamburger, a mini-spectacle on a great big bun. ✉*11480 N. Torrey Pines Rd.* ☎*858/777–6635* ▤*AE, D, DC, MC, V.*

$$$
Fodor's Choice
★
✕**George's California Modern.** Formerly George's at the Cove, a $2.6 million makeover brought a new name and sleek updated look to this eternally popular restaurant overlooking La Jolla Cove. Hollywood types and other visiting celebrities can be spotted in the sleek main dining room with its wall of windows. Simpler, more casual preparations of fresh seafood, beef, and lamb reign on the new menu chef Trey Foshee enlivened with seasonal produce from local specialty growers. Give special consideration to imaginatively garnished, citrus-cured yellowtail, succulent garlic-roasted chicken, chickpea-crusted petrale sole, and spice-braised Duroc pork shoulder. For more informal dining and a sweeping view of the coast try the rooftop Ocean Terrace. ✉*1250 Prospect St.* ☎*858/454–4244* ⌕*Reservations essential* ▤*AE, D, DC, MC, V* ◷*No lunch.*

$$$
Fodor's Choice
★
✕**Nine-Ten.** Many long years ago, the elegant Grande Colonial Hotel in the heart of La Jolla "village" housed a drug store owned by actor Gregory Peck's father. In the sleekly contemporary dining room that now occupies the space, acclaimed Chef Jason Knibb serves satisfying seasonal fare at breakfast, lunch, and dinner. At night the perfectly executed menu can take extravagant turns, as with the appetizers of Maine scallops with cauliflower custard, brown butter, and capers, or lobster risotto, and creative ones, as with the entrées of duck breast with forbidden black rice and sous vide salmon in an orange–olive oil emulsion. Pastry Chef Amy O'Hara is newly arrived from San Francisco, and skilled at creating ephemeral and delicious desserts; her caramelized bananas with coconut ice cream is sublime. ✉*910 Prospect St.* ☎*858/964–5400* ▤*AE, D, DC, MC, V.*

$
✕**Rimel's Rotisserie.** An affordable option in often pricey La Jolla, this comfy spot sometimes serves seafood caught that morning by fishermen

who work for the owner. Other than market-priced "fresh catches" and the $21 filet mignon, most items come in under $10, such as grilled mahimahi tacos (served with rice, beans, and a powerful green chili-garlic sauce), grain-fed chicken grilled on a mesquite-fire rotisserie, and "steaming rice bowls" that actually are plates spread with jasmine rice and wok-cooked meats and seafood with a variety of vegetables. This is one of La Jolla's better choices for families. ⊠*1030 Torrey Pines Rd.* ☎*858/454–6045* ⊟*AE, D, DC, MC, V.*

¢ ✗**Chicago On A Bun.** Fans of Chicago-style hot dogs head here when they get a craving for Windy City sidewalk cuisine. The decor—mostly built around Chicago Cubs memorabilia—is imported from the City of the Broad Shoulders, as are the Vienna-brand beef hot dogs, and even the steamed poppyseed buns. Garnish a dog your way, or take it Chicago-style, which means piled with mustard, onion, relish, chopped tomatoes, tiny hot peppers, celery salt, dill pickles—and never ketchup. A basket of fried-to-order potato chips is almost obligatory with hot dogs, juicy Italian beef sandwiches, or chili cheeseburgers. At its most ambitious, the menu at this great budget choice offers impressive bar-becued ribs. ⊠*8935 Towne Center Dr.* ☎*858/622–0222* ⊟*MC, V.*

ASIAN

$$$ ✗**Cafe Japengo.** Framed by marbled walls and accented with bamboo trees and unusual black-iron sculptures, this Pacific Rim restaurant serves Asian-inspired cuisine with many North and South American touches. The spicy kimchee crab cocktail and the lobster salad with pineapple-honey dressing are guaranteed to wake up your mouth. There's also a selection of grilled, wood-roasted, and wok-fried entrées; try the braised short ribs with saffron fettuccine or the sake-marinated prawns. The sushi is always fresh, and many regard it as the liveliest sushi bar in town. Service can be slow, but the pace in the bar, crowded with young locals on the make, is fast and lively. If you savor quiet, avoid weekend evenings. ⊠*Aventine Center, 8960 University Center La.* ☎*858/450–3355* ⊟*AE, D, DC, MC, V* ☉*No lunch weekends.*

$$$ ✗**Roppongi Restaurant and Sushi Bar.** A hit from the moment it opened, Roppongi serves global cuisine with strong Asian notes. The contemporary dining room, done in wood tones and accented with a tropical fish tank, Buddhas, and other Asian statuary, has a row of comfortable booths along one wall. It can get noisy when crowded; tables near the bar are generally quieter. Order the imaginative Euro-Asian tapas as appetizers, or combine them for a full meal. Equally delicious are the Roppongi crab stack and the Asian pear arugula salad. Good entrées are wasabi-crusted filet mignon and hibachi-grilled sea bass. The creative sushi bar rocks. ⊠*875 Prospect St.* ☎*858/551–5252* ⊟*AE, D, DC, MC, V.*

$$ ✗**Zenbu.** There's a cool California vibe to this cozy, moodily lighted
Fodor'sChoice sushi and seafood restaurant that serves some of the freshest fish in town and attracts a who's who of La Jolla. Restaurateur Matt Rimel runs a commercial fishing company, and uses his connections to bring varied seafood from all over the world that excels whether raw or cooked. Seasonal specialties include buttery Croatian and Spanish *otoro* tuna belly and local sea urchin fresh from its spiny shell. Sushi,

which can be pricey, ranges from simple nigiri to beautiful sashimi plates and original rolls like Salmon Spider, which combines soft-shell crab with fresh salmon. Cooked dishes run from noodle bowls and Montana prime sirloin seared at the table on a hot stone to whole fried rockfish or local spiny lobster dynamite. ⊠*7660 Fay Ave., Suite 1* ☎*858/454–4540* ▭*AE, D, DC, MC, V* ⊗*No lunch.*

CAFÉ

$ ╳ **Michele Coulon Dessertier.** A "dessertier" confects desserts, a job that Michele Coulon does exceedingly well with organic produce and imported chocolate in the back of a small, charming shop in the heart of La Jolla. Moist chocolate-chip scones, the colorful raspberry pinwheel *bombe* (a molded dessert of cake, jam, almond macaroons, and ice-cream filling), the berry-frangipane tart, and a decadent chocolate mousse cake are a few treats. This is not just a place for dessert, however. Lunch is served weekdays (the store is open 9–4), and the simple menu includes quiche Lorraine (baked fresh daily) and salads. ⊠*7556 Fay Ave.* ☎*858/456–5098* ▭*AE, D, MC, V* ⊗*Closed Sun. No dinner.*

> ## WHEN THE GRUNIONS RUN
>
> A generations-old San Diego tradition is heading to the beach during certain high tides—preferably when the moon is full—to hunt grunion. These small, barely edible fish come ashore during mating periods and "run" on the beach, causing great excitement among spectators. As the fish flop across the sand in search of adventure (as it were), bold individuals chase them down and bravely scoop up a few with their hands—catching them by any other means is illegal. Beach-area businesses and eateries often know the date of the next run.

DELI

$ ╳ **Elijah's.** This large, somewhat sterile-looking, brightly lighted delicatessen is in the La Jolla village area near I–5. Prominent are towering sandwiches, blintzes, smoked fish plates, and specialties like "mishmosh" soup, which combines noodles, matzo balls, and shredded crepes in a big bowl of steaming chicken broth. Count on hearty breakfast, reliable chopped liver, and dinners like chicken-in-the-pot and savory beef brisket. The restaurant makes impressive Reuben sandwiches, a combination of corned beef, sauerkraut, Swiss cheese, and Thousand Island dressing on rye bread. Service is quick and friendly. One of San Diego's best art-movie theaters is 50 feet away. ⊠*8861 Villa La Jolla Dr.* ☎*858/455–1462* ▭*AE, D, MC, V.*

FRENCH

$$$$ ╳ **Marine Room.** Gaze at the ocean from this venerable La Jolla Shores mainstay and, if it's during an especially high tide, feel the waves race across the sand and beat against the glass. Long-running chef Bernard Guillas takes a bold approach to combining ingredients. Creative seasonal menus score with "trilogy" plates that combine three meats, sometimes including game, in distinct preparations. Exotic ingredients show up in a variety of dishes, including zatar-spiced prawns, hibiscus

infusion with ahi tuna, and rosehips with a rack of lamb. ⊠*2000 Spin-drift Dr.* ☎*858/459–7222* ▤*AE, D, DC, MC, V.*

$$$ ✗**Tapenade.** Named after the Provençal black olive–and–anchovy paste, Tapenade specializes in the fresh cuisine of the south of France. The sunny cuisine matches the unpretentious, light, and airy room, lined with 1960s French movie posters, in which it is served. Fresh ingredients, a delicate touch with sauces, and an emphasis on seafood characterize the menu, which changes frequently. If you're lucky, it may include boar stewed in red wine (possibly the single best entrée in San Diego), lobster in a lobster-corn sauce flavored with Tahitian vanilla, pan-gilded sea scallops, and desserts like chocolate fondant. The two-course "Riviera Menu" served at lunch for $19.95 is a fabulous steal. ⊠*7612 Fay Ave.* ☎*858/551–7500* ▤*AE, DC, MC, V* ◷*No lunch weekends.*

ITALIAN

$$ ✗**Barolo.** This cozy, candlelighted restaurant in the Golden Triangle's Renaissance Towne Center boasts specialties like veal scallops with pesto and goat cheese and pear–stuffed ravioli. The mixed green salad with shrimp and avocado nicely kicks off a meal that may go on simply to a sausage pizza or roasted salmon. Ask for a banquette table and enjoy the suave, eager-to-please service. ⊠*8935 Towne Center Dr.* ☎*858/622–1202* ▤*AE, D, MC, V* ◷*No lunch weekends.*

$$ ✗**Trattoria Acqua.** Reservations are a good idea for this Mediterranean-inspired bistro above La Jolla Cove. On the lower level of Coast Walk center, this romantic eatery has dining rooms that are semi-open to the weather and the view, yet sufficiently sheltered for comfort. Choose from New Zealand mussels baked with crumbs, chopped almonds, and herbs; a lobster potpie crowned with puff pastry; and *agnolotti* pasta stuffed with wild mushrooms and black truffles. The superb wine list earns kudos from aficionados. ⊠*1298 Prospect St.* ☎*858/454–0709* ▤*AE, DC, MC, V.*

$ ✗**Barbarella.** With the sunny patio brightened by year-round blooms and the menu of casual Cal-Italian fare, it's not hard to see why Barbarella attracts many visitors to the La Jolla Shores area. For locals, the other part of the charm is blond owner Barbara Beltaire, who works the room joking with regulars and even swiping a french fry or two. The warm woodsy room is accented with original art by local artists and a mosaic-tile pizza oven decorated by Nikki de Saint Phalle. The seasonal menu ranges from crispy wild-mushroom pizzas, rock shrimp, and zucchini fritti in a silver cup, to oversize burgers topped with marinated red onions and blue cheese, and grilled salmon with pesto. Barbarella is packed on weekends, so reservations are a must. ⊠*2171 Avenida de la Playa* ☎*858/454–4373* ▤*AE, MC, V.*

$ ✗**Osteria Romantica.** The name means "Romantic Inn," and with a sunny location a few blocks from the beach in La Jolla Shores, the look does suggest a trattoria in Positano. The kitchen's wonderfully light hand shows up in the tomato sauce that finishes the scampi La Jolla Shores and other dishes, and in the pleasing Romantica salad garnished with figs and walnuts. Savory pasta choices include lobster-filled *mezzelune* (half moons) in saffron sauce, and wonderfully rich spaghetti *alla carbonara,* while main events might be chicken with fennel or a nice plate of breaded veal scallops crowned with chopped arugula and tomatoes. The warm, informal service suits the neighborhood. ⊠*2151 Avenida de la Playa* ☎*858/551–1221* ▤*AE, D, DC, MC, V.*

JAPANESE

$ ✕**Sushi on the Rock.** Regulars will stand outside this hip California-style sushi restaurant waiting for it to open so they can nail a seat for the daily happy hour from 5 to 6:30. There's something fun and nonthreatening about Sushi on the Rock, from the young friendly sushi chefs to the comically named specialties, like the crab-stuffed mushrooms better known as Monkey Balls. Loads of original rolls include the Barrio Roll stuffed with fried white fish and spicy tomato salsa, the Ashley Roll that pairs seared tuna with soft-shell crab and tangy whole-grain mustard sauce, and the Bruce Lee with spicy crab, tuna, and avocado. Japanese-inspired dishes include pot stickers, Asian-style Caesar salad, and panko-crusted sea bass. ⊠*7734 Girard Ave.* ☎*858/456–1138* ⚑*Reservations not accepted* ▤*AE, D, MC, V* ⊘*No lunch weekends.*

SEAFOOD

$$$ ✕**Blue Coral Seafood & Spirits.** This upscale, fairly new seafood restaurant at the Hyatt Aventine complex is off to a swimming start with its menu of fresh fish, inventive cocktails, and modern decor highlighted by a blue coral–inspired glass sculpture. At the bar, natural juices and fruit-infused spirits enliven cocktails such as the Blueberry Drop and the Coral Cocktail. Settle into one of the raised half-moon banquettes to experience a creative menu of classically inspired dishes, such as clam chowder spiked with herbs and bacon or a three-way crab tasting; à la carte entrées include subtle petrale sole in chive butter, pepper-crusted mahimahi, and tender filet mignon with balsamic sauce. Sides include addictive blue-cheese-and-apple slaw and lobster macaroni and cheese. A fantastic list of 60 wines by the glass makes for interesting reading and sipping; be sure to make reservations, because it's already a "spot" Thursday through Saturday. ⊠*8990 University Center La.* ☎*858/453–2583* ▤*AE, D, DC, MC, V* ⊘*No lunch.*

$$ ✕**Whisk'n'ladle.** The former Fresh has been re-christened Whisk'n'ladle by the young owner who wants to add a sense of comfortable whimsy to his centrally located restaurant. The menu still offers local seafood and seasonal produce, mostly in a small-plates format. Appetizers such as asparagus with Manchego cheese and romesco sauce or seared scallops lead into larger plates like pappardelle Bolognese and short ribs with spicy carrots and polenta. By all means request a patio table when reserving at this hip, popular eatery that doubles as a fashion show of some of La Jolla's ladies who lunch. And the bar is worth a visit, too, with its original menu of cocktails like the Cucumber Honey Mimosa or Lavender Cosmopolitan made with fresh herbs and fruit. ⊠*1044 Wall St.* ☎*858/551–7575* ▤*AE, D, DC, MC, V.*

$ ✕**El Pescador.** This low-key fish market and café in the heart of La Jolla village is popular with locals for its simply prepared fresh fish. Try a fillet—maybe halibut, mahi, salmon, or tuna—lightly grilled and piled on a soft torta roll with shredded lettuce, tomato, and onions. Other choices include ceviche, Dungeness crab salad, sautéed mussels with sourdough bread, and excellent fish tacos. Seats are few, and tables often end up being shared, but the food is worth the wait. ⊠*627 Pearl St.* ☎*858/456–2526* ▭*AE, D, MC, V.*

MISSION BAY & BEACHES

This area is all about the casual beach scene, and for the most part the food here is similarly laid-back. Burgers and tacos are easy to find, but so are sushi and Thai food. Many of the restaurants here are really bars at heart that serve food and then quickly transform around 9 PM.

AMERICAN

$$$ ✕**Jordan.** With some 300 seats, this ocean-facing restaurant in the beach-chic boutique-style Tower23 Hotel might seem overwhelming, but the seating is divided between a long, narrow outdoor terrace (sit here!) and a series of relatively intimate indoor rooms. New chef David Warner presents modern steak house fare including chops and steaks with sauces of the diner's choosing, lightened with lots of seasonal produce and a sushi menu. Breakfast and lunch have a similar appeal, with dishes like crabcake eggs Benedict with citrus hollandaise and a Portobello mushroom sandwich or a stunning Cobb salad laden with shrimp, scallops, and local fish. On Friday and Saturday the bar is the place to see and be seen in Pacific Beach for under-thirty types, and it's jammed after 9 PM. ⊠*723 Felspar St., Pacific Beach* ☎*858/270–5736* ▭*AE, D, DC, MC, V.*

¢ ✕**Hodad's.** No, it's not a flashback. The 1960s live on at this fabulously funky burger joint founded in that era: an unrepentant hippy crowd sees to it. Walls are covered with license plates, and the amiable servers with tattoos. Still, this is very much a family place, and Hodad's clientele often includes toddlers and octogenarians. Huge burgers are the thing, loaded with onions, pickles, tomatoes, lettuce, and condiments, and so gloriously messy that you might wear a swimsuit so you can stroll to the beach for a bath afterward. The mini-hamburger is good, the double bacon cheeseburger absolutely awesome, as are the onion rings and seasoned potato wedges. ⊠*5010 Newport Ave., Ocean Beach* ☎*619/224–4623* ▭*AE, MC, V.*

CUBAN

$ ✕**Andres' Restaurant.** For more than two decades, Andres' was San Diego's sole outpost for solid, savory Cuban cuisine. In a nondescript building in the Morena Boulevard home-furnishings district near Pacific Beach, Andres' is not much to look at, although the enclosed-patio dining room is comfortable, and servers smile as they place heaped-high plates of breaded steak, roast pork, and grilled marinated fish in front of impressed diners. For Cuban home cooking at its best, order the *picadillo,* a ground-beef hash with bold and piquant flavors and avoid the often-overcooked pollo asado. Like all entrées, they're accompanied by oceans of delicious black beans and mountains of rice. Nothing ever changes here, which is the way regulars like it. ⊠*1235 Morena Blvd., Morena District* ☎*619/275–4114* ▭*AE, D, DC, MC, V* ⊗*Closed Sun.*

Talking Tacos

Even though terms like tacos, burritos, enchiladas, and tostadas are as common as macaroni and cheese to San Diegans, don't count on widespread agreement among residents as to what they mean. Authentic cuisine brought from Mexico is quite at odds with Southern California's home-grown "Cal-Mex" style of cooking, although both can be delicious.

An authentic taco never takes the form of a folded, fried-hard shell stuffed with ground beef, golden Cheddar cheese, sour cream, chopped lettuce, and tomatoes. Even so, this is the version many novices encounter the first time around, and as San Diegans say, finding one is "no problemo." If you meet a soft torti-lla—more authentically made from corn-flour dough (*masa*) than from white flour—rolled around a filling and served fresh, fragrant, and hot, it's a lot closer to the real thing. Fill-ings can be shredded beef or chicken, or slowly simmered tongue in green sauce, or grilled or deep-fried fish or seafood, or just about any savory tid-bit. Garnishes usually include a drizzle of salsa and a squeeze of tart Mexican lime (a citrus different from the large lime commonly found in the United States), along with cilantro sprigs and chopped onion. Sliced radishes, again topped with lime and a sprinkle of salt, are served on the side.

Tacos El Gordo (✉ *689 H St., Chula Vista* ☎ *619/691–8848*), a well-known Tijuana taco franchise, moved across the border to Chula Vista and National City several years ago, bringing authentic street-style carne asada and seasoned pork adobada tacos on small freshly made tortillas. Most casual San Diego restaurants, the best being El Pescador in La Jolla,

Zocalo Grill in Old Town, and The Brigantine chain,offer some version of the fish taco, either with batter-fried whitefish or grilled fish topped with a mayonnaise based tangy white sauce, shredded cabbage, lime, and salsa. Many residents think of San Diego as the fish taco capital of the planet, but that title really belongs to Ensenada, a port city about 60 mi south of the California border. There, arranged cheek-by-jowl with the sizeable, attractively stocked, and decidedly aromatic waterside fish market, are a good 100 stands offering a kaleido-scope of tacos, each slightly different from the others and all accompanied by a slightly varied selection of condiments.

In San Diego, to be "one taco shy of a combination plate" is to be, shall we say, rather divorced from reality. A combination plate is anchored by such constants as delicately flavored rice and *frijoles refritos,* smooth, creamy, well-cooked beans that must be draped with melted shredded cheese and usually support a small raft of shredded lettuce dabbed with a bit of sour cream. Any empty spaces (you shouldn't see more of the plate than the rim) will be hidden by the pre-ferred combination of tacos, enchila-das, chiles rellenos, and burritos. What are those? Enchiladas can be filled with cheese, chicken, or beef and topped with savory, mostly mild red or green chile sauce. Chiles rellenos are mild, deep-fried peppers stuffed with cheese. Burritos are tortillas filled with beans and shredded meat. It's good, filling food, and you'll enjoy it. And that's the whole enchilada.

—David Nelson

LATIN AMERICAN

$ ✕**Isabel's Cantina.** A funky mix of Asian and Latin fare mingles on the inventive menu at this popular beachy restaurant created by chef and cookbook author Isabel Cruz. A huge teak Buddha reposes coolly in one corner, playing yin to the yang of spicy Latin-inspired fare. The day starts early with coconut French toast, carnitas pork scramble with guacamole and black beans, and healthy egg-white dishes. Lunch and dinner dishes include crispy wontons with ahi tuna, steak and chicken lettuce wraps, fragrant Buddha bowls of soba noodles and vegetables in coconut and lemongrass broth, spicy roasted Dragon chicken, and grilled salmon with house-made salsas. Save room for the house-made sautéed bananas and decadent flourless chocolate cake. Chef's table dinners offer a chance to learn about Cruz's approach to cuisine while having a unique dining experience in the kitchen. ⊠*966 Felspar St., Pacific Beach* ☎*858/272–8400* ⊟*AE, MC, V.*

GERMAN

$$ ✕**Kaiserhof.** Without question this is the best German restaurant in San Diego County, and the lively bar and beer garden work to inspire a sense of *Gemütlichkeit* (happy well-being). Tourist board–style posters of Germany's romantic destinations hang on the wall, Spaten and Paulaner flow from the tap. Gigantic portions are accompanied by such side dishes as potato pancakes, bread dumplings, red cabbage, and spaetzle. Entrées include sauerbraten, Wiener schnitzel, goulash, a great Reuben sandwich, and smoked pork chops, plus excellent daily specials such as crisp pork schnitzel with tart red cabbage. Weekday happy hour includes German beers on tap and a generous buffet. Reservations are a good idea. ⊠*2253 Sunset Cliffs Blvd., Ocean Beach* ☎*619/224–0606* ⊟*AE, MC, V* ☉*Closed Mon. No lunch Tues.–Thurs.*

ITALIAN

$$ ✕**Caffe Bella Italia.** Contemporary Italian cooking as prepared in Italy—an important point in fusion-mad San Diego—is the rule at this simple restaurant near one of the principal intersections in Pacific Beach. The menu presents Neapolitan-style macaroni with sausage and artichoke hearts in spicy tomato sauce, pizzas baked in a wood-fired oven, pappardelle with a creamy Gorgonzola and walnut sauce, plus formal entrées like chicken breast sautéed with balsamic vinegar, and slices of rare filet mignon tossed with herbs and topped with arugula and Parmesan shavings. Impressive daily specials include beet-stuffed ravioli in creamy saffron sauce. ⊠*1525 Garnet Ave., Pacific Beach* ☎*858/273–1224* ⊟*AE, D, DC, MC, V* ☉*No lunch Sun. and Mon.*

$ ✕**The Venetian.** The spacious back room of this neighborhood restaurant is actually a sheltered garden that you can enjoy in all weather. The menu takes a personal view of Italian cuisine, with house specialties like seafood pasta in tangy marinara sauce, and bow-tie pasta tossed with prosciutto, peas, mushrooms, and a rose-tinted cream sauce. The well-priced selection of veal, chicken, and seafood dishes is excellent, but many regulars settle for the lavishly garnished antipasto salad and one of the tender-crusted pizzas. ⊠*3663 Voltaire St., Ocean Beach* ☎*619/223–8197* ⊟*AE, D, DC, MC, V.*

2

JAPANESE

$$ ✕**Sushi Ota.** Wedged into a minimall between a convenience store and a looming medical building, Sushi Ota initially seems less than auspicious. Still, San Diego–bound Japanese business people frequently call for reservations before boarding their trans-Pacific flights. Look closely at the expressions on customers' faces as they stream in and out of the doors, and you can see the eager anticipation and satisfied glows that are products of San Diego's best sushi. Besides the usual California roll and tuna and shrimp sushi, sample the sea urchin or surf clam sushi, and the soft-shell crab roll or the omakase menu. Sushi Ota offers the cooked as well as the raw. There's additional parking behind the mall. It's hard not to notice that Japanese speakers get the best spots, and servers can be abrupt. ✉*4529 Mission Bay Dr., Pacific Beach* ☎*858/270–5670* ⌚*Reservations essential* ⊟*AE, D, MC, V* ⊘*No lunch Sat.–Mon.*

MEXICAN

$ ✕**Gringo's Cantina.** About a stone's throw from the ocean in the heart of lively Pacific Beach, this sizeable restaurant often seems to be having a party. A good variety of margaritas and fine tequilas helps fuel the atmosphere, but so does a menu cleverly divided between Mexican casual fare like quesadillas, enchiladas, burritos, and fajitas, and authentic regional specialties from the Mexican heartland. The latter includes dishes like *chiles en nogada* (meat-stuffed chilies in a walnut-cream sauce) and oven-roasted pork chops in Oaxacan-style mole sauce. The dressed up *queso fundido,* or melted Oaxacan cheese with crumbled chorizo sausage, makes a great shared starter. Make reservations, because this place is hot. ✉*4474 Mission Blvd., Pacific Beach* ☎*858/490–2877* ⊟*AE, D, MC, V.*

SEAFOOD

$$$ ✕**Red Marlin.** A multimillion-dollar renovation of the Hyatt Regency Mission Bay has turned a historic restaurant, soaring ceilings, and 120-degree views of Mission Bay into a bright and modern space specializing in seafood. Start with a pot of mussels in a yellow curry, a blue crab cake with preserved lemon and a salad, then move on to smoked salt-and-chile-dusted sea scallops, or a natural corn-fed rib-eye steak for two. ✉*1441 Quivira Rd., Mission Bay* ☎*619/221–4868* ⊟*AE, D, DC, MC, V.*

THAI

$ ✕**Lanna.** This small, attractive Thai restaurant loads its tables with lush full-bloom roses, and even scatters rose petals on most plates. On the eastern edge of Pacific Beach, Lanna serves a number of house specialties that are not found elsewhere, such as "talay Thai," a batter-fried fish fillet topped with a green-apple salad, onions, and cashews, and spice-braised duck in a deep, dark, wonderfully fragrant red curry sauce. The kitchen demonstrates considerable talent, and servers are both prompt and gracious. ✉*4501 Mission Bay Dr., Pacific Beach* ☎*858/274–8424* ⊟*MC, V.*

MISSION VALLEY

Big chain restaurants like the Cheesecake Factory, King's Fish House, and PF Chang's dominate the dining scene in this very developed area; the rents are high and developers tend to favor big names. The signature retail cafés tucked away inside large department stores, specifically Nordstrom's and Neiman Marcus, make good convenient options.

AMERICAN

$$ ✕**The Zodiac.** Men like to lunch at this elegant room in the luxurious Neiman Marcus department store as much as the ladies, who sometimes watch informal modeling while enjoying cool chardonnay and the restaurant's signature Mandarin orange soufflé with rich chicken salad on the side. Salads abound, but there's serious competition from the dressy lobster club sandwich, sea scallops, and Gorgonzola-crusted filet mignon. The desserts are as self-indulgent as some of the well-heeled patrons, and this is by far the best place to dine in Fashion Valley, which is universally regarded as San Diego's leading shopping center. ⊠*Neiman Marcus, Fashion Valley, 7027 Friars Rd.* ☎*619/692–9100* ⊟*AE, MC, V* ⊗*Closed Sun. No dinner.*

$ ✕**Mr. Peabody's.** Burgers and beer are an unbeatable combination anywhere, but especially within a stone's throw of the pricey Fashion Valley mall. Friendly and informal, this bustling eatery is fine for kids during lunch, but perhaps not after that. The attractions range from juicy half-pound burgers that rank among the best in Southern California, to a variety of tacos and a convincing, gently priced rib-eye steak. Order a basket of excellent fries or onion rings for the table, but not both, because the portions are beyond huge. ⊠*6110 Friars Rd.* ☎*619/542–1786* ⚱*Reservations not accepted* ⊟*MC, V.*

$ ✕**Ricky's Family Restaurant.** Chain feederies haven't driven out all of San Diego's old-line family restaurants, and this unpretentious place on the quiet fringe of Mission Valley remains dear to the city's heart. A traditional three-meals-daily restaurant, Ricky's serves big portions of unassuming, well-prepared, all-American cooking, but is famed for its breakfasts, when savory corned-beef hash and fluffy, strawberry-crowned Belgian waffles are the rule. The spectacular apple pancake, a soufflé-like creation that takes 20 minutes to bake, arrives burning hot and is irresistible to the last molecule of molten cinnamon sugar. Ricky's popularity never wanes. ⊠*2181 Hotel Circle S* ☎*619/291–4498* ⊟*MC, V.*

ITALIAN

$$ ✕**Prego Ristorante.** Since 1990, this Tuscan-style villa in Hazard Center has drawn diners searching for good Italian fare in Mission Valley. With a polished service staff, Prego greets the budget-conscious with excellent pizzas, including an unusual pie topped with meaty Portobello mushrooms and goat cheese. More formal meals might consist of linguine sauced with prawns and Manila clams, lobster-filled agnolotti pasta, plump mesquite-grilled pork chops, and the day's meats and poultry from the rotisserie. The pastry case is packed with luscious sweets. The restaurant also offers one of the most comfortable bars in the valley. ⊠*1370 Frazee Rd.* ☎*619/294–4700* ⊟*AE, D, DC, MC, V.*

JAPANESE

$ ✕**Oki Ton Japanese Bistro.** The best Japanese fare in Mission Valley is found in Oki Ton, a good-looking but informal eatery in the imposing Fenton Marketplace center just off busy Friars Road. The sushi chefs acquit themselves well with specialty rolls like the "inside-out" dragon roll of eel, avocado, shrimp tempura, and crab. The heaped sushi combination plate satisfies nicely, and the kitchen does equally well with an excellent chicken teriyaki, grilled salmon with ginger sauce, and a katsu platter of crisply breaded pork, chicken breast, and prawns. The filling meals include Japanese pickles, rice, salad, and the special house miso soup. ✉*2408 Northside Dr.* ☎*619/284–8036* ▤*AE, D, DC, MC, V.*

SEAFOOD

$ ✕**King's Fish House.** This warehouse-size restaurant remains wildly popular with shoppers at Mission Valley's many malls, owing to extremely friendly and efficient service, tanks filled with lively lobsters and Dungeness crabs, and a daily-changing menu with a fine selection of freshly shucked oysters. Specialties include New Orleans–style barbecued shrimp and a full-size New England clambake complete with red potatoes and sweet corn on the cob. Fish and shellfish are char-grilled, deep-fried, sautéed, steamed, and skewered, and the menu obliges meat eaters with a convincing cheeseburger, roasted chicken, and grilled sirloin. When jammed, the scene recalls a train station—and sounds like one, too. ✉*825 Camino de la Reina N* ☎*619/574–1230* ▤*AE, DC, MC, V.*

$ ✕**Little Fish Market.** This spin-off of downtown's Fish Market is custom-designed for the restaurant row at the Fenton Marketplace near Qualcomm Stadium. The restaurant recently upgraded to full-service status (you used to order at the counter), and transformed the dining room into a much more comfortable space, although it remains quite informal. The menu includes shellfish cocktails, smoked-fish plates, sushi, chowder served in a bread bowl, and more significant meals of deep-fried and charbroiled fish and shellfish. ✉*2401 Fenton Pkwy.* ☎*619/280–2277* ⏷*Reservations not accepted* ▤*AE, D, DC, MC, V.*

OLD TOWN

The historic adobe buildings clustered in the center of Old Town is where California first started; it's the first permanent encampment of Spanish settlers. Obviously, it's Mexican food that reigns here, though many of the restaurants that were once independently owned have been taken over by an out-of-state company that runs themed areas. Still, Old Town offers a few choices for affordable and authentic cuisine.

MEXICAN

$$ ✕**El Agave.** A Mexico City native brings authentic regional Mexican fare to what's an otherwise touristy area. Quesadillas filled with Manchego and squash blossoms; shrimp in bright, smoky guajillo chiles; and chicken in a slow-simmered mole are some of the tempting dishes that await. Try one of the more than 100 tequilas, such as the arti-

sanal tequilas made from 100% blue agave. ⊠ *2304 San Diego Ave.* ☎ *619/220–0692* ⊟ *AE, MC, V.*

$$ ✗ **Zocalo Grill.** Try for a table by a fireplace on the covered terrace, but the contemporary cuisine tastes just as good anywhere in the spacious and handsome eatery. Instead of cooking the carnitas (in this case, chunks of pork) the traditional way, simmering them in well-seasoned lard, Zocalo braises them in a mixture of honey and Guinness beer and serves the dish with mango salsa and avocado salad.

OLD VINES
Napa and Sonoma counties in Northern California might get all the publicity when it comes to wine, but California viticulture got its start in San Diego—Old Town to be exact. There are no vines there anymore, but the San Diego Wine & Culinary Center (⊠ *200 Harbor Dr.* ☎ *619/231–6400*) pours wines from all of the best vintners in the region.

Recommended starters include artichoke fritters and crisp shrimp skewers with pineapple-mango relish. The Seattle surf and turf roasts wild salmon and forest mushrooms on a cedar plank. This is one of the best bets in Old Town. ⊠ *2444 San Diego Ave.* ☎ *619/298–9840* ⊟ *AE, DC, MC, V.*

THAI

¢ ✗ **Saffron Noodles and Saté.** Comfortable outdoor tables on a narrow sidewalk and inexpensive prices make this and the neighboring Saffron Thai Grilled Chicken takeout worth a short detour from Old Town. The simple menu has spicy and mild noodle soups; stir-fried noodles with chicken, beef, pork, or shrimp; and a couple of uncommon Vietnamese and Thai-Indian noodle dishes bathed with aromatic sauces. Go next door for the namesake grilled half chicken served with jasmine rice, tart-sweet cucumber salad, and savory housemade peanut sauce. The room has a Zen feeling but is sunny and comfortable. ⊠ *3737 India St.* ☎ *619/574–7737* ⊟ *MC, V.*

UPTOWN

It's a wonder the streets of central Hillcrest and Uptown don't collapse beneath the weight of all the restaurants, as the district has become a center for diverse independent and ethnic dining and entertainment. It's an easy walking neighborhood that's open to everyone but is considered the center of San Diego's gay community. Farther east, new eateries continue to open in the North Park dining district along 30th Street.

AMERICAN

$ ✗ **Corvette Diner Bar & Grill.** A San Diego County favorite for children's parties and other family occasions, Corvette Diner showcases a real Corvette (changed yearly) in a kitschy, 1950s-style dining room dominated by vintage movie posters and singing servers. The menu has what you'd expect—macaroni and cheddar, plump burgers, piled-high deli sandwiches, spaghetti and meatballs, greasy chili-cheese fries, and thick milk shakes. The daily "Blue Plate Specials" are well-priced classics like grilled pork chops and "picnic basket" fried chicken. ⊠*3946 5th Ave., Hillcrest* ☎*619/542–1476* ⊟*AE, D, MC, V.*

$ ✕**Dish.** Part of the new 15,000-square-foot nightclub Universal by the creators of the popular Stingaree in downtown, Dish offers upscale urban comfort food for brunch, lunch, and dinner. The sexy decor in vibrant shades of red and orange offset by gilt and natural driftwood is the setting for Chef Antonio Friscia's menu of lobster macaroni and cheese, Wiener schnitzel with naturally raised pork, and braised chicken enchiladas. Lunch offerings include grilled sandwiches and vegetarian pizza, and brunch brings Frangelico French toast, quiche, and custom Bloody Marys and mimosas. ⊠*1220 University Ave., Hillcrest* ☎*619/296–3474* ⊟*AE, MC, V.*

$ ✕**Hash House A Go Go.** Expect to wait an hour or more for weekend breakfast at this trendy Hillcrest eatery, whose walls display photos of farm machinery and other icons of Middle America, but whose menu takes an up-to-the-minute look at national favorites. The oversize portions are the main draw here; at breakfast, huge platters carpeted with fluffy pancakes sail out of the kitchen, while at noon customers favor the overflowing chicken potpies crowned with flaky pastry. The parade of old-fashioned good eats continues at dinner with hearty meat and seafood dishes, including the grand sage-flavored fried chicken, bacon-flavored waffles, and hot-maple-syrup combinations. ⊠*3628 5th Ave., Hillcrest* ☎*619/298–4646* ⊟*AE, MC, V.*

$ ✕**Hob Nob Hill.** That Hob Nob never seems to change suits San Diego just fine; this is the type of place where regulars delight in ordering the same meal they've been ordering for 20 years. With its dark-wood booths and patterned carpets, the restaurant seems suspended in the 1950s, but you don't need to be a nostalgia buff to appreciate the bargain-price American home cooking—dishes such as pecan rolls, fried chicken, and corned beef like your mother never really made. The crowds line up morning, noon, and night. Reservations are suggested for Sunday breakfast. ⊠*2271 1st Ave., Middletown* ☎*619/239–8176* ⊟*AE, D, MC, V.*

$ ✕**The Linkery.** The menu at this earthy farm-to-table-style restaurant reads like a who's who of seasonal produce and the area's top organic farms. Housemade sausages such as chicken cordon bleu and smoky poblano pork lend the casual restaurant its name, but there's lots of vegetarian fare, too, including grilled Blue Lake beans with organic shoyu cask–aged soy sauce and lasagna stuffed with garden vegetables. Entrées include wild pan-seared fluke in blood-orange vinaigrette and a ranch-style ham and egg sandwich. The well-chosen wine and beer list includes cask-conditioned ales and even mead. ⊠*3794 30th St., North Park* ☎*619/255–8778* ⊟*AE, MC, V*

CAFÉS

¢ ✕**Bread & Cie.** There's a brisk East Coast air to this artsy, urban bakery
FodorsChoice and café that put itself on the map by being one of San Diego's first and best artisan bread bakers. Owner Charles Kaufman is a former New Yorker and filmmaker, who gave Bread & Cie a sense of theater by putting bread ovens imported from France on center stage. The mix includes warm foccacia covered in cheese and vegetables, crusty

loaves of black olive bread, gourmet granola with Mediterranean yogurt, bear claws, and first-rate cinnamon rolls. Lunch on house-made quiche, paninis filled with pastrami, turkey, and pesto, or Brie and honey, washed down with tea, coffee, and upscale soft drinks. ✉ *350 University Ave., Hillcrest* ☎ *619/683–9322* ▭ *D, MC, V.*

ECLECTIC

$$$ ✕ **Laurel.** Proprietor Tracy Borkum has returned this old favorite to top-tier status by installing a fresh "Swinging London" look and creative, Mediterranean-inspired cuisine. Cozy up to the long curving bar for sparkling wine cocktail or an appetizer such as Indian-spiced lamb sliders. The menu changes seasonally and features items such as Loch Duart salmon with white asparagus; pear, bacon, and blue-cheese flatbread; and short-rib spring rolls. Borkum wisely retained the butterscotch pot de crème from the original menu, and Laurel remains especially popular with guests attending theatrical events in nearby Balboa Park. ✉ *505 Laurel St., Banker's Hill* ☎ *619/239–2222* ▭ *AE, D, DC, MC, V* ⊗ *No lunch.*

$$ ✕ **The Prado.** This beautiful restaurant in the House of Hospitality on Balboa Park's museum row brings an inventive, contemporary menu to an area where picnic lunches or hot dogs from a nearby cart are the only other options. The striking Spanish–Moorish interior has original painted ceilings and elaborate glass sculptures, and the bar is a fashionable pre- and post-theater destination for light nibbles with a Latin and Asian twist and creative drinks. In the dining room, servers offer dishes that range from a dressy "farmer's salad" to saffron linguine with shellfish of the day, Colorado rack of lamb, and roasted sea bass. ✉ *1549 El Prado, Balboa Park* ☎ *619/557–9441* ▭ *AE, D, MC, V.*

INDIAN

$ ✕ **Bombay Exotic Cuisine of India.** Notable for its elegant dining room with a waterfall, Bombay employs a chef whose generous hand with raw and cooked vegetables gives each course a colorful freshness reminiscent of California cuisine, though the flavors definitely hail from India. Try the tandoori lettuce-wrap appetizer and any of the stuffed *kulchas* (a stuffed flatbread). The unusually large selection of curries may be ordered with meat, chicken, fish, or tofu. The curious should try the *dizzy noo shakk*, a sweet and spicy banana curry. Try a *thali*, a plate that includes an entrée, traditional sides, naan, dessert, and tea. ✉ *Hillcrest Center, 3960 5th Ave., Suite 100, Hillcrest* ☎ *619/298–3155* ▭ *AE, D, DC, MC, V.*

$ ✕ **India Princess.** Notable for intricately prepared dishes, India Princess offers a menu with many well-prepared specialties. A long, narrow

---

SAN DIEGO'S BOUNTY

Sunny San Diego is one of the premier agricultural areas in the country. Visit a farmer's market and have a taste: spring is the season for cherimoyas and strawberries, summer brings peaches and boysenberries, autumn is the time for apples and pears, and winter is abundant with tangerines and grapefruit. There's a different market every day of the week; check the list of farmer's markets around the county at ⊕www.sdfarmbureau.org.

front room leads to the much more comfortable back room, a rather intimate cave perfumed by spicy scents, and enlivened by explosive sizzling sounds when red-hot metal platters of meats cooked in a traditional tandoor oven arrive from the kitchen. Head straight for the generous buffet, or if ordering à la carte, dishes to try include the succulent lamb dumplings called *nargisi kofta,* sautéed shrimp *jalfarezee,* and the *kadai* chicken (cooked in a round-bottom pan like a wok). Vegetarians will be pleased with the many offerings. The mint *paratha* bread is fragrant and excellent. ⊠*3925 4th Ave., Hillcrest* ☎*619/291–5011* ▭*AE, MC, V.*

ITALIAN

$$ ✕**Busalacchi's Ristorante.** This long-running hit on the fringe of Hillcrest offers a romantic, low-key dining room and a stylish, sheltered patio that overlooks busy 5th Avenue. The lengthy menu zeroes in on elegant, fully flavored Sicilian specialties—it may be the only place in San Diego offering an *insalata di citrioli,* a salad of cucumbers, corn, tomatoes, and Gorgonzola. The pasta dishes include familiar favorites, but classically Sicilian is the rigatoni in an aromatic sausage-caper sauce; the stuffed, breaded-veal *spiedini* (on skewers) also is superb. ⊠*3683 5th Ave., Hillcrest* ☎*619/298–0119* ▭*AE, DC, MC, V* ⊗*No lunch weekends.*

$$ ✕**Sambuca Italian Bistro.** This cozy, candlelit restaurant, with reasonable prices and a well-prepared menu, differs more than a bit from the competition. Dishes marked "signature" are particularly noteworthy, like the Sambuca shrimp appetizer with a lime-garlic sauce. Creamy flavors make the four-cheese fusilli pasta with lobster an extravagant treat, while there's delicious subtlety to the roasted chicken with brandied Gorgonzola sauce. There are daily specials on weekdays. ⊠*3888 4th Ave., Hillcrest* ☎*619/298–8700* ▭*AE, D, MC, V.*

$ ✕**Pizzeria Arrivederci.** The wood-burning oven in this restaurant by a native of Sorrento adds an authentic toasty flavor to pizzas topped with forest mushrooms and smoky *scamorza* cheese, or perhaps *alla messicana,* a Mexican-style pie whose topping includes pork sausage, cilantro, and crushed red peppers. The list of imaginative pizzas is long (yes, you can get a pepperoni pizza, too), but there are also expertly made pastas such as penne in creamy vodka sauce with smoked salmon, and penne in pungent puttanesca sauce. Start with a well-priced glass or bottle of wine and a plate of roasted peppers with anchovies or the shrimp and white-bean salad with arugula. The young waiters from Italy treat guests well. ⊠*3789 4th Ave., Hillcrest* ☎*619/542–0293* ▭*AE, D, DC, MC, V.*

MEXICAN

$ ✕**Baja Betty's.** A margarita and a combination plate speak to the soul of many a San Diegan. Pair this duo with a sizzling scene and smoking music and you come up with a gay-friendly hot spot like Baja Betty's, which offers dozens of tequilas—some quite spectacular—and a long list of potent cocktails built upon them. The salsa similarly sizzles, and can dress everything from the excellent *carnitas* quesadilla, filled with shredded pork, to the "flamenco" flautas, filled with a choice of shredded beef or chicken. Large portions, good cooking, friendly servers, low prices, and a party mood make this a find. ⊠*1421 University Ave., Hillcrest* ☎*619/269–8510* ⊟*AE, D, DC, MC, V.*

$ ✕**Ortega's, A Mexican Bistro.** Californians have long flocked to Puerto
Fodor'sChoice Nuevo, the "lobster village" south of San Diego in Baja California.
★ When a member of the family that operates several Puerto Nuevo restaurants opened Ortega's, it became an instant sensation, since it brought no-nonsense, authentic Mexican fare straight to the heart of Hillcrest. The specialty of choice is a whole lobster prepared Baja-style and served with superb beans, rice, and made-to-order tortillas, but there are other fine options, including melt-in-the-mouth carnitas (slowly cooked pork), made-at-the-table guacamole, and grilled tacos filled with *huitlacoche* corn mushrooms and Mexican herbs. The pomegranate margaritas are a must, as is the special red salsa if you like authentic spice. ⊠*141 University Ave., Hillcrest* ☎*619/692–4200* ⊟*AE, MC, V.*

¢ ✕**El Zarape.** There's a humble air to this cozy Mexican taqueria, but one bite of the signature scallop tacos and you'll realize something special is happening in the kitchen. Seared bay scallops mingle with tangy white sauce and shredded cheese in a satiny corn tortilla. Or perhaps you'll prefer sweet pieces of lobster meat in oversize quesadillas; burritos filled with chiles rellenos; or the original beef, ham, and pineapple Aloha burrito. No matter, nearly everything is fantastic at this busy under-the-radar eatery that's part of a developing independent restaurant row in University Heights. Mexican beverages, including the sweet-tart hibiscus-flower drink *jamaica* and the cinnamon rice drink *horchata,* and house-made flan and rice pudding round out the menu. ⊠*4642 Park Blvd., University Heights* ☎*619/692–1652* ⊟*AE, MC, V.*

MIDDLE EASTERN

¢ ✕**Mama's Bakery & Lebanese Deli.** This little house converted into a restaurant serves some of the best authentic Lebanese fare in San Diego County. The key is the sajj, a super-heated oven that's used to cook a flatbread by the same name. The warm herbed bread might be wrapped around garlicky marinated chicken, hummus and vegetables, or made into the Manakeesh Ultimate, a combination of labne yogurt cheese, herbs, tomatoes, olives, and fresh mint. Heartier plates usually include housemade hummus along with grape leaves, fried eggplant with baba ganoush, or seasoned kafta ground beef with rice, salad, and pita bread. For dessert, try some of the buttery baklava. ⊠*4237 Alabama St., North Park* ☎*619/688–0717* ⊟*MC, V.*

Where to Stay

WORD OF MOUTH

"For beach access, check out hotels on Pacific Beach or Mission Beach. Some hotels on Mission Bay are also within walking distance of Mission Beach. All three areas are quite close to SeaWorld and not too far from the Zoo."

—mscarls

"I would try to stay on Shelter Island. Minimal parking charges, convenient location, and right across from the Harbor."

—tchoiniere

"[The Hotel Circle area] is the economy place to stay in San Diego. They are mostly decent hotels for a place to sleep. . . . If you want a hotel to enjoy the beauty of San Diego, that is not the place."

—ltt

BEST BETS FOR SAN DIEGO LODGING

Here are our top lodging recommendations by price and experience. The very best properties—in other words, those that provide a particularly remarkable experience in their price range—are designated in the listings with a Fodor's Choice logo.

Fodor'sChoice ★

Britt Scripps Inn, $$
Catamaran Resort Hotel, $$$
Grande Colonial, $$$
Hard Rock Hotel, $$$
Heritage Park Inn, $$
Hotel Del Coronado, $$$
Hotel Solamar, $$$
Lodge at Torrey Pines, $$$$
The Sofia Hotel, $$
U.S. Grant, $$$$
Westgate Hotel, $$$

Best By Price

¢

Hotel Occidental

$

La Jolla Cove Suites
Western Inn Old Town

$$

Bahia Resort Hotel
Britt Scripps Inn
The Dana on Mission Bay
Heritage Park Inn
The Sofia Hotel

$$$

Catamaran Resort Hotel
Grande Colonial
Hard Rock Hotel
Hotel Del Coronado
Hotel Solamar
Westgate Hotel

$$$$

Hotel Parisi
The Ivy
La Valencia
Lodge at Torrey Pines
U.S. Grant

Best By Experience

BEST HOTEL BAR

Hotel Solamar
The Grande Colonial
The Ivy
La Valencia
The Pearl

BEST BEACH

Hotel Del Coronado
La Jolla Shores Hotel
Paradise Point Resort & Spa
Tower 23

BEST FOR KIDS

The Catamaran
Coronado Island Marriott Resort
Hyatt Regency Mission Bay Marina & Spa
Loews Coronado Bay Resort
Paradise Point Resort & Spa

BEST FOR ROMANCE

Hotel Del Coronado
Hotel Parisi
Hotel Solamar
The Ivy
The Lodge at Torrey Pines

BEST VIEWS

Best Western Island Palms Hotel & Marina
Crystal Pier Hotel
Hilton San Diego Resort
Sheraton San Diego Hotel & Marina
Tower 23

MOST TRENDY

Hard Rock Hotel
The Ivy
The Keating

The Pearl
Tower 23

BEST LOBBY

The Lodge at Torrey Pines
Hotel Solamar
Hyatt Regency Mission Bay Marina & Spa
The W
Westgate Hotel

BEST POOL

Hotel Solamar
Hyatt Regency Mission Bay Marina & Spa
The Ivy
Loews Coronado Bay Resort

BEST NEW HOTELS

Hard Rock Hotel
The Ivy
The Pearl Hotel
Sofia Hotel

BEST OLD HOTELS

Glorietta Bay Inn
Heritage Park Inn
Hotel Del Coronado
La Valencia
Westgate Hotel

BEST KEPT SECRET

Best Western Hacienda Suites-Old Town
Best Western Island Palms
Britt Scripps Inn
The Sofia Hotel
La Jolla Cove Suites

WHERE SHOULD I STAY?

	Neighborhood Vibe	Pros	Cons
Coronado	A picturesque city with historic and resort hotels, beaches, and tourist-oriented restaurants.	Beautiful, wide beaches are good for families and escapes.	If you plan to do most sightseeing in San Diego, you'll spend a lot of time commuting across the bridge or on the ferry.
Downtown	An action-packed area with a mixed bag of budget chain, boutique, and business hotels.	Lots of restaurants, nightclubs, bars, and shopping. Won't need a car to get to many attractions.	Can be congested and noisy. Parking is expensive.
Harbor & Shelter Island and Point Loma	Point Loma is a mostly residential area of older homes; Shelter and Harbor Islands are devoted to recreational areas.	Near the airport and the bay. Great city views. Convenient for boaters.	Isolated from the rest of the city. Has few exciting hotel and restaurant choices.
La Jolla	"The jewel of San Diego," a beautiful coastal area with a range of high end hotels and a few value choices.	Close or right on the beach. Some of the best restaurants and shopping in the county.	Often congested and parking can be near impossible. Very expensive.
Mission Bay & Beaches	A relaxed and casual beach area with many water and sport activities.	Right on the water. Great values. Close to Sea-World.	Some parts of Mission Bay are seedy. Area is somewhat removed from central San Diego.
Mission Valley & Hotel Circle	Chockablock with big box shopping centers and malls, car lots, and chain hotels.	Centrally located. Affordable. Great for business travelers.	Area lacks character; you'll mostly find chain hotels and restaurants.
Old Town	Home to the most popular park in the California state system (Old Town San Diego State Historic Park). Historic lodgings and some modestly priced chain hotels.	Centrally located. Tourist-friendly shops and restaurants. Lots to see and do.	Not much going on at night. Kitschy.
Uptown	A hip residential area in the heart of San Diego's gay community with small independently owned hotels and inns.	Close to the zoo and Balboa Park. Vibrant neighborhood with unique shops and restaurants.	Area can be congested. Not many hotel options.

3

Updated by
Maria C. Hunt

"WHEN I LOOK AT SAN DIEGO, it feels like Miami did years ago, with the vitality and anticipation to take off," said Rande Gerber, famous bar and lounge designer responsible for both bars at the new Hard Rock San Diego. And he's right. This ain't just your family-friendly San Diego any more. Seen for years as the home of SeaWorld and the San Diego Zoo, the city's new class of boutique hotels is gaining attention from the hip jet-set crowd. Features like see-through showers at the Ivy, Sunday afternoon rehab pool parties at the Hard Rock Hotel, and the edgy Italian chic Pininfarina design at the Keating now mingling with kiddie pools and ho-hum chains. Facing this sexy hotel boom, classic hotels are upping the ante by adding sleek modern decor and such amenities as spas, flat-screen TVs, and wireless Internet service.

San Diego is divided into many different enclaves, so to avoid sitting in traffic, figure out first what you want to see and do. If you want to luxuriate by the water, choose a hotel in La Jolla, Coronado, Mission Beach, or Pacific Beach. La Jolla, home to historic landmark hotels such as the Grande Colonial and La Valencia, offers many romantic and upscale ocean-view hotels and some of the area's best restaurants and specialty shopping. But it's easy to find a water view in any price range: surfers make themselves at home at Tower 23 and Diamond Head Inn in Pacific Beach. If you're arriving by boat or plan to do some sportfishing, check out the hotels located near marinas in Shelter Island, Point Loma, or Coronado.

Mission Valley and downtown are ideal for business travelers; there are plenty of well-known chain hotels with conference space, modern business centers, and executive floors. When the work is done, join the trendsetters flocking to downtown's Gaslamp Quarter for the mix of expense account–worthy restaurants and boutique-style hotels. Here, your hotel is as much a place to rest your head as it isn't; settle in at the stylish Ivy Hotel or the pool-topped Hotel Solamar if you want to be in the middle of the action.

And of course, San Diego is still as much a playground for families as for hipsters; choose a hotel in Mission Beach, historic Old Town, or Mission Valley, areas that offer good-value accommodations with extras like sleeper sofas, and are close to the Zoo and SeaWorld.

WHAT IT COSTS					
	¢	$	$$	$$$	$$$$
Hotels	under $100	$100–$199	$200–$299	$300–$400	over $400

Prices are for a standard double room in high (summer) season, excluding 10.5% tax.

CORONADO

$$$$ 🏨 **Coronado Island Marriott Resort.** Near San Diego Bay, this snazzy hotel has rooms with great downtown skyline views. A $15 million renovation in 2007 brings a revamped lobby with sofas for lounging, grounds with tropical plants, a redesigned pool area with firepits, and large rooms and suites in low-slung buildings redone in a cheerful island-inspired fashion. The resort runs $6 water taxis that drop you off downtown. **Pros:** Spectacular views, hotel spa, close to water taxis. **Cons:** Not in downtown Coronado, difficult to find. ⊠ *2000 2nd St.* ☎ *619/435–3000 or 800/543–4300* ⊕ *www.marriotthotels.com/sanci* ⚲ *273 rooms, 27 suites* ⚷ *In-room: Wi-Fi. In-hotel: restaurant, room service, bar, tennis courts, pools, gym, spa, beachfront, water sports, bicycles, laundry service, concierge, parking (fee), no-smoking rooms* ▭ *AE, D, DC, MC, V.*

$$$ 🏨 **El Cordova Hotel.** Built as a countryside mansion in 1902, this two-story Spanish-style building was converted into a hotel in 1930. Its quaint Old Mexico courtyard is ringed by shops and cafés. Most rooms are suites, and you can walk to the beach from here. **Pros:** Centrally located, near dining and shops. **Cons:** Understaffed, few amenities, overpriced. ⊠ *1351 Orange Ave. 92118* ☎ *619/435–4131* ⊕ *www. elcordovahotel.com* ⚲ *8 rooms, 32 suites* ⚷ *In-room: kitchen (some). In-hotel: pool* ▭ *AE, D, MC, V.*

$$$ 🏨 **Glorietta Bay Inn.** The main building on this property is an Edwardian-style mansion built in 1908 for sugar baron John D. Spreckels, who once owned much of downtown San Diego. Rooms in the mansion and in the newer motel-style buildings are quaintly furnished, some have patios or balconies. The inn is adjacent to the Coronado harbor and near many restaurants and shops, but is much smaller and quieter than the Hotel Del across the street. Tours ($12) of the island's historical buildings depart from the inn three mornings a week. Continental breakfast and afternoon ginger snaps and lemonade are served daily. **Pros:** Great views, friendly staff, close to beach. **Cons:** Mansion rooms are small, lots of traffic nearby. ⊠ *1630 Glorietta Blvd.* ☎ *619/435–3101 or 800/283–9383* ⊕ *www. gloriettabayinn.com* ⚲ *100 rooms* ⚷ *In-room: kitchen (some), refrigerator, DVD, dial-up. In-hotel: pool, bicycles, no elevator, laundry service, concierge, parking (fee), no-smoking rooms* ▭ *AE, MC, V.*

> ## HOME, SWEET HOME
>
> The Glorietta Bay Inn, which was once the home of San Diego sugar baron John D. Spreckels, features a brass cage elevator, a marble staircase with curving bronze railings, a solarium, and stained-glass windows. Designed by architect Harrison Albright, the Italian Renaissance house cost all of $35,000 when it was built in 1906.

$$$
Fodor'sChoice
★ 🏨 **Hotel Del Coronado.** The Victorian-styled "Hotel Del," situated along 28 oceanfront acres, is as much of a draw today as it was when it opened in 1888. The resort is always alive with activity, as guests—including U.S. presidents, European royalty, and celebrities—and tourists marvel at the fanciful architecture, surrounding sparkling sand, and gorgeous ocean views. About half of the resort's accommodations are

in the more charming, original Victorian building, where each room is unique in size and footprint. Rooms in the California Cabana buildings and Ocean Towers, built in the mid-1970s, have a Pottery Barn–style look with marble bathrooms. These rooms are closer to the pool and the beach, making them a good option for families with children. In 2007 the hotel added several luxury enhancements, including a new spa with an infinity pool and Beach Village: 78 lavish beachfront villas and cottages that feature fully equipped kitchens, fireplaces, spa-style baths with soaking tubs, and private ocean-view terraces. **Pros:** Romantic, on the beach, hotel spa. **Cons:** Some rooms are small, expensive dining, public areas are very busy. ⊠ *1500 Orange Ave.* ☎ *800/468–3533 or 619/435–6611* ⊕ *www.hoteldel.com* ⊅ *757 rooms, 65 suites, 43 villas, 35 cottages* ⚐ *In-room: safe, refrigerator (some), Ethernet. In-hotel: 5 restaurants, room service, bars, pools, gym, spa, beachfront, water sports, bicycles, children's programs (ages 4–12), laundry service, concierge, airport shuttle, parking (fee), no-smoking rooms* ⊟ *AE, D, DC, MC, V.*

$$$ ⊡ **Loews Coronado Bay Resort.** You can park your boat at the 80-slip marina of this romantic retreat, set on a secluded 15-acre peninsula on the Silver Strand. After a $6 million redecoration in 2006, rooms glow in sand and sea hues, and feature upgraded beds with sea-grass headboards; all have furnished balconies with water views. Get out there on one of the resort's rented watercraft or luxuriate by the tropical oasis that surrounds three pools. The 10,000-square-foot Sea Spa offers a garden with alfresco showers and Watsu water massages. One treatment room, catering to teens, is splashed with a Southern California theme—surfboards, palm trees, and the ocean. **Pros:** Great restaurants, lots of activities, lobby worth lingering in. **Cons:** Far from anything, somewhat confusing layout. ⊠ *4000 Coronado Bay Rd.* ☎ *619/424–4000 or 800/815–6397* ⊕ *www.loewshotels.com* ⊅ *403 rooms, 37 suites* ⚐ *In-room: safe, dial-up. In-hotel: 3 restaurants, room service, bars, tennis courts, pools, gym, spa, beachfront, water sports, bicycles, children's programs (ages 4–12), laundry service, concierge, parking (fee), no-smoking rooms* ⊟ *AE, D, DC, MC, V.*

$$ ⊡ **La Avenida Inn.** An old-school motor lodge surrounding a pool landscaped with palms and tropical flowers, this inn caters to a budget crowd in a tony area. It's the most economical choice on this half of the island, offering clean and simply furnished rooms. The big plus here is that it's a half-block from historic Hotel Del Coronado and one block from the beach. Continental breakfast is served daily, and double-pane windows with plantation shutters in the rooms reduce the street noise. **Pros:** Affordable, good location, pool. **Cons:** Few amenities, busy area, somewhat dated rooms. ⊠ *1315 Orange Ave.* ☎ *619/435–3191 or 800/437–0162* ⊕ *www.laavenidainn.com* ⊅ *27 rooms, 2 suites* ⚐ *In-room: Wi-Fi. In-hotel: pool, no elevator, parking (no fee)* ⊟ *AE, MC, V* ⊠�‖ *CP.*

$ ⊡ **Cherokee Lodge.** This small inn, brought across the bay more than a century ago by barge, exudes elegance and charm with armoires, embroidered couches, polished headboards, and beautiful woodwork. Continental breakfast vouchers for a nearby restaurant are included.

Pros: Nicely landscaped, quaint rooms, quiet neighborhood. **Cons:** Somewhat hard to find, manager not always on-site, no front lobby. ✉ *964 D Ave.* ☎ *619/437–1967 or 877/743–6213* ⊕ *www.cherokeelodge.com* 🛏 *12 rooms* ♿ *In-room: no a/c, refrigerator, dial-up, Wi-Fi. In-hotel: no elevator, laundry facilities, no-smoking rooms* ⊟ *AE, D, DC, MC, V.*

$ 🍽 **Crown City Inn & Bistro.** On Coronado's main drag, the Crown City Inn is close to shops, restaurants, and the beach. For the price, it's easily one of the best deals on the island. This two-story motor inn lacks the amenities and prestige of Coronado's bigger and better-known lodgings, though it has many return guests. A public park is across the street. **Pros:** Affordable, on-site restaurant. **Cons:** Few amenities, somewhat dated rooms, a hike from downtown. ✉ *520 Orange Ave.* ☎ *619/435–3116* ⊕ *www.crowncityinn.com* 🛏 *33 rooms* ♿ *In-room: refrigerator. In-hotel: restaurant, room service, pool, bicycles, no elevator, laundry facilities, parking* ⊟ *AE, D, DC, MC, V.*

DOWNTOWN

$$$$ 🍽 **The Ivy.** Opened in May 2007, the Ivy is a lively and luxurious haven for the travel elite. The high-style lobby has a sexy feel with Zebrawood millwork and tall columns wrapped in braided leather. Upon arrival, a butler escorts guests directly to their rooms, where a personalized snack awaits, along with a glass-enclosed bath, flat-screen TV, walnut floors and cabinetry, and a natural palette of modern and classic furnishings. After mixing a drink in the room's fully stocked bar, guests can dine at the Quarter Kitchen restaurant, sampling a menu of fresh coastal cuisine. Stop off for a nightcap at the rooftop bar or in the exclusive Envy nightclub down below, offering Vegas-inspired entertainment and bottle service. **Pros:** Central location, great scene, luxurious rooms. **Cons:** Spotty service, pricey attitude. ✉ *650 F St., Downtown* ☎ *619/814–1000* ⊕ *www.ivyhotel.com* 🛏 *159 rooms, 17 suites* ♿ *In-room: Ethernet, Wi-Fi. In-hotel: restaurant, room service, bar, pool, laundry service, concierge, public Internet, public Wi-Fi, parking (fee), some pets allowed, no-smoking rooms* ⊟ *AE, D, DC, MC, V.*

$$$$ 🍽 **The Keating Hotel.** The Keating's 116-year-old historic exterior looks nothing like its new sexy interior, remade into a hotel in 2006. Guests are greeted with a sports car–red lobby that leads to 35 rooms designed by Pininfarina, the Italian company that makes Ferraris and Maseratis. The contemporary set will appreciate the room's minimalist open floor plan that showcases stainless bath fixtures, a blue resin walk-through shower, and a personalized "sip and crave" beverage and snack bar. Upon check-in, you're given a 15-minute lesson on how to use all the room's gadgets, which include a Bang & Olufsen sound system, plasma TV, and personal espresso maker. For appetizers and cocktails, head downstairs to the Lounge. A historic redbrick bank vault, part of the San Diego Trust & Savings Bank that once occupied the building, now holds a selection of wines from Italy. **Pros:** Great location, boutique hotel, many amenities. **Cons:** Industrial-feeling rooms, small lobby. ✉ *432 F St., Downtown* ☎ *619/814–5700 or 877/753–2846*

KNOW-HOW

San Diego has hotels in abundance, including several newly opened in the last few years. When you make reservations, ask about specials. Hotel packages are your best bet; deals range from arts and culture escapes to relaxing spa weekends and special event getaways. Check hotel Web sites for Internet specials and try to call a hotel directly; sometimes your effort will result in a lower rate. Several properties in the Hotel Circle area of Mission Valley offer reduced rates and even free tickets to the San Diego Zoo, Wild Animal Park, SeaWorld, Legoland, and other attractions. Many hotels also promote discounted weekend packages to fill rooms after convention and business customers leave town. Since the weather is great year-round, don't expect substantial discounts in winter. You can save on hotels and attractions by visiting the San Diego Convention & Visitors Bureau Web site (www.sandiego.org) for a free Vacation Planning Kit with a Travel Value Coupon booklet.

PRICES

The lodgings we list run from bare-bones basic to lavishly upscale. Note that even in the most expensive areas, you can find some more affordable rooms. High season is summer, and rates are lowest in the fall. If an ocean view is important, request it when booking, but be aware that it will cost significantly more than a non-ocean-view room.

We always list a property's facilities, but we don't specify whether you'll be charged extra to use them; when pricing accommodations, always ask what's included. Our price categories are based on a hotel's standard double room (or suites, in all-suites properties) in non-holiday high season. Assume that hotels operate on the **European Plan** (EP, with no meals) unless we specify otherwise.

RESERVATIONS

Book well in advance, especially if you plan to visit in summer, which is the busy season for most hotels. In spring and fall, conventions can fill every downtown hotel room. Special sports events such as golf or tennis tournaments also mean that host resorts and nearby hotels are fully booked.

SERVICES

You can assume that all rooms have private baths, phones, TVs, and air-conditioning unless otherwise noted. Downtown hotels once catered primarily to business travelers, though the new boutique hotels are attracting hip young leisure travelers to the area, while those at Mission Bay, in coastal locations such as Carlsbad and Encinitas, and at inland resort areas offer golf and other sports facilities, spa services, children's activities, and more.

⊕ *www.thekeating.com* ⇆ *26 rooms, 9 suites* ⌂ *In-room: safe, DVD, Wi-Fi. In-hotel: bar, room service, laundry service, concierge, parking (fee), no-smoking rooms* ▤ *AE, D, DC, MC, V.*

$$$$

Fodor's Choice

★

☷ **U.S. Grant.** Stepping into the regal U.S. Grant not only puts you in the lap of luxury, but also back into San Diego history; the 99-year-old building is on the National Register of Historic Sites. A 2006 remodeling reintroduced the hotel's original grandeur and opulence. The lobby is a confection of luxurious French fabrics, crystal chandeliers, and

Italian Carrera–marble floors. Guests sip tea and martinis here Thursday through Sunday afternoons. Rooms feature custom Italian linens, operatic lighting, and original French and Native American artwork, and the sunny baths are elegantly designed with marble-tile shower enclosures and stone sinks. The Grant Grill restaurant reopened in January 2007, boasting a fusion of grilled specialties and fresh regional cuisine. The venue's 1940s-style New York decor has a glamorous appeal, with African mahogany walls and plush seating. **Pros:** Modern rooms, great location, near shopping and restaurants. **Cons:** The hotel's many special events get hectic. ⊠ *326 Broadway, Downtown* ☎ *619/232–3121 or 800/237–5029* ⊕ *www.usgrant.net* ⮐ *270 rooms, 47 suites* ⚷ *In-room: safe, Ethernet, Wi-Fi. In-hotel: restaurant, room service, bar, gym, laundry service, concierge, public Wi-Fi, airport shuttle, parking (fee), no-smoking rooms* ▤ *AE, D, DC, MC, V.*

$$$$ ⚏ **W Hotel.** Come here for the trendy decor and neon drinks, not the service. The W chain's urban finesse adapts to San Diego with nautical blue-and-white rooms with beach-ball pillows and goose-down comforters. The Beach bar has a heated sand floor and fire pit, but the pool is tiny by San Diego standards. The lobby doubles as the futuristic Living Room lounge, a local hipster nightspot where nonguests have to wait behind a velvet rope. Be sure to get a room on an upper floor—the leather- and black-clad crowd parties into the night. The hotel restaurant, Rice, serves stylish Asian and Latin cuisine, and the Away Spa caters to both body and spirit. **Pros:** Large lobby, modern rooms, spa. **Cons:** Spotty service, not centrally located. ⊠ *421 West B St., Downtown* ☎ *619/398–3100 or 877/822–0000* ⊕ *www.whotels. com/sandiego* ⮐ *258 rooms, 16 suites* ⚷ *In-room: safe, DVD, dial-up, Wi-Fi. In-hotel: restaurant, room service, bars, gym, spa, concierge, parking (fee), no-smoking rooms* ▤ *AE, D, MC, V.*

$$$$ ⚏ **Westin Gaslamp Quarter.** You know you're here when you see the startling lighted blue obelisk fronting this high-rise hotel. Inside, it's all understated cream-color marble and curved staircases—and guest rooms are freshly redecorated in a stylish urban design. The lobby lounge is packed every night with business travelers and weary shoppers back from the adjacent Horton Plaza. **Pros:** Modern decor, good location. **Cons:** Lots of hustle and bustle. ⊠ *910 Broadway Circle, Gaslamp Quarter* ☎ *619/239–2200 or 888/625–5144* ⊕ *www.westin.com* ⮐ *450 rooms, 8 suites* ⚷ *In-room: safe, dial-up. In-hotel: 2 restaurants, room service, bar, pool, gym, laundry service, concierge, parking (fee), no-smoking rooms* ▤ *AE, D, DC, MC, V.*

$$$$ ⚏ **Westin San Diego.** After a $15 million spring 2007 renovation that turned the former Wyndham into a Westin, this hotel boasts new furnishings throughout, Heavenly Beds, and premium Steakman shower heads, making it a good choice for business travelers as well as vacationers who want to be near downtown shopping and restaurants. Though not large, the standard rooms have crisp white and dark-wood decor, and many of the upper-floor rooms have panoramic views. The large health club is fully equipped and rarely crowded. **Pros:** Good location, large gym, new decor. **Cons:** Smallish rooms, busy area. ⊠ *400 W. Broadway, Gaslamp Quarter* ☎ *619/239–4500 or 800/996–3426* ⊕ *www.westin.com/sandiego*

Where to Stay Downtown

🛏436 rooms, 6 suites 🛆In-room: dial-up. In-hotel: restaurant, room service, bar, pool, gym, laundry service, concierge, airport shuttle, parking (fee), no-smoking rooms ☰AE, D, DC, MC, V.

$$$ 🏨 **Doubletree Downtown.** Dwarfing the many two-story Victorian homes in the area, this 22-story former Radisson has plenty of rooms with unobstructed views of San Diego Bay and the downtown skyline. Thanks to a $10 million renovation in mid-2007, rooms now have a modern look with new Sweet Dreams beds, carpeting, furniture, and granite counter tops in the bath. Yet some fixtures near the pool still show their age. Although the hotel is practically adjacent to a freeway off-ramp, the noise level is tolerable. The airport and Little Italy's restaurants and coffeehouses are nearby. **Pros:** Good views, updated rooms, most rooms have balconies. **Cons:** Near freeway, busy location. ✉1646 Front St., Downtown ☎619/239–6800 or 800/333–3333 ⊕www.radisson.com 🛏313 rooms, 20 suites 🛆In-room: dial-up. In-hotel: restaurant, room service, bar, pool, gym, concierge, public Wi-Fi, airport shuttle, parking (fee) ☰AE, D, DC, MC, V.

$$$ 🏨 **Embassy Suites–San Diego Bay.** The front door of each spacious, contemporary suite opens out onto a 12-story atrium, and rooms facing the harbor have spectacular views. A 2008 bathroom renovation brings new granite counters, motion lights, and curved shower rods to add more room. Other new features include a 24-hour business center and Precor equipment and padded floors in the fitness center. A cooked-to-order breakfast and afternoon cocktails are complimentary, as are airport transfers and a daily newspaper. The convention center, the Embarcadero, Seaport Village, and a trolley station are nearby. **Pros:** New bathrooms, upgraded gym, good location. **Cons:** Busy location, wildly varying room rates. ✉601 Pacific Hwy., Embarcadero ☎619/239–2400 or 800/362–2779 ⊕www.embassy-suites. com 🛏337 suites 🛆In-room: refrigerator, dial-up, Wi-Fi. In-hotel: restaurant, room service, bar, pool, gym, bicycles, laundry facilities, laundry service, concierge, airport shuttle, parking (fee), no-smoking rooms ☰AE, D, DC, MC, V.

$$$ 🏨 **Hard Rock Hotel.** Self-billed as a hip playground for rock stars and
Fodor'sChoice people who just want to party like them, the new Hard Rock Hotel
★ is conveniently located near PETCO Park overlooking glimmering San Diego Bay. The interior oozes laid-back sophistication, and guest rooms with cantilever furniture include branded Sleep Like a Rock beds, minibars, flat-screen TVs, and modern baths. At turn-down you get local CDs, rock candy, and Rolling Stone magazine. For the true rock-star experience, choose from one of 17 Rock Star suites, each with individual decor, including one designed by pop group the Black-Eyed Peas. Rande Gerber puts his signature on two bars: the swank Sweetwater Saloon on the ground floor and Moonstone on the fourth-floor pool deck. Restaurants on-site include sushi mecca Nobu, Mary Jane's Coffee Shop, and a Pinkberry frozen yogurt shop. **Pros:** Central location, great scene, luxurious rooms. **Cons:** Pricey drinks, some attitude. ✉207 5th Ave., Gaslamp Quarter ☎ 619/702–3000 or 866/751–7625 ⊕www.hardrockhotelsd.com 🛏244 rooms, 176 suites 🛆 In-room: safe, refrigerator, Ethernet, Wi-Fi. In-hotel: 2 restaurants, room service,

bars, pool, gym, spa, laundry service, concierge, public Internet, public Wi-Fi, parking (fee), no-smoking rooms ☐*AE, D, DC, MC, V.*

$$$ 🏨**Hilton San Diego Gaslamp Quarter.** Step into the modern and sophisticated lobby with its cozy lounge spaces and wood accents, and you'll know this isn't your usual Hilton. Rooms have pillow-top mattresses, down comforters, and free Internet. The 5th Avenue Loft rooms, a boutique hotel within this hotel, are urban retreats with extra-high ceilings, tall windows, Frette linens, and keyed access; some have whirlpool tubs. An outdoor terrace off the New Leaf lounge is furnished like a comfy living room and has a fire pit. And you can't beat the location: the San Diego Trolley whizzes by, the convention center is across the street, and nightlife and restaurants are just outside your door. **Pros:** Good decor, upscale lofts, near restaurants and shops. **Cons:** Noisy area, somewhat gritty. ✉*401 K St., Gaslamp Quarter* ☎*619/231–4040 or 800/445–8667* ⊕*www.sandiegogaslampquarter.hilton.com* ⏴*240 rooms, 13 suites, 30 lofts* ⏶*In-room: safe (some), Ethernet. In-hotel: restaurant, room service, bar, pool, gym, laundry service, concierge, public Wi-Fi, parking (fee), no-smoking rooms* ☐*AE, D, DC, MC, V.*

$$$ 🏨**Hotel Solamar.** For its first entry onto San Diego's hotel scene, the
Fodor'sChoice Kimpton boutique hotel chain redid an old warehouse, hitting the right
★ notes with striking, high style. The lobby features a wall of lighted sea shells against an indigo background. Off to the side, a fireplace lounge offers a complimentary wine hour every afternoon. Guest rooms reflect this urban escape's fun side with polka-dot bed throws, Frette 350-thread-count sheets, and zebra- or leopard-print hotel robes. The flat-screen TVs have DVD/CD players and connect to the Yoga Channel; Wi-Fi is available throughout the hotel. Some rooms offer deep Japanese-style Jacuzzi tubs and some have patios opening onto the pool area, which may get noisy in the evenings—at night, the pool rocks with a rollicking party scene at JBar, lighted by fire pits and illuminated palm trees. Check out the hotel's restaurant, Jsix, which offers a diverse, creative seasonal menu. All this is complemented by Kimpton's excellent service. **Pros:** Great restaurant, good service, upscale rooms. **Cons:** Busy valet parking, bars are crowded on weekends. ✉*435 6th Ave., Gaslamp Quarter* ☎*619/531–8740 or 877/230–0300* ⊕*www.hotelsolamar.com* ⏴*235 rooms, 16 suites* ⏶*In-room: safe, DVD, Wi-Fi. In-hotel: 2 restaurants, room service, bars, pool, gym, laundry service, concierge, public Wi-Fi, parking (fee), pets allowed* ☐*AE, D, DC, MC, V.*

$$$ 🏨**Manchester Grand Hyatt San Diego.** Built primarily for business travelers, this hotel between Seaport Village and the convention center is the largest in San Diego, and its 40- and 33-story towers make it the West Coast's tallest waterfront hotel. The interior combines old-world opulence with California airiness; palm trees pose next to ornate tapestry couches in the light-filled lobby. All the British Regency–style guest rooms have

---

HIGH IN THE SKY

The Manchester Grand Hyatt, designed by architects Skidmore, Owings & Merrill, is the tallest building on the West Coast, at 497 feet. The top floor lounge offers panoramic views for miles.

water views and windows that open and iPod docking stations. Stay in the newer Seaport Tower for more recently updated rooms. The hotel's Business Plan includes access to a desk area and office supplies. The trolley station is one block away, and the Gaslamp's clubs and restaurants are within walking distance. **Pros:** Great views, conference facilities, good location. **Cons:** Very busy, some rooms dated. ✉*1 Market Pl., Embarcadero* ☎*619/232–1234 or 800/233–1234* ⊕*www.manchestergrand.hyatt.com* ⇦*1,625 rooms, 95 suites* ⌂*In-room: safe, refrigerator, dial-up. In-hotel: 3 restaurants, room service, bars, tennis courts, pool, gym, spa, laundry service, concierge, executive floor, parking (fee), no-smoking rooms* ▤*AE, D, DC, MC, V.*

$$$ 🏨**Omni San Diego Hotel.** The product of burgeoning downtown growth, this modern masterpiece occupies the first 21 floors of a 32-story high-rise overlooking PETCO Park baseball stadium. Though built for the business traveler, the hotel attracts a fair share of sports fans (it's connected to the stadium by a sky bridge). The modern lobby is simply stunning; all rooms have windows that open to the breeze, and most have views of the ocean, bay, the downtown skyline, or the PETCO outfield. Pleasantly decorated, rooms include DVD players and soothing sound machines. The pool terrace has a stone fireplace, outdoor dining, and a tanning area. **Pros:** Baseball game views, good location, modern setting. **Cons:** Busy, crowded during baseball season. ✉*675 L St., Gaslamp Quarter* ☎*619/231–6664 or 800/843–6664* ⊕*www.omnisandiegohotel.com* ⇦*478 rooms, 33 suites* ⌂*In-room: safe, DVD, dial-up, Wi-Fi. In-hotel: restaurant, room service, bar, pool, gym, laundry service, concierge, public Wi-Fi, parking (fee), some pets allowed (fee), no-smoking rooms* ▤*AE, D, DC, MC, V.*

$$$ 🏨**San Diego Marriott Hotel and Marina.** This 25-story twin-tower hotel next to the convention center has everything a businessperson—or leisure traveler—could want. As a major site for conventions, the complex can be hectic and impersonal, and the hallways can be noisy. Lending some tranquillity are the lagoon-style pools nestled between cascading waterfalls. The standard rooms are smallish, but pay a bit extra for a room with a balcony overlooking the bay and you can have a serene, sparkling world spread out before you. The fine dining restaurant Molly's and its gourmet shop are worth a visit. Seaport Village and a trolley station are nearby. **Pros:** Great location, many amenities, good restaurant. **Cons:** Small rooms, very busy. ✉*333 W. Harbor Dr., Embarcadero* ☎*619/234–1500 or 800/228–9290* ⊕*www.marriotthotels.com/sandt* ⇦*1,300 rooms, 54 suites* ⌂*In-room: refrigerators (some), dial-up. In-hotel: 2 restaurants, room service, bars, tennis courts, pools, gym, laundry facilities, concierge, executive floor, parking (fee), no-smoking rooms* ▤*AE, D, DC, MC, V.*

$$$

Fodor'sChoice

★

🏨**Westgate Hotel.** A modern high-rise near Horton Plaza hides what must be the most opulent Old World–style hotel in San Diego. The lobby, modeled after the anteroom at Versailles, is done in antiques and Baccarat chandeliers. Rooms are individually furnished with Italian marble counters and bath fixtures with 24-karat-gold overlays. From the ninth floor up the views of the harbor and city are breathtaking, but some views have been obscured by newer buildings. Afternoon tea, with or without champagne, is served in the lobby to the accompaniment of piano and harp music. The San Diego Trolley stops right outside the door. **Pros:** Elegant rooms, grand lobby, near shopping. **Cons:** Formal atmosphere, somewhat gritty neighborhood. ✉ *1055 2nd Ave., Gaslamp Quarter* ☎ *619/238–1818, 800/221–3802* ⊕ *www.westgatehotel.com* ⬚ *223 rooms* ⚏ *In-room: DVD, Ethernet. In-hotel: 2 restaurants, room service, bar, gym, spa, concierge, airport shuttle, parking (fee), no-smoking rooms* ⊟ *AE, D, DC, MC, V.*

> ### HEY BIG SPENDER!
>
> When the Westgate Hotel was built in 1970 for a cost of $14.5 million, it was the most expensive hotel built in the United States to date. Part of that grand sum was spent on antiques such as a $150,000 marble and bronze fireplace from the 1700s, a $50,000 rosewood bombe chest, and assorted Aubusson tapestries and Baccarat crystal chandeliers.

$$ ▦**The Bristol.** Pop art by Peter Max and Andy Warhol on the walls marks the style of this splashy boutique hotel. Rooms are decorated in sleek earthy tones accented with bright colors or stripes on pillows and chairs. They also feature flat-screen TVs and iPod docks, bathrobes, and CD players. The ballroom with a twinkly starlight ceiling is worth a peek. The San Diego Trolley stops right outside at First and Broadway, but beware, the Greyhound bus depot across the street is noisy. **Pros:** Modern rooms, centrally located, good value. **Cons:** Noisy area, somewhat seedy area. ✉ *1055 1st Ave., Downtown* ☎ *619/232–6141 or 888/745–4393* ⊕ *www.thebristolsandiego.com* ⬚ *102 rooms* ⚏ *In-room: Wi-Fi. In-hotel: restaurant, bar, gym, public Wi-Fi, parking (fee), no-smoking rooms* ⊟ *AE, D, DC, MC, V.*

$$ ▦**Courtyard San Diego Downtown.** Marriott took a venerable 1928 bank building and transformed it into a Spanish-style hotel that caters to business travelers. Under a two-story painted ceiling, the marble lobby is a breathtaking architectural space where ornate, numbered teller cages still stand at check-in, separating the lobby from the Lincoln Bar. Rooms are simply furnished and serviceable. There are some Jacuzzi rooms, and the Presidential Suite has a balcony overlooking the bay. **Pros:** Central location, historic building, free HBO. **Cons:** Simple rooms, somewhat seedy area. ✉ *530 Broadway, Downtown* ☎ *619/446–3000 or 800/321–2211* ⊕ *www.marriott.com/sancd* ⬚ *230 rooms, 15 suites* ⚏ *In-room: refrigerator (some), Ethernet. In-hotel: restaurant, room service, bar, gym, laundry facilities, laundry service, concierge, parking (fee), no-smoking rooms* ⊟ *AE, D, DC, MC, V* ⦿CP.

$$ ▦**Holiday Inn San Diego on the Bay.** A December 2007 renovation brought new beds and bath fixtures to this hotel on the Embarcadero, overlooking San Diego Bay. The hotel, made up of three high-rise towers reached by dated elevators, has spacious rooms with balconies and hard-to-beat views. Although the hotel grounds are nice, if fairly sterile, the bay is just across the street and offers boat rides, restaurants, and picturesque walking areas. The hotel is very close to the airport and Amtrak station. The English-style Elephant and Castle Pub is a great place for food, drink, and meeting people. **Pros:** Large rooms, great

views. **Cons:** Not centrally located. ✉*1355 N. Harbor Dr., Embarcadero* ☎*619/232–3861 or 800/877–8920* ⊕*www.holiday-inn.com* ⤴*600 rooms, 10 suites* ⚒*In-room: Wi-Fi. In-hotel: 3 restaurants, room service, bar, pool, gym, laundry facilities, public Wi-Fi, airport shuttle, parking (fee), no-smoking rooms* ▭*AE, D, DC, MC, V.*

$$ 🏨**Horton Grand Hotel & Suites.** A Victorian confection, the Horton Grand comprises two 1880s hotels moved brick by brick from nearby locations and fit together. The delightfully retro rooms are furnished with period antiques, ceiling fans, and gas-burning fireplaces. The choicest rooms overlook a garden courtyard that twinkles with miniature lights. The hotel is a charmer, but service can be erratic. **Pros:** Near shops and restaurants, balconies, historic property. **Cons:** Spotty service, area sometimes noisy. ✉*311 Island Ave., Gaslamp Quarter* ☎*619/544–1886 or 800/542–1886* ⊕*www.hortongrand.com* ⤴*108 rooms, 24 suites* ⚒*In-room: refrigerator (some), Wi-Fi. In-hotel: restaurant, bar, parking (fee), no-smoking rooms* ▭*AE, DC, MC, V.*

$$ 🏨**Little Italy Inn.** This Old World–style bed-and-breakfast, in a renovated 1910 property, has 23 unique, well-appointed rooms. Wide hallways lead to rooms with luxury touches like wood floors, whirlpool tubs, plush robes, and free bottles of water. The cafés, boutiques, and bakeries of Little Italy are steps away, though traffic is loud getting onto the nearby freeway ramp. The lowest-price rooms have shared baths; DVD players, irons, ironing boards, hair dryers, and refrigerators are available upon request. **Pros:** Good location, historic property, free HBO. **Cons:** Some shared baths, no parking, loud traffic area. ✉*505 W. Grape St., Little Italy* ☎*619/230–1600 or 800/518–9930* ⊕*www. littleitalyinn.com* ⤴*23 rooms* ⚒*In-room: safe, Wi-Fi. In-hotel: No elevator, public Wi-Fi, no smoking rooms* ▭*AE, D, MC, V* ⏷*CP.*

$$ 🏨**Porto Vista Hotel & Suites.** A $15 million renovation turned this former budget motel into a contemporary hotel with two additional buildings, a restaurant and lounge with a view of the city and harbor, a business center, and a fitness center with an 18-person whirlpool. Still, there's a down-at-heels edge to the lobby furniture. All rooms are outfitted with pillowtop beds, many have balconies with views, and some suites offer mini-kitchens. The hotel is in a relatively quiet location. **Pros:** New decor and fitness center. **Cons:** Overpriced. ✉*1835 Columbia St., Little Italy* ☎*619/544–0164 or 800/800–8000* ⊕*www.portovistasandiego.com* ⤴*193 rooms* ⚒*In-room: refrigerator (some) kitchen (some), Wi-Fi. In-hotel: restaurant, room service, laundry facilities, airport shuttle, parking (fee), no-smoking rooms* ▭*AE, D, DC, MC, V* ⏷*CP.*

$$ 🏨**Ramada Inn Gaslamp/Convention Center.** Found on the northern end of the Gaslamp, this historic, 10-story building was San Diego's tallest when it opened in 1913. It's close to restaurants, nightclubs, and shops on 4th and 5th avenues, but you escape the racket when you enter the lobby, adorned with overstuffed chairs and a big crystal chandelier. Good value and location make up for the small rooms, which were upgraded in 2007 with new beds and furnishings. The suites come with robes, coffeemakers, and in some cases hot tubs and big-screen TVs. **Pros:** Historic building, central location. **Cons:** Small rooms, in the middle of bars. ⊠*830 6th Ave., Gaslamp Quarter* ☎*619/531–8877 or 800/664–4400* ⊕*www.stjameshotel.com* ➳*95 rooms, 4 suites* ⌂*In-room: Ethernet. In-hotel: restaurant, room service, parking (fee), no-smoking rooms* ⊟*AE, D, DC, MC, V.*

$$ 🏨**San Diego Marriott Gaslamp Quarter.** This 22-story hotel is in the midst of all the Gaslamp's restaurants and boutiques, a short walk to the trolley station, convention center, and PETCO Park. It has sweeping views of downtown and the waterfront as well as right into the ballpark; be sure to visit Altitude, the rooftop bar, for the panorama. Rooms offer luxury linens, 27-inch flat-screen TVs, a laptop safe, and gourmet coffee. There's wireless Internet throughout. The restaurant, Soleil @ K, emphasizes simply prepared fresh produce and meats. **Pros:** Good views, modern decor, central location. **Cons:** Rooftop bar can get rowdy. ⊠*660 K St., Gaslamp Quarter* ☎*619/696–0234* ⊕*www. sandiegogaslamphotel.com* ➳*291 rooms, 15 suites* ⌂*In-room: safe, refrigerator, Ethernet. In-hotel: restaurant, room service, bars, gym, concierge, executive floors, public Wi-Fi, parking (fee)* ⊟*AE, D, DC, MC, V.*

$$ 🏨**The Sofia Hotel.** A major remodeling in 2006 transformed the former
Fodor's Choice Pickwick into a practical and stylish downtown destination. The Sofia's rooms are small, but clever details help guests feel looked after; rooms feature pillow-top mattresses, flat-screen TVs, contemporary bath fixtures, and a mini-refrigerator and microwave for doggie-bag leftovers. Green features include motion-sensor heating and light controls. The four slightly larger VIP suites offer an extra sitting area and soaking tubs in the bathrooms. Weary travelers will benefit from spending time in the Zen-like yoga studio or getting an in-room massage. The fireside lobby invites guests to curl up with a book or chat with other visitors. The hotel is a short walk from the convention center, Gaslamp District, and Horton Plaza shopping. **Pros:** Upscale room amenities, historic building, near shops and restaurants. **Cons:** Next to bus station, busy area. ⊠*150 W. Broadway, Downtown* ☎*800/826–0009* ⊕*www. thesofiahotel.com* ➳*212 rooms, 4 suites* ⌂*In-room: safe, refrigerator, Ethernet, Wi-Fi. In-hotel: restaurant, gym, laundry service, concierge, public Internet, public Wi-Fi, parking (fee), some pets allowed (fee), no-smoking rooms* ⊟*AE, D, DC, MC, V.*

$ 🏨**500 West.** An $8 million renovation in 2004 transformed San Diego's historic 1924 Armed Services YMCA Building into this hip, urban boutique hotel. Catering to the style-conscious, the hotel has tiny rooms big on quality, with flat-screen TVs, platform beds, Michael Graves–designed lighting, and a postmodern decor. It has mostly single rooms and very few doubles, and all rooms share detached private bathrooms. The Grand Central Café serves breakfast and lunch daily, and the hotel lobby has wireless Internet. Weekly tenants can use a gourmet kitchen equipped with a Viking range and Sub-Zero fridge; there's also a common area with tables and vending machines. The YMCA gym is still downstairs, and may account for the sometimes funny smell in the lobby; guests can use it for $5 a day or $15 a week. **Pros:** Near shops and restaurants, modern room decor, kitchen. **Cons:** Small rooms, few double rooms, above YMCA. ⊠*500 W. Broadway, Downtown*

☎619/234–5252 or 866/500–7533 ⊕*www.500westhotel.com* ☞*259 rooms* ⚙*In-room: Wi-Fi. In-hotel: restaurant, bar, gym, laundry facilities, public Wi-Fi.* ▤*MC, V.*

$ 🏨**Gaslamp Plaza Suites.** On the National Register of Historic Places, this 11-story structure a block from Horton Plaza was built in 1913 as one of San Diego's first "skyscrapers." The public areas have old marble, brass, and mosaics. Although most rooms are rather small, they are well decorated with dark-wood furnishings that give the hotel an elegant flair. You can enjoy the view and a complimentary Continental breakfast on the rooftop terrace. Book ahead if you're visiting in summer. **Pros:** Historic building, good location, well priced. **Cons:** Books up early, smallish rooms. ✉*520 E St., Gaslamp Quarter* ☎619/232–9500 or 800/874–8770 ⊕*www.gaslampplaza.com* ☞*12 rooms, 52 suites* ⚙*In-room: refrigerator, DVD. In-hotel: restaurant, bar, laundry service, parking (fee), no smoking rooms* ▤*AE, D, DC, MC, V* ▢*CP.*

¢ 🏨**Hotel Occidental.** A block from Balboa Park, this is a bare-bones place, but a heck of a deal. All rooms are done in pale colors with bright accents and have kitchenettes with refrigerators and microwaves, flat-screen TVs, and DVD players; there's also a DVD movie library. Parking is limited, but public transit is nearby. Complimentary Continental breakfast is served in the café from 7 to 11 AM daily. Save your pennies and book a room with no (that is, with a shared) bathroom for only $59 single, $69 double. **Pros:** Kitchenettes, free local calls and breakfast, near park. **Cons:** Plain rooms, limited parking. ✉*410 Elm St., Downtown* ☎619/232–1336 or 800/205–9897 ⊕*www.hoteloccidental-sandiego.com* ☞*52 rooms, 2 suites* ⚙*In-room: safe, kitchen, refrigerator, DVD, Wi-Fi. In-hotel: no elevator, laundry facilities, public Wi-Fi* ▤*AE, MC, V.*

HARBOR & SHELTER ISLANDS AND POINT LOMA

$$$ 🏨**Sheraton San Diego Hotel & Marina.** Of this property's two high-rises, the smaller, more intimate Bay Tower has larger rooms, with separate areas suitable for business entertaining; the Marina Tower has better sports facilities. Rooms throughout are decorated with plush, contemporary furnishings. Views from the upper floors of both sections are superb, but because the Bay Tower is closer to the water it has fine outlooks from the lower floors, too. The Club and executive level offers free Continental breakfast and afternoon appetizers, and free high-speed Internet access. **Pros:** Water views, near marina, near airport. **Cons:** Not centrally located. ✉*1380 Harbor Island Dr., Harbor Island* ☎619/291–2900 or 888/625–5144 ⊕*www.sheraton.com* ☞*1,044 rooms, 50 suites* ⚙*In-room: safe, Ethernet. In-hotel: 3 restaurants, room service, bars, tennis courts, pools, gym, bicycles, laundry service, concierge, executive floor, public Wi-Fi, airport shuttle, parking (fee), no-smoking rooms* ▤*AE, D, DC, MC, V.*

$$ 🏨**Bay Club Hotel & Marina.** Rooms in this appealing low-rise Shelter Island property are large, light, and furnished with rattan tables and chairs and Polynesian tapestries; all have balconies with views of either the bay or the marina. A buffet breakfast and shuttle service to and

from the airport or Amtrak station are included. **Pros:** Water views, large rooms, good service. **Cons:** Not centrally located, somewhat dated rooms. ✉*2131 Shelter Island Dr., Shelter Island* ☎*619/224–8888 or 800/672–0800* ⊕*www.bayclubhotel.com* ➾*95 rooms, 10 suites* ⌂*In-room: safe, refrigerator, Wi-Fi. In-hotel: restaurant, room service, bar, pool, gym, concierge, airport shuttle, parking (fee), public Wi-Fi, no-smoking rooms* ▤*AE, D, DC, MC, V* ⌺*BP.*

$$ 🖼**Best Western Island Palms Hotel & Marina.** This waterfront inn, with an airy lobby brightened by skylights, a waterfall, and a Thai theme expressed in gilt carvings and golden statues, is a good choice if you have a boat to dock: the adjacent marina has guest slips. Both harbor- and marina-view rooms are available. Standard accommodations are average size; if you're traveling with family or more than one friend, the two-bedroom suites with kitchens are a good deal. The hotel will ferry guests to the cruise ship terminal and train station. **Pros:** Near water, great rooms views. **Cons:** Not centrally located, somewhat confusing area, average-size rooms. ✉*2051 Shelter Island Dr., Shelter Island* ☎*619/222–0561 or 800/345–9995* ⊕*www.islandpalms.com* ➾*114 rooms, 60 suites* ⌂*In-room: kitchen (some), refrigerator, Wi-Fi. In-hotel: restaurant, bar, tennis courts, pools, gym, bicycles, laundry service, parking (no fee), public Wi-Fi, no-smoking rooms* ▤*AE, D, DC, MC, V.*

$$ 🖼**Holiday Inn Express–SeaWorld Area.** In Point Loma near the West Mission Bay exit off I–8, this is a surprisingly cute and quiet lodging option despite proximity to bustling traffic. The three-story building is only about a half-mile from both SeaWorld and Mission Bay. Geared towards leisure travelers, rooms offer firm and soft pillows, and include standard sleeper sofas. Hot buffet breakfast is included. **Pros:** Near SeaWorld, free breakfast, good service. **Cons:** Not a scenic area, somewhat hard to find. ✉*3950 Jupiter St., Sports Arena* ☎*619/226–8000 or 800/320–0208* ⊕*www.hiexpress.com* ➾*71 rooms, 2 suites* ⌂*In-room: refrigerator, Ethernet. In-hotel: pool, laundry facilities, laundry service, public Wi-Fi, parking (no fee), no-smoking rooms* ▤*AE, D, DC, MC, V* ⌺*CP.*

$$ 🖼**Humphrey's Half Moon Inn & Suites.** This sprawling South Seas–style resort has grassy open areas with palms and tiki torches. A $20 million upgrade in early 2008 put new bedding, carpeting, flat-screen TVs, microwaves, and granite vanities in guest rooms. The rooms, some with kitchens and some with yacht-harbor or bay views, are decorated in a subtle natural color scheme. The Grand Marina Suite can accommodate up to eight in 1,000 square feet with a full kitchen. Locals throng to Humphrey's for the brunch, jazz lounge, and the outdoor jazz and pop concerts from May through October. **Pros:** Water views, near marina, nightlife on property. **Cons:** Vast property, not centrally located. ✉*2303 Shelter Island Dr., Shelter Island* ☎*619/224–3411 or 800/542–7400* ⊕*www.halfmooninn.com* ➾*128 rooms, 54 suites* ⌂*In-room: safe, kitchen (some), refrigerator, Ethernet, dial-up. In-hotel: restaurant, room service, bar, pool, gym, bicycles, no elevator, laundry facilities, airport shuttle, parking (fee), no-smoking rooms.* ▤*AE, D, DC, MC, V.*

CLOSE UP

Family-Friendly Hotels

Got kids in tow? San Diego is designed for family fun; the year-round sunny, warm weather ensures lots of play days. The focus is on outdoor activities, such as surfing or swimming, but be sure to spend a day at Balboa Park's gardens, museums, and IMAX theater. Many hotels let kids under 18 stay free—just ask. And check into kids' activity programs, family-size suites, in-room Nintendo, or kitchenettes. Shop around for hotel packages, which often include tickets to local attractions.

Some of the high-end properties give kids the special treatment with children's programs; most occur in summer, some year-round. The famous **Hotel Del Coronado** has tons of activities, from surfing lessons, treasure hunts, and kayak tours to making sand candles on the resort's white-sand beach. The **Loews Coro-**

nado Bay Resort has welcome gifts for children, a kids-only pool, a game library, and special menus. Some recreational fun is offered seasonally, such as sunset sails and gondola rides. And kids can bring their pets.

Across the bay, resorts on family-friendly Mission Bay cater to young ones. The **Hilton San Diego Resort** holds a summer Kid's Kamp (ages 5–12, $10 per child per hour) with koi fish feeding, sand-castle building, and scavenger hunts. There's a special children's wading pool, a lawn croquet course, a sand volleyball court, and plenty of water-sport rentals, paddle boats, and Jet Skis. At the **Lodge at Torrey Pines'** library, kids over age 12 can play pool or watch movies borrowed from the concierge; it's open from 8 AM until 11 PM.

—Lenore Greiner

$$ 🏨 **Kona Kai Resort.** This 11-acre property blends Spanish and Mediterranean styles. The spacious and light-filled lobby, with its neoclassical end tables, velvet sofas, and Oriental carpets over faded terra-cotta tiles, opens onto a lush esplanade that overlooks the hotel's adjacent marina. The rooms are well appointed, if a bit small, though most have balconies and look out onto either the marina or San Diego Bay. The attractive hotel is popular for business meetings. In summer, a two- to four-night minimum stay might be in effect. **Pros:** Quiet area, near marina, water views. **Cons:** Not centrally located, small rooms. ✉*1551 Shelter Island Dr., Shelter Island* ☎619/221–8000 or 800/566–2524 ⊕*www.resortkonakai.com* ☞*129 rooms, 5 suites* ₺*In-room: refrigerator, Wi-Fi. In-hotel: restaurant, room service, bar, tennis courts, pools, gym, spa, beachfront, bicycles, public Wi-Fi, airport shuttle, parking (fee), no-smoking rooms* ▤*AE, D, DC, MC, V.*

$$ 🏨 **The Pearl Hotel.** This previously vintage motel received a makeover, turning it into a retro-chic beach bungalow, decorated with kitschy lamps and original art by local children. Most rooms only have one bed, but contain amenities like plasma-screen TVs and Roku Soundbridge Internet radio; DVD players are available for rent. On Wednesday nights movies are shown on the back wall of the kidney-shaped pool. **Pros:** Near marina, restaurant on-site (dinner only). **Cons:** Not centrally located, one bed in rooms. ✉*1410 Rosecrans St., Point Loma* ☎877/732–7573 ⊕*www.thepearlsd.com* ☞*23 rooms* ₺*In-room:*

Wi-Fi. In-hotel: restaurant, bar, pool, bicycles, no elevator, parking (fee), public Wi-Fi, no-smoking rooms ☰AE, D, DC, MC, V.

$$ 📷**Vagabond Inn–Point Loma.** This two-story budget motel is safe, clean, and comfortable, close to the airport, yacht clubs, and Cabrillo National Monument—and the popular Point Loma Seafoods is next door. A daily newspaper and Continental breakfast are included. **Pros:** Near airport and restaurants. **Cons:** Few amenities, spotty service. ✉*1325 Scott St., Point Loma* ☎*619/224–3371 or 800/522–1555* ⊕*www.vagabondinn.com* 🛏*40 rooms* ♿*In-room: kitchen (some), refrigerator (some). In-hotel: pool, no elevator, parking (no fee), no-smoking rooms* ☰*AE, D, DC, MC, V* ⦿*CP.*

$ 📷**Ramada Limited San Diego Airport.** The location is convenient, although on a busy street, and the simply decorated rooms with bay views are quite a deal. Continental breakfast, daily newspaper, and local calls are complimentary. There's a heated pool and a bay-view bar with billiards. **Pros:** Quiet area, near airport, free breakfast. **Cons:** Few amenities, little nightlife in area. ✉*1403 Rosecrans St., Point Loma* ☎*619/225–9461 or 888/298–2054* ⊕*www.ramada.com* 🛏*80 rooms* ♿*In-room: refrigerator. In-hotel: bar, pool, laundry facilities, public Wi-Fi, airport shuttle, parking (no fee), no-smoking rooms* ☰*AE, D, DC, MC, V* ⦿*CP.*

LA JOLLA

$$$$ 📷**Hotel Parisi.** A Zen-like peace welcomes you in the lobby, which has a skylighted fountain and is filled with Asian art. The studio-style suites are decorated according to the principles of feng shui; you can order a massage, a yoga session, or the on-staff psychologist from room service. Favored by celebrities, the hushed, earth-tone suites have flat-screen TVs, granite bathrooms, Frette linens, and ergonomic tubs. The rooms are set back enough from the street noise, but in the ocean-view suites you have to look over buildings across the street to view the Pacific. A European buffet breakfast is served daily. **Pros:** Upscale amenities, modern decor, centrally located. **Cons:** One-room "suites," snooty staff. ✉*1111 Prospect St.* ☎*858/454–1511* ⊕*www.hotelparisi.com* 🛏*24 suites* ♿*In-room: safe, DVD, Wi-Fi. In-hotel: room service, parking (fee), no-smoking rooms* ☰*AE, D, MC, V* ⦿*CP.*

$$$$ 📷**La Valencia.** This pink Spanish-Mediterranean confection drew Hollywood film stars in the 1930s and '40s with its setting and views of La Jolla Cove. Many rooms, although small, have a recently updated black, white, and neutral color scheme with colorful accents, mod brocade-pattern chairs, and flat-screen TVs. The personal attention provided by the staff, as well as the plush robes and grand bathrooms, make the stay even more pleasurable. The hotel is right in the middle of the shops and restaurants of La Jolla village. Rates are lower if you're willing to look out on the village rather than the ocean. Be sure to have a cocktail while gazing at the ocean in Le Sala and stroll the tiered gardens in back. **Pros:** Upscale rooms, views, near beach. **Cons:** Expensive, lots of traffic. ✉*1132 Prospect St.* ☎*858/454–0771 or 800/451–0772* ⊕*www.lavalencia.com* 🛏*93 rooms,10 suites, 15 villas* ♿*In-room: safe, DVD, Wi-Fi. In-hotel: 3 restaurants, room service,*

bar, pool, gym, laundry service, concierge, parking (fee), no-smoking rooms ⊟*AE, D, MC, V.*

$$$$ 🏨**Lodge at Torrey Pines.** This beautiful Craftsman-style lodge sits on a
FodorśChoice bluff between La Jolla and Del Mar and commands a coastal view. You
★ know you're in for a different sort of experience when you see the Scottish kilted doorman. The warm and understated rooms are spacious and furnished with antiques and reproduction turn-of-the-20th-century pieces. The service is excellent, and the restaurant, A. R. Valentien (named after a San Diego plein-air artist of the early 1900s), serves fine California cuisine. Beyond the grounds are the Torrey Pines Golf Course and scenic trails that lead to the Torrey Pines State Beach and Reserve. The village of La Jolla is a 10-minute drive away. **Pros:** Upscale rooms, good service, near golf. **Cons:** Not centrally located, expensive. ✉*11480 N. Torrey Pines Rd.* ☎*858/453–4420 or 800/995–4507* ⊕*www.lodgetorreypines.com* ➼*164 rooms, 6 suites* ♿*In-room: safe, kitchen (some), Ethernet. In-hotel: 2 restaurants, bars, golf course, pool, gym, spa, public Wi-Fi, parking (fee), no-smoking rooms* ⊟*AE, D, DC, MC, V.*

$$$$ 🏨**Scripps Inn.** You'd be wise to make reservations well in advance for this small, quiet inn tucked away on Coast Boulevard; its popularity with repeat visitors ensures that it's booked year-round. Lower weekly and monthly rates (not available in summer) make it attractive to long-term guests. Rooms are done in a beige beachy style, with plantation shutters, and all have ocean views; some have fireplaces and flat-screen TVs. Continental breakfast is served in the lobby each morning. **Pros:** Beach access, intimate, free parking. **Cons:** Spotty service, busy area. ✉*555 S. Coast Blvd.* ☎*858/454–3391* ⊕*www.jcresorts.com* ➼*7 rooms, 7 suites* ♿*In-room: safe, kitchen (some), DVD (some), Wi-Fi. In-hotel: no elevator, parking (no fee), no-smoking rooms* ⊟*AE, D, DC, MC, V* ⦿*CP.*

$$$ 🏨**Estancia La Jolla Hotel & Spa.** La Jolla's newest resort was once the site of a famous equestrian ranch, Blackhorse Farms, where Thoroughbreds were trained. This hotel has a rustic elegance, rambling California rancho–style architecture, and courtyards with bubbling fountains. Rooms have marble baths and come with robes and slippers and 24-hour room service. The resort offers free high-speed and wireless Internet, a pool with private cabanas, and a spa where guests can be pampered with an outdoor massage in a private garden of eucalyptus, citrus, and lavender. Besides spa packages, the resort offers golf getaways at the nearby Torrey Pines Golf Course. **Pros:** Upscale rooms, spa, landscaped grounds. **Cons:** Spotty service, not centrally located. ✉*9700 N. Torrey Pines Rd.* ☎*858/550–1000 or 877/437–8262* ⊕*www.estancialajolla.com* ➼*200 rooms, 10 suites* ♿*In-room: safe, Wi-Fi. In-hotel: 3 restaurants, room service, bar, pool, gym, spa, laundry service, concierge, public Wi-Fi, parking (fee), no-smoking rooms* ⊟*AE, D, MC, V* ⦿*CP.*

$$$ 🏨**Grande Colonial.** This white wedding cake–style hotel has ocean views
FodorśChoice and is in the heart of La Jolla village. Built in 1913 and expanded and
★ redesigned in 1925–26, the Colonial is graced with charming European details: chandeliers, a marble hearth, mahogany railings, oak furnishings, and French doors. In 2007, 18 club-level suites that include

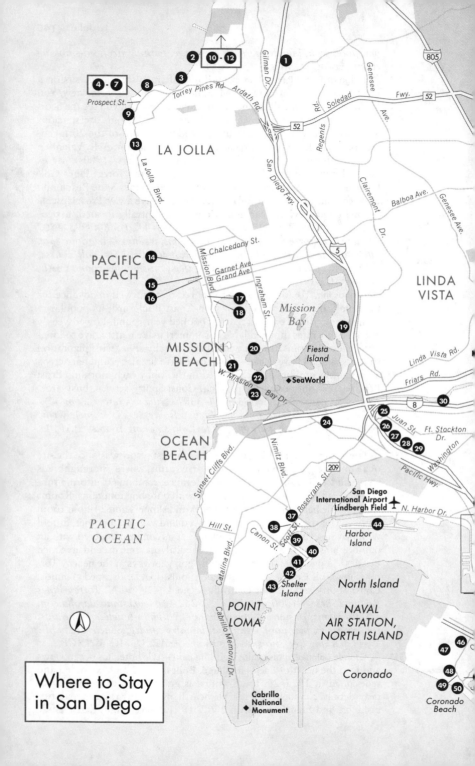

Where to Stay
in San Diego

3

LODGING ALTERNATIVES

APARTMENT RENTALS

If you're planning an extended stay or need lodgings for four or more people, consider an apartment rental. Oakwood Apartments rents comfortable furnished apartments in the Mission Valley, La Jolla, downtown, Carmel Valley, Chula Vista, and Coronado areas with maid service and linens; there's a one-week to 30-day minimum stay depending on locations. Several hotels also offer special weekly and monthly rates, especially in the beach communities. Rental apartments and condominiums are available through realtors who specialize in Mission Beach, Pacific Beach, La Jolla's Golden Triangle–University City area, Carlsbad, and Escondido. In addition, there are six Residence Inns by Marriott in San Diego; these sometimes offer good value for families traveling on weekends.

International Agents **Hideaways International** (☎603/430–4433 or 800/843–4433 ⊕ www.hideaways.com); annual membership $185. **Vacation Home Rentals Worldwide** (☎201/767–9393 or 800/633–3284 ⊕ www.vhrww.com).

Local Agents **Oakwood Apartments** (☎800/888–0808 ⊕ www.oakwood.com). **Penny Realty** (☎800/748–6704 ⊕ www.missionbeach.com). **San Diego Vacation Rentals** (☎800/222–8281 ⊕ www.sdvr.com).

BED & BREAKFASTS

San Diego is known more for its resorts and chain properties, but the city has several bed-and-breakfasts, most of which are in private homes and are well maintained and accommodating. Historic Julian, in the mountains east of San Diego, has many (see Chapter 7). The San Diego Bed & Breakfast Guild lists a number of high-quality member inns. The Bed & Breakfast Directory for San Diego, maintained by a guild member, covers San Diego County.

Reservation Services **Bed & Breakfast Directory for San Diego** (☎800/619–7666 ⊕ www.sandiegobandbguild.com). **San Diego Bed & Breakfast Guild** (☎619/523–1300 or 800/619–7666 ⊕ www.bandbguildsandiego.org). **Julian Bed and Breakfast Guild** (☎888/765–4333 ⊕ www.julianbnbguild.com).

HOME EXCHANGES

If you would like to exchange your home for someone else's, join a home-exchange organization, which will send you its listings of available exchanges, regularly updated, for a year and will include your own listing in at least one of them. It's up to you to make specific arrangements.

Exchange Clubs **HomeLink USA** (☎954/566–2687 or 800/638–3841 ⊕ www.homelink.org); $90 yearly for a listing and online access; $50 additional to receive directories. **Intervac U.S.** (☎800/756–4663 ⊕ www.intervacus.com); $126 yearly for a listing, online access, and a catalog; $79 without catalog.

complimentary valet parking, luxury bath products, snack baskets, and full breakfast were added in areas called the Little Hotel by the Sea and Garden Terrace Suites done in cheerful tones of tangerine and lime. The hotel's restaurant, Nine-Ten, run by chef Jason Knibb, is well liked by locals for its fresh, seasonal California cuisine. **Pros:** Near shopping, near beach, superb restaurant. **Cons:** Somewhat busy street. ✉ *910 Prospect St.* ☎ *858/454–2181 or 800/826–1278* ⊕ *www.thegrandecolonial.com* ⇌ *52 rooms, 41 suites* ⇘ *In-room: safe, kitchen (some), Wi-Fi. In-hotel: restaurant, room service, bar, pool, concierge, parking (fee), no-smoking rooms* ⊟ *AE, D, DC, MC, V.*

3

$$$ ⊡**Hilton La Jolla Torrey Pines.** The hotel blends discreetly into the Torrey Pines cliff top, overlooking the Pacific Ocean and the 18th hole of the Torrey Pines Golf Course, site of the 2008 U.S. Open. Oversize accommodations are simple but elegant; most have balconies or terraces. The menu at the hotel's restaurant, the Torreyana Grille, changes with the seasons. **Pros:** Ocean view, near golf, large rooms. **Cons:** Not centrally located. ✉ *10950 N. Torrey Pines Rd.* ☎ *858/558–1500 or 800/774–1500* ⊕ *www.hilton.com* ⇌ *382 rooms, 12 suites* ⇘ *In-room: safe, Wi-Fi. In-hotel: restaurant, room service, bars, tennis courts, pool, gym, laundry service, concierge, public Wi-Fi, parking (fee), no-smoking rooms* ⊟ *AE, D, DC, MC, V.*

$$$ ⊡**Hotel La Jolla.** Rooms will have a modern beach feel, including high-end bedding, new beds, data ports for laptops, and flat-screen TVs thanks to a major renovation beginning in fall 2008. The ocean-view restaurant Clay's on the top floor serves seasonal California cuisine and hosts jazz artists, and the happy hours are a scene. **Pros:** Water views, large rooms, centrally located. **Cons:** On busy intersection, ongoing renovations. ✉ *7955 La Jolla Shores Dr.* ☎ *800/666–0261* ⊕ *www. hotellajolla.com* ⇌ *104 rooms, 4 suites In-room: safe, DVD, Wi-Fi. In-hotel: restaurant, room service, bar, concierge, parking (fee), no-smoking rooms* ⊟ *AE, D, MC, V* ⦿*CP.*

$$$ ⊡**Hyatt Regency La Jolla.** The Hyatt is in the Golden Triangle area, about 10 minutes from the beach and the village of La Jolla. The post-modern design of architect Michael Graves's striking lobby continues in the spacious rooms, where warm cherrywood furnishings contrast with austere gray closets. Fluffy down comforters and cushy chairs and couches make you feel right at home, though, and business travelers appreciate the endless array of office and in-room services. The hotel's four trendy restaurants include Cafe Japengo. Rates are lowest on weekends. **Pros:** Many restaurants, modern rooms, upscale amenities. **Cons:** Busy hotel, not centrally located. ✉ *Aventine Center, 3777 La Jolla Village Dr.* ☎ *858/552–1234 or 800/233–1234* ⊕ *www.hyatt. com* ⇌ *419 rooms, 20 suites* ⇘ *In-room: safe, Ethernet, Wi-Fi. In-hotel: 4 restaurants, room service, bars, tennis courts, pool, gym, concierge, laundry service, parking (fee), no-smoking rooms* ⊟ *AE, D, DC, MC, V.*

$$$ ⊡**La Jolla Inn.** One block from the beach and near some of the best shops and restaurants, this European-style inn with a delightful staff sits in a prime spot in the village of La Jolla. Many rooms have sweeping ocean views from their balconies; one spectacular penthouse suite

faces the ocean, the other the village. Enjoy the delicious complimentary Continental breakfast in your room or on the upstairs sundeck. **Pros:** Near beach, good service, free parking. **Cons:** Busy area, dated rooms. ✉*1110 Prospect St.* ☎*858/454–0133 or 888/855–7829* ⊕*www.lajollainn.com* ⬦*21 rooms, 2 suites* ⬦*In-room: kitchen (some), refrigerator, Ethernet, Wi-Fi. In-hotel: no elevator, laundry facilities, laundry service, parking (no fee), no-smoking rooms* ☰*AE, D, DC, MC, V* ⍾*CP.*

WORD OF MOUTH

"There are several different areas to stay in so you should decide that first (La Jolla, Mission Bay, Downtown, Coronado, UTC-Golden Triangle, Hotel Circle). In my opinion La Jolla is the nicest area to stay in (but probably the most expensive and it can be difficult to get into and out of the area) while the Hotel Circle area is the least desirable (nothing but streets lined with chain hotels)."

—saps

$$$ 🛏 **La Jolla Shores Hotel.** One of the few San Diego hotels actually on the beach, La Jolla Shores is located at La Jolla Beach and Tennis Club. There's a great beach scene here: you can stroll past launching kayakers, scuba divers, and locals walking their dogs, and you may even catch a swimsuit fashion shoot. Reflecting San Diego's Spanish past, the hotel's palms, fountains, red-tile roofs, and Mexican tile work lend character to the low-lying compound, which could use some interior updating. A $1.4 million room renovation in early 2008 lends a Tommy Bahama theme with new bedding, wall coverings, and flat-screen TVs to the beachfront and coastal-view rooms. Tennis lessons are available. **Pros:** On beach, great views, quiet area. **Cons:** Not centrally located, unrenovated rooms are dated. ✉*8110 Camino del Oro* ☎*858/459–8271 or 866/782–7979* ⊕*www.ljshoreshotel.com* ⬦*127 rooms, 1 suite* ⬦*In-room: kitchen (some), refrigerator, Ethernet. In-hotel: restaurant, room service, bar, tennis courts, pool, gym, beachfront, laundry service, parking (fee), no-smoking rooms* ☰*AE, D, DC, MC, V.*

$$ 🛏 **Holiday Inn Express–La Jolla.** Many rooms at this modest property in the southern section of La Jolla are remarkably large, with huge closets. In 2007 the hotel lobby and rooms received new decor, including beds, furniture, and floor coverings. It's not in the heart of La Jolla, but this is a good value for families who want to stay in La Jolla and still have a few dollars left over for shopping and dining. Continental breakfast is included. **Pros:** Large rooms, recent upgrades, good value. **Cons:** Not centrally located, pricey for a chain hotel. ✉*6705 La Jolla Blvd.* ☎*858/454–7101 or 800/451–0358* ⊕*www.hiexpress. com* ⬦*57 rooms, 15 suites* ⬦*In-room: kitchen (some), refrigerator, dial-up. In-hotel: pool, laundry service, parking (no fee), no-smoking rooms* ☰*AE, D, DC, MC, V* ⍾*CP.*

$ 🛏 **La Jolla Cove Suites.** It may lack the charm of some properties in this exclusive area, but this motel with studios and suites (some with spacious oceanfront balconies) gives its guests the same first-class views of La Jolla Cove at lower rates. The beach is across the street and down a short cliff, and snorkelers and divers can take advantage of lockers and outdoor showers. Continental breakfast is served in the sunroom. The underground lot is also a bonus in a section of town where a parking spot is a prime commodity. **Pros:** Good value, ocean views, some large rooms. **Cons:** Dated rooms, busy street. ⊠*1155 Coast Blvd.* ☎*858/459–2621 or 800/248–2683* ⊕*www.lajollacove. com* ⇆*25 rooms, 90 suites* &*In-room: no a/c (some), safe, kitchen (some), Wi-Fi. In-hotel: pool, laundry service, parking (fee), some pets allowed (fee), no-smoking rooms* ⊟*AE, D, DC, MC, V* |⊙|*CP.*

MISSION BAY & THE BEACHES

$$$$ ⊞**Tower23.** A neo-modern masterpiece with a beachy vibe, this 2005-vintage boutique hotel is a San Diego rarity, the first beachfront hotel to be built in the last 10 years. Its namesake is a lifeguard tower that gets repositioned up and down the beach, so don't look for it out front. Tower23 caters to surfer dudes and babes alike, but be aware that the service of its youthful staff can be spotty. (surf's up?) Rooms gleam in seawater-blues, sand, and moss-green with teak furnishings; the suites feature Jacuzzi tubs and step-in rain showers. You get all the toys here: high-definition, flat-screen TVs with Bose concert sound, DVD players, XBox video games, two-line cordless phones, and free Wi-Fi that reaches to the beach. All rooms have balconies and patios. Catch the sunset at the indoor–outdoor Tower Bar with its tiny sushi bar or on the Tower Deck with a fire pit. The pool, alas, is only ornamental, but you do have the ocean. The restaurant, JRDN, offers outdoor dining and cutting-edge, expensive cuisine. **Pros:** Beach views, good location, hip decor. **Cons:** Spotty service, busy area. ⊠*723 Felspar St., Pacific Beach* ☎*866/869–3723* ⊕*www.tower23hotel.com* ⇆*38 rooms, 6 suites* &*In-room: safe, DVD, Wi-Fi. In-hotel: restaurant, room service, bar, beachfront, laundry service, concierge, public Wi-Fi, parking (fee), no-smoking rooms, some pets allowed (fee)* ⊟*AE, D, MC, V.*

$$$ ⊞**Catamaran Resort Hotel.** Exotic macaw parrots perch in the lush
Fodor'sChoice   lobby of this appealing hotel on Mission Bay. Tiki torches light the
★   way through grounds thick with tropical foliage to the six two-story buildings and the 14-story high-rise. The South Seas theme continues in the room design, while the Catamaran Spa, where the almost 10,000-square-feet facilities are devoted to treatments such as Lomi Lomi massage and seaweed body wraps has an Asian decor accented by beautiful mosaics, Buddhas, and gilt ceilings. The fitness center offers sweeping views of Mission Bay's beach; yoga and Pilates take place outside on the secluded lawn. A classical or jazz pianist plays nightly at the Moray Bar; the Atoll Restaurant serves fine cuisine, but the highlight is the Sunday brunch featuring Hawaiian dancers. Among the resort's many water-oriented activities are free cruises on Mission Bay aboard the *Bahia Belle* stern-wheeler. **Pros:** Recently upgraded rooms, spa, free cruises. **Cons:** Not centrally located. ⊠*3999 Mission Blvd., Mission Beach* ☎*858/488–1081 or 800/422–8386* ⊕*www.catamaranresort.com* ⇆*313 rooms* &*In-room: safe, kitchen (some), refrigerator (some), Ethernet, Wi-Fi. In-hotel: restaurant, room service, bar, pool, gym, spa, beachfront, bicycles, parking (fee), no-smoking rooms* ⊟*AE, D, DC, MC, V.*

$$$ ⚏**Crystal Pier Hotel.** Crystal Pier, a Pacific Beach landmark, had its grand opening in 1927; 10 years later, the first of the cottages were built. They are rustic little oases with a charm all their own. True, they lack some of the amenities of comparably priced hotels, but you're paying for character and proximity to the ocean—the blue-and-white cottages here are literally on the pier. Most units sleep four but cost the same no matter what the occupancy; only one suite has air-conditioning. Call four to six months in advance for reservations. There's a minimum stay requirement of three nights from mid-June through September, two nights the rest of the year. The cottages are a bargain in off-season. **Pros:** Ocean view, historic hotel, on beach. **Cons:** Few amenities, no a/c in most, reservations fill up fast. ✉ *4500 Ocean Blvd., Pacific Beach* ☎ *858/483–6983 or 800/748–5894* ⊕ *www.crystalpier. com* ⇆ *23 cottages, 6 suites* ♿ *In-room: no a/c (some), kitchen (some). In-hotel: beachfront, public Wi-Fi, parking (no fee), no-smoking rooms* ▤ *D, MC, V.*

$$$ ⚏**Hilton San Diego Resort & Spa.** Tropical plants, bridges, and ponds surround the villas—some with fire pits on the patio—at this deluxe resort; rooms and suites in the high-rise have views of Mission Bay. Accommodations done in a chic, modern style are well appointed, with wet bars, coffeemakers, and spacious bathrooms; all have patios or balconies. Children stay free, and there's weekend Kids Kamp for children over five. The sports facilities are excellent, and aquatic sports equipment is available for rent at the resort's own boat dock on the beach. The Bayside Terrace Grill serves California coastal cuisine. The full-service spa specializes in sports and therapeutic massages. **Pros:** Modern rooms, water views, beach activities. **Cons:** Not centrally located. ✉ *1775 E. Mission Bay Dr., Mission Bay* ☎ *619/276–4010 or 800/445–8667* ⊕ *www.hiltonfamily.com* ⇆ *357 rooms, 9 suites* ♿ *In-room: refrigerator, Ethernet. In-hotel: 2 restaurants, room service, bars, tennis courts, pools, gym, spa, beachfront, bicycles, children's programs (ages 5–12), laundry service, concierge, public Wi-Fi, parking (fee), no-smoking rooms* ▤ *AE, D, DC, MC, V.*

$$$ ⚏**Hyatt Regency Mission Bay Spa & Marina.** A $65 million renovation in 2007 turned this venerable Mission Bay hotel into a modern and stunning property with many amenities. Rooms are in several low-level, lanai-style units, though there are marina suites and Tower rooms with spectacular views of the bay. Rooms feature a neutral color scheme and clean-lined furniture, quilt top beds, flat-screen TVs, iPod docking stations, and refrigerators, and most offer balconies with a view of the garden, bay, ocean, or swimming pool courtyard (pools have 120-foot water slides, plus a smaller slide on the kiddie pool). The new Red Marlin restaurant serves seasonal, seafood-heavy cuisine with 180-degree water views; the eco-friendly spa uses all natural organic products. The hotel offers a casually elegant Sunday champagne brunch. Year-round sportfishing charters, water taxis to SeaWorld, and winter whale-watching expeditions are other features. **Pros:** Modern decor, eco-spa, water views. **Cons:** Slightly hard to navigate surrounding roads, thin walls, not centrally located. ✉ *1441 Quivira Rd., Mission Bay* ☎ *619/224–1234 or 800/233–1234* ⊕ *www.hyatt.com* ⇆ *354*

rooms, 76 suites ⟠*In-room: refrigerators, Ethernet, Wi-Fi. In-hotel: 2 restaurants, room service, bar, pools, gym, spa, laundry service, concierge, parking (fee), no-smoking rooms* ▭*AE, D, DC, MC, V.*

$$$ 🏨 **Pacific Terrace Hotel.** Travelers love this terrific beachfront hotel and the blue ocean views from most rooms, a perfect place for watching sunsets over the Pacific. Don't be put off by the copper lettering changing colors. In 2007 rooms were redecorated in a tropical plantation theme with new beds, marble counters, plantation shutters, iPod docking stations, and flat-screen plasma TVs. Private balconies (or patios) and coffeemakers come with every room; eight of the suites have indoor hot tubs. Continental breakfast is complimentary, as is the daily delivery of *USA Today*. Even the smallest room is fairly large. The friendly, casual staff makes for a comfortable stay. **Pros:** Beach views, large rooms, friendly service. **Cons:** Busy area, lots of traffic. ⊠*610 Diamond St., Pacific Beach* ☎*858/581–3500 or 800/344–3370* ⊕*www. pacificterrace.com* ⥈*73 rooms, 12 suites* ⟠*In-room: safe, refrigerator, DVD, Wi-Fi. In-hotel: pool, gym, laundry service, parking (fee), no-smoking rooms* ▭*AE, D, DC, MC, V* ⊚*CP.*

$$$ 🏨 **Paradise Point Resort & Spa.** The beautiful landscape at this 44-acre resort on Vacation Isle has been the setting for a number of movies. The botanical gardens have ponds, waterfalls, footbridges, waterfowl, and more than 600 varieties of tropical plants, a convincing backdrop for the Balinese spa. Many recreation activities are offered, including five pools, and there's access to a marina. The rooms' bright fabrics and plush carpets are cheery and many overlook the water. **Pros:** Water views, pools, good service. **Cons:** Not near commercial areas, summer minimum stays, motel-thin walls. ⊠*1404 W. Vacation Rd., Mission Bay* ☎*858/274–4630 or 800/344–2626* ⊕*www.paradisepoint.com* ⥈*462 cottages* ⟠*In-room: safe, refrigerator, Ethernet. In-hotel: 3 restaurants, room service, bars, tennis courts, pools, gym, spa, beachfront, bicycles, concierge, parking (fee), no-smoking rooms* ▭*AE, D, DC, MC, V.*

$$ 🏨 **Bahia Resort Hotel.** This huge complex on a 14-acre peninsula in Mission Bay Park has studios and some suites with kitchens; many have wood-beam ceilings and a tropical theme. The hotel's Victorian-style stern-wheeler, the *Bahia Belle*, offers guests complimentary cruises on the bay at sunset. Room rates are reasonable for a place so well located—within walking distance of the ocean—and with so many amenities, including use of the facilities at its sister hotel, the nearby Catamaran. **Pros:** Bay cruises, good value, free parking. **Cons:** Not centrally located ⊠*998 W. Mission Bay Dr., Mission Bay* ☎*858/488–0551 or 800/576–4229* ⊕*www.bahiahotel.com* ⥈*243 rooms, 77 suites* ⟠*In-room: kitchen (some), refrigerator, Ethernet. In-hotel: restaurant, room service, bars, tennis courts, pool, gym, concierge, public Wi-Fi, parking (no fee)* ▭*AE, D, DC, MC, V.*

$$ 🏨 **The Dana on Mission Bay.** There's a modern chic to the earth-toned lobby of this beach hotel, making it feel you've arrived somewhere much more expensive. The resort's rooms all have sofa sleepers—great for families—and bay views. The Bay View suites also have wet bars with granite counters and two flat-screen TVs. Some rooms are fairly

standard hotel fare; be sure to ask for one of the newer Courtyard rooms, which are in two-story buildings without elevators. Sea-World and the beach are within walking distance. The Marina Village Conference Center across the street offers meeting and banquet rooms with bay views. **Pros:** Free parking, water views, two pools. **Cons:** Slightly confusing layout, not centrally located. ⊠*1710 W. Mission Bay Dr., Mission Bay* ☎*619/222–6440 or 800/445–3339* ⊕*www.thedana.net* ↩*259 rooms, 12 suites* ⌂*In-room: refrigerator, Wi-Fi. In-hotel: 2 restaurants, room service, bar, pools, bicycles, laundry service, public Wi-Fi, airport shuttle, parking (fee), no-smoking rooms* ▤*AE, D, DC, MC, V.*

WORD OF MOUTH

"You will be fairly centrally located if you stay in the Mission Valley or Hotel Circle areas, although remember you will run into a lot of work traffic in the mornings and evenings. I don't know about prices, but hotels in the Mission Bay area are also well located for you. (Don't confuse Mission Bay with Mission Beach. Mission Beach is out of the way. It is Mission Bay area that is convenient.) Have fun!"   —Melissa5

$$ \text{Surfer Beach Hotel.} $$

$$ 🔲 **Surfer Beach Hotel.** Choose this place for its great location—right on bustling Pacific Beach. Guest rooms were updated in 2006 but are still rather simple, though they include pillow-top beds, upholstered headboards, and retro accents and flat-screen TVs. Most have balconies, but can look out on an ugly rooftop; get a higher room to take advantage of the ocean view. The slightly larger junior suites have leather sofas for lounging and wet bars with microwaves, refrigerators, and coffeemakers. While the two-bedroom Sunset Suite has bare bones decor, it includes a full kitchen and large sundeck that's perfect for warm-weather get-togethers. Take a break from the crowds on the beach and relax by the hotel's outdoor swimming pool. World Famous, the on-site restaurant, specializes in seafood and steaks and also serves up breakfast and lunch with an ocean view. **Pros:** Beach location, view rooms, pool. **Cons:** Busy area, dated rooms. ⊠*711 Pacific Beach Dr., Pacific Beach* ☎*858/483–7070 or 866/251–2764* ⊕*www.surferbeachhotel. com* ↩*52 rooms, 16 suites* ⌂*In-room: refrigerator, Wi-Fi. In-hotel: restaurant, bar, pool, beachfront, laundry facilities, concierge, parking (fee), some pets allowed, no-smoking rooms* ▤*AE, D, DC, MC, V.*

MISSION VALLEY & HOTEL CIRCLE

$$$ 🔲 **Crowne Plaza San Diego.** After an $8 million renovation in mid-2007, the former Red Lion Hanalei Hotel is now a member of the Hotel Intercontinental chain. Upgraded rooms feature a cheerful tropical plantation-style decor and a signature sleep program with quiet zones, relaxation CDs, eye masks, and lavender spray. The hotel is good for business travelers, but also appeals to vacationers, with the pool, nearby golf course, shopping, and free shuttle to Old Town and Fashion Valley mall. **Pros:** Near shopping, close to airport, updated rooms. **Cons:** Near freeway, dated public areas, spotty service. ⊠*2270 Hotel Circle North* ☎*619/297–1101* ⊕*www.ichotelsgroup.com* ↩*407 rooms, 15 suites* ⌂*In-room: safe, refrigerators (some), Ethernet (some), Wi-Fi.*

In-hotel: restaurant, room service, bar, pool, gym, spa, laundry facilities, laundry service, concierge, executive level, public Wi-Fi, parking (fee), no-smoking rooms ▭*AE, D, DC, MC, V.*

$$$ ⬚ **Doubletree Hotel San Diego Mission Valley.** Near the Fashion Valley shopping mall and adjacent to the Hazard Center—which has a seven-screen movie theater, four major restaurants, a food pavilion, and more than 20 shops—the Doubletree is also convenient to Route 163 and I–8. A San Diego Trolley station is within walking distance. Public areas done in a neoclassical style are bright and comfortable, well suited to this hotel's large business clientele. A complimentary Continental breakfast and happy hour are provided for executive floor guests. **Pros:** Centrally located, large rooms, executive floor. **Cons:** Dated bathrooms, few amenities. ✉*7450 Hazard Center Dr.* ☎*619/297–5466 or 800/222–8733* ⊕*www.doubletree.com* ⟋*294 rooms, 6 suites* ⌂*In-room: Wi-Fi. In-hotel: restaurant, room service, bar, tennis courts, pools, gym, laundry facilities, laundry service, concierge, executive floor, public Wi-Fi, airport shuttle, parking (fee), no-smoking rooms* ▭*AE, D, DC, MC, V.*

$$ ⬚ **The Hilton San Diego Mission Valley.** After an $11 million renovation in September 2006, the Hilton's central location and upgraded amenities make it a magnet for business travelers. The spacious lobby offers a convenient car-rental desk and automated kiosks for quick check-out and airline check-in before heading to the airport. Rooms are redecorated in classic coastal style and feature improved lighting, Hilton's "Suite Dreams" beds with upgraded linens, and modernized baths with large granite counters. Executive rooms include wired Internet for added security, upgraded bath amenities, and access to a chic private lounge on the top floor that serves a breakfast buffet and evening hors d'oeuvres. Stish restaurant also serves three meals a day. Travelers with children will enjoy the pool; it has plenty of lounge chairs and three cabanas for added privacy. **Pros:** Near shopping, close to airport, spacious rooms. **Cons:** Near freeway, few good restaurants nearby. ✉*901 Camino del Rio S* ☎*619/543–9000* ⊕*www.hilton.com* ⟋*349 rooms* ⌂*In-room: safe, Ethernet (some), Wi-Fi. In-hotel: restaurant, room service, bar, pool, gym, laundry service, concierge, executive floor, public Internet, public Wi-Fi, parking (fee), no-smoking rooms* ▭*AE, D, DC, MC, V.*

$$ ⬚ **San Diego Marriott Mission Valley.** This 17-floor high-rise is well equipped for business travelers—the front desk provides 24-hour fax and photocopy services, and rooms come with desks. The hotel is in the middle of the San Diego River valley near Qualcomm Stadium and the Rio Vista Plaza shopping center, minutes from the Mission Valley and Fashion Valley malls. There's free transportation to the malls, and the San Diego Trolley stops across the street. Rooms are comfortable (with individual balconies) and the staff is friendly. **Pros:** Near shopping, centrally located, good business center. **Cons:** Skimpy amenities. ✉*8757 Rio San Diego Dr.* ☎*619/692–3800 or 800/228–9290* ⊕*www.marriott.com* ⟋*350 rooms, 5 suites* ⌂*In-room: dial-up. In-hotel: restaurant, room service, bar, pool, gym, laundry service, concierge, executive floor, parking (fee), no-smoking rooms* ▭*AE, D, DC, MC, V.*

$$ ▦ **Sheraton San Diego Mission Valley.** This Sheraton San Diego property caters to business travelers, but visitors will like the guest rooms outfitted with fresh carpeting, linens, and furnishings in rich contemporary hues. The lobby presents a nautical theme that includes potted palms and overstuffed armchairs with twisted-rope accents. Room amenities include spacious showers with curved bars and granite vanities. Executive floor guests also receive a Continental breakfast and a hosted happy hour. **Pros:** Centrally located, pets allowed. **Cons:** Few amenities. ⊠*1433 Camino del Rio S 92108* ☎*619/260–0111 or 800/325–3535* ⊕*www.sheraton.com* ⊲*245 rooms, 15 suites* ☐*In-room: Ethernet. In-hotel: restaurant, room service, bar, pool, gym, laundry service, concierge, executive floor, public Wi-Fi, airport shuttle, parking (fee), some pets allowed (fee), no-smoking rooms* ▭*AE, D, DC, MC, V.*

OLD TOWN

$$ ▦ **Best Western Hacienda Suites–Old Town.** Surrounded by colorful gardens with hot-pink bougainvillea, this white stucco hotel with balconies and Spanish-tile roofs is in a quiet part of Old Town, away from the freeway and the main retail bustle. The layout is somewhat confusing, and accommodations are not large enough to earn the "suite" label the hotel gives them, but they're decorated in tasteful Southwestern style and are well equipped. **Pros:** On-site restaurant, morning coffee, good location. **Cons:** Confusing layout, small suites. ⊠*4041 Harney St.92110* ☎*619/298–4707 or 800/888–1991* ⊕*www.bestwestern. com* ⊲*169 rooms* ☐*In-room: no a/c, refrigerator, VCR, Ethernet. In-hotel: restaurant, room service, bar, pool, gym, laundry service, concierge, public Wi-Fi, airport shuttle, parking (fee), no-smoking rooms* ▭*AE, D, DC, MC, V.*

$$ ▦ **Courtyard San Diego Old Town.** This hotel on the site of the 1850 Gila House Hotel has Spanish colonial–style fountains and courtyards, and rooms with pleasant floral blue and gold color schemes with red accents. Transfers to the airport, the zoo, and SeaWorld are complimentary. **Pros:** Good value, near attractions. **Cons:** Not centrally located, few amenities. ⊠*2435 Jefferson St.* ☎*619/260–8500 or 800/255–3544* ⊕*www.marriott.com/sanot* ⊲*160 rooms, 16 suites* ☐*In-room: Ethernet. In-hotel: restaurant, bar, pool, gym, laundry facilities, laundry service, public Wi-Fi, airport shuttle, parking (fee), no-smoking rooms* ▭*AE, D, DC, MC, V.*

$$ ▦ **Heritage Park Inn.** The beautifully restored mansions in Heritage Park
Fodor's Choice   include this inn's romantic main 1889 Queen Anne–style house, as
★   well as the Italianate but plainer house of 1887 that serves as its extension. Rooms range from smallish to ample, and most are bright and cheery. A two-bedroom suite is furnished with period antiques, and there are also two junior suites. A full breakfast and afternoon tea are included. There's a two-night minimum stay on weekends, and weekly and monthly rates are available. Classic vintage films are shown nightly in the parlor on a small film screen. **Pros:** Historic area, tea service. **Cons:** Weekend minimum stay, no parking. ⊠*2470 Heritage Park Row* ☎*619/299–6832 or 800/995–2470* ⊕*www.heritageparkinn. com* ⊲*9 rooms, 3 suites* ☐*In-room: refrigerators (some). In-hotel: no*

elevator, public Wi-Fi, no-smoking rooms ⊟*AE, D, MC, V* ⋅⊙⋅*BP.*

$ ⊞**Holiday Inn Express–Old Town.** Already an excellent value for Old Town, this cheerful property throws in such perks as Continental breakfast and afternoon snacks. Rooms have a European look; a $1 million renovation in 2007 added new carpet, linens, and bathroom granite and fixtures. When you've had enough of the heated pool off the shaded courtyard, you can

tackle the historic park's attractions and restaurants nearby. Priority Club members receive amenity bags with bottled water, granola bars, and fresh fruit. **Pros:** Good value, complimentary afternoon snack, Continental breakfast. **Cons:** Smallish rooms. ⊠*3900 Old Town Ave.* ☎*619/299–7400 or 800/465–4329* ⊕*www.hioldtownhotel.com* ⇆*125 rooms, 4 suites* ⋄*In-room: refrigerator, Ethernet. In-hotel: pool, laundry facilities, laundry service, public Wi-Fi, airport shuttle, parking (fee), no-smoking rooms* ⊟*AE, D, DC, MC, V* ⋅⊙⋅*CP.*

$ ⊞**Western Inn–Old Town.** The three-story Western Inn, decorated in a vaguely Spanish motif, is close to shops and restaurants, but far enough away from the main tourist drag that you don't have to worry about noise and congestion. The rooms won't win any design awards with their non-matching multifloral decor, but they have new carpeting and furniture as of early 2008 and some have microwaves. There's a free Continental breakfast, and a barbecue area where you can cook for yourself. Bus, trolley, and Coaster stations are a few blocks away. **Pros:** Good location, quiet, free Continental breakfast. **Cons:** Dated rooms, no restaurant, not centrally located. ⊠*3889 Arista St.* ☎*619/298–6888 or 888/475–2353* ⊕*www.westerninn.com* ⇆*29 rooms, 6 suites* ⋄*In-room: refrigerator (some), Wi-Fi. In-hotel: public Wi-Fi, parking (fee), no-smoking rooms* ⊟*AE, D, DC, MC, V* ⋅⊙⋅*CP.*

UPTOWN

$$ ⊞**Balboa Park Inn.** This all-suites B&B occupies four Spanish colonial-style 1915 residences connected by courtyards. Prices are reasonable for romantic one- and two-bedroom suites, done in Italian, French, Spanish, or early-California style. Some rooms have fireplaces, whirlpool tubs, patios, and kitchens. A generous, complimentary Continental breakfast is delivered to your room on Monday–Saturday mornings; you also get a newspaper. The lack of off-street parking is inconvenient, but the San Diego Zoo is a 10-minute walk away. **Pros:** Good value, good location, Continental breakfast. **Cons:** No parking, busy area. ⊠*3402 Park Blvd., North Park* ☎*619/298–0823 or 800/938–8181* ⊕*www.balboaparkinn.com* ⇆*26 suites* ⋄*In-room: kitchen (some), refrigerator. In-hotel: no-smoking rooms* ⊟*AE, D, DC, MC, V* ⋅⊙⋅*CP.*

$$ Britt Scripps Inn. A block west of Balboa Park, in prominent Banker's
Fodor's Choice   Hill, this inn occupies the former mansion of the Scripps newspaper
★   family. A $6 million investment has turned the beautifully maintained
1887 Queen Anne into a stunning example of lavish Victorian decor.
The carved oak woodwork shines throughout, and the two-story
stained-glass window is magnificent. In the nine guest rooms, antique
beds with monumental headboards, claw-foot tubs, rain-head showers,
heated towel racks, plush robes, and high-thread-count linens spell old-
fashioned luxury, while high-tech updates such as flat-screen TVs, free
Wi-Fi, and multi-line phones are artfully hidden. Rates include a full
American breakfast and afternoon wine and cheese in the parlor. Stroll
the grounds to visit the first camphor tree in North America, planted
in 1865. A 10-minute walk across Cabrillo Bridge places you in Balboa
Park. **Pros:** Intimate, historic building, upscale amenities. **Cons:** Not
near nightlife. ⊠ *406 Maple St., North Park* ☎ *888/881–1991* ⊕ *www.
brittscripps.com* ⇦ *9 rooms* & *In-room: DVD, Wi-Fi. In-hotel: no ele-
vator, concierge, public Wi-Fi, parking (no fee), no-smoking rooms*
⊟ *AE, DC, MC, V* ⎟○⎟*BP.*

Nightlife &
the Arts

NIGHTLIFE

Updated by
AnnaMaria
Stephens

Years ago, San Diego scraped by on its daytime offerings. Fun after sundown consisted of neighborhood dives and a scattering of dance clubs and live music venues. That sleepy beach town vibe is as long gone as the red light district that once thrived where the tourist-friendly, nightlife-packed Gaslamp Quarter now stands.

Downtown is the obvious neighborhood for party animals of all breeds. Its streets are lined with sleek lounges, massive nightclubs, and quirky dive bars. The Gaslamp Quarter is the main event, with the most bars and clubs located on its 16-block stretch. The late-night commotion is spreading to East Village, the area surrounding PETCO Park, where new bars seem to crop up every other weekend. A few neighborhoods on the outskirts of downtown—Golden Hill and North and South Park, in particular—offer plenty of hip underground treasures for intrepid visitors.

The beach areas tend to cater to the casual and collegiate, though certain haunts have their share of former flower children and grizzled bikers. Hillcrest is the heart of San Diego's gay community, and home to loads of gay-popular bars. Coffeehouses are another important element of San Diego nightlife culture, especially for the under-21 set. Singer Jewel got her start in local coffee shops, and plenty of other acts have launched to fame from an active area music scene, including pop-punkers Blink-182 and Grammy-winning gospel group Nickel Creek.

Locals rely on alt-weeklies like the *Reader* and *San Diego CityBeat*, as well as glossy monthlies like *San Diego* and *Riviera* magazines for nightlife info. You can't buy booze after 2 AM, which means last call is around 1:40. Smoking is only allowed outside, and even then it can be tricky. And be sure to hail a taxi if you've tied one on—drunk driving laws in California are stringent.

CASUAL BARS & PUBS

Aero Club (⊠*3365 India St., Mission Hills* ☎*619/297–7211*), named for its proximity to the airport, draws in twenty- and thirty-somethings with its killer jukebox (everything from the Clash to Modest Mouse), pool tables, dominoes, and 20 beers on tap (including a few local brews). Drinks are cheap, which makes it a common place to fuel up before heading downtown. Don't miss the cool fighting warplanes mural.

Bar Basic (⊠*410 10th Ave., East Village* ☎*858/581–5960*) is the place to liquor up before a Padres game. Right across from PETCO Park, the always-bustling Basic is true to its name with the simple pleasures it dishes up: cold drinks and hot pizza. The garage-style doors at this former warehouse roll up and keep the industrial-chic space ventilated during the balmy summer season.

★ **Bar Pink** (⊠*3829 30th St., North Park* ☎*619/564–7194*) is the only place in town to drink $2 Tecates in a bar co-owned by Rocket From the Crypt frontman John "Speedo" Reis. Cheap drinks, live music, and a hip crowd explain the line that's usually waiting outside.

Barefoot Bar and Grill (⊠ *Paradise Point Resort & Spa, 1404 W. Vacation Rd., Mission Bay* ☎ *858/581– 5960*), a beachfront watering hole and hotel bar with a tiki feel, attracts flocks of singles, especially on Sunday nights in spring and summer. Live music and happy-hour specials fill the joint up early, making for long latecomer lines. ■**TIP**➔ Make a splashy appearance and roll up in your boat—you can dock at the bar.

Dick's Last Resort (⊠ *345 4th Ave., Gaslamp Quarter* ☎ *619/231– 9100*) is not for Emily Post adher-

ents. The surly waitstaff and abrasive service are part of the gimmick. The rudeness notwithstanding, fun-loving party people pile into this barnlike restaurant and bar. Dick's has live music nightly, a solid beer list, and buckets of greasy grub. True to its name, Dick's is a suitable "last resort" after a long night of drinking.

★ **East Village Tavern & Bowl** (⊠ *930 Market St., East Village* ☎ *619/677– 2695*) means no more hauls to the suburbs for a night of blue-collar bliss. This laid-back hot spot, which opened in 2007, has several lanes for bowling (with an expansion in the works). Reservations are definitely recommended. Renting lanes is pricey during prime times, but if you consider that some nearby clubs charge a Jackson just for admission, East Village Tavern seems suddenly reasonable. The expansive bar area screens sports on fancy flat screens and the jukebox plays an assortment of alt- and classic rock.

El Agave Tequileria (⊠ *2304 San Diego Ave., Old Town* ☎ *619/220– 0692*) won't give you a hazy hangover after a night of cheap shots. Tequila—which in Mexico has a history dating back to the Aztecs—is made from the Agave cactus. Agave means "admirable," and El Agave's selection is exactly that. The restaurant's bar stocks hundreds of top-shelf brands that are as sip-worthy as the finest cognac.

Karl Strauss' Brewing Company (⊠ *1157 Columbia St., Downtown* ☎ *619/234–2739* ⊠ *1044 Wall St., La Jolla* ☎ *858/551–2739*) was the first microbrewery in San Diego. The original locale draws an after-work downtown crowd and later fills with beer connoisseurs from all walks of life; the newer La Jolla version draws a mix of locals and tourists. Beer-to-go by the gallon is a very popular choice. The vaguely German-inspired pub food here is above average.

CLOSE UP

Cocktails with a View

ROOFTOP BARS
Altitude Skybar (Gaslamp Quarter)
Beach at the W Hotel (Downtown)
'Canes Bar and Grill (Mission Beach)
Eden at the Ivy Hotel (Gaslamp Quarter)
Jbar (Gaslamp Quarter)
Moonstone Lounge at the Hard Rock
Hotel (Gaslamp Quarter)
Stingaree (Gaslamp Quarter)
Top of the Park (Hillcrest)

OUTDOOR PATIOS
Barefoot Bar and Grill (Mission Bay)
Brockton Villa (La Jolla)
Dick's Last Resort (Gaslamp Quarter)
ENO at the Hotel Del (Coronado)

Humphrey's by the Bay (Shelter Island)
Jack's La Jolla (La Jolla)
JRDN (Pacific Beach)
Lei Lounge (University Heights)
Moondoggies (Pacific Beach)
Pacific Beach Bar & Grill (Pacific
Beach)
Pannikin (La Jolla)
The Pearl Hotel (Point Loma)
Shakespeare Pub & Grille (Mission
Hills)
Starlite (Mission Hills)
Universal (Hillcrest)
Urban Mo's (Hillcrest)
The Vine (Ocean Beach)
The Wine Cabana (Old Town)

The Local (✉ *1065 Fourth Ave., Downtown* ☎ *619/231–4774*) is a kick-back beach bar in the middle of the city. Flip-flops are totally acceptable at the Local, where tasty bar grub goes down good with the regional beers on tap. It's a favorite happy hour haunt for downtown professionals and dwellers.

Live Wire (✉ *2103 El Cajon Blvd., North Park* ☎ *619/291–7450*) is an underground hole-in-the-wall popular with the twentysomething pierced and tattooed set. DJs spin everything from punk to funk during the week and on occasional weekends. A well-stocked (and very loud) jukebox and TVs screening movies or music videos are the only other entertainment in this hip dive, unless you count people-watching. Cocktails come in pint glasses, so pace yourself—the police lie in wait on nearby side streets.

Moondoggies (✉ *832 Garnet Ave., Pacific Beach* ☎ *858/483–6550*) is not just for Gidget anymore, but is home to a mixed, laid-back crowd of people who don't mind bumping into each other or minor beer spills. A large, airy sports bar feel is heightened by the dozens of TVs in every available spot. Many TVs show surf and skate videos that remind you that the beach is only two blocks away. A large, heated outdoor patio draws smokers. On Fridays, local rock, funk, or reggae bands play here.

Moose McGillycuddy's (✉ *535 5th Ave., Gaslamp Quarter* ☎ *619/702–5595*) is a major pick-up palace for college students and military (translation: a young crowd that gets pretty inebriated as the night wears on). A DJ spins house and Top 40 dance music to power the dance floor while the staff serves drinks and Mexican food.

Nunu's (⊠*3537 5th Ave., Hillcrest* ☎*619/295–2878*) might be the most popular mainstream bar in très gay Hillcrest, but don't expect a glitzy facade. This retro-cool hangout with intentionally dated decor sits within the tatty walls of a white-brick box that probably hasn't had a face-lift since the LBJ administration.

O'Hungry's (⊠*2547 San Diego Ave., Old Town* ☎*619/298–0133*) is famous for its yard-long beers and sing-alongs. The seafaring decorative scheme inside is quite a contrast to the Mexican-theme Old Town San Diego State Historic Park just outside the doors. Be sure to drink up quickly—this landmark saloon closes at midnight.

Pacific Beach Bar & Grill (⊠*860 Garnet Ave., Pacific Beach* ☎*858/272–4745*) is a block away from the beach. The popular nightspot has a huge outdoor patio, so you can enjoy star-filled skies as you party. The lines here on weekends are generally the longest of any club in Pacific Beach. There's plenty to see and do, from billiards and satellite TV sports to an interactive trivia game. The grill takes orders until 1 AM, so it's a great place for a late-night snack.

Pacific Shores (⊠*4927 Newport Ave., Ocean Beach* ☎*619/223–7549*) isn't going for classy with its acid-trip mermaid mural, but hey, it's OB—a surf town populated by leftovers from the '60s, man. A laid-back but see-and-be-seen crowd congregates here for relatively inexpensive drinks (no beers on tap though) and Sinatra-esque tunes on the jukebox.

Patrick's II (⊠*428 F St., Gaslamp Quarter* ☎*619/233–3077*) serves up live jazz, blues, and rock in an intimate Irish setting.

RT's Longboard Grill (⊠*1466 Garnet Ave., Pacific Beach* ☎*858/270–4030*) appeals to the young, tanned beach crowd that comes by to schmooze and booze under the indoor palapas that give this lively bar a south-of-the-border feel.

Shakespeare Pub & Grille (⊠*3701 India St., Mission Hills* ☎*619/299–0230*) captures all the warmth and camaraderie of a traditional pub in England—except that here you can enjoy consistently sunny and warm weather on the sprawling patio. The bar hands pour from a long list of imported ales and stouts, and it's the place to watch soccer matches.

Tavern at the Beach (⊠*1200 Garnet Ave., Pacific Beach* ☎*858/272–6066*), streaked with purple neon, draws fun-loving college students. Drink specials and socializing are the main attractions, although if you get bored you can always watch one of the 48 TVs.

Typhoon Saloon (⊠*1165 Garnet Ave., Pacific Beach* ☎*858/373–3444*) is an obligatory stop for college-age singles club-hopping on weekend nights. There are several levels, four bars, and two small dance floors. DJs play a Top 40 mix.

Fodor'sChoice **The Waterfront** (⊠*2044 Kettner Blvd., Little Italy* ☎*619/232–9656*)
★ is San Diego's oldest neighborhood bar. It's not actually on the waterfront, but has been the workingman's refuge in Little Italy since the days when the area was the Italian fishing community. Because the

bar is considered a local landmark, developers actually constructed an apartment building around it rather than tear it down. It's also famous for its bar burgers, and it's still the hangout of working-class heroes, even if most of the collars are now white. There's live jazz and blues many evenings.

Whiskey Girl (✉ *600 5th Ave., Gaslamp Quarter* ☎ *619/236–1616*) is popular with the happy-hour sports crowd because of its three dozen flat-screen and two big-screen TVs. On Tuesday through Thursday, bands play retro disco, R&B, and '80s music; DJs play the rest of the week. This place has long been a major stop on the bachelorette party circuit.

COFFEEHOUSES

Starbucks serves good brew, but for true coffee klatch culture, Californians love their independent cafés and coffeehouses. San Diego's got plenty, especially in the Hillcrest and North Park neighborhoods. Many offer tasty fare (from light pastries to full meals) alongside every possible caffeinated concoction. Some offer terrific live entertainment, too. And, if a coffee buzz isn't the kind you're looking for, a handful even serve wine and beer. Hookah lounges are another popular bar-alternative. Smoking shisha from a hookah hose can be an unusual conversation starter.

★ **Brockton Villa Restaurant** (✉ *1235 Coast Blvd., La Jolla* ☎ *858/454–7393*), a palatial café overlooking La Jolla Cove, has indoor and outdoor seating, as well as scrumptious desserts and coffee drinks; the beans are roasted in San Diego. It closes at 9 most nights.

Café Bassam (✉ *3088 5th Ave., Hillcrest* ☎ *619/557–0173*) offers a Parisian-inspired coffee-sipping experience, and there's also a selection of wine and about 150 teas. It's open until 1:30 AM most nights.

Claire de Lune (✉ *2906 University Ave., North Park* ☎ *619/688–9845*), on a corner in artsy North Park, is revered for its redesign of the historic Oddfellows building. High ceilings and huge arched windows give this wooden-floored hangout a funky charm. There are sofas and armchairs for lounging as well as tables for studying. Local musicians and poets take the stage on various nights.

Cream Coffee Bar (✉ *4496 Park Blvd., University Heights* ☎ *619/260–1917*) resembles a makeshift study hall by day. The café is popular with laptop users writing term papers and surfing the net with the free Wi-Fi. The music is loud and the employees deliberately unenthused, but the coffee is flavorful. Cream also serves wine.

Fodor'sChoice **Extraordinary Desserts** (✉ *2929 5th Ave., Hillcrest* ☎ *619/294–2132*
★ ✉ *1430 Union St., Little Italy* ☎ *619/294–7001*) lives up to its name, which explains why there's a line at this café, even though it has ample seating. Paris-trained Karen Krasne turns out award-winning cakes, tortes, and pastries of exceptional beauty (many are decorated with fresh flowers). The Japanese-theme patio invites you to linger over yet another

coffee drink. A branch in Little Italy has a patio with teak chairs, a bar serving wine and bubblies, and a wider selection of savory nibbles.

Fumari (✉330 G St., Downtown ☎619/238–4949) is a dark and cozy spot for savoring shesha. The richly flavored tobaccos are worth the exorbitant price tag (around $14 for a bowl), and the chill café ambience makes it easy to hang out and hookah the evening away.

Gelato Vero Caffe (✉3753 India St., Mission Hills ☎619/295–9269) is where a mostly young crowd gathers for some authentic Italian ice cream and a second-floor view of the downtown skyline. The place is usually occupied by regulars who stay for hours at a time.

Javanican (✉4338 Cass St., Pacific Beach ☎858/483–8035) serves the young beach-community set. Aside from a good cup of joe, live acoustic entertainment is a draw. Adventurous musicians can sign up to play at the open mike Monday nights. Other local musicians headline throughout the week.

Living Room (✉1018 Rosecrans St., Point Loma ☎619/222–6852) is in an old house not far from the water. The wooden floors creak and there are plenty of cubbyholes for the studious college students who are regulars here. It's a great place to catch a caffeine buzz before walking along Shelter Island. There are several other locations, including popular branches in Old Town and La Jolla.

Pannikin (✉7467 Girard Ave., La Jolla ☎858/454–5453) is a bright coffeehouse with indoor and outdoor seating. Among the regulars are folks who have been shopping and sightseeing in La Jolla's village. Several locations are scattered throughout the county; The Leucadia outpost (a stone's throw from Lou's Records) is also a locals' and visitors' favorite.

Twiggs Bakery & Coffeehouse (✉4590 Park Blvd., University Heights ☎619/296–0616) is full of the din of conversation when music isn't playing. Poetry readings and musicians playing their acoustic originals make this venue a true bohemian experience. The free open mike night on Wednesday is always popular.

Upstart Crow (✉835 West Harbor Dr., Seaport Village ☎619/232–4855) is a bookstore and coffeehouse in one. The secluded upstairs space contains the java joint and is ideal for chatting or perusing the book that you just bought. Irreverent gifts are sold, too.

Urban Grind (✉3797 Park Blvd., Hillcrest ☎619/299–4763) ranks among the city's most gay-popular java joints, and is a great place to meet locals, read a book, work on your laptop (free Wi-Fi), or simply people-watch. It's open until 11 PM, with a wine bar on Friday and Saturday nights.

Zanzibar Coffee Bar and Gallery (✉976 Garnet Ave., Pacific Beach ☎858/272–4762), a cozy, dimly lighted spot along Pacific Beach's main strip, is a great place to mellow out and eavesdrop, or to just watch the club-hopping singles make their way down the street.

COMEDY & CABARET

★ **Comedy Store La Jolla** (⊠ *916 Pearl St., La Jolla* ☎ *858/454–9176*), like its sister establishment in Hollywood, hosts some of the best national touring and local talent. Cover charges range from nothing on open mike nights to $20 or more for national acts. A two-drink minimum applies for all shows. Seating is at bistro-style tables.

Lips (⊠ *3036 El Cajon Blvd., North Park* ☎ *619/295–7900*) serves you dinner while female impersonators entertain (minimum $15 per person). The place is always a hit for birthdays and bachelorette parties, but fair warning to the conservative—the scene can get raunchy. The motto, "where the men are men and so are the girls," says it all.

National Comedy Theatre (⊠ *3717 India St., Mission Hills* ☎ *619/295–4999*) has competitive improv comedy contests on Friday and Saturday nights.

COUNTRY–WESTERN

★ **In Cahoots** (⊠ *5373 Mission Center Rd., Mission Valley* ☎ *619/291–1184*), with its great sound system, large dance floor, and DJ, is the destination of choice for cowgirls, cowboys, and city slickers alike. Free dance lessons are given every day, when seasoned two-steppers strut their stuff. Happy hour seven days a week is one of this bar's many lures. Tuesday is country karaoke night.

Wagon Wheel (⊠ *8861 N. Magnolia Ave., Santee* ☎ *619/448–8550*) has served as East County's country-music headquarters since 1943. Line dancers kick up their heels when a house band plays on the second and fourth Saturday night of each month. On Sundays between 5 and 10 PM, the bar admits all ages for Family Day.

DANCE CLUBS

Bar Dynamite (⊠ *1808 W. Washington St., Mission Hills* ☎ *619/295–8743*) is affectionately known to regulars as Bar D, and in its heyday was the hottest underground dance club around. It's still a pretty good bet for booty-shaking classic hip-hop, as well as mashups, reggae, and funk, and the cover rarely tops $5.

★ **Beauty Bar** (⊠ *4746 El Cajon Blvd., City Heights* ☎ *619/516–4746*), part of a small chain with locations in New York and Hollywood, is pretty much hipster headquarters in Uptown San Diego. Live bands and cutting-edge DJs keep the young and beautiful in good spirits—or as happy as sullen hipsters with high-maintenance haircuts can possibly be, anyway. It's a really fun place to dance if you can look past the attitude.

Belo San Diego (⊠ *919 4th Ave., Gaslamp Quarter* ☎ *619/231–9200*) is another mega-sized, Vegas-style dance club. A bumpin' sound system and big-name DJs (Steve Aoki, for example) make this riotously colored club (imagine Austin Powers waving a decor wand around) a hit. People pay $20 a pop to get in.

Cafe Sevilla (⊠*555 4th Ave., Gaslamp Quarter* ☎*619/233–5979*) brings a Latin flavor to the Gaslamp Quarter with its mix of contemporary and traditional Spanish and Latin American music. Get fueled up at the tapas bar before venturing downstairs for dancing. This is the best place in San Diego to take salsa lessons.

> **I'M ON THE LIST**
>
> Why spend money on cover charges when you can get yourself on the guest list? Do a little pre-planning—visit the club's Web site or call ahead to find out who's promoting a particular night. Usually all it takes is a quick e-mail signup to save your cash for cocktails.

★ **Envy at the Ivy** (⊠*630 F St., Gaslamp Quarter* ☎*619/814–1000*) is a glamorous new addition to the Gaslamp nightlife scene, a cavernous downstairs space with a decidedly naughty feel. Big money went into this multi-level dance club, and the steep cover and pricey drinks will remind you of that again and again. But it's one of the few places in town where you can bump and grind with sports stars and visiting celebs. Plus, the cocktail waitresses are outfitted like Catwoman. Also tempting is The Ivy's Enticements program, which includes chef demos, wine tasting, and poker and pole-dancing lessons. You don't have to be a VIP to participate, but you do have to RSVP. Call the hotel for more info.

Kava Lounge (⊠*2812 Kettner Blvd., Middletown* ☎*619/543–0933*), a free-spirited underground dance club, is a favorite of the nightlife-lovin' counterculture. The crowd is always eclectic and open-minded. DJs spin everything from downtempo to breakbeat, and organic cocktails keep sweaty bodies cool when the dance floor heats up.

★ **On Broadway** (⊠*615 Broadway, Gaslamp Quarter* ☎*619/231–0011*), a huge club in a former bank building, builds suspense with its velvet rope and suited security crew. On Friday and Saturday nights—the only nights it's open—sexily clad young professionals wait in a line that sometimes reaches around the block. Even the steep cover charges do little to discourage clubbers from waiting an hour or more. Drinks are pricey, and when the club is packed it can be near-impossible to order one from the sometimes unfriendly staff. But the cool decor—marble floors, Greek columns, and original vault doors mixed with modern design elements—make it worth a visit, as do the computerized light shows, Leviathan sound system, and skilled DJs.

Stingaree (⊠*6th Ave. and Island St., Gaslamp Quarter* ☎*619/544–0867*), a posh Gaslamp Quarter destination, occupies a historic warehouse in the former Red Light District. The owners spent a gazillion dollars creating this smashing three-story space with translucent "floating" staircases and floor-to-ceiling water walls. There's a high-end restaurant and a dance club inside (the music tends to be of the Top 40 variety). Dress nicely—the air of exclusivity at this hangout is palpable, and to further prove the point, drinks cost a fortune.

Whistle Stop Bar (⊠ *2236 Fern St., South Park* ☎ *619/284–6784*) is the place to get your groove on to indie, electro, and hip-hop, plus live bands on occasion. It's a bitty-but-banging locals' favorite just a few minutes from downtown, and though it gets hot and crowded, the dance floor is always happening on weekends. Plus, the cover's only five bucks.

GAY

Baja Betty's (⊠ *1421 University Ave., Hillcrest* ☎ *619/269–8510*) draws plenty of gay customers, although it's quite popular with everyone in the Hillcrest area. It's a low-key but rather elegant space with chandeliers and soft lighting, and it stocks some 75 brands of tequila and mixes plenty of fancy cocktails.

★ **Bourbon Street** (⊠ *4612 Park Blvd., University Heights* ☎ *619/291–0173*) is a popular place to meet old friends or make new ones. Several scenes exist in this one bar. The front area is a karaoke spot. The outdoor courtyard draws crowds that gather to watch and comment on whatever is showing on the large-screen TV. Weekends, a back area known as the Stable Bar has DJs who turn the small room into a makeshift dance floor.

Flicks (⊠ *1017 University Ave., Hillcrest* ☎ *619/297–2056*), a hip video bar that's popular with the see-and-be-seen crowd, plays music and comedy videos on four big screens. Drink specials vary each night.

Lei Lounge (⊠ *4622 Park Blvd., University Heights* ☎ *619/813–2272*) is fabulous, dah-ling, and a welcome addition to the neighborhood's gay-popular offerings. The tropical-themed lounge is like a mini-vacay, with cabanas, fire pits, palm trees, frou-frou cocktails, tasty tapas, and DJ-spun music. It's paradise for an afternoon or evening—or both.

Martinis Above Fourth (⊠ *3940 4th Ave., 2nd floor, Hillcrest* ☎ *619/400–4500*), with its swank lounge, presents live piano and cabaret to a friendly crowd. Swill cocktails inside or on the patio, and consider a meal afterward—Martinis is also a restaurant serving contemporary American fare.

Numbers (⊠ *3811 Park Blvd., North Park* ☎ *619/294–9005*) has a dance floor as well as giant-screen TV, six pool tables, darts, and daily drink specials.

Rich's (⊠ *1051 University Ave., Hillcrest* ☎ *619/295–2195*), a popular dance club, hosts frequent male revues. The dancing and music here are some of the best in the city, making Rich's popular not only with gay men but also plenty of lesbians and straight revelers.

★ **Top of the Park** (⊠ *525 Spruce St., Hillcrest* ☎ *619/291–0999*) is held only on Friday evenings, but this festive after-work cocktail party on the rooftop of the gay-popular Park Manor Suites hotel is de rigueur with the locals. It's a great way to kick off the weekend, and the views of downtown and Balboa Park are stupendous.

Fodor'sChoice
★

Universal (⌧*525 Spruce St., Hillcrest* ☎*619/291–0999*), which opened in Spring 2008, is the latest project from the team that created Stingaree and Bar West. The "omnisexual" club, outfitted in high-gloss black and snakeskin, has a dance floor and enclaves for lounging. It's connected through a fire pit–centric garden patio to a restaurant, Dish,

where a diverse crowd (gay, straight, who knows) nibbles on upscale comfort food. Bottle service at the bar features a variety of tasty mixers suited to the type of liquor requested.

Urban Mo's Bar and Grill (⌧*308 University Ave., Hillcrest* ☎*619/491–0400*) rounds up country-music cowboys for line dancing and two-stepping on its wooden dance floor—but be forewarned, yee-hawers, Mo's can get pretty wild on Western nights. There are also techno and pop nights, but Mo's real allure is in the creative drinks (Parker Posey Cosmo, for example) and the breezy patio where love (or something like it) is usually in the air.

JAZZ

Fodor'sChoice
★

Anthology (⌧*1337 India St., Little Italy* ☎*619/595–0300*) is a much-needed new arrival on the live music scene. This classy joint would make the Rat Pack proud—especially the fine-tuned acoustics. The sleek, three-story club books acts ranging from Herb Alpert to Ozomatli, though the lineup is primarily jazz.

Croce's (⌧*802 5th Ave., Gaslamp Quarter* ☎*619/233–4355*), the intimate jazz cave of restaurateur Ingrid Croce (widow of singer-songwriter Jim Croce), books superb acoustic-jazz musicians.

Dizzy's (⌧*Harbour Towers, 200 Harbor Dr., Downtown* ☎*858/270–7467*) is one of the few venues in town that's totally devoted to music and the arts. The popular joint had to vacate its downtown digs when the building required extensive renovations. It's since taken up residence in the San Diego Wine & Culinary Center. During the week you can count on the best in jazz, visual and performance-art shows, and the occasional spoken-word event. Refreshments are sold, including wine, which is an improvement over the old location.

Humphrey's by the Bay (⌧*2241 Shelter Island Dr., Shelter Island* ☎*619/224–3577*), surrounded by water, is the summer stomping ground of musicians such as the Cowboy Junkies and Chris Isaak. From June through September this dining and drinking oasis hosts the city's best outdoor jazz, folk, and light-rock concert series. The rest of the year the music moves indoors for some first-rate jazz most Sunday, Monday, and Tuesday nights, with piano-bar music on most other nights.

Clay's La Jolla (✉7955 *La Jolla Shores Dr., La Jolla* ☎858/459–0541) is the reincarnation of one of San Diego's most famous jazz venues, which closed in the mid-1990s, then returned half a decade later in a slightly different format. Perched on the top floor of the Hotel La Jolla, Clay's delivers an ocean view and a lineup of mostly jazz musicians (and the occasional DJ) Wednesday through Sunday.

LIVE MUSIC CLUBS

★ **Belly Up Tavern** (✉143 *S. Cedros Ave., Solana Beach* ☎858/481–8140), a fixture on local papers' "best of" lists, has been drawing crowds of all ages since it opened in the mid-'70s. The "BUT's" longevity attests to the quality of the eclectic entertainment on its stage. Within converted Quonset huts, critically acclaimed artists play everything from reggae and folk to—well, you name it.

★ **'Canes Bar and Grill** (✉3105 *Oceanfront Walk, Mission Beach* ☎858/ 488–1780) is closer to the ocean than any other music venue in town. Step outside for a walk on the beach, where the sounds of the national rock, reggae, and hip-hop acts onstage create a cacophony with the crashing waves. Step back inside to enjoy some of the cooler bands to pass through town.

Fodor'sChoice **Casbah** (✉2501 *Kettner Blvd., Middletown* ☎619/232–4355), near
★ the airport, is a small club with a national reputation for showcasing up-and-coming acts. Nirvana, Smashing Pumpkins, and the White Stripes all played the Casbah on their way to stardom. Within San Diego, it's widely recognized as the headquarters of the indie rock scene. You can hear every type of band here—except those that sound like Top 40.

Ché Café (✉*Bldg. 161, UCSD campus, La Jolla* ☎858/534–2311), a good old-fashioned bastion of counterculture at University of California at San Diego, presents some of the edgiest music around. The all-ages café is also home to a restaurant serving vegan and vegetarian food, and it hosts countless events, parties, and workshops related to leftist politics and activism.

Dream Street Live (✉2228 *Bacon St., Ocean Beach* ☎619/222–8131) is the place to see up-and-coming (or good enough to drink to) local rock and alternative bands. The music is on the heavy side, and the biker and rocker crowd that hangs out here can have a scary look about them. This is not the place for a quiet evening out.

4th & B (✉345 *B St., Downtown* ☎619/231–4343) is a live-music venue housed in a former bank that is only open when a concert is booked. All styles of music and occasional comedy acts take the stage.

★ **House of Blues** (✉1055 *5th Ave., Downtown* ☎619/299–2583), the nationally renowned chain of blues and rock clubs, opened a spectacular space in downtown San Diego in summer 2005. There's something going on here just about every night of the week, and Sunday's gospel brunch is one of the hottest events in town.

Over the Border (✉ *3008 Main St., Chula Vista* ☎ *619/427–5889*) is the home of *rock en español* in San Diego. Cover bands usually play the weekends, but some of the top Latin Rock bands make this unassuming cinderblock club a destination for concertgoers from both sides of the border.

710 Beach Club (✉ *710 Garnet Ave., Pacific Beach* ☎ *858/483–7844*), a surprisingly spacious beach bar, hosts well-known local and, occasionally, national bands playing rock, reggae, and especially potent blues. This is a good place to enjoy a drink before or after a nice walk on the boardwalk or on Crystal Pier, literally just steps away.

Soma (✉ *3350 Sports Arena Blvd., Sports Arena* ☎ *619/226–7662*) is a name that has been associated with the San Diego music scene since the '80s. Now near the Sports Arena area, this all-ages club occupies a former cinema multiplex converted into two concert halls. A smaller room features local acts, while the huge main hall hosts some of the top touring indie rock and punk bands. Regardless of the room, the young crowds love their mosh pits. There's no seating, and when packed Soma can feel like a sauna, so the uninitiated are advised to stand on the sidelines.

Tio Leo's (✉ *5302 Napa St., Bay Park* ☎ *619/542–1462*) is a throwback to the days when lounges were dark and vinyl-filled. The crowd is retro-attired as well. The lounge is in a Mexican restaurant, and an incredible variety of country, rockabilly, zydeco, blues, jazz, and swing acts graces the small stage, making it a regular destination for partnered dancers.

Winston's (✉ *1921 Bacon St., Ocean Beach* ☎ *619/222–6822*) is a sure bet for quality music in Ocean Beach. In a bowling alley–turned–rock club, Winston's hosts local bands, reggae groups, and, occasionally, 1960s-style bands. The crowd, mostly locals, is typically mellow, but can get rowdy.

NIGHT BAY CRUISES

Bahia Belle (✉ *998 W. Mission Bay Dr., Mission Bay* ☎ *858/539–7779*) is a Mississippi-style stern-wheeler offering relaxing evening cruises along Mission Bay that include cocktails, dancing, and live music (these floating bars are fondly known by locals as booze cruises). Cruises run from Wednesday through Sunday in summer and Friday and Saturday in winter (but no cruises in December and January). The $6 fare is less than most nightclub covers.

Hornblower Cruises (✉ *1066 N. Harbor Dr., Downtown* ☎ *800/668–4322*) makes nightly dinner-dance cruises aboard the *Lord Hornblower*—passengers are treated to fabulous views of the San Diego skyline.

★ **San Diego Harbor Excursion** (✉ *1050 N. Harbor Dr., Downtown* ☎ *619/234–4111 or 800/442–7847*) welcomes guests aboard with a glass of champagne as a prelude to nightly dinner-dance cruises.

PIANO BARS

Inn at the Park (✉3167 5th Ave., Hillcrest ☎619/296–0057), at the Park Manor Suites, offers large booths to settle into as a piano player entertains nightly beginning at 7 PM. This gay-popular venue makes for a nice stop after a day in Balboa Park.

★ **Jack's La Jolla** (✉7863 Girard Ave., La Jolla ☎858/456–8111) mixes several appealing elements into one: unstuffy beach bar (with steel-drum music), picturesque sidewalk café, inspired restaurant, and wine bar. But where nightlife is concerned, this swish establishment is best known for its live piano tunes.

Red Fox Steak House (✉2223 El Cajon Blvd., North Park ☎619/297–1313) is dearly loved by locals, and not just the AARP-ers who regularly flock there to sing Sinatra tunes to tickled ivories and the occasional impromptu horn section. This old-school piano lounge—typically referred to as Red Fox Room—is dimly lit, which is wise since the waitresses are as old as the patrons. But a hip, young crowd happily mingles with people their grandparents' age—and they sometimes even join in the serenade.

Shout! House (✉655 4th Ave., Gaslamp Quarter ☎619/231–6700), where dueling pianos and rock-and-roll sing-alongs make for a festive, even boisterous, evening, is open Tuesday through Sunday—so make reservations or come early to get a good seat.

Westgate Hotel Plaza Bar (✉1055 2nd Ave., Gaslamp Quarter ☎619/238–1818) is one of the most elegant settings in San Diego. "Old Money" is evoked with leather-upholstered seats, marble tabletops, and a grand piano.

TRENDY LOUNGES

★ **Airport Lounge** (✉2400 India St., Middletown ☎619/685–3881) sits, appropriately, right beneath the flight path of Lindbergh Field—you can actually watch the planes landing just overhead from the courtyard out back. This is truly an homage to airplanes: the staff dress in pilots' and flight attendants' garb, and the decor suggests a super-hip, futuristic airplane. It's gimmicky but loads of fun.

Altitude Skybar (✉660 K St., Gaslamp Quarter ☎619/696–0234), at the San Diego Marriott Gaslamp Quarter, occupies the hotel's 22nd-story rooftop. It's a great spot not only to people-watch but also to admire the city skyline.

Bar West (✉959 Hornblend St., Pacific Beach ☎619/273–4800), the brainchild of the guy who opened downtown's successful Stingaree, brings an infusion of class to style-starved PB. An unusually attractive crowd hangs out against a backdrop of unusually attractive modern design, but it's not all perfection. You actually have to pay to step onto the small, roped-off dance floor.

Bitter End (⊠770 5th Ave., Gaslamp Quarter ☎619/338–9300) is a tri-level martini bar and dance club that draws a crowd any night of the week. With its dark, molded wood paneling and a few over-stuffed armchairs, at times you get the feeling you're in your rich uncle's study. But your uncle prob-ably wouldn't make you stand in the long lines that form here on weekends. The martinis are potent, and a stylish, dressy crowd keeps the night interesting.

4

Cafe Japengo (⊠8960 University Center La., La Jolla ☎858/450–3355) is the post-work socializing spot for young La Jolla profession-als. A sushi bar is one draw, but most come here for the singles scene that plays itself out nightly.

Confidential (⊠901 4th Ave., Gaslamp Quarter ☎619/696–8888), opened by a team of investors that includes former reality-TV star (of *The Bachelor* fame) Andrew Firestone, is a posh, high-profile lounge that rakes in its fair share of local movers and shakers and those simply hoping to rub shoulders with them. The loft space with soaring ceilings, clean lines, and leather sofas is attached to a chichi restaurant serving world-beat tapas.

Hard Rock Hotel (⊠207 5th Ave., Gaslamp Quarter ☎619/702–3000) was hyped for what seemed like years before it even opened its doors in late 2007. International nightlife impresario Rande Gerber (aka Mr. Cindy Crawford) created two of the bars at this destination hotel, including the loungey Sweetwater Saloon off the lobby and the roof-top Moonstone Lounge. Also slated to open by late 2008 are the live music venue Folsom and Woodstock, the hotel's 9,000-square-foot outdoor event space. If you can't be a rock star, you might as well party like one.

FodorśChoice **Eden at the Ivy and Ultra Lounge** (⊠630 F St., Gaslamp Quarter
★ ☎619/814–1000) offer a chiller version of nightlife for Ivy visitors. Sink into a deep leather couch in the posh lobby Ultra Lounge or head upstairs to the spacious rooftop Eden, where you can swill cocktails poolside while gazing at gorgeous people or views of the city—both are in abundance.

Jbar (⊠435 6th Ave., Gaslamp Quarter ☎619/531–8744), the trendy poolside bar on the fourth floor of the Kimpton Group's swank Hotel Solamar, is a sexy spot for people-watching while sipping sangria or mango piña coladas, or noshing on snacks from the "slow food" menu. On cool evenings you can warm up before the roaring fire pit.

Jose's Court Room (✉ *1037 Prospect St., La Jolla* ☎ *858/454–7655*) is a hit with yuppies from La Jolla and other neighboring beach communities. This small but clean hole-in-the-wall's lack of space gives suave singles an excuse to get up close and personal.

★ **JRDN** (✉ *723 Felspar St., Pacific Beach* ☎ *866/869–3723*), pronounced "Jordan," occupies the ground floor of Pacific Beach's swankest boutique hotel, Tower23. The contemporary lounge captures both the laid-back personality of the neighborhood and the increasingly sophisticated sensibility of San Diego, with its sleek walls of windows and expansive patio overlooking the Pacific Beach boardwalk.

> **C'MON, GET HAPPY!**
>
> Buffalo wings and dollar-off beers belong to the happy hour of yore. These days, chic spas across the county are clued in to what women (and more than a few men) really crave during the early evening hours: pampering and relaxation. Try Glamour Mondays at the Keating Hotel's Minus 1 Lounge—a martini and a manicure for under $20. The Beauty Bar also buffs and polishes at vintage manicurist carts weekly during the early evening hours.

Minus 1 (✉ *432 F St.,, Gaslamp Quarter* ☎ *619/814–5700*), the bar at the ultra-contemporary, Italian-designed Keating Hotel, draws wealthy Euros and scantily clad women. It's pricey and pretentious (don't you dare wear flip-flops), but Minus 1 is putting the red light back in the Gaslamp (literally—the lighting is red).

Onyx Room/Thin (✉ *852 5th Ave., Gaslamp Quarter* ☎ *619/235–6699*) is the hippest split-level in town. Although Onyx and Thin are separate clubs, the fact that they share the same owners and building makes for many options as you move back and forth between the two, sampling each bar's distinctive look and feel. Onyx is downstairs and feels like two bars in one. In front there's a mood-lighted cocktail lounge, and in the next room acid-jazz bands and DJs keep the crowds dancing on the tiny dance floor. Every Tuesday, Onyx hosts a free jazz jam by local maestro Gilbert Castellenos. Thin, the upstairs venue, has a stainless-steel–heavy interior that could be the inside of a UFO. Thin is more conducive to the conversation-minded, although a DJ spins down-tempo acid jazz and funk tunes on weekends. Weekend cover charges allow entrance to both clubs.

★ **The Pearl Hotel** (✉ *1410 Rosecrans St., Point Loma* ☎ *619/226–6100*) references late '60s Palm Springs with shag carpet, clean lines, and lots of wood accents. The lobby bar is almost as fabulous as the outdoor pool area, where inflatable balls bob in illuminated water and vintage flicks show on a huge screen. And feel free to drink to excess. After midnight, when the bar closes, you can stay over at a discounted rate if there are unbooked rooms available.

Fodor'sChoice **Starlite** (✉ *3175 India St., Mission Hills* ☎ *619/358–9766*) stops bargo-
★ ers in their tracks with its stellar interior design, which includes rock walls, luxe leather booths, and a massive mirror-mounted chandelier. A hexagonal wood-plank entryway leads to a sunken white bar, where

sexy tattooed guys and girls mix up creative cocktails like the Starlite Mule, which is served in a copper mug. Live bands and DJs alternate during the week; otherwise, an iPod plays wonderfully eclectic playlists of old-timey music. During warmer months, procuring a spot on the outside wood-decked patio is an art form.

> ### NECTAR OF THE HIPSTER?
>
> The Starlite Mule—a got-kick signature concoction of organic vodka, ginger beer, bitters, and fresh lime juice—is just one of the reasons people pack it in at this hard-to-find hotspot (look for the sign).

U-31 (⊠3112 *University Ave., North Park* ☎619/584–4188) ratchets up this neighborhood's nightlife potential with a spacious layout and stylish, custom-designed interior. Located at University and 31st, the aptly named U-31 is loungey except when DJs command patrons to the dance floor or on Mondays, when the brave and alcoholically emboldened battle for victory at mechanical bull riding.

★ The **W Hotel** (⊠421 *West B St., Downtown* ☎619/398–3100) has three bars, and even after several years on the scene, they continue to lure the young bar-hopping set. The ground level Living Room, recently renovated by *Queer Eye*'s Thom Filicia, encourages lounging with plush chairs and couches. The scene is always charged at Magnet, adjacent to Rice restaurant. Have a late-night nosh and head for the beach—or, more accurately, Beach, the W's open-air rooftop with private beach cabanas, fire pits, and tons of heated sand covering the floor. Get here before 9 pm on weekends to avoid a queue.

WINE BARS

The Cask Room (⊠550 *Park Blvd., Downtown* ☎619/822–1606) won't strike visitors as an oenophiles-only kind of place. It's a low-key but sophisticated environment for learning the ins-and-outs of wine tasting or just for savoring a fine glass of white or red. The staff is friendly and accommodating—don't be afraid to ask for samples before ordering. You might even end up chatting with the friendly owners.

ENO at the Hotel Del Coronado (⊠1500 *Orange Ave., Coronado* ☎619/522–8490), one of the renovated Hotel Del's new offerings, is a stylish contemporary wine bar serving fine wines, artisanal cheeses, and gourmet chocolates—three of life's most sensual culinary indulgences.

The Grape (⊠823 *5th Ave., Downtown* ☎619/238–8010) is a pleasant place to swing by before or after dinner. The long, narrow wine bar could do without the cheesy wine-themed decor (aren't grape lights passé?), but the mile-long wine list and lively ambience make up for it. Skip the unremarkable nibbles.

The Vine (⊠1851 *Bacon St., Ocean Beach* ☎619/222–8463) is a romantic little wine bar in Ocean Beach, of all places. Alongside a small-plates food menu, the Vine offers a solid selection of moderately priced wines by the glass. For a perfect afternoon, grab a seat on the patio, order a cheese plate, and raise a toast to Dionysus as your wine opens up in the tangy sea air.

The Wine Cabana (✉ *2539 Congress St., Old Town* ☎ *619/574–9463*), a newcomer to San Diego's wine bar scene, is on the small side inside, but the outdoor patio saves the day with semi-private cabanas for groups to hang out in. On Dog Day Afternoons, you can even bring your pooch. A nice and affordable selection of wines and a variety of flights and tastings has quickly garnered the Wine Cabana a regular clientele.

★ **Wine Steals** (✉ *1243 University Ave., Hillcrest* ☎ *619/295–1188*) puts to rest the notion of wine drinkers as dull snobs. On busy nights the Hillcrest location crackles with excitement—you can actually hear the din of conversation from half a block away. A wide assortment of reasonably priced wines draws patrons in while freshly baked pizza keeps tummies in top form for imbibing. A second Wine Steals is located in Point Loma.

THE ARTS

Locals like to gripe about the state of the arts scene in San Diego. Some even believe that we're culturally anemic because of a countywide overdose on sunshine—who wants to sit inside and paint (or act or dance) when it's so beautiful out nearly every day? But the city does have a thriving arts scene, featuring both seasoned heavyweights and up-and-coming lightweights. National touring companies perform regularly at the 3,000-seat Civic Theatre and in Escondido at the California Center for the Arts. Programs at San Diego State University, the University of California at San Diego, private universities, and community colleges host a range of artists, from well-known professionals to students. The *San Diego Union-Tribune* lists attractions and complete movie schedules (the U-T's Web site, ⊕ *www. SignOnSanDiego.com*, posts searchable listings). The *Reader* weekly devotes an entire section to upcoming cultural events, as does *San Diego CityBeat*. For a monthly outlook, consult *San Diego* magazine, or the younger, hipper *Riviera* magazine. Flipping through community micromags or perusing stacks of printed postcards found in most coffeehouses can unearth some intriguing underground happenings. You can also scan arts listings and book tickets through the Web site of **San Diego Art + Sol** (⊕ *www.sandiegoartandsol.com*), which is produced by a partnership of organizations, including the City of San Diego Commission for Arts and Culture and the San Diego Convention & Visitors Bureau.

Book tickets well in advance, preferably at the same time you make hotel reservations. Outlets selling last-minute tickets do exist, but you risk paying top rates or getting less-than-choice seats—or both.

You can buy half-price tickets to most theater, music, and dance events on the day of performance at **Times Arts Tix** (✉ *Horton Plaza, Gaslamp Quarter* ☎ *619/497–5000*). Advance full-price tickets are also sold here. **Ticketmaster** (☎ *619/220–8497*) sells tickets to many performances.

CLOSE UP

Art and Entertainment

A couple of venues in San Diego host monthly nighttime events meant to lure the city's culturati—especially of the younger variety.

The Museum of Contemporary Art, San Diego puts on **Thursday Night Thing** (☎ 858/454–3541 ⊕ www. mcasd.org) the first Thursday of every month (except January) at its downtown location. Events are related to current exhibits, such as casual Q&As with artists, but the museum bumps up the entertainment quotient with bands in the outdoor plaza, DJs in the galleries, and no-host cocktail bars. Past TNTs have included live graffiti and breakdancing, art-making activities (photo booths with zany props, postcards from recycled materials), and 3-D night.

The San Diego Museum of Art hosts a sundown series called **Culture & Cocktails** (☎619/232–7931 ⊕ www.sdma.org) to coincide with major new exhibitions. For a $10 admission, visitors can enjoy a complimentary themed cocktail (a "Bombay Sapphire" for a recent Indian art-related exhibit) and nibbles, DJs and live entertainment (a Bollywood film, for example), plus a much cooler crowd than the tired daytime tourists dragging their kids from gallery to gallery.

Two artsy neighborhoods host monthly community nighttime art walks. For six years, **Ray at Night** (⊕ www.rayatnight.com) takes place on the second Saturday of every month on Ray Street in North Park, one of San Diego's hippest, most up-and-coming neighborhoods. Galleries stay open late and often offer drinks and light bites, as well as scintillating cultural conversation. Après art, the neighborhood bars are always packed. Up in Solana Beach, the third Thursday of the month brings **Cedros Gallery Nights**. Galleries and boutiques keep their doors open, and locals head out to mingle. Design aficionados will especially enjoy it, as Solana Beach is one of San Diego's primary design districts.

Service charges vary according to the event, and most tickets are nonrefundable.

DANCE

★ **California Ballet Company** (☎858/560–6741) performs high-quality contemporary and classical works September–May. The *Nutcracker* is staged annually at the **Civic Theatre** (✉*3rd Ave. and B St., Downtown*); other ballets are presented at the **East County Performing Arts Center** (✉*210 E. Main St., El Cajon* ☎619/440–2277) and at **Copley Symphony Hall** (✉*750 B St., Downtown* ☎619/235–0804).

City Ballet (✉*North Park Theatre, 2895 University Ave., North Park* ☎858/272–8663) holds performances at the **Stephen and Mary Birch North Park Theatre** and other area venues from November through May.

Eveoke Dance Theater (✉*2811-A University Ave., North Park* ☎619/ 238–1153), San Diego's major avant-garde dance company, performs a regular season of dance theater works, produces several special events, and presents community-focused classes and exhibitions.

Jean Isaacs' San Diego Dance Theater (☎*858/484–7791*) has earned serious kudos for its diverse company and provocative programming, which includes everything from Mexican waltzes to modern jazz. The company performs at different venues around the city.

Malashock (☎*619/260–1622*), the city's esteemed modern dance company, presents edgy, intriguing works at venues throughout the city; Malashock has often collaborated on performances with the San Diego Opera, the San Diego Symphony, and other important cultural institutions.

San Diego Ballet (✉*2650 Truxton Rd., Downtown* ☎*619/294–7378*) brings a vast repertory of classic and contemporary ballets to several venues countywide, as well as in-studio performances.

FILM

Landmark Theatres (☎*619/819–0236*), known for first-run foreign, art, American independent, and documentary offerings, operates the following three theaters in the San Diego area: **La Jolla Village Cinemas** (✉*8879 Villa La Jolla Dr., La Jolla*) is a modern multiplex set in a shopping center. **Hillcrest Cinemas** (✉*3965 5th Ave., Hillcrest*) is a posh multiplex right in the middle of uptown's action. **Ken Cinema** (✉*4061 Adams Ave., Kensington*) is considered by many to be the last bastion of true avant-garde film in San Diego. It plays a roster of art and revival films that changes almost every night (many programs are double bills). It publishes its listings in the *Ken,* a small newspaper distributed in nearly every coffeehouse and music store in the county.

In its 226-seat theater, the **Museum of Photographic Arts** (✉*1649 El Prado, Balboa Park* ☎*619/238–7559*) runs a regular film program that includes classic American and international cinema by prominent filmmakers, as well as the occasional cult film. Each screening is preceded by an informative introduction from the museum staff.

The 500-seat **Sherwood Auditorium** (✉*700 Prospect St., La Jolla* ☎*858/454–3541*), at the Museum of Contemporary Art, hosts foreign and classic film series and special cinema events, including the wildly popular Festival of Animation in October and November.

Science, space-documentary, observation-of-motion, and sometimes psychedelic films are shown on the IMAX screen at the **Reuben H. Fleet Science Center** (✉*1875 El Prado, Balboa Park* ☎*619/238–1233*).

MUSIC

Balboa Theatre (✉*868 4th Ave., Gaslamp Quarter* ☎*619/570–1100*) reopened in 2007 after remaining shuttered for more than two decades. The renovated theater dates from the glamorous 1920s, and in addition to its architectural splendor, offers unsurpassed sound.

Coors Amphitheatre (✉*2050 Entertainment Cir., Chula Vista* ☎*619/ 671–3500*), the largest concert venue in town, can accommodate

20,000 concertgoers with reserved seats and lawn seating. It presents top-selling national and international acts during its late-spring to late-summer season.

Fodor'sChoice **Copley Symphony Hall** (✉*750 B St., Downtown* ☎*619/235–0804*) has
★ great acoustics surpassed only by an incredible Spanish Baroque interior. Not just the home of the San Diego Symphony Orchestra, the renovated 2,200-seat 1920s-era theater has also presented such popular musicians as Elvis Costello and Sting.

Cox Arena (✉*San Diego State University, 5500 Canyon Crest Dr., College Area* ☎*619/594–6947*) attracts top-name acts like Eric Clapton and Depeche Mode to its 12,500-person confines.

East County Performing Arts Center (✉*210 E. Main St., El Cajon* ☎*619/558–0206*) hosts a variety of performing arts events, but mostly music. Internationally touring jazz, classical, blues, and world-beat musicians have ensured its popularity among locals.

★ **La Jolla Athenaeum Music & Arts Library** (✉*1008 Wall St., La Jolla* ☎*858/454–5872*) is a membership-supported, nonprofit library with an exceptional collection of books, periodicals, CDs, and other media related to arts and music. The Athenaeum also hosts jazz and chamber music concerts throughout the year.

La Jolla Music Society (☎*858/459–3728*) presents internationally acclaimed chamber ensembles, orchestras, and soloists at Sherwood Auditorium, the Civic Theatre, Copley Symphony Hall, and the Stephen and Mary Birch North Park Theatre.

Open-Air Theatre (✉*San Diego State University, 5500 Campanile Dr., College Area* ☎*619/594–6947*) presents top-name rock, reggae, and popular artists in summer concerts under the stars.

San Diego Chamber Orchestra (☎*858/350–0290*), a 30-plus member ensemble, performs three times a month, October–April, in a number of different venues, including St. Paul's Cathedral downtown and Sherwood Auditorium in La Jolla.

★ **San Diego Opera** (✉*Civic Theatre, 3rd Ave. and B St., Downtown* ☎*619/533–7000*) draws international artists. Its season runs January–May. Past performances have included *Die Fledermaus, Faust, Idomeneo,* and *La Bohème,* plus concerts by such talents as the late Luciano Pavarotti.

San Diego Sports Arena (✉*3500 Sports Arena Blvd., Sports Arena* ☎*619/224–4171*) holds 13,000-plus fans for big-name concerts.

San Diego State University School of Music and Dance (☎*619/594–1696*) presents concerts in many genres, including jazz, classical, and world music, in different venues on campus.

San Diego Symphony Orchestra (✉*750 B St., Downtown* ☎*619/235–0804*) puts on special events year-round, including classical concerts and summer and winter pops. Concerts are held at Copley Symphony

Hall, except the Summer Pops series, which is held on the Embarcadero, beyond the San Diego Convention Center on North Harbor Drive.

Sherwood Auditorium (✉ *700 Prospect St., La Jolla* ☎ *858/454–3541*), a 500-seat venue in the Museum of Contemporary Art, hosts classical and jazz events.

★ **Spreckels Organ Pavilion** (✉ *Balboa Park* ☎ *619/702–8138*) holds a giant outdoor pipe organ donated to the city in 1914 by sugar magnates John and Adolph Spreckels. The beautiful Spanish Baroque pavilion hosts concerts by civic organist Carol Williams on most Sunday afternoons and on most Monday evenings in summer. Local military bands, gospel groups, and barbershop quartets also perform here. All shows are free.

Spreckels Theatre (✉ *121 Broadway, Downtown* ☎ *619/235–9500*), a designated-landmark theater erected in 1912, hosts comedy, dance, theater, and concerts. Good acoustics and old-time elegance make this a favorite local venue.

THEATER

California Center for the Arts, Escondido (✉ *340 N. Escondido Blvd., Escondido* ☎ *760/839–4138*) presents mainstream theatrical productions such as *Grease* and *The Odd Couple*.

Coronado Playhouse (✉ *1835 Strand Way, Coronado* ☎ *619/435–4856*), a cabaret-type theater near the Hotel Del Coronado, stages regular dramatic and musical performances.

Cygnet Theatre (✉ *6663 El Cajon Blvd., East San Diego* ☎ *619/337–1525*) shows a mix of contemporary hits, modern classics, and offbeat comedies and musicals. The company recently expanded with its 2008 acquisition of Old Town Theatre.

Diversionary Theatre (✉ *4545 Park Blvd., University Heights* ☎ *619/220–0097*) is San Diego's premier gay and lesbian company. It presents a range of original works that focus on gay and lesbian themes.

FodorsChoice **La Jolla Playhouse** (✉ *University of California at San Diego, 2910 La* ★ *Jolla Village Dr., La Jolla* ☎ *858/550–1010*) crafts exciting and innovative productions under the new artistic direction of Christopher Ashley, May through March. Many Broadway shows, such as *Tommy* and *Jersey Boys,* have previewed here before heading for the East Coast. The playhouse has three stages: the Mandell Weiss Theatre has the main stage, the Mandell Weiss Forum is a thrust stage, and the Sheila and Hughes Potiker Theatre, opened in 2005, is a black-box theater.

★ **Lamb's Players Theatre** (✉ *1142 Orange Ave., Coronado* ☎ *619/437–0600*) has a regular season of five productions from February through November and stages a musical, Festival of Christmas, in December. An American Christmas is the company's dinner-theater event at the Hotel Del Coronado.

Lyceum Theatre (⊠*79 Horton Plaza, Gaslamp Quarter* ☎*619/544–1000 or 619/231–3586*) is the home of the San Diego Repertory Theatre, and also presents productions by visiting theater companies.

Lynx Performance Theatre (⊠*2653-R Ariane Dr., La Jolla* ☎*619/889–3190*) is a progressive theater space known for presenting often controversial and edgy works.

Lyric Opera San Diego (⊠*North Park Theatre, 2891 University Ave., North Park* ☎*619/239–8836*) presents a variety of operas, operettas, and other musical theater productions including several Gilbert and Sullivan works each season at the Stephen and Mary Birch North Park Theatre.

Marie Hitchcock Puppet Theatre (⊠*2125 Park Blvd., Balboa Park* ☎*619/544–9203*) entertains with amateur and professional puppeteers and ventriloquists five days a week. The cost is just a few dollars for adults and children alike. If you feel cramped in the 200-seat theater, don't worry; the shows rarely run longer than a half hour.

North Coast Repertory Theatre (⊠*987 Lomas Santa Fe Dr., Solana Beach* ☎*858/481–1055*) shows a diverse mix of comic and dramatic works in its 194-seat space. The emphasis is on contemporary productions, but it's been known to stage some classics, too.

Fodor'sChoice
★ **Old Globe Theatre** (⊠*1363 Old Globe Way, Balboa Park* ☎*619/234–5623*) is the oldest professional theater in California, presenting classics, contemporary dramas, and experimental works at the historic Old Globe and its sister theaters, the intimate Cassius Carter Centre Stage and the outdoor Lowell Davies Festival Theater. The Old Globe also mounts a popular Shakespeare Festival every summer at Lowell Davies.

Old Town Theatre (⊠*4040 Twiggs St., Old Town* ☎*619/688–2494*) is a 248-seat theater that formerly catered to tourists and mature crowds with its boisterous, crowd-pleasing revues (*Forbidden Broadway: Special Victims Unit,* for example). It is now operated by Cygnet Theatre Company, one of the more interesting small San Diego theater groups.

Poway Center for the Performing Arts (⊠*15498 Espola Rd., Poway* ☎*858/748–0505*), an ambitious theater in suburban San Diego, presents musical comedy and other lighthearted, family-friendly fare.

San Diego Civic Theatre (⊠*3rd Ave. and B St., Downtown* ☎*619/570–1100*), in addition to being the home of the San Diego Opera, presents musicals and other major Broadway-style productions throughout the year.

San Diego Junior Theater (☎*619/239–8355*) stages youth productions year-round at the Casa del Prado Theatre in Balboa Park and the Firehouse in La Jolla. It also offers educational programs in acting, singing, and dancing for kids ages 3–18.

San Diego Repertory Theatre (⊠*Lyceum Theatre, 79 Horton Plaza, Gaslamp Quarter* ☎*619/231–3586*), San Diego's first resident acting company, performs contemporary works year-round.

San Diego State University Drama Department (⊠*Don Powell Theatre and elsewhere on campus, 5500 Campanile Dr., College Area* ☎*619/594–6947*) presents contemporary and classic dramas.

★ **Sixth@Penn Theatre** (⊠*3704 6th Ave., at Pennsylvania Ave., Hillcrest* ☎*619/688–9210*) performs superbly rendered classics and cutting-edge, provocative plays, often with gay and lesbian themes.

Starlight Musical Theatre (⊠*Starlight Bowl, 2005 Pan American Plaza, Balboa Park* ☎*619/544–7827*), a summertime favorite, is a series of musicals performed in an outdoor amphitheater mid-June–early October. Because of the theater's proximity to the airport, actors often have to freeze mid-scene while a plane flies over.

Sushi Performance & Visual Art (⊠*390 11th Ave., East Village* ☎*619/235–8466*), a nationally acclaimed group, provides an opportunity for well-known performance artists to do their thing at a variety of venues around town. As of this writing, they were looking for a permanent home downtown, so stay tuned.

UCSD Theatre (⊠*University of California at San Diego, 2910 La Jolla Village Dr. and Expedition Way, La Jolla* ☎*858/534–4574*) presents productions by students in the university's theater department September–May.

Welk Resort Theatre (⊠*8860 Lawrence Welk Dr., Escondido* ☎*760/749–3448 or 888/802–7469*), a famed dinner theater about a 45-minute drive northeast of downtown on I–15, puts on polished Broadway-style productions.

Sports & the Outdoors

WORD OF MOUTH

"I would recommend heading up to Torrey Pines and watching the parasailers jumping off the cliffs. Or sign up and do it! My hubby and 13-year-old daughter did it and it was amazing."

—buzymom3

"La Jolla Shores is a nice beach. The tidepools are fun at Cabrillo, check the tide schedule in the paper or on the Internet for lowest tide times. The cove is pretty and you may see the seals before they are "removed", but it is more of a looking beach than a hanging out beach."

—tinabina

Updated by
Jane Onstott

SAN DIEGO HAS A REPUTATION as an active, outdoors-oriented community. That makes sense, since virtually nowhere else in the United States offers such perfect weather in combination with so many places to play, and in such a lovely locale. San Diego has miles of beaches and bays, numerous lakes, mountains to climb, and deserts to explore. Visit wide expanses of parks where you can perfect your disc golf game, or some 90 actual golf courses. With balmy average temps and less than a foot of rain per year, the lure to go play outside is hard to resist.

The ocean especially is one of San Diego's most popular natural attractions. Surfers, swimmers, kayakers, divers, snorkelers, sailboarders, and even kiteboarders have 70 mi of shorefront to explore. You can rent equipment and take lessons in any one of these sports or simply enjoy a fishing or whale-watching excursion aboard a charter boat. Even if you're inclined to do no more than sightsee, you can take a low-impact sunset stroll on a wide, sandy beach or explore secluded coves at low tide. At the end of the day at any beach in the county, you'll see a daily ritual as locals cease all activity to watch the orange orb of the sun slip silently into the blue-gray Pacific.

BASEBALL

Long a favorite spectator sport in San Diego, where games are rarely rained out, baseball gained even more popularity in 2004 with the opening of PETCO Park, a stunning 42,000-seat facility right in the heart of downtown. In March 2006, the semi-finals and the final game of the first-ever World Baseball Classic, scheduled to be a quadrennial event fielding teams from around the world, took place here. The **San Diego Padres** (✉ *100 Park Blvd., Downtown* ☎ *619/795–5000 or 877/374–2784* ⊕ *www. sandiegopadres.com*) slug it out for bragging rights in the National League West from April into October—they won the division in 2005 and 2006. Tickets are usually available on game day, but games with such rivals as the Los Angeles Dodgers and the San Francisco Giants often sell out quickly. For an inexpensive day at the ballpark, go for the $7 ($5 on the day of game) park pass and have a picnic on the grass, while watching the play on one of several giant-screen TVs.

FodorsChoice ★

> ### PETCO PARK TOURS
>
> Most San Diegans love the PETCO baseball park, but it wasn't always so. After voters narrowly approved the project, more than a dozen lawsuits stalled construction for years. Issues were traffic, downtown congestion, and the fact that San Diego already had a perfectly serviceable baseball stadium. Take a tour before any home game and see whether the $450-million-plus price tag was worth it.

BASKETBALL

Although there have been a few attempts to bring pro and semi-pro basketball to San Diego, no team has endured. Diehard basketball fans instead rely on college teams to give them a fix. The **San Diego State University Aztecs** (✉ *Cox Arena, College Ave. Exit off I–8, San Diego*

State University ☎619/283–7378 ⊕www.goaztecs.com) compete from November through March in the Western Athletic Conference with such powers as the University of Utah and Brigham Young University. The **University of San Diego Toreros** (✉*Jenny Craig Pavilion, 5998 Alcalá Park, Linda Vista* ☎619/ 260–4803 ⊕www.usdtoreros.com) take on West Coast Conference opponents Pepperdine University, the University of San Francisco, and the University of California at Santa Barbara, among others.

BEACHES

> ### TOP 5 SPORTS & BEACHES
>
> ■ Ride your bike along the picturesque Silver Strand bike path, nine miles each way.
>
> ■ Rent roller blades and skim along the Mission Bay boardwalk.
>
> ■ Hug a Torrey pine (found few places in the world) at the namesake state park in La Jolla.
>
> ■ Watch the surfers at Swami's beach from the Self-Realization Foundation's meditation gardens on the cliffs above.
>
> ■ Play disc golf at Balboa Park's Morley Field.

5

Water temperatures are generally chilly, ranging from 55°F to 65°F from October through June, and 65°F to 73°F from July through September. But this doesn't stop many people from taking a refreshing dip.For a surf and weather report, call ☎ 619/221–8824. Pollution, which has long been a problem near the Mexican border, is inching north and is generally worse near river mouths and storm-drain outlets. The weather page of the *San Diego Union-Tribune* includes pollution reports along with listings of surfing and diving conditions.

Overnight camping is not allowed on any San Diego city beach, but there are campgrounds at some state beaches throughout the county (☎800/444–7275 for reservations ⊕ www.reserveamerica.com). Lifeguards are stationed at city beaches from Sunset Cliffs up to Black's Beach in the summertime, but coverage in winter is provided by roving patrols only. Leashed dogs are permitted on most San Diego beaches and adjacent parks from 6 PM to 9 AM; they can run unleashed anytime at Dog Beach at the north end of Ocean Beach, and from Memorial Day through Labor Day, at Rivermouth in Del Mar. It's rarely a problem, however, to take your pet to isolated beaches in winter.

Pay attention to signs listing illegal activities; undercover police often patrol the beaches, carrying their ticket books in coolers. Glass containers are prohibited on all San Diego beaches if their purpose is to carry alcohol, and fires are allowed only in fire rings or elevated barbecue grills. Alcoholic beverages—including beer—are completely banned on city beaches. Drinking in beach parking lots, on boardwalks, and in landscaped areas is also illegal. Although it may be tempting to take a starfish or some other sea creature as a souvenir from a tide pool, it upsets the delicate ecological balance and is illegal, too.

Finding a parking spot near the ocean can be hard in summer, but for the time being, unmetered parking is at all San Diego city beaches.

Del Mar has a pay lot and metered street parking around the 15th Street Beach.

The beaches below are listed from south to north, starting near the Mexican border. County Highway S21 runs along the coast between Torrey Pines State Beach and Reserve and Oceanside, although its local name, Old Highway 101 or Coast Highway 101, for example, varies by community. Most of the beaches north of Del Mar are plagued by erosion and bluff failure. It's always wise to stay clear of the bluffs, whether you're above or below them.

SOUTH BAY

Border Field State Beach. This southernmost San Diego beach is different from most California beaches; there are no lifeguards and the fence marking off the south end of the parking lot also marks the U.S.–Mexican border. The beach is part of Border Field State Park, a marshy area with wide chaparral and wildflowers, a favorite among horseback riders and hikers. The park contains much of the Tijuana River Estuary, a haven for migrating birds. Access to the park is often closed to motor vehicles because of lack of manpower; you can park about a mile away at the entrance to the state beach and walk along the salt flats, about a mile. When open, the park has barbecue grills, plentiful parking, and restrooms. Beware: in winter the grounds are often posted with contamination signs because of sewer runoff from Tijuana. ✛ *Exit I–5 at Dairy Mart Rd. and head west along Monument Rd., South San Diego.*

☾ **Imperial Beach.** In July or early August this classic Southern California beach is the site of one of the nation's largest sand-castle competitions (*www.usopensandcastle.com*). The rest of the year, this laid-back town is a great place for long walks away from crowds. The beach break here is often excellent, but sewage contamination can be a problem, especially in winter and after heavy rains. There are lifeguards, restrooms, parking, and plenty of eateries nearby. A walk on the pier (with its own seafood restaurant), the southernmost in California, allows views of Mexico to the south and Point Loma to the north. A walk on the beach south toward Border Field State Beach or north towards Coronado is a great way to experience a quiet, uncrowded shore—not always an easy thing to do. ✛ *Take Palm Ave. west from I–5 until it hits water, South Bay.*

CORONADO

☾ **Silver Strand State Beach.** This quiet Coronado beach is ideal for families. The water is relatively calm, lifeguards and rangers are on duty year-round, and there are places to Rollerblade or ride bikes. Four parking lots provide room for more than 1,000 cars. RV sites at a state campground ($25) are available by reservation (☎ 800/444–7275 ⊕ *www. reserveamerica.com*). Foot tunnels under Route 75 lead to a bayside beach, which affords great views of the San Diego skyline. ✛ *From San Diego–Coronado Bridge, turn left onto Orange Ave., which becomes Rte. 75, and follow signs* ☎ 619/435–5184.

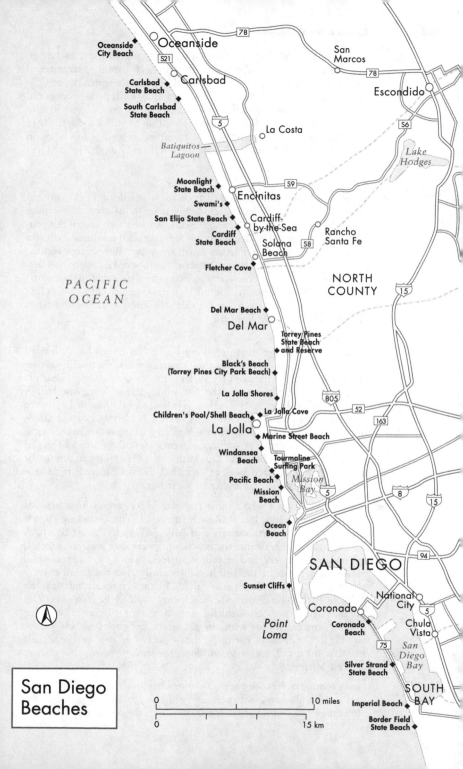

San Diego
Beaches

PACIFIC
OCEAN

NORTH
COUNTY

SAN DIEGO

Point
Loma

SOUTH
BAY

San
Diego
Bay

Batiquitos
Lagoon

Lake
Hodges

Mission
Bay

Oceanside City Beach
Oceanside
Carlsbad State Beach
Carlsbad
South Carlsbad State Beach
La Costa
San Marcos
Escondido
Moonlight State Beach
Encinitas
Swami's
San Elijo State Beach
Cardiff-by-the-Sea
Cardiff State Beach
Solana Beach
Rancho Santa Fe
Fletcher Cove
Del Mar Beach
Del Mar
Torrey Pines State Beach and Reserve
Black's Beach (Torrey Pines City Park Beach)
La Jolla Shores
Children's Pool/Shell Beach
La Jolla Cove
La Jolla
Marine Street Beach
Windansea Beach
Tourmaline Surfing Park
Pacific Beach
Mission Beach
Ocean Beach
Sunset Cliffs
Coronado
National City
Chula Vista
Coronado Beach
Silver Strand State Beach
Imperial Beach
Border Field State Beach

S21
78
78
S6
S9
5
S8
15
805
52
163
5
8
15
94
5
75

0   10 miles
0   15 km

☙ ★ **Coronado Beach.** With the famous Hotel Del Coronado as a backdrop, this stretch of sandy beach is one of San Diego County's largest and most picturesque. It's perfect for sunbathing, people-watching, or Frisbee. Exercisers include Navy SEAL teams, as well as the occasional Marine Recon unit, who have training runs on the beaches in and around Coronado. Parking can be difficult on the busiest days. There are plenty of restrooms and service facilities, as well as fire rings on the north end. ⊹ *From the bridge, turn left on Orange Ave. and follow signs.*

POINT LOMA

Sunset Cliffs. Beneath the jagged cliffs on the west side of the Point Loma peninsula is one of the more secluded beaches in the area. A few miles long, it's popular with surfers and locals. At the south end of the peninsula, near Cabrillo Point, tide pools teeming with small sea creatures are revealed at low tide. Farther north the waves lure surfers and the lonely coves attract sunbathers. Stairs at the foot of Pescadero and Bermuda avenues provide beach access, as do some (treacherous at points) cliff trails. There are no facilities. A visit here is more enjoyable at low tide; check the local newspaper for tide schedules. ⊹ *Take I–8 west to Sunset Cliffs Blvd. and head west.*

SAN DIEGO

Ocean Beach. Much of this mile-long beach is a haven for volleyball players, sunbathers, and swimmers. The area around the municipal pier at the south end is a hangout for surfers and transients; the pier itself is open to the public 24 hours a day for fishing and walking, and there's a restaurant at the middle. The beach is south of the channel entrance to Mission Bay. You'll find fire rings as well as plenty of casual places to grab a snack on adjoining streets; limited parking is available. Swimmers should beware of strong rip currents around the main lifeguard tower. There's a dog beach at the north end where Fido can run leash-free. ⊹ *Take I–8 west to Sunset Cliffs Blvd. and head west. A right turn off Sunset Cliffs Blvd. takes you to the water.*

★ **Mission Beach.** San Diego's most popular beach draws huge crowds on hot summer days, but is lively year-round. The 2-mi-long stretch extends from the north entrance of Mission Bay to Pacific Beach. A wide boardwalk paralleling the beach is popular with walkers, joggers, roller skaters, bladers, and bicyclists. Surfers, swimmers, and volleyball players congregate at the south end. Scantily clad volleyball players practice on Cohasset Court year-round. Toward its north end, near the Belmont Park roller coaster, the beach narrows and the water becomes rougher. The crowds grow thicker and somewhat rougher as well. For parking, you can try for a spot on the street, but your best bets are the two big lots at Belmont Park. ⊹ *Exit I–5 at Grand Ave. and head west to Mission Blvd. Turn south and look for parking near roller coaster at West Mission Bay Dr.*

Pacific Beach/North Pacific Beach. The boardwalk of Mission Beach turns into a sidewalk here, but there are still bike paths and picnic tables along the beachfront. Pacific Beach runs from the north end of Mission

Beach to Crystal Pier. North Pacific Beach extends from the pier north. The scene here is particularly lively on weekends. There are designated surfing areas, and fire rings are available. Parking can be a challenge, but there are plenty of restrooms, showers, and restaurants in the area. ✛ *Exit I–5 at Grand Ave. and head west to Mission Blvd. Turn north and look for parking.*

LA JOLLA

The beaches of La Jolla combine unusual beauty with good fishing, scuba diving, and surfing. On the down side, they are crowded and have limited parking. Don't think about bringing your pet; dogs aren't even allowed on the sidewalks above some beaches here.

> ## THE GREEN FLASH
>
> Some people think it's a phony phenomenon, but the fleeting "green flash" is real, if rare. On a clear day and under certain atmospheric conditions, higher frequency green light causes a brief green flash at the moment when the sun sinks into the sea. Where's a good spot to look for it? How about the Green Flash restaurant, right on the boardwalk in Pacific Beach.

Tourmaline Surfing Park. This is one of the area's most popular beaches for surfing and sailboarding year-round. No swimming is allowed, and surfing etiquette is strongly enforced by the locals in and out of the water. There's a 175-space parking lot at the foot of Tourmaline Street that normally fills to capacity by midday. ✛ *Take Mission Blvd. north (it turns into La Jolla Blvd.) and turn west on Tourmaline St.*

Windansea Beach. If the scenery here seems familiar, it's because Windansea and its habitués were the inspiration for Tom Wolfe's satirical novel *The Pump House Gang,* about a group of surfers who protect their surf-turf from outsiders. The beach's sometimes towering waves (caused by an underwater reef) are truly world-class. With its incredible views and secluded sunbathing spots set among sandstone rocks, Windansea is also one of the most romantic of West Coast beaches, especially at sunset. ✛ *Take Mission Blvd. north (it turns into La Jolla Blvd.) and turn west on Nautilus St.*

Marine Street Beach. Wide and sandy, this strand often teems with sunbathers, swimmers, walkers, and joggers. The water is known as a great spot for bodysurfing, although the waves break in extremely shallow water and you'll need to watch out for riptides. ✛ *Accessible from Marine St., off La Jolla Blvd.*

Children's Pool. Because of the pool's location at the tip of the La Jolla peninsula, you can actually look east for unmatched panoramic views of the coastline and ocean. This shallow cove, protected by a seawall, has small waves and no riptide. The area just outside the pool is popular with scuba divers who explore the offshore reef when the surf is calm. Groups of harbor seals hang out along the beach, claiming it as their own during the winter pupping season. Court battles are currently raging between animal protection groups and citizens who want the pinnipeds to share the sand and stop fouling the water with their waste. Most recent court ruling (March 2008): seals: 1, kids, 0. Get back to

5

your corners, guys. ✛ *Follow La Jolla Blvd. north. When it forks, stay to left, then turn right onto Coast Blvd.*

Shell Beach. North of Children's Pool is a small cove, accessible by stairs, with a relatively secluded beach. The exposed rocks off the coast have been designated a protected habitat for sea lions; you can watch them sun themselves and frolic in the water. ✛ *Continue along Coast Blvd. north from Children's Pool.*

Fodor's Choice **La Jolla Cove.** This is one of the prettiest spots on the West Coast. A
★ palm-lined park sits on top of cliffs formed by the incessant pounding of the waves. At low tide the tide pools and cliff caves provide a destination for explorers. Divers, snorkelers, and kayakers can explore the underwater delights of the San Diego–La Jolla Underwater Park Ecological Reserve. The cove is also a favorite of rough-water swimmers. ✛ *Follow Coast Blvd. north to signs, or take La Jolla Village Dr. exit from I–5, head west to Torrey Pines Rd., turn left, and drive downhill to Girard Ave. Turn right and follow signs.*

☾ ★ **La Jolla Shores.** On summer holidays all access routes are usually closed, so get here early—this is one of San Diego's most popular beaches. The lures are an incredible view of La Jolla peninsula, a wide sandy beach, an adjoining grassy park, and the gentlest waves in San Diego. In fact, several surf schools teach here and kayak rentals are nearby. A concrete boardwalk parallels the beach. Arrive early to get a parking spot in the lot at the foot of Calle Frescota. ✉ *8200 Camino del Oro* ✛ *From I–5 take La Jolla Village Dr. west and turn left onto La Jolla Shores Dr. Head west to Camino del Oro or Vallecitos St. Turn right.*

★ **Black's Beach.** The powerful waves at this beach, officially known as Torrey Pines City Park Beach, attract world-class surfers, and its relative isolation appeals to nudist nature lovers (although by law nudity is prohibited) as well as gays and lesbians. Access to parts of the shore coincides with low tide. There are no lifeguards on permanent duty, although they do patrol the area between spring break and mid-October. Strong rip currents are common—only experienced swimmers should take the plunge. Storms have weakened the cliffs in the past few years; they're dangerous to climb and should be avoided. Part of the fun here is watching hang gliders and paragliders ascend from the glider port atop the cliffs. ✛ *Take Genesee Ave. west from I–5 and follow signs to glider port; easier access, via a paved path, available on La Jolla Farms Rd., but parking is limited to 2 hrs.*

DEL MAR

★ **Torrey Pines State Beach and Reserve.** One of San Diego's best beaches encompasses 12,000 acres of bluffs and bird-filled marshes. A network of meandering trails leads to the sandy shoreline below. Along the way enjoy the rare Torrey pine trees, found only here and on Santa Rosa Island, offshore. The large parking lot is rarely full; there are bathrooms, showers, and lifeguards on patrol. Guided tours of the nature preserve here are offered on weekends. Torrey Pines tends to get crowded in summer, but more isolated spots heading south under the cliffs you'll run into isolated Black's Beach, *above.* ✛ *Take Carmel*

Valley Rd. Exit west from I–5, turn left on Rte. S21 ☎*858/755–2063* ⊕ *www.torreypine.org* ✉*Parking $10.*

Del Mar Beach. The numbered streets of Del Mar, from 15th north to 29th, end at a wide beach popular with volleyball players, surfers, and sunbathers. Parking can be a problem in town; there's metered parking along the beach, making it challenging to stay for more than a few hours. The portion of Del Mar south of 15th Street is lined with cliffs and rarely crowded. Leashed dogs are permitted on most sections of the beach year-round; from October through May, dogs may run free at Rivermouth, Del Mar's northernmost beach. During the annual summer meeting of the Del Mar Thoroughbred Club, horse players sit on the beach in the morning, working on the *Daily Racing Form* before heading across the street to the track. Food, accommodations, and shopping are all within an easy walk of the beach. Because parking is at a premium, it's a great idea to bring a bike to cruise around the city before or after the beach. ✛ *Take Via de la Valle Exit from I–5 west to Rte. S21 (also known as Camino del Mar in Del Mar) and turn left.*

5

SOLANA BEACH
Most of the beaches in this little city are nestled under cliffs, and access is limited to private stairways. However, there's a new pay lot with restrooms and easy beach access at the north end of town. At the west end of Lomas Santa Fe Drive you'll find access to a small beach, known locally as **Fletcher Cove.** Also here are restrooms and a parking lot. During low tide it's an easy walk under the cliffs to nearby beaches. High tide can make some of the beach impassable. Tides and surf conditions are posted at a kiosk by the parking lot. ✛ *From I–5 take Lomas Santa Fe Dr. west.*

CARDIFF-BY-THE-SEA
Cardiff State Beach. This beach, popularly known as George's, begins at the parking lot immediately north of the cliffs at Solana Beach. A reef break draws surfers, although this cobbly beach otherwise is not particularly appealing. However, a walk south will give you great access to some of the secluded coves of Solana Beach. Pay attention to the incoming tide or you may have to wade or swim back to the parking lot. ✛ *From I–5 turn west on Lomas Santa Fe Dr. to Rte. S21 (Old Hwy. 101) and turn right* ☎*760/753–5091* ✉*Parking $6 (weekdays), $8 (weekends).*

San Elijo State Beach. There are campsites (☎*800/444–7275* ⊕ *www. parks.ca.gov for reservations*) atop a scenic bluff at this park, which also has a store and shower facilities plus beach access for swimmers and surfers. Sites run $25–$35. ✛ *From I–5 exit at Encinitas Blvd, head west. Turn left (south) on South Coast Hwy. for about 2 mi* ☎*760/753–5091* ✉*Parking $6 (weekdays), $8 (weekends) per car, or park free nearby on U.S. 101.*

ENCINITAS
★ **Swami's.** Palms and the golden lotus-flower domes of the nearby Self-Realization Center temple and ashram earned this picturesque beach its name. Extreme low tides expose tide pools that harbor anemones,

starfish, and other sea life. Remember to look but don't touch; all sea life here is protected. The beach is also a top surfing spot; the only access is by a long stairway leading down from cliff-top Seaside Road-side Park, where there's free parking. On big swells, the bluffs are lined with gawkers watching the area's best surfers take on, and be taken down by, one of the best big waves in the county. Offshore, divers do their thing at North County's only underwater park, Encinitas Marine Life Refuge. ✛ *Follow Rte. S21 north from Cardiff, or exit I–5 at Encinitas Blvd., go west to Rte. S21, and turn left.*

Moonlight State Beach. Large parking areas and lots of facilities make this beach, tucked into a break in the cliffs, an easy getaway. To combat erosion, sand is trucked in every year. The volleyball courts on the north end attract many competent players, including a few professionals who live in the area. It's easily accessible from the Encinitas Coaster train station. ✛ *Take Encinitas Blvd. exit from I–5 and head west to 3rd St. Turn left. Parking lot is on your right at top of hill.*

CARLSBAD

Carlsbad State Beach/South Carlsbad State Beach. Erosion from winter storms has made the southern Carlsbad beaches rockier than most beaches in Southern California. This is particularly true of South Carlsbad, a stretch of which is named in honor of Robert C. Frazee, a local politician and civic booster. Still, it's a good swimming spot, there are fine street- and beach-level promenades outside downtown Carlsbad, and for self-contained RVs there's overnight camping (☎ *800/444-7275*). No overnight camping is allowed at Carlsbad State Beach, farther to the north, but there's a fishing area and a parking lot. A cement walkway borders the beach and continues into downtown Carlsbad, too. The south swell here means good summer surf when other San Diego beaches are bereft. The beach here has separate swimming and surfing sections, and showers ✛ *Exit I–5 at La Costa Ave. and head west to Rte. S21. Turn north and follow coastline* ☎ *760/438–3143.*

OCEANSIDE

Swimmers, surfers, and U.S. Marines (from nearby Camp Pendleton) often come to play on **Oceanside's beaches.** The surf is good around the Oceanside Pier near the foot of Mission Avenue and on either side of the two jetties. Self-serve RV camping is permitted in the parking lot at the northernmost end of Harbor Beach. There's no tent camping. There are plenty of pay lots and meters around the pier and also in the Oceanside Harbor area. ✛ *Take Vista Way west from I–5 to Rte. S21 (Coast Hwy.) and turn right. Best access points are from Cassidy St., Oceanside Pier, and Oceanside Harbor area. For direct access to Oceanside Harbor, take Harbor Dr. exit from I–5 and follow signs.*

BICYCLING

BIKE PATHS

On any given summer day, **Route S21** (or Old Highway 101) from La Jolla to Oceanside looks like a freeway for cyclists. It's easily the most popular and scenic bike route around, never straying more than a quarter-mile from the beach. Although the terrain is fairly easy, the long, steep Torrey Pines grade is world famous for weeding out the weak. Another Darwinian challenge (survival of the fittest) along this route is dodging slow-moving pedestrians and cars pulling curbside to park in towns like Encinitas, Del Mar, and Oceanside. Experienced cyclists follow **Lomas Santa Fe Drive** in Solana Beach east into Rancho Santa Fe, perhaps even continuing east on Del Dios Highway, past Lake Hodges, to Escondido. These roads can be narrow and winding in spots.

For more leisurely rides, Mission Bay has miles and miles of cement paths bordering big green lawns, children's playgrounds, and picnic spots. **San Diego Harbor** is a scenic place to pedal past big boats and cruise ships. **Mission Beach Boardwalk** is truly a scene; with babes on blades and bikes—in bikinis of course—often slowing foot and bike traffic to a crawl. San Diego also has a **velodrome** in the Morley Field section of Balboa Park. Often thought of as only for racing, this .3-km, light-banked, elliptical cycling track is more like a lap pool for bicyclists of all types who come for community, not competition. For those who want to take their biking experience to the extreme, the **Kearny BMX** (⊠ *3170 Armstrong St., Kearny Mesa* ☎*619/561–3824* ⊕*www. kearnybmx.com*) has a dirt track where BMXers rip it up, racing three times a week, with time for practice beforehand.

BIKE TOURS AND RENTALS

Bike Tours San Diego (⊠*509 5th Ave., Downtown* ☎*619/238–2444* ⊕*www.bike-tours.com*) rents all types of bikes and conducts biking tours in the downtown waterfront and Gaslamp area, to and around Coronado Island, up to Cabrillo National Monument, and elsewhere
★ in the city. **Hike Bike Kayak San Diego** (⊠*2246 Ave. de la Playa, La Jolla* ☎*858/551–9510 or 866/425–2925* ⊕*www.hikebikekayak.com*) offers a wide range of guided bike tours, from easy excursions around Mission Bay and Coronado Island to slightly more rigorous trips through coastal La Jolla. Mountain-biking tours are also available, and the company also rents bikes of all types (and can van-deliver them to your hotel).

Cheap Rentals Mission Beach (⊠*3689 Mission Blvd., Mission Beach* ☎*858/488–9070 or 800/941–7761* ⊕*www.cheap-rentals.com*) is right on the boardwalk and has great daily and weekly prices for bike rentals, including beach cruisers, tandems, hybrids, and 2-wheeled baby carriers. **Holland's Bicycles** (⊠*977 Orange Ave., Coronado* ☎*619/435–3153* ⊕*www.hollandsbicycles.com*) is a great rental source on Coronado Island and has a second location at the ferry landing (☎ *619/435–7180*), so you can jump on your bike as soon as your cross the harbor from downtown San Diego. **Wheel Fun Rentals** (⊠*1355 N. Harbor Dr., Downtown* ☎*619/239–3347* ⊕*www.wheelfunrentals.com*

THE GREAT WIDE OPEN

A $7 round-trip ferry ride transports you and your bike from downtown San Diego to hyper-flat, super-cruisable Coronado, with a wide, flat beach, the historic Hotel Del Coronado (an unbeatable background for photos), and the beautifully manicured gardens of its many residential streets.

5

com), at the downtown Holiday Inn, rents surreys, cruisers, mountain bikes, tandems, and electric bicycles, among other 2-, 3-, and 4-wheeled contraptions. Wheel Fun has a number of other locations around San Diego; call or visit the Web site for details.

DIVING

DIVE SITES

Enthusiasts the world over come to San Diego to snorkel and scuba-dive off La Jolla and Point Loma. At La Jolla Cove you'll find the 6,000-acre

★ **San Diego–La Jolla Underwater Park Ecological Preserve.** Because all sea life is protected here, it's the best place to see large lobster, sea bass, and sculpin, as well as numerous golden garibaldi, the state marine fish. It's common to see hundreds of beautiful (and harmless) leopard sharks schooling at the north end of the cove, near La Jolla Shores, especially in summer. Farther north, off the south end of Black's Beach, the rim of **Scripps Canyon** lies in about 60 feet of water. The canyon plummets to more than 900 feet in some sections.

The HMCS *Yukon,* a decommissioned Canadian warship, was intentionally sunk off **Mission Beach** to create a diving destination. A mishap caused it to settle on its side, creating a surreal, M. C. Escher–esque diving environment. This is a technical dive and should be attempted by experienced divers only; even diving instructors have become disoriented inside the wreck. Another popular diving spot is **Sunset Cliffs** in Point Loma, where the sea life and flora are relatively close to shore. Strong rip currents make it an area best enjoyed by experienced divers, who mostly prefer to make their dives from boats. Farther offshore, the Point Loma Kelp Beds harbor a nice variety of both plants and animals. It's illegal to take any wildlife from the ecological preserves in La Jolla or near Cabrillo Point. Spearfishing requires a license (available at most dive stores), and it's illegal to take out-of-season lobster and game fish. The *San Diego Union-Tribune* includes diving conditions on its weather page. For recorded diving information, contact the **San Diego City Lifeguard Service** (☎619/221–8824).

DIVE TOURS AND OUTFITTERS

Diving Locker (✉6167 *Balboa Ave., Clairemont Mesa* ☎858/292–0547 ⊕*www.divinglocker.com*) has been a fixture in San Diego since 1958, making it the city's longest-running dive shop. **Ocean Enterprises Scuba Diving** (✉7710 *Balboa Ave., Ste. 101, Clairemont Mesa* ☎858/565–6054 ⊕*www.oceanenterprises.com*) provides everything you need to plan a diving adventure, from equipment to instruction. **Scuba San Diego** (✉1775 *E. Mission Bay Dr., Mission Bay* ☎619/260–1880 ⊕*www.scubasandiego.com*) is well regarded for its top-notch instruction and certification programs, as well as for guided dive tours of La Jolla Cove and La Jolla Canyon, and unguided charter boat trips to La Jolla's Wreck Alley or to the Coronado Islands (in Mexico, just south of San Diego).

FISHING

San Diego's waters are home to a plethora of game species and you never know what you'll hook. Depending on the season, a half- or full-day ocean charter trip could bring in a yellowfin, dorado, sea bass, or halibut. Longer trips to Mexican waters can net you bigger game like a marlin or a bigeye tuna. Pier fishing doesn't offer as much potential excitement, but it's the cheapest ocean fishing option available. No license is required to fish from a public pier, such as the Ocean Beach, Imperial Beach, and Oceanside piers.

Public lakes are frequently stocked with a variety of trout and large-mouth bass, but also have resident populations of bluegill and catfish. A fishing license from the **California Department of Fish and Game** (✉*4949 Viewridge Ave., San Diego* ☎*858/467–4201* ⊕*www.dfg. ca.gov*), available at most bait-and-tackle and sporting-goods stores, is required for fishing from the shoreline. Nonresidents can purchase an annual license or a 10-day, 2-day, or 1-day short-term license. Children under 16 do not need a license.

Note that city reservoirs no longer sell snacks, drinks, bait, or fishing licenses, nor do they rent pedal boats or electric motors. Make sure to obtain your fishing license in advance. They also accept cash only for day-use fees.

County-operated **Lake Jennings** (✉*10108 Bass Rd., Lakeside* ☎*858/ 694–3049* ⊕*www.lakejennings.org*) is stocked with trout during the winter and catfish during the summer months; it's a popular fly-fishing spot. Like Lake Jennings, **Lake Morena** (✉*2550 Lake Morena Dr., Campo* ☎*858/694–3049* ⊕*www.lakemorena.com*) is open for fishing and camping. City-operated reservoirs, like **Sutherland** (open March through September, Friday through Sunday; ✉*22850 Sutherland Dam Rd.* ☎*619/668–2050*) is a good spot for catching trout and bass, but has no campgrounds. For information, call 619/668–3274. Three fresh-water lakes—**Dixon, Hodges, and Wohlford**—surround the North County city of Escondido. On the south shore of Lake Wohlford, camping is allowed at the **Oakvale RV Park** (☎*760/749–2895*); there's a supply store and a boat ramp. On the north shore, there's camping at **Lake Wohlford Resort** (☎*760/749–2755*), and **Lake Wohlford Cafe** (☎*760/749–6585*) has live worms (not on the menu, of course) and limited other fishing supplies, and rents rowboats and motorboats. **Dixon Lake Campground** (☎*760/741–3328, 760/839–4680 ranger station*) is city-administered and offers amenities similar to those of Lake Wohlford.

Fisherman's Landing (✉*2838 Garrison St., Point Loma* ☎*619/221–8500* ⊕*www.fishermanslanding.com*) has a fleet of luxury vessels from 57 feet to 124 feet long, offering long-range multiday trips in search of yellowfin tuna, yellowtail, and other deep-water fish. Whale-watching and sometimes whale-petting trips are also available. **H&M Landing** (✉*2803 Emerson St., Point Loma* ☎*619/222–1144* ⊕*www.hmlanding.com*) schedules fishing trips, plus whale-watching excursions from December through March. **Seaforth Boat Rentals** (✉*1641 Quivira Rd., Mission*

5

Bay ☎619/223–1681 or 888/834–2628 ⊕*www.seaforthboatrental.com*) can arrange a charter for an ocean adventure or rent you a sailboat, powerboat, or skiff from their Mission Bay, Coronado, or downtown San Diego location. **Helgren's Sportfishing** (✉*315 Harbor Dr. S, Oceanside* ☎*760/722–2133* ⊕*www.helgrensportfishing.com*) is your best bet in North County, offering the full assortment of trips from Oceanside Harbor.

> ### GO FISH
>
> The California Department of Fish and Game issues "Fishing Passports" showing 150 different species of fresh and saltwater fish and shellfish found throughout the state. Fishing aficionados can catch (and hopefully, release) in San Diego County many of the species listed, receiving a stamp for each species caught. See www.dfg.ca.gov for info.

FOOTBALL

The **San Diego Chargers** (✉*9449 Friars Rd., Mission Valley* ☎*619/280–2121 or 877/242–7437* ⊕*www.chargers.com*) of the National Football League fill Qualcomm Stadium from August through December. Games with AFC West rivals the Oakland Raiders are particularly intense.

★ The **San Diego State University Aztecs** (☎*619/283–7378 or 877/737–8039* ⊕*www.goaztecs.com*) compete in the Mountain West Conference and attract the most loyal fans in town, with attendance rivaling that of the NFL Chargers. The biggest game of the year is always a showdown with Brigham Young University. Like the Chargers, the Aztecs also play their home games at Qualcomm Stadium. The **Holiday Bowl** (☎*619/283–5808*), one of college football's most-watched playoff games, takes place in Qualcomm Stadium around the end of December.

FRISBEE GOLF

This is like golf, except it's played with Frisbees. A course, laid out at Morley Field in Balboa Park, is open seven days a week from dawn to dusk. Frisbees are available to rent for a small fee, and there's also a small fee for using the course on a first-come, first-served basis. Rules are posted. Directions to the field are available from the **Balboa Park Disc Golf Course** (☎*619/692–3607* ⊕*www.morleyfield.com*).

GOLF

On any given day, it would be difficult to find a better place to play golf than San Diego. The climate—generally sunny, without a lot of wind—is perfect for the sport, and there are some 90 courses in the area, appealing to every level of expertise. Experienced golfers can play the same greens as PGA-tournament participants, and beginners or rusty players can book a week at a golf resort and benefit from expert instruction. You'd also be hard-pressed to find a locale that has more scenic courses—everything from sweeping views of the ocean to verdant hills inland.

During busy vacation seasons it can be difficult to get a good tee-off time. Call in advance to see if it's possible to make a reservation. You don't necessarily have to stay at a resort to play its course; check if the one you're interested in is open to nonguests. Most public courses in the area provide a list of fees for all San Diego courses. The **Southern California Golf Association** (☎818/980–3630 ⊕*www.scga.org*) publishes an annual directory ($15) with detailed and valuable information on all clubs. Another good resource for golfers is the **Public Links Golf Association of Southern California** (☎714/994–4747 ⊕*www.plga.org*), which details the region's public courses on its Web site.

★ The PGA **Buick Invitational** (☎619/281–4653 ⊕*www.buickinvitational. com*) brings the pros to the Torrey Pines Golf Course in late January or early February.

COURSES

The following is not intended to be a comprehensive list, but provides suggestions for some of the best places to play in the area. The adult public's green fees are included for each course; carts (in some cases mandatory), instruction, and other costs are additional. Rates go down during twilight hours.

★ **Arrowood Golf Course** (✉*5201A Village Dr., Oceanside* ☎*760/967– 8400* ⊕*www.arrowoodgolf.com*) is a peaceful coastal links that opened in 2005 in Oceanside, right beside a nature preserve. It's one of the most scenic new layouts in the region. Green fees: $85–$110.

The **Balboa Park Municipal Golf Course** (✉*2600 Golf Course Dr., Balboa Park* ☎619/239–1660 ⊕*www.balboaparkgolf.com*) is in the heart of Balboa Park, making it convenient for downtown visitors. Green fees: $21–$35.

★ **Coronado Municipal Golf Course** (✉*2000 Visalia Row, Coronado* ☎619/435–3121 Ext. 4 ⊕*www.golfcoronado.com*) has 18 holes, a driving range and putting green, equipment rentals, and a snack bar and sit-down restaurant. Views of San Diego Bay and the Coronado Bridge from the back 9 make it popular—but rather difficult to get on unless you reserve a tee time, 3 to 14 days in advance, for an additional $38. Green fees themselves are $25.

★ **Cottonwood at Rancho San Diego Golf Club** (✉*3121 Willow Glen Rd., El Cajon* ☎619/442–9891 or 800/455–1902 ⊕*www.cottonwood- golf.com*) has a driving range, rentals, a restaurant, and two 18-hole courses. The Monte Vista course is the less challenging of the two. Ivanhoe often hosts tournaments. Both are good walking courses, and have nice practice putting greens. Green fees: $35–$60. On weekend mornings tee times include non-optional cart rental. Guaranteed tee times can be made up to 60 days in advance for $10.

Eastlake Country Club (✉*2375 Clubhouse Dr., Chula Vista* ☎619/482– 5757 ⊕*www.eastlakecountryclub.com*) has 18 holes, a driving range, equipment rentals, and a snack bar. A fun course for golfers of almost all levels of expertise, it's not overly difficult despite the water hazards. Green fees: $69–$89.

Encinitas Ranch (✉1275 *Quail Gardens Dr., Encinitas* ☎760/944–1936 ⊕*www.jcgolf.com*), tucked away in the former flower fields of coastal North County, is a hilly course that offers beautiful views of the Pacific as you play its championship 18 holes. Green fees: $77–$97.

Mission Bay Golf Resort (✉2702 *N. Mission Bay Dr., Mission Bay* ☎858/581–7880) has 18 holes, a driving range, equipment rentals, and a snack bar. A not-very-challenging executive (par 3 and 4) course, Mission Bay is lighted for night play with final tee time at 7:45 PM. Green fees: $22–$28.

Mount Woodson Golf Club (✉16422 *N. Woodson Dr., Ramona* ☎760/ 788–3555 ⊕ *www.jcgolf.com/courses-woodson.php*) has 18 holes, equipment rentals, a golf shop, and a snack bar. This heavily wooded course in the hilly area off Highway 67 has scenic views and wooden bridges. Green fees: $72–$92, with a discount for SoCal residents.

FodorsChoice **Torrey Pines Golf Course** (✉11480 *N. Torrey Pines Rd., La Jolla* ☎858/
★   452–3226 or 800/985–4653 ⊕*www.torreypinesgolfcourse.com*) has a driving range and equipment rentals, and is one of the best public golf courses in the United States. Home to the 2008 U.S. Open and the site of the Buick Invitational since 1968, Torrey Pines has views of the Pacific from many of its 36 holes. The par-72 South Course receives rave reviews from the touring pros. Designer by Rees Jones, it has more length and more challenges than the North Course and, fittingly, commands higher green fees. It's not easy to get a good tee time here, as professional brokers buy up the best ones. A full-day or half-day Instructional Golf Playing Package includes cart, green fee, and a golf-pro escort for the first 9 holes. Green fee on the South Course run $145–$181, the North Course $51–$64.

RESORTS

Barona Creek (✉1932 *Wildcat Canyon Rd., Lakeside* ☎619/387–7018 ⊕*www.barona.com*) in East County is one of the newer resorts in the area. Hilly terrain and regular winds add to the challenge. Fast greens will test your finesse. If your game is on, you can always see if your luck holds in the adjacent casino. Green fees: $120–$200.

★ **Carlton Oaks Lodge and Country Club** (✉9200 *Inwood Dr., Santee* ☎619/ 448–4242 ⊕*www.carltonoaksgolf.com*) has 18 holes, a driving range, equipment rentals, a clubhouse, a restaurant, and a bar. Many local qualifying tournaments are held at this difficult Pete Dye–designed course with lots of trees and water hazards. Carts are included. Green fees: $70–$90. County residents get a break.

Doubletree Golf Resort San Diego (✉14455 *Peñasquitos Dr., Rancho Peñasquitos* ☎858/672–9100 ⊕*www.doubletree.com*), a fairly hilly, well-maintained course in inland North County, has 18 holes, a driving range, equipment rentals, and a clubhouse with restaurant. Green fees: $60–$80.

FodorsChoice **Four Seasons Aviara Golf Club** (✉7100 *Four Seasons Point, Carlsbad*
★   ☎760/603–6800 ⊕*www.fourseasons.com*) is a top-quality course

with 18 holes (designed by Arnold Palmer), a driving range, equipment rentals, and views of the protected adjacent Batiquitos Lagoon and the Pacific Ocean. Carts fitted with GPS systems that tell you the distance to the pin, among other features, are included in the cost. Green fees: $215–$235.

★ **La Costa Resort and Spa** (⊠ *2100 Costa del Mar Rd., Carlsbad* ☎ *760/ 438–9111 or 800/854–5000* ⊕ *www.lacosta.com*), one of the premier golf resorts in Southern California, has two 18-hole PGA-rated courses, a driving range, a clubhouse, equipment rentals, an excellent golf school, and a pro shop. After a full day on the links you can wind down with a massage, steam bath, and dinner at the exclusive spa resort that shares this verdant property. Green fees: $195–$205, with a discount for resort guests.

Morgan Run Resort and Club (⊠ *5690 Cancha de Golf, Rancho Santa Fe* ☎ *858/756–2471* ⊕ *www.morganrun.com*), a very popular walking course near polo grounds and stables, has 27 holes (for members, members' guests, and resort guests only) that can be played in three combinations of 9; a driving range; equipment rentals; and a pro shop. Green fees: $100–$120 for resort guests.

★ **Rancho Bernardo Inn and Country Club** (⊠ *17550 Bernardo Oaks Dr., Rancho Bernardo* ☎ *858/675–8470 Ext. 1* ⊕ *www.ranchobernardo-inn.com*) has an 18-hole course, driving range, equipment rentals, and a restaurant; the course is managed by JC Golf, which has a golf school as well as several other respected courses throughout Southern California open to guests of Rancho Bernardo Inn. The restaurant here, El Bizcocho, lays out one of the best Sunday brunches in the county. Green fees: $85–$110.

Redhawk (⊠ *45100 Redhawk Pkwy., Temecula* ☎ *951/302–3850 or 800/451–4295* ⊕ *www.redhawkgolfcourse.com*) has 18 holes in an arboretum-like setting, a driving range, a putting green, and a restaurant. The par-72 course offers enough challenges to have earned a four-star rating from *Golf Digest* and a top 10 ranking from *California Golf Magazine*. Green fees: $70–$90.

★ **Sycuan Resort & Casino** (⊠ *3007 Dehesa Rd., El Cajon* ☎ *619/442–3425 or 800/457–5568* ⊕ *www.sycuanresort.com*) comes highly recommended by anyone who's played here, and is one of *Golf Digest*'s favorites. There are 54 holes, a driving range, equipment rentals, tennis courts, a lodge, and restaurants. Hackers will love the executive par-3 course; seasoned golfers can play the championship courses. Green fees: $18–$92.

HANG GLIDING & PARAGLIDING

The **Torrey Pines Gliderport** (⊠ *2800 Torrey Pines Scenic Dr., La Jolla* ☎ *858/452–9858* ⊕ *www.flytorrey.com*), perched on the cliffs overlooking the ocean north of La Jolla, is one of the most spectacular spots to hang glide in the world. It's for experienced pilots only, but hang gliding and paragliding lessons and tandem rides for inexperienced gliders are available. Lookie loos can grab a bite at the snack shop after parking in the large dirt lot, but barriers keep them from looking right over the cliff for the best view of their airborne fellows.

HIKING & NATURE TRAILS

San Diego has plenty of open space for hiking. From beachside bluffs and waterfront estuaries to the foothills and trails of the nearby Laguna Mountains and the desert beyond, the county has several vegetation and climate zones. Those who lack the time to explore the outskirts will find a day hike through the canyons and gardens of Balboa Park or the riparian riverbeds of Mission Trails Park a great way to escape to nature without leaving the city. A list of scheduled walks appears in the "Night and Day" section of the Thursday *San Diego Union-Tribune* and in the *Reader* weekly.

Guided hikes are conducted regularly through Los Peñasquitos Canyon Preserve and the Torrey Pines State Beach and Reserve.

The **San Dieguito River Park** (✉ *18372 Sycamore Creek Rd., 21 mi north of San Diego on I–5 to Lomas Santa Fe Dr., east 1 mi to Sun Valley Rd., north into park, Solana Beach* ☎ *858/674–2270* ⊕ *www.sdrp. org*) is a 55-mi corridor that begins at the mouth of the San Dieguito River in Del Mar and heads from the riparian lagoon area through coastal sage scrub and mountain terrain to end in the desert just east of Volcan Mountain near Julian. It's open to hikers, bikers, and horses. The **Tijuana Estuary** (✉ *301 Caspian Way, Exit I–5 at Coronado Ave., head west to 3rd St., turn left onto Caspian, which leads into estuary parking lot, Imperial Beach* ☎ *619/575–3613* ⊕ *www.tijuanaestuary. com*), mostly contained within Border Field State Park, is one of the last extant riparian environments in Southern California. The freshwater and saltwater marshes give refuge to migrant and resident waterfowl. Equestrian trails fringe the south end of the Tijuana Estuary in Border Field State Park. The visitor center is open Wednesday through Sunday. **Mission Trails Regional Park** (✉ *1 Father Junípero Serra Trail, Mission Valley* ☎ *619/668–3281* ⊕ *www.mtrp.org*), which encompasses nearly 6,000 acres of wooded hillsides, grasslands, chaparral, and riparian streams, is only 8 mi northeast of downtown. Trails range from easy to difficult; they include one with an impressive view of the city from Cowles Mountain and another along a historic missionary path. Lake Murray is at the southern edge of the park, just off Highway 8. At ★ more than 600,000 acres, **Anza-Borrego Desert State Park** (✉ *200 Palm Canyon Dr., Borrego Springs* ☎ *760/767–5311* ⊕ *www.parks.ca.gov*) is the nation's largest desert state park. There are 500 mi of dirt roads and countless trails for hiking, which is especially popular during the two-week desert wildflower bloom, which happens each year between early February and late April—the exact timing depends on winter rains, so it's best to call the park ahead of time for advice. The park is about a two-hour drive east of downtown San Diego, at the far eastern end of San Diego County.

★ **Hike Bike Kayak San Diego** (✉ *2246 Ave. de la Playa, La Jolla* ☏ *858/ 551–9510 or 866/425–2925* ∰ *www.hikebikekayak.com*) does guided treks through Torrey Pines State Beach and Reserve, and Mission Trails Regional Park, the latter including Cowles Mountain and Fortuna Mountain.

HORSEBACK RIDING

Bright Valley Farms (✉ *12310 Campo Rd., Spring Valley* ☏ *619/670– 1861* ∰ *www.brightvalleyfarms.com*) offers lessons and rents horses to ride on the winding trails of the Sweetwater River Valley. **Sweet Water Farms** (✉ *3051 Equitation La., Bonita* ☏ *619/475–3134* ∰ *www. sweetwaterhorses.com*) provides trail rides through the stunning nature trails of inland San Diego County's Bonita area and offers horse camping as well.

JET SKIING

Jet Skis can be launched from most ocean beaches, although you must ride beyond surf lines, and some beaches have special regulations governing their use. The only freshwater lake that allows Jet Skis is **El Capitan Reservoir**, 30 mi northeast of the city near Lake Jennings. Take I–8 north to Lake Jennings Park Road, head east on El Monte Road, and follow signs; there's a day-use fee of $5 per person. Waveless Mission Bay and the small **Snug Harbor Marina** (✉ *4215 Harrison St., Carlsbad* ☏ *760/434–3089*), east of the intersection of Tamarack Avenue and I–5 in Carlsbad, are favorite spots. **San Diego Jet Ski Rentals** (✉ *1636 Grand Ave., Pacific Beach* ☏ *858/272–6161*) rents Jet Skis. They are open daily in summer; other times of year, call ahead for a reservation. **Seaforth Boat Rentals** (✉ *1715 Strand Way, Coronado* ☏ *619/437–1514 or 888/834–2628* ✉ *1641 Quivira Rd., Mission Bay* ☏ *619/223–1681* ✉ *333 West Harbor Dr. Gate 1, Downtown* ☏ *619/239–2628*) rents Yamaha Waverunners for 2 or 3 people.

JOGGING

The most popular run downtown is along the **Embarcadero,** which stretches for 2 mi around the bay. There are uncongested sidewalks all through the area, but the alternative in the downtown area is to head east to **Balboa Park,** where trails snake through the canyons. Joggers can start out from any parking lot, but it's probably easiest to start anywhere along the 6th Avenue side. Entry to the numerous lots is best where Laurel Street connects with 6th Avenue. There's also a fitness circuit course in the park's **Morley Field** area. **Mission Bay** is renowned among joggers for its wide sidewalks and basically flat landscape. Trails head west around Fiesta Island, providing distance as well as a scenic route. **Del Mar** has the finest running trails along the bluff; park your car near 15th Street and run south along the cliffs for a gorgeous view of the ocean. The **Mission Beach boardwalk** is a great place to run while soaking up the scenery and beach culture. Organized runs occur almost every weekend. They're listed in *Competitor* magazine, which is available free at bike and running shops. **Roadrunner Sports** (✉*5553 Copley Dr., Kearny Mesa* ☎*858/974–4475* ⊕*www.roadrunnersports. com*) has all the supplies and information you'll need for running in San Diego.

ROCK CLIMBING

★ **Mission Trails Regional Park** (✉*1 Father Junípero Serra Trail, Mission Valley* ☎*619/668–3281* ⊕*www.mtrp.org*) has a huge quantity of bouldering, top-roping, and single-pitch climbs. With plenty of belay stations and holds that are regularly changed, the three locations of **Solid Rock Gym** (✉*2074 Hancock St., Old Town* ☎*619/299–1124* ✉*13026 Stowe Drive, Poway* ☎*858/748–9011* ✉*992 Rancheros Dr., San Marcos* ☎*760/480–1429* ⊕*www.solidrockgym.com*) appeal to all skill levels with indoor top-roping, bouldering, and lead climbing areas. In addition to day-use fees they rent equipment and offer lessons. **Vertical Hold Sport Climbing Center** (✉*9580 Distribution Ave., Mira Mesa* ☎*858/586–7572* ⊕*www.verticalhold.com*) is the largest full-service indoor rock-climbing gym in Southern California. It offers lessons, equipment rentals, and party packages.

ROLLERBLADING & ROLLER-SKATING

The miles and miles of sidewalks of **Mission Bay Aquatic Park** are perfect for Rollerblading and skating; you can admire the sailboats and kites while you get some exercise. **Bikes and Beyond** (✉*1201 1st Ave., Coronado* ☎*619/435–7180*) is the place to go to rent skates, blades, and bikes to cruise the beachwalk of Coronado. **Cheap Rentals Mission Beach** (✉*3689 Mission Blvd., Mission Beach* ☎*858/488–9070 or 800/941–7761* ⊕*www.cheap-rentals.com*) has good prices for Rollerblades, especially for the full day; rental comes with helmet and knee and elbow pads. **Skateworld** (✉*6907 Linda Vista Rd., Linda Vista* ☎*858/560–9349* ⊕*www.sandiegoskateworld.com*) has several public sessions daily on weekends, with adults-only skating on Tuesday evenings. In addition to private group sessions for bladers and skaters they offer a really-and-truly women's roller derby (the season is February through May). If you want to learn to make legal roller derby hits, avoid penalties, and take a fall, join their RD boot camp.

SAILING & BOATING

The city's history is full of seafarers, from the ships of the 1542 Cabrillo expedition to the America's Cup that once had a home here. Winds in San Diego are fairly consistent, especially in winter. You can rent a slip at one of several marinas if you're bringing your own boat. If not, you can rent vessels of various sizes and shapes—from small paddleboats to sleek 12-meters and kayaks to Hobie Cats—from specialized vendors. In addition, most bayside resorts rent equipment for on-the-water adventures. Most of what's available from these outlets is not intended for the open ocean, which is wise, considering the potential danger for the inexperienced. The **Bahia Resort Hotel** (⊠*998 W. Mission Bay Dr., Mission Bay* ☎*858/488–2582* ⊕ *www.bahiahotel.com*) and

★ its sister location, the **Catamaran Resort Hotel** (⊠*3999 Mission Blvd., Mission Beach* ☎*858/488–2582*), rent paddleboats, kayaks, powerboats, and sailboats from 14 to 22 feet. The Bahia also rents out a ski boat. **Harbor Sailboats** (⊠*2040 Harbor Island Dr., Harbor Island* ☎*619/291–9568 or 800/854–6625* ⊕*www.harborsailboats.com*) rents sailboats from 22 to 47 feet long for open-ocean adventures. **Seaforth Boat Rentals** (⊠*1715 Strand Way, Coronado* ☎*619/437–1514 or 888/834–2628* ⊠ *1641 Quivira Rd., Mission Bay* ☎*619/223–1681* ⊠*333 W. Harbor Dr. Gate 1, Downtown* ☎*619/239–2628*) has kayaks, Jet Skis, fishing skiffs, and power boats from 10 feet to 20 feet in length as well as sailboats from 16 to 36 feet. They also can hook you up with a skipper. **Hike Bike Kayak San Diego** (⊠*2246 Ave. de la Playa, La Jolla* ☎*858/551–9510 or 866/425–2925* ⊕*www.hikebikekayak. com*) offers several kayak tours, from easy excursions in Mission Bay that are well-suited to families and beginners to more advanced jaunts, where kayakers paddle with leopard sharks or whale-watch (from a safe distance). Moonlight tours are also offered; during the summer months a cruise into the bay to see SeaWorld's impressive fireworks shows over the water can be thrilling. **Carlsbad Paddle Sports** (⊠*2002 S. Coast Hwy., Oceanside* ☎*760/434–8686* ⊕*www.carlsbadpaddle. com*) handles kayak sales, rentals, and instruction for coastal North County.

Contact **California Cruisin'** (⊠*1450 Harbor Island Dr., Downtown* ☎*619/296–8000 or 800/449–2248* ⊕*www.californiacruisin.com*) for yachting charter excursions and dinner cruises. **Hornblower Cruises and Events** (⊠*1066 N. Harbor Dr., Embarcadero* ☎*619/686–8700 or 888/467–6256* ⊕*www.hornblower.com*) operates harbor cruises, sunset cocktail and dining cruises, whale-watching excursions, and yacht charters. **San Diego Harbor Excursion** (⊠*1050 N. Harbor Dr., Embarcadero* ☎*619/234–4111 or 800/442–7847* ⊕*www.sdhe.com*) has two-

★ hour dinner and brunch cruises and a ferry to Coronado. **Classic Sailing Adventures** (⊠*2051 Shelter Island Dr., Shelter Island* ☎*619/224–0800 or 800/659–0141* ⊕*www.classicsailingadventures.com*) offers more intimate sails aboard their 38-foot sailboat for champagne sunset cruises in summer, or daytime sightseeing (whale-watching in winter). For information, including tips on overnight anchoring, contact the **Port of San Diego Mooring Office** (☎*619/686–6227*). For additional information contact the **San Diego Harbor Police** (☎*619/686–6272*).

SKATEBOARD PARKS

Skateboarding culture has always thrived in San Diego, and recent changes in liability laws have encouraged a jump in the number of skate parks. A good number of top pro skateboarders live in San Diego and often practice and perfect new moves at local skate parks. Pads and helmets (always a good idea anywhere) are required at all parks.

Escondido Sports Center (✉3315 Bear Valley Pkwy., Escondido ☎760/839–5425 ⊕www.escondido.org) has a 22,000-square-foot skate park that includes a mini-ramp, street course, and vertical ramp. **Magdalena Ecke Family YMCA** (✉200 Saxony Rd., Encinitas ☎760/942–9622) is very popular among the many pros in this beach town. It has a competition street course, two cement pools, and a classic vertical ramp, installed for the 2003 X games. **Ocean Beach Skatepark at Robb Field** (✉2525 Bacon St., Ocean Beach ☎619/525–8486) is the largest park in the city. It has a huge street plaza, bowls, ledges, grind rails, and quarterpipes.

> **GREAT LEAP**
>
> San Diego skateboarder Danny Way, who already held world records for distance and height on a skateboard, set a new world record on July 9, 2005, when he became the first person to jump over the Great Wall of China without the use of a motorized vehicle, and live to tell the tale.

SURFING

If you're a beginner, consider paddling in the waves off Mission Beach, Pacific Beach, Tourmaline Surfing Park, La Jolla Shores, Del Mar, or Oceanside. More experienced surfers usually head for Sunset Cliffs, the La Jolla reef breaks, Black's Beach, or Swami's in Encinitas. All necessary equipment is included in the cost of all surfing schools. Beach area Y's offer surf lessons and surf camp in the summer months, and during
★ spring break. **Hike Bike Kayak San Diego** (✉2246 Ave. de la Playa, La Jolla ☎858/551–9510 or 866/425–2925 ⊕www.hikebikekayak.com) gives group and private lessons in La Jolla, year-round. If you know what you're doing but didn't bring your stick, they rent boards, too. **Kahuna Bob's Surf School** (☎760/721–7700 or 800/524–8627 ⊕www.kahunabob.com) conducts two-hour lessons in coastal North County seven days a week. They offer surf camp in summer for the children. **San Diego Surfing Academy** (☎760/230–1474 or 800/447–7873 ⊕www.surfacademy.com) has private lessons anytime, group lessons twice daily during the warmer months, and five-day surf camps for teens, kids, and adults. The academy, which has called San Diego home for more than a dozen years, is based at South Carlsbad State Beach. **Surf**
★ **Diva Surf School** (✉2160 Avenida de la Playa, La Jolla ☎858/454–8273 ⊕www.surfdiva.com) offers clinics, surf camps, surf trips, and private lessons especially formulated for girls and women. Clinics and trips are for women only, but guys can book private lessons from the nationally recognized staff.

Many local surf shops rent both surf and bodyboards. **Cheap Rentals Mission Beach** (✉3689 Mission Blvd., Mission Beach ☎858/488–9070 or 800/941–7761 ⊕www.cheap-rentals.com) is right on the boardwalk, just steps from the waves. They rent wetsuits, bodyboards, and skimboards in addition to soft surfboards and long and short fiberglass rides. **Star Surfing Company** (✉4652 Mission Blvd., Pacific Beach ☎858/273–7827 ⊕www.starsurfingco.com) can get you out surfing around the Crystal Pier, with wetsuits, bodyboards, and surfboards.

Hansen's (✉*1105 S. Coast Hwy. 101, Encinitas* ☎*760/753–6595 or 800/480–4754* ⊕*www.hansen-surf.com*) is just a short walk from Swami's beach. One of San Diego's oldest and most popular surf shops, it has an extensive selection of boards, wetsuits and clothing for sale, and a rental department as well.

SWIMMING

Built in 1925, Belmont Park's 58-yard-long **Plunge** (✉*3115 Mission Blvd., Mission Beach* ☎*858/488–3110* ⊕*www.belmontpark.com*) is the largest heated indoor swimming pool in Southern California. The **Copley Family YMCA** (✉*3901 Landis St., North Park* ☎*619/283–2251*) has a heated, indoor pool with hours for lap swimming and free swim. The **Bud Kearns Memorial Pool** (✉*2229 Morley Field Dr., Balboa Park* ☎*619/692–4920*) is operated from May to October by the City of San Diego; some years it opens as early as March and stays open through the end of the year, so call to get the current schedule.

The **Magdalena Ecke Family YMCA** (✉*200 Saxony Rd., Encinitas* ☎*760/942–9622* ⊕*www.ecke.ymca.org*) is convenient for swimming in North County with two pools, one cooler pool for aerobics classes and lap swim, and the other, warmer pool for free swimming. In between the two pools is a "wet pad" with sprinklers. The indoor pool area has a retractable roof that opens in fair weather.

TENNIS

Most of the more than 1,300 courts around the county are in private clubs, but a few are public. The **Balboa Tennis Club at Morley Field** (✉*2221 Morley Field Dr., Balboa Park* ☎*619/295–9278* ⊕*www.balboatennis.com*) has 25 courts, 19 of them lighted. The Tennis Cafe serves snacks, soups, and sandwiches. Courts are available on a first-come, first-served basis for a daily $5-per-person fee. Heaviest usage is 9 AM–11 AM and after 5 PM; at other times you can usually arrive and begin playing. Pros offer clinics and classes. The **La Jolla Tennis Club** (✉*7632 Draper Ave., La Jolla* ☎*858/454–4434* ⊕*www.ljtc.org*) has nine public courts near downtown La Jolla; five are lighted; the daily fee is $5. The club is initiating a reservations system (call from 12 to 72 hours ahead to reserve a court) on a trial basis. The 12 lighted courts at the privately owned **Peninsula Tennis Club** (✉*Robb Field, Ocean Beach* ☎*619/226–3407*) are available to the public for $5 per person daily.

> ### SURFING IS SWELL
>
> In San Diego the biggest swells usually occur in winter, although good-size waves can form year-round. Generally, swells come from a northerly direction in winter, although in summer they tend to come from the south. Certain surf spots are better on different swells. In winter, try beaches like Swami's or Black's Beach. Summer spots are La Jolla's Windansea and nearby Tourmaline Surfing Park. Surf the Web at www.sandiegoinsidertours.com to learn more.

5

Several San Diego resorts have top-notch tennis programs staffed by big-name professional instructors. **Rancho Valencia Resort** (⊠ *5921 Valencia Circle, Rancho Santa Fe* ☎ *858/759–6224* ⊕ *www.ranchovalencia.com*), which is among the top tennis resorts in the nation, has 17 hard courts and several instruction programs. Tennis shoes and tennis attire (no T-shirts) are required.

Fodor'sChoice

★ **La Costa Resort and Spa** (⊠ *2100 Costa Del Mar Rd., Carlsbad* ☎ *760/438–9111* ⊕ *www.lacosta.com*), site of the annual Acura Tennis Classic, has 17 hard and clay courts, seven of them lighted, plus professional instruction, clinics, and workouts.

VOLLEYBALL

Ocean Beach, South Mission Beach, Del Mar Beach, Moonlight Beach, and the western edge of Balboa Park are major congregating points for volleyball enthusiasts. These are also the best places to find a pickup game. Contact the **San Diego Volleyball Club** (☎ *858/385–1855* ⊕ *www.sdvbc.org*) to find out about organized games and tournaments.

WATERSKIING

Mission Bay is popular for waterskiing, although the bay is often polluted, especially after a heavy rain. As a general rule, it's best to get out early, when the water is smooth and the crowds are thin. Boats and equipment can be rented from **Seaforth Boat Rentals** (⊠ *1715 Strand Way, Coronado* ☎ *619/437–1514 or 888/834–2628* ⊠ *1641 Quivira Rd., Mission Bay* ☎ *619/223–1681* ⊠ *333 West Harbor Dr., Gate 1, Downtown* ☎ *619/239–2628*).

WINDSURFING

Also known as sailboarding, windsurfing is a sport best practiced on smooth waters, such as Mission Bay. More experienced windsurfers will enjoy taking a board out on the ocean. Wave jumping is especially popular at the Tourmaline Surfing Park in La Jolla and in the Del Mar area, where you can also occasionally see kiteboarders practice their variation on the theme. Sailboard rentals and instruction are available at the **Bahia Resort Hotel** (⊠ *998 W. Mission Bay Dr., Mission Bay* ☎ *858/488–2582* ⊕ *www.bahiahotel.com*). The **Catamaran Resort Hotel** (⊠ *3999 Mission Blvd., Mission Beach* ☎ *858/488–1081*), a sister location of the Bahia Resort Hotel, offers similar services.

Shopping

WORD OF MOUTH

"Horton Plaza … is an unusual mall in downtown San Diego. It looks somewhat like a Dr. Seuss children's book with stairways branching off in every direction, vivid colors and designs. Definitely worth seeing."

—San_Diego_Mom

"On to Coronado! We checked out the hotel and beach and walked around the main drag, doing lots of window shopping. This is a really fun area and I wouldn't mind coming back here some day to relax."

—aggiegirl

Updated
by Amanda
Knoles

SAN DIEGO'S RETAIL VENUES ARE as diverse as the city's vibrant neighborhoods. From La Jolla's tony boutiques to the outlet malls at San Ysidro, you'll find stores that appeal to every taste and budget. Trendsetters will have no trouble finding must-have handbags and designer apparel at the world-class Fashion Valley mall in Mission Valley, a haven for luxury brands such as Hermès, Jimmy Choo, and Carolina Herrera. The upscale mall with more than 200 retailers is anchored by six department stores including Neiman Marcus, Nordstrom, and Saks Fifth Avenue. La Jolla's chic boutiques offer a more intimate shopping experience along with some of the classiest clothes, jewelry, and footwear in the county.

Into kitschy gifts and souvenirs? Seaport Village has an abundance of quirky shops that won't disappoint, plus you'll be able to enjoy the coastal breezes while you shop for that Coronado Bridge snow globe. The Gaslamp Quarter, downtown's trendy hot spot, is where you'll find independent shops selling urban apparel, unique home decor, and vintage treasures. If you can't find it in the boutiques, head for Westfield Horton Plaza, the downtown mall boasting more than 180 stores and 22 eateries. Nearby Little Italy is the place to find contemporary art and home decor.

The beach towns have the best swimwear and sandals, and Uptown is known for its mélange of funky bookstores, offbeat gift shops, and nostalgic collectibles. Old Town is a must for pottery, ceramics, jewelry, and handcrafted baskets.

Shopping hours vary, but malls and major shopping centers typically stay open until at least 9 PM, and independent stores are usually open from 10 to 6 daily. Visit ⊕ *www.sandiego.citysearch.com* and ⊕ *www. signonsandiego.com* for more details on local shops and sales. The *San Diego Union Tribune* and the *San Diego Reader* frequently offer discount coupons.

CORONADO

Coronado's resort hotels attract tourists in droves, but somehow the town has managed to avoid being overtaken by chain stores. Instead, shoppers can browse a variety of family-owned shops and dine at sidewalk cafés along Orange Avenue, stroll through the arcade at the historic Hotel Del Coronado, or take in the specialty shops at the Ferry Landing Marketplace.

SHOPPING CENTERS

Fodor'sChoice **Ferry Landing Marketplace.** A staggering view of San Diego's downtown
★ skyline across the bay, 30 boutiques, and a Tuesday afternoon Farmers' Market provide a delightful place to shop while waiting for a ferry. **Men's Island Sportswear** (☎619/437–4696) is a unique spot with hats, tropical sportswear, and accessories. ⊠1201 1st St., at B Ave. ☎619/435–8895 ⊕www.coronadoferrylanding.com.

SPECIALTY STORES

Friendly shopkeepers make the boutiques lining **Orange Avenue,** Coronado's main drag, a good place to browse for clothes, home decor, gift items, and gourmet foods.

BOOKSTORE **Bay Books.** This old-fashioned book-
★ store is the spot to sit, read, and sip coffee on an overcast day by the sea. International travelers will love the large selection of foreign-language magazines and newspapers, and there's a section in the back devoted to children's books and games. There are plenty of secluded reading nooks and a sidewalk reading area with a coffee bar. ⊠*1029 Orange Ave.* ☎*619/435–0070* ⊕*www.baybookscoronado.com.*

CLOTHING & **Dale's Swim Shop.** All things beachy
ACCESSORIES catch your eye in this shop crammed with swimsuits, hats, sunglasses, and sunscreen. ⊠*1150 Orange Ave.* ☎*619/435–1757.*

Kippys. Madonna and Liz Hurley have been photographed in the high quality leather belts from this shop. Fringed suede vests, sexy leather pants, and beaded denim are all here. ⊠*1114 Orange Ave.* ☎*619/435–6218* ⊕*www.kippys.com.*

Orange Blossoms Shop. The shop's casual wear for women and girls includes embellished tees, frilly tops, and colorful handmade sweaters. ⊠*952 Orange Ave.* ☎*619/437–8399* ⊕*www.orangeblossomsshop. com.*

GOURMET **In Good Taste.** Come here for smooth-as-silk chocolates and fudge, spe-
FOODS cialty cheeses, wine, truffles, and fresh bread. ⊠*1146 Orange Ave.* ☎*619/435–8356.*

HOME **The Attic.** The Attic is stocked with lots of Victoriana, white-painted fur-
ACCESSORIES niture, quilts, and linens. Be sure to go around the corner on 10th Street
& GIFTS to its sister shop, **10th Street Attic,** for more of the same one-of-a-kind merchandise. ⊠*1011 Orange Ave.* ☎*619/435–5432.*

Fodor'sChoice **Hotel Del Coronado.** At the dozen gift shops within the peninsula's main
★ historic attraction, you can purchase everything from sportswear to designer handbags, jewelry, and antiques. ⊠*1500 Orange Ave.* ☎*619/435–6611* ⊕*www.hoteldel.com/shopping.*

La Provençale. The shop carries imported linens, tableware, fashion accessories, and paintings, all in sunny colors. ⊠*1122 Orange Ave.* ☎*619/437–8881.*

TOP 5 SHOPPING

■ **Fashion Valley.** This is the mall Carrie Bradshaw would shop at.

■ **Gaslamp Quarter.** The plethora of trendy boutiques take you from casual tourist to head-turning hottie.

■ **La Jolla.** Shop like the rich and famous while enjoying breathtaking ocean views.

■ **Old Town.** Who needs a trip to Mexico when you can shop 'til you drop at Bazaar del Mundo.

■ **Seaport Village.** Souvenir heaven: The world's hottest salsas, seashell jewelry, and snow globes are all here.

6

Seaside Home. Sophisticated bedding, crystal, porcelain, and home accessories are sold here. There's another branch in La Jolla village. ✉ *1053 B Ave.* ☎ *619/435–8232* ⊕ *www.seasidehomecoronado.com.*

Seaside Papery. This sister store of Seaside Home offers a selection of high-end wedding invitations, greeting cards, wrapping papers, and luxury personal stationery. ✉ *1162 Orange Ave.* ☎ *619/435–5565* ⊕ *www.seasidepapery.com.*

Ye Olde Flower Shoppe. In addition to fresh-cut floral bouquets and arrangements, this charming shop offers dish gardens, greeting cards, candles, gift baskets, and decorative accessories. ✉ *1330 Orange Ave.* ☎ *800/323–0885* ⊕ *yeoldeflowershoppe.com* ⊙ *Closed Sun.*

DOWNTOWN

EMBARCADERO

Spanning 14 acres and offering more than 50 shops and 17 eateries, Embarcadero's Seaport Village is the most popular destination in this marina neighborhood. The picturesque shopping center caters to tourists with a heavy concentration of souvenir shops, but you'll also find toys, art, jewelry, apparel for the whole family, and nostalgic collectibles.

SHOPPING CENTERS

Seaport Village. Quintessentially San Diego, this waterfront complex of more than 67 shops and restaurants has sweeping bay views, fresh breezes, and great strolling paths. Horse and carriage rides, an 1895 Looff carousel, and frequent public entertainment are side attractions. The Seaport is within walking distance of hotels, the San Diego Convention Center, and San Diego Trolley, and there's also an easily accessible free parking lot. **Discover Nature** (☎ *619/231–1299*) is where you can find gifts for the office, table-top fountains, wind chimes,
★ and jewelry. **Kite Flite** (☎ *877/234–8229*) carries a huge inventory of kites in every size, shape, and price range, and they'll let you try before you buy. **Latitudes** (☎ *619/235–0220*) sells casual beachwear for men and women. **San Diego Surf Co.** (☎ *619/696–8967*) has all the top brands in beachwear and surf apparel. **Seaport Village Shell Company** (☎ *619/234–1004*) carries shells, coral, jewelry, and craft items. **Upstart Crow** (☎ *619/232–4855*) offers a terrific selection of books, journals, gifts, and greeting cards. The outdoor coffee bar is great for people-watching while you grab a snack. **Wyland Galleries** (☎ *619/544–9995*) offers the marine-life art of Wyland; there's another branch in La Jolla. ✉ *W. Harbor Dr. at Kettner Blvd.* ☎ *619/235–4014* ⊕ *www.spvillage.com.*

Shopping Blitz Tour

SHOPPING SAFARI

Horton Plaza, San Diego's colorful downtown mall, is a great place to begin your shopping adventure. Parking is free for three hours with a store purchase, or you can get there by trolley or bus. There are more than 180 stores to browse through including Abercrombie and Fitch, Nordstrom, and Macy's. Arden B, Planet Funk, and BCBG Maxazria are great for hip fashions and clubwear. Horton Toy & Doll is a delight for all ages, and you'll find cool skate and surf apparel for teens at Pac Sun. Grab a quick lunch at Nordstrom Café or one of the many eateries in the food court before heading over to the **Gaslamp Quarter**, an easy stroll north. Between Sixth and Tenth Avenues, explore fun boutiques like Buzz, Five and a Dime, and Urchin. Irresistible indulgences for yourself or someone special await at La Paperie, Z Galerie, and Bubbles Boutique. Lucky Dog even has pampering treats for the pooch you left back home.

GO FLY A KITE

Head over to **Seaport Village** and stop in to Kite Flite. They'll let you test-drive any kite you like just outside their door. Once you've bought your favorite one, take it to adjacent Embarcadero Park and watch your new toy soar in the sea breezes. Carefully pack your cool kite into its bag and check out Upstart Crow for books and gifts. Enjoy a coffee and snack on the outdoor patio or kick back in one of the comfy lounge chairs inside.

SAIL AWAY

Stroll down to the Broadway Pier (1050 N. Harbor Dr.) and take the fifteen-minute ferry ride to **Coronado Island**. (Ferries depart daily every hour from 9 to 9 and a round-trip ticket is $6.) The postcard view of the skyline and the majestic Coronado Bridge is worth the trip in itself. The Ferry Landing Marketplace features 30 fun stores selling everything from wind chimes and wildlife art to music boxes and casual clothing. Next take the Coronado Shuttle to Orange Avenue, the city's main drag for shopping, dining and people-watching. Stop in at Dale's Swim Shop for beach gear, Seaside Papery for stylish stationery, and visit In Good Taste for gourmet chocolates, fine cheeses, and wine. Follow the crowd to the Hotel Del Coronado and enjoy a leisurely tour of the lobby and grounds before heading downstairs to the shopping arcade. Designer handbags, toys, fine menswear, sexy lingerie, home decor, and fabulous jewelry are a few of the temptations you'll find hard to resist. Exit the shops and walk out onto the beach path for one of the most glorious ocean views in all of San Diego. A tropical drink or smoothie at the Sundeck Bar and Grill is a must before heading back to the ferry for your return trip to the mainland.

6

GASLAMP QUARTER

Here you'll find the usual mall denizens as well as hip fashion boutiques and gift shops, even for your pup. The historic heart of San Diego has recently seen an explosion of specialty shops, art galleries, and boutiques take up residence in the Victorian buildings and renovated warehouses along 4th and 5th avenues. Some stores in this area tend to close early, starting as early as 5 PM.

SHOPPING CENTERS

Westfield Horton Plaza. Within walking distance of most downtown hotels, Horton Plaza is bordered by Broadway, 1st Avenue, G Street, and 4th Avenue. The multilevel shopping, dining, and entertainment complex is an open-air visual delight, with a terra-cotta color scheme and flag-draped facades. There are department stores, including Macy's and Nordstrom; fast-food counters; upscale restaurants; the Lyceum Theater; cinemas; a game arcade; and 140 other stores. Park in the plaza garage and any store where you make a purchase will validate
★ your parking ticket, good for three free hours. The **San Diego City Store** (☎619/238–2489) sells city artifacts and memorabilia, such as street signs and parking meters. The yellow SURFING OK sign is a typical San Diego–inspired souvenir. ⊠324 Horton Plaza ☎619/238–1596 ⊕www.westfield.com/hortonplaza.

SPECIALTY STORES

CLOTHING & **Blends.** Minimalist decor provides a perfect backdrop for the wild col-
ACCESSORIES ors and patterns featured on limited-edition sneakers from Nike, Reebok, Vans, and other in-demand brands. Prices are steep, but the styles are unique. ⊠726 Market St. ☎619/233–6126.

Designer Millinery. Owner Diana Cavagnaro, who has taught millinery for more than 14 years at a local college, has been in the hat business for more than 25 years. This shop displays her whimsical, lavish creations as well as scarves and hat blocks, but is by appointment only. ⊠311 4th Ave. ☎619/239–4287.

Le Travel Store. Among the travel accessories sold here are luggage, totes, guidebooks, and maps. ⊠745 4th Ave. ☎619/544–0005.

Lucky Brand Jeans. Shop here for women's, men's, kids', and even baby's jeans, as well as hip fashions. ⊠621 5th Ave. ☎619/230–9260.

Quiksilver Boardriders Club. This shop features Quiksilver's full line of surf clothing, shoes, and accessories, and their famous surfboards. ⊠402 5th Ave. ☎619/234–3125.

Ron Stuart. Sharp-dressed men flock to this men's shop for Manzoni suits, Tommy Bahama shirts, and expert tailoring on-site. ⊠225 A St. ☎619/232–8850 ⊕www.ronstuartmensclothing.com ⊙Closed Sun.

Splash Wearable Art. The reasonably priced clothing includes one-of-a-kind things not found at the malls, such as dresses crafted from Balinese fabrics and a fine collection of hand-beaded evening wear. ⊠376 5th Ave. ☎619/233–5251.

Urban Outfitters. Street-vibe fashions, accessories, and shoes for men and women, plus home decor and whimsical gift items. ⊠665 5th Ave. ☎619/231–0102 ⊕www.urbanoutfitters.com.

Urchin Boutique. A sassy mix of urban and hippie chic, this boutique features Christie's of London hats, Lips jeans, and apparel from up and coming designers. ⊠911 6th Ave. ☎619/269–3742 ⊕www.urchin-style.com ⊙Closed Sun.–Tues.

Villa Moda. You'll find the finest designer wear for women in this upscale boutique. ⊠*363 5th Ave.* ☎*619/236–9068* ⊕*www.villamoda.com.*

Western Hat Works. Western Hat Works has been selling every kind of hat from fedora to Stetson since 1922. ⊠*433 E St.* ☎*619/234–0457.*

GALLERIES **The Art of Tim Cantor.** The artist works in a private studio in the back of this gallery showcasing his intense, mysterious works in oil and sculpture. ⊠*527 4th Ave.* ☎*619/235–6990* ⊕*www.timcantor.com.*

CJ Gallery. This gallery in the historic Whitney Building specializes in contemporary fine art. ⊠*343 4th Ave.* ☎*619/595–0048* ⊕*www.cjart-gallery.com.*

Michael J. Wolf Fine Arts. In the historic Brunswick Building, the Gaslamp's oldest art gallery presents the work of emerging contemporary artists. ⊠*363 5th Ave., Ste. 102* ☎*619/702–5388* ⊕*www.mjwfinearts.com.*

Opium Gallery. Furniture and accessories from the world over are sold here. ⊠*425 Market St.* ☎*619/234–2070.*

HOME
ACCESSORIES
& GIFTS
Bubbles Boutique. You'll find stuff for use beyond the bathtub, although the selection of hand-crafted soaps and bath treats is pleasingly broad. There are also sugar and salt body scrubs, body moisturizers, and manly shaving gels, pajamas, robes, and slippers. ⊠*226 5th Ave.,* ☎*866/236–9003* ⊕*www.bubblesboutique.com.*

★ **Cuban Cigar Factory.** As Cuban cigar makers hand-roll the goods for this factory, the largest maker of hand-rolled cigars on the West Coast, satisfied smokers puff around tables sampling the product. Tobacco grown from Cuban seed in the Dominican Republic, Central America, and elsewhere goes into the cigars, sold in boxes of 10 and 25 along with accessories such as humidors. ⊠*551 5th Ave.* ☎*619/238–2496* ⊕*www.cubancigarfactory.com.*

Lucky Dog Pet Boutique. If nothing is too good for Fifi or Fido, prove it with a fashionable sweater, raincoat, or pair of shoes. The dog gifts here even include hats, bags, and perfume. If your pooch is in tow, they'll take his photo for their photo gallery. ⊠*415 Market* ☎*619/696–0364* ⊕*www.shopluckydog.com.*

San Diego Wine & Culinary Center. Promoting the bountiful produce, wine, food, and chefs of San Diego, the center offers cooking classes and wine tastings. Stock up on locally made olive oils, jams, and sauces to take home. ⊠*200 Harbor Dr., in Harbor Club Towers* ☎*619/231–6400* ⊕*www.sdwineculinary.com.*

Z Gallerie. Everything for the hip home is here, from fine art to artful tabletop accessories, bed linens, and draperies. ⊠*611 5th Ave.* ☎*619/696–8137* ⊕*www.zgallerie.com.*

SAN DIEGO'S EAST VILLAGE

Just a hop, skip, and a jump from the Gaslamp Quarter, the up and coming East Village offers a variety of shops catering to local hipsters and fashion-savvy visitors (especially from 8th to 10th avenues between Broadway and J Street). Here are some of our favorites:

Buzz. This men's lifestyle boutique offers the latest denim, hoodies, casual shirts, and accessories from Diesel, Earnest Sewn, and Converse by John Varvatos. They also stock a limited selection of books, magazines, and CDs. ⊠ *630 10th Ave.* ☎ *619/955-7805* ⊕ *www.buzzclothing.com* ☉ *Closed Mon.*

The District. Friendly stylists help customers choose perfect outfits from lines like Kasil denim, Red Monkey, Giorgio Brutini, and Kendra Scott. Hot buys are leather cuff watches and stylish handbags. ⊠ *1020 8th Ave.* ☎ *619/231-9533* ⊕ *www.thedistrictsd.com* ☉ *Closed Sun.*

Five and A Dime. A popular hangout for hipsters, this boutique features labels like Crooks & Castles, Godwin, One People Project, and Bad Company. Choose from a great selection of hats, shoes, sweaters, and tees for guys and gals, and be sure to check out the weird toys. ⊠ *701 8th St.* ☎ *619/236-0364* ⊕ *www.5andadime.com.*

LITTLE ITALY

Boasting more than 33,500 square feet of retail, Little Italy is an especially fun place to visit during holiday celebrations and special events like the ArtWalk and jazz festival. Many shops have a strong European ambience, and shoppers will find an enticing array of wares, from colorful ceramics and hand-blown glassware to modern home accents and designer shoes. The stretch along Kettner Boulevard and India Street from Laurel to Date Street is the Art & Design District.

SPECIALTY STORES

CLOTHING **Niche.** This upscale boutique has a great selection of designer shoes and apparel for women, plus adorable children's outfits. ⊠ *621 W. Fir St.* ☎ *619/615–0782* ⊕ *www.nicheboutique.com* ☉ *Closed Mon.*

Station. Find cutting-edge fashions and accessories for men and women from names like Ella Moss, Tracy Reese, Three Dot, and Tank Farm. ⊠ *414 W. Cedar St.* ☎ *619/544–1100* ⊕ *www.stopatstation.com.*

GALLERIES **Boomerang for Modern.** Thoroughly mid-20th-century modern design is celebrated here. Aficionados will discover now-classic furniture and accessories produced by Charles and Ray Eames and George Nelson. Small exhibitions showcase vintage and recent works in the modernist spirit, many by local artists. ⊠ *2475 Kettner Blvd.* ☎ *619/239–2040* ⊕ *www.boomerangformodern.com.*

Masquerade Art of Living. Masquerade's collections include fine art and wearable art, as well as mirrors, lamps and other home accessories, and gifts. ⊠ *1608 India St.* ☎ *619/235–6564* ⊕ *www.masqueradeartofliving.com.*

Mixture. Housed in a 1940s brick warehouse, Mixture blends art and high design for the home. You'll find high-style bedding, rugs, glassware, and bath and body products here, along with original art and sculpture. ⊠*2210 Kettner Blvd.* ☎*619/239–4788* ⊕*www.mixture-home.com.*

Kettner Arts Complex. Several fine-art galleries are in this building, including **CJ Kuhl Gallery** (☎*619/696–7230* ⊕*www.cjkuhl.com*) and **David Zapf Gallery** (☎*619/232–5004*). ⊠*2400 Kettner Blvd.*

HOME ACCESSORIES & GIFTS

Bella Stanza. The elegant Italian handmade gifts for the home include a large collection of colorful ceramics, glass, and art pieces. ⊠*1501 India St., No. 120* ☎*619/239–2929* ⊕*www.bellastanzagifts.com.*

Blick Art Materials. Besides supplying local artists with their tools, Blick Art Materials also carries fine stationery, beautiful leather-bound journals, and a fine selection of art books. ⊠*1844 India St.* ☎*619/687–0050* ⊕*www.dickblick.com.*

Che Bella Nido. Surrounded by a lovely garden and patio, this warm and inviting shop is filled with home decor and accessories including gorgeous ceramic vases and bowls, fragrant candles, Portuguese linens, and coffee table books. ⊠*611 W. Fir St.* ☎*619/232–1111* ⊕*www.chebellanido.com* ☽*Closed Sun.*

Disegno Italia. You've got to see the intensely creative design of these Italian-made home and office accessories. The sculptural kitchen gadgets are modern art. Where else can you find a can opener that looks like a parrot? ⊠*1605 India St.* ☎*619/515–0191* ⊕*www.disegno-italiano.biz.*

Simply Italian. The fine selection of furniture and accessories for the home hand-crafted by Italian artisans includes Murano glass chandeliers and lava-stone and majolica tables from Naples. ⊠*1646 India St.* ☎*619/702–7777* ⊕*www.simply-italian.com.*

Urban Skin Care. Treat yourself to an energizing facial and shop for skin care products from Dermalogica, Kinerase, Obagi, and Tricomin. ⊠*2326 India St.* ☎*619/233–0306* ⊕*www.urbanskincare.com.*

Zazou Home. A former 1908 paint factory houses this lifestyle store offering contemporary art, architectural finds, and objects of desire. ⊠*2136 Kettner Blvd.* ☎*619/234–3841* ⊕*www.zazouhome.com.*

LA JOLLA

Known as San Diego's Rodeo Drive, La Jolla's chic boutiques, art galleries, and gift shops line narrow twisty streets that are often celebrity-soaked. Prospect Street and Girard Avenue are the primary shopping stretches, and North Prospect is chockablock with art galleries. The Upper Girard Design District stocks home decor accessories and luxury furnishings. Parking is tight in the village and store hours vary widely, so it's wise to call in advance. Most shops on Prospect Street stay open until 10 PM on weeknights to accommodate evening strollers. On the east side of I–5, office buildings surround Westfield UTC, where you'll find department and chain stores.

SHOPPING CENTERS

Westfield UTC. Formerly University Towne Center, this handy outdoor mall east of La Jolla village has more than 150 shops and 24 eateries, plus an ice-skating rink. Department stores include Nordstrom, Macy's, and Sears Roebuck. **Charles David** (☎858/625–0275) sells high-fashion women's shoes. **Chuao Chocolatier** (☎858/546–1463 ⊕*www. chuaochocolatier.com*), pronounced "chew-wow," is an artisanal chocolate factory named after a region in Venezuela that produces the world's most highly prized cacao beans. **Naartjie** (☎858/625–0940) sells stylish clothing and accessories for babies and children. **Papyrus** (☎858/458–1399) carries a collection of San Diego postcards, whimsical notecards, gifts, and fine stationery. ✉*4545 La Jolla Village Dr., between I–5 and I–805* ☎*858/546–8858* ⊕*www.westfield.com/utc*.

★ **Coast Walk Plaza.** This seaside shopping area has breathtaking views, great paths for strolling, and benches perfect for people-watching. **Antique Maps, Inc.** (☎858/551–8500) boasts one of the most extensive collections of antique maps and atlases in the country. **Cherubs' Cottage** (☎858/459–3518) is brimming with gifts and accessories for every room in the home. Along with attractive vases, candleholders, and tableware, you'll find greeting cards, stationery, an eclectic selection of books for all ages, and gourmet food items. **Gaia Day Spa** (☎858/456–8797) features a tempting array of organic lotions and potions perfect for pampering facials and body treatments at home. Brands include Gaia, Jurlique, Sacred Earth, Aqua Dessa, and Sonoma Lavender. Aromatherapy candles, pillows, robes and inspirational books and CDs are also available. **Suzan's Silver and Amber Jewelry** (☎858/454–9808) specializes in affordably priced contemporary jewelry handcrafted from sterling silver and semi-precious stones. ✉ *1298 Prospect, at Roslyn Lane and Coast Blvd. S.* ☎*619/235–4014*

SPECIALTY STORES

BOOKSTORE **Warwick's.** An upscale bookstore and La Jolla fixture since 1896, Warwick's often hosts big-name author signings. ✉*7812 Girard Ave.* ☎*858/454–0347*.

CLOTHING **Ascot Shop.** The classic Ivy League look is king in this traditional haberdashery that sells menswear by Talbott, but also gives you the option of loosening up with a Hawaiian shirt. Local stockbrokers are the store's biggest customers. ✉*7750 Girard Ave.* ☎*858/454–4222*.

Donna Marsh. Spanning 5,500 square feet with separate rooms for career apparel, evening wear, and casual attire, this upscale women's boutique showcases fashions from

GO DIRECTLY TO PARK PLACE

The locals seem to have a monopoly on all the free parking spots in La Jolla, so do yourself a favor and park at one of the Prospect Avenue garages, between Wall and Silverado streets, or along Herschel, Girard, and Fay avenues. Rates range from $1.50 for 20 minutes to a maximum of $15 per day. After 4 PM, there is a flat rate of $8.

more than 120 designers. The premium denim area features hot styles from Paige, Habitual, Not Your Daughter's Jeans, and Tag. ✉*7712 Fay Ave.* ☎*858/454–3003* ⊕*www.donnamarshlajolla.com.*

★ **Elizabeth's Closet.** Specializing in chic apparel and accessories for men and women, this luxury boutique offers an impressive array of designers including Nanette Lepore, Hale Bob, and Catherine Malandrino. Owner Elizabeth Patterson, a former model and assistant to designer Nicole Miller, shares insider fashion tips at weekly trunk shows. ✉*1274 Prospect St.* ☎*858/459–4673* ⊕*www.shopelizabeths.com.*

Jep Clothing Boutique. Known for its avant-garde fashions, helpful staff, and laid-back atmosphere, Jep features upscale brands for men and women from names like Ella Moss, John Varvatos, Kasil, and L.A.M.B., plus sought after fragrances, jewelry, and accessories. ✉*7501 La Jolla Blvd.* ☎*858/551–0600* ⊕*www.jepboutique.com.*

La Jolla Surf Systems. One block from La Jolla Shores Beach, this La Jolla institution for vivid California beach and resort wear has been in business since 1979. Tame the waves with surfboards by Olas or Tuberville and boogie boards by BZ and Morey. This shop also rents surfboards and boogie boards, beach chairs, umbrellas, and snorkel gear. ✉*2132 Avenida de la Playa* ☎*858/456–2777.*

Let's Go La Jolla. Boasting an upscale fashion collection spread over two levels, this trend-savvy store offers top name designs in denim, casual, and formal wear for men and women. ✉*7863 Girard Ave.* ☎*858/459–2337* ⊕*www.letsgoclothing.com.*

Neroli Lingerie. This is the place for French lingerie by Aubade, Huit, and Simone Perele. If you're lucky, you'll land here during one of the boutique's frequent fashion shows. ✉*7944 Girard Ave.* ☎*858/456–9618.*

Nicole Miller. A favorite of San Diego's best-dressed women, this chic boutique is a great place to spot vacationing celebrities. Give your wardrobe a boost with figure-flattering dresses and tops, tailored trousers, and sexy evening frocks. ✉*1275 Prospect St.* ☎*858/454–3434* ⊕*www.nicolemiller.com.*

Rangoni of Florence. This boutique carries its own house brand, Rangoni of Florence, as well as other, medium-price European men's and women's footwear brands including Amalfi, Donald Pliner, and Cole Haan, all fashioned in Italy. ✉*7870 Girard Ave.* ☎*858/459–4469.*

Shades of Bettie. Named for pinup queen Bettie Page, this funky store specializes in retro fashions and accessories. Shop for '40s-style dresses, vintage-inspired purses, tees with tattoo designs, and leopard-print totes. ✉*1295 Prospect St. #108* ☎*619/850–4491* ⊘*Closed Tues. and Weds.*

GALLERIES & **Africa and Beyond.** This gallery carries Shona stone sculpture, textiles, CRAFTS crafts, masks, and jewelry. ✉*1250 Prospect St.* ☎*858/454–9983.*

The Artful Soul. Jewelry, handbags, and gifts by more than 130 contemporary crafts artists, many local. ⊠7660-A Fay Ave. ☎858/459–2009.

Fingerhut Gallery. Fingerhut carries the art of Dr. Seuss and Grace Slick alongside works by Peter Max and etchings and lithographs by Picasso, Chagall, and Toulouse Lautrec. ⊠1205 Prospect St. ☎858/456–9900.

★ **Gallery Eight.** Hand-blown glass, quilted silk jackets from India, and ceramics with a botanical motif are on display. ⊠7464 Girard Ave. ☎858/454–9781.

Prospect Place Fine Art. Etchings and lithographs by 19th- and 20th-century masters include works by Miró, Matisse, Rufino Tamayo, and Chagall. ⊠1268 Prospect St. ☎858/459–1978.

★ **Vetro.** Vetro means "glass" in Italian, but the word doesn't do justice to the stunning collection of colorful, vintage handblown glass lamps, bottles, vases, and other pieces from around the world. ⊠7605 Girard Ave. ☎858/729–0045 ⊕www.vetrocollections.com.

Wyland Galleries. California artist Wyland is famous for his artworks depicting whales and other marine life. The gallery showcases his bronzes, original paintings, and limited-edition work. There's also a gallery in Seaport Village. ⊠1025 Prospect St., Ste. 100 ☎858/459–8229.

HOME
ACCESSORIES
& GIFTS

Alexander Perfumes and Cosmetics. Products rarely seen in the United States are available in this European-style perfumery, which claims to have the largest selection of fragrances in California. Its cosmetic lines include Lancaster, Darphin, and Orlane. ⊠7914 Girard Ave. ☎858/454–2292.

Everett Stunz. This store stocks the finest in luxury home linens, robes, and sleepwear in cashmere, silk, or Swiss cotton. ⊠7613 Girard Ave. ☎800/883–3305.

★ **La Mano.** Save yourself a trip to La Serenissima and explore the wide selection of delightful papier-mâché and ceramic Venetian Carnival masks, many handmade. You'll also find the traditional Carnival costumes, including black hooded capes, for rent. ⊠1298 Prospect St. ☎858/454–7732 ⊕www.lamanomasks.com.

Muttropolis. Dogs will love the very chic chew toys, such as a Chewy Vuitton purse or a Cosmo-paw-litan. They'll also love the accessories, such as high-fashion coats and hoodies for strutting La Jolla's sun-splashed streets. There's haute cat-ture for felines here as well, and lots of catnip toys. ⊠7755 Girard Ave. ☎858/459–9663 ⊕www.shop.muttropolis.com.

Seaside Home. You'll find the same upscale bedding, crystal, porcelain, and home accessories here as in the sister store on Coronado Island. ⊠7509 Girard Ave. ☎858/454–0866 ⊕www.seasidehome-coronado.com.

🕓 **Toys, Etc.** A huge selection of educational toys, dolls, train sets, and games make this shop a must for children, parents, and anyone still a kid at heart. ✉ *7836 Herschel Ave.* ☎ *858/459–5104.*

JEWELRY **Fogel's Antique Beads.** Among the European precious beads from the 1920s are dazzling Austrian and Czech crystal beads. Restringing is done here. ✉ *1128 Wall St.* ☎ *858/456–2696.*

Philippe Charriol Boutique. Charriol's U.S. flagship store features the limited-edition La Jolla watch, an 18-karat white gold bracelet that opens to reveal a mother-of-pearl face on a black satin strap, and also sells watches, necklaces, and bracelets in the Swiss brand's stainless-steel and Celtic cable designs. There are fine leather goods and writing instruments as well. It's open noon–6 daily. ✉ *1227 Prospect St.* ☎ *858/551–4933 or 800/872–0172.*

Pomegranate. Antique and estate jewelry is paired here with fashions by Eileen Fisher and Harari. ✉ *1152 Prospect St.* ☎ *858/459–0629.*

MISSION VALLEY

6

Situated northeast of downtown near I–8 and Route 163, Mission Valley boasts two major shopping centers and a few smaller strip malls. Crème de la crème Fashion Valley features an impressive roster of high-end department stores and luxury boutiques. It's one of only three shopping malls in the world to have Neiman Marcus, Saks Fifth Avenue, Nordstrom, and Bloomingdale's under one roof. At Westfield Mission Valley mainstream mainstays like Macy's and Old Navy, plus bargain-hunter favorites like Loehmann's and Nordstrom Rack, abound. The San Diego Trolley and city buses make stops at both centers.

SHOPPING CENTERS

FodorsChoice **Fashion Valley.** San Diego's best and most upscale mall has a contempo-
★ rary Mission theme, lush landscaping, and more than 200 shops and restaurants. Acclaimed retailers like Bloomingdale's, Neiman Marcus, and Tiffany are here, along with boutiques from fashion darlings like Michael Kors, Jimmy Choo, Carolina Herrera, and James Perse. **Na Hoku** (☎ *619/294–7811*), a Hawaiian jewelry store, has Tahitian black pearls and pendants fashioned as exotic flowers. **Smith & Hawkin** (☎ *619/298–0441*) stocks fancy gardening supplies, teak furniture, and gifts. ✉ *7007 Friars Rd.* ☎ *619/688–9113* ⊕ *www.shopfashion-valleymall.com.*

Park in the Valley. This U-shaped mall is across the street from West-field Mission Valley. It's anchored by **OFF 5th** (☎ *619/296–4896*), where fashions by Ralph Lauren, Armani, and Burberry seen last season in Saks Fifth Avenue are sold this season at Costco prices. ✉ *1750 Camino de la Reina.*

> **SHOPPER'S PARADISE**
>
> More than 18 million shoppers visit Fashion Valley shopping center each year. That's more than the combined attendance of Sea World, Legoland, the San Diego Padres, San Diego Chargers, and San Diego Zoo.

Westfield Mission Valley. The discount stores at San Diego's largest outdoor mall sometimes reward shoppers with the same merchandise as that sold in Fashion Valley, the mall up the road, but at lower prices. Shops include Macy's Home Store; Loehmann's; Bed, Bath and Beyond; Nordstrom Rack; Charlotte Russe; and Frederick's of Hollywood. ✉ *1640 Camino del Rio N* ☎ *619/296–6375* ⊕ *www. westfield.com/missionvalley.*

FAMILY COMFORTS

The Family Lounge at Westfield Mission Valley shopping center is a lifesaver for parents shopping with kids. Along with private nursing areas, baby changing stations, and bottle warmers, the lounge has a TV with DVD player, and children's books and toys. It's located near the restrooms by the Food Court.

SPECIALTY SHOPS

D'Angelo Couture. Wedding gowns, bridesmaid dresses, and bridal accessories are their specialty, but this high-end boutique is also a great spot to shop for fancy club wear and elegant evening gowns. ✉ *1400 Camino de la Reina, Ste. 120, at Mission Center Rd.* ☎ *619/497–1949* ⊕ *www.dangelocouture.com* ⊘ *Closed Sun.*

MISSION BAY & BEACHES

Mission, Grand, and Garnet are the big shopping avenues in the beach towns. Souvenir shops are scattered up and down the boardwalk, and along Mission Boulevard you'll find surf, skate, and bike shops, bikini boutiques, and stores selling hip T-shirts, jeans, sandals, and casual apparel. Garnet Avenue is the hot spot for resale boutiques, thrift stores, and pawnshops. The Ocean Beach Antique District in the 4800 block of Newport Avenue invites browsing with several buildings housing multiple dealers under one roof. Independent stores showcase everything from vintage watches and pottery to linens and retro posters.

SPECIALTY SHOPS

CLOTHING **Men's Fashion Depot.** San Diego insiders head for this warehouse-style men's store for discounted suits and affordable tuxedos. Speedy alterations are available. ✉ *3730 Sports Arena Blvd., Mission Bay* ☎ *619/222–9570* ⊕ *www.mensfashiondepot.signonsandiego.com.*

Pilar's Beach Wear. This is California's largest selection of major-label swimsuits, including the sexy styles featured in *Sports Illustrated*'s swimsuit issue. ✉ *3745 Mission Blvd., Mission Beach* ☎ *858/488–3056* ⊕ *www.pilarsbeachwear.com.*

Raw Clothing. A local favorite for 16 years, this beachside shop offers hip casual wear for the whole family. Find Roxy swimwear, Juicy Couture accessories, and hot denim styles from Chip & Pepper. ✉ *940 Garnet Ave., Pacific Beach* ☎ *858/483–9111* ⊕ *www.rawclothing.com.*

The River. Inspired by California's surf and skate culture and located just two blocks from the ocean, this fun store offers casual wear for all ages, including nostalgic brands like OP and hip new lines like Element and Jedidiah. ✉*1020 Garnet Ave., Pacific Beach* ☎*858/270–3022* ⊕*www.theriverclothing.com.*

HOME
ACCESSORIES
& GIFTS

Great News Discount Cookware. Cooks drool over the discount kitchen tools and gadgets, especially over the mandolines and chinois. There's a cooking school in the back, an extensive selection of cookbooks, and excellent customer service. ✉*1788 Garnet Ave., Pacific Beach* ☎*858/270–1582* ⊕*www.great-news.com.*

Mallory's OB Attic. Mallory's handles collectibles, antiques, and used furniture. ✉ *4921 Newport Ave., Ocean Beach* ☎*619/223–5048.*

OLD TOWN

Located north of downtown off I–5, Old Town is tourist-focused, but the festival-like ambience and authentic Mexican restaurants also make it a popular destination for locals. At Old Town Historic Park, you'll feel like a time traveler as you visit shops housed in restored adobe buildings. Farther down the street you'll find stores selling Mexican blankets, piñatas, and glassware. Old Town Festival Marketplace offers live entertainment, local artists selling their wares from carts, and a market crammed with unique apparel, home decor, toys, jewelry, and food. Dozens of stores sell San Diego logo merchandise and T-shirts at discounted prices, and you'll find great deals on handcrafted jewelry, art, and leather accessories.

6

SHOPPING CENTERS

★ **Bazaar del Mundo Shops.** An arcade with a Mexican villa theme shares the corner of Taylor and Juan with the Guadalajara Restaurant and offers a variety of riotously colorful gift shops such as **Ariana,** for ethnic and artsy women's fashions; **Artes de Mexico,** which has a fine array of handmade Latin American crafts and Guatemalan weavings; and **The Gallery** which has handmade jewelry, Native American crafts, collectible glass, and original seriographs by John August Swanson. The **Laurel Burch Galleria** carries the complete collection of this northern California artist's signature jewelry, accessories, and totes. ✉*4133 Taylor St.* ☎*619/296–3161* ⊕*www.bazaardelmundo.com.*

Old Town Festival Marketplace. Featuring a variety of Latin-inspired shops, carts, and local artisans, this eclectic market offers everything from silver jewelry to dolls, gourmet foods, home decor and apparel. ✉*4010 Twiggs St.* ☎*619/278–0955.*

Plaza del Pasado. Found within the Old Town San Diego State Historic Park, the Plaza del Pasado has the easy feel of Old California. Friendly shopkeepers dressed as Californios host a collection of boutiques and eateries around a flower-filled square, which has been designed in keeping with Old Town's early California days, from 1821 to 1872. Similarly, the nearly dozen shops stock items reminiscent of that era. Stroll through shops such as **Tienda Nueva,** a gift shop with resort wear, hats, and dolls; **Casa de Serrano,** for candles, Mexican crafts, earthenware, and ceramics; **Tienda de la Luz,** selling handblown glass and paper crafts; and **Tienda del Posado**, for weavings, gemstone jewelry, and leather goods. **Designs in Shell** sells handmade kaleidoscopes from 30 international artists. **La Panaderia** offers baked goods made using early Mexican cooking methods. Two restaurants, Casa de Reyes and the Cosmopolitan, serve Mexican food. Shops are open daily 10–10 April–December; 10–6 January–March. ⊠ *2754 Calhoun St. 866/378-2943* ⊕ *www.plazadelpasado.com.*

OFF THE BEATEN PATH

Kobey's Swap Meet. Not far from Old Town is San Diego's premier flea market. The open-air weekend event seems to expand every week, with sellers displaying everything from futons to fresh strawberries. The back section, with secondhand goods, is a bargain-hunter's delight. The swap meet is open Friday–Sunday 7–3; admission is 50¢ on Friday and $1 on weekends, children under 11 free; parking is free. ⊠ *San Diego Sports Arena parking lot, 3500 Sports Arena Blvd., Sports Arena* ☎ *619/226-0650.*

SPECIALTY SHOPS

GALLERIES & CRAFTS

Chuck Jones' Studio Gallery. This gallery, often crowded at night with after-dinner strollers, is devoted to the extensive animation art of the late Chuck Jones, cartoon director at Warner Bros. from 1938 to 1962 and creator of the Road Runner and Wile E. Coyote among other characters. ⊠ *2501 San Diego Ave.* ☎ *619/294-9880.*

Variations Imports. Shop here for wall decor, clocks, candleholders, Asian figurines, and unusual imports from around the world. ⊠ *3975 Twiggs St.* ☎ *619/260-1008* ⊕ *www.variationsimports.com.*

★ **Gallery Old Town.** The rare collection of photojournalism by Alfred Eisenstaedt, Margaret Bourke-White, and Gordon Parks occupies a historic building on one of San Diego's oldest streets. ⊠ *2513 San Diego Ave.* ☎ *619/296-7877.*

HOME ACCESSORIES & GIFTS

Apache Indian Arts Center. Southwestern Indian jewelry, paintings, sculpture, and Pueblo baskets are sold here. ⊠ *2425 San Diego Ave.* ☎ *619/296-9226.*

★ **Bailey & McGuire Pottery.** Situated in a historic adobe building, this shop selling authentic Mexican pottery also boasts an indoor gallery with crafts from international artists. ⊠ *2769 San Diego Ave.* ☎ *619/295-0306.*

The Diamond Source. Specializing in fashionable diamond and precious gemstone jewelry, this shop features unique designs from master jeweler Marco Levy. ⊠ *2474 San Diego Ave.* ☎ *619/299-6900* ⊕ *www. thediamondsource.com.*

Ye Olde Soap Shoppe. This shop carries hand-fashioned soaps, as well as a full line of soap-making supplies, including kits, herbs, and vegetable bases. ⊠ *2497 San Diego Ave.* ☎ *619/543-1300* ⊕ *www.soap-making.com.*

SOUTH BAY

California's southern cities, Chula Vista and San Ysidro, are accessible via The San Diego Trolley or an easy drive south down I–5. Chula Vista has become a shopping destination with its modern and family-friendly shopping center Otay Ranch Town Center. Located a short drive from Knott's Soak City USA theme park, it offers inexpensive and mid-range shopping, dining, and entertainment options. The Shops at Las Americas, one of San Diego's most popular outlet malls, attract visitors from throughout the region, including south of the border; plan to spend a day to make a dent in its offerings. Las Americas can be reached via a short walk from the San Ysidro trolley station. By car take the Camino de la Plaza exit off I–5, the last in the U.S.; it has secured parking lots.

SHOPPING CENTER

Otay Ranch Town Center. San Diego's newest shopping center is anchored by Macy's and Barnes & Noble, with more than 100 retailers including Chloe Accessories, Sephora, Anthropologie, H&M, and Sigrid Olsen. The open-air plaza offers lots of fun activities for families, including a chalk garden and popper fountain for kids, a 12-screen AMC movie theater, an adjacent dog park, and several popular restaurants including Cheesecake Factory, California Pizza Kitchen, and King's Fish House. ⊠*2015 Birch Rd, Chula Vista* ☎*619/472–8679* ⊕*otayranchtowncenter.com.*

Shops at Las Americas. Set right against the international border in San Ysidro, this outlet mall has approximately 120 shops, including two duty-free outlets, and a clutch of fast-food and sit-down restaurants. The usual brand names are here, everything from Adidas and Aerosoles to Zales. One of the largest outlets in the world, the **Nike Factory Store** (☎*619/428–8849*) sells shoes, clothing, and accessories. And California's only **Neiman Marcus Last Call** (☎*619/690–5600*) is here, too. The 2,000-square-foot **Ritmo Latino** store, selling a huge selection of Latin music CDs, reflects the mall's bicultural and binational customer base. ⊠*4211 Camino de la Plaza* ☎*619/934–8400* ⊕*www.lasamericas.com.*

UPTOWN

Hillcrest has many avant-garde apparel shops alongside gift, book, and music stores. North Park, east of Hillcrest, is a retro buff's paradise with many resale shops, trendy boutiques, and stores that sell a mix of old and new. University Avenue offers a mélange of affordably priced furniture, gift, and specialty stores appealing to college students, singles, and young families. South Park's 30th , Juniper, and Fern streetshave everything from the hottest new denim lines to baby gear and craft supplies. The shops and art galleries in upscale Mission Hills, west of Hillcrest, have a modern and sophisticated ambience that suits the well-heeled residents just fine.

SPECIALTY STORES

BOOKSTORE **Obelisk.** The shelves here hold a bounty of gay and lesbian literature, cards, and gifts. ⊠ *1029 University Ave., Hillcrest* ☎ *619/297–4171.*

CLOTHING **Firefly.** Fitness wear is the specialty at this shop run by a yoga instructor. Find workout and lounge attire from Raw 7 and Tattoo. Accessories include yoga mats, workout gear, and stress-reducing CDs. ⊠ *928 Fort Stockton Dr., Mission Hills* ☎ *619/299–4359* ⊕ *www. catchthespark.com.*

★ **The Jeanery, UTC.** Specializing in casual men's clothing from an international array of brands, this ultra-cool boutique entertains customers with an on-site DJ. Premium denim from names like Nudie, Replay, and Energie is featured alongside Ben Sherman and Fred Perry shirts, Sendra boots, and Philippe Starck watches. ⊠ *7007 Friars Rd., Ste.220, University Heights* ☎ *858/450–6600* ⊕ *www.jeanery.com.*

Kate Ross. Known for premium denim lines like Paige, Odyn, and Joe's, this cool boutique for men and women also stocks Ben Sherman shirts and must-have tops from Ella Moss, Tank Farm, and Kanvas. ⊠ *3013 University Ave., Hillcrest* ☎ *619/501–6318* ⊕ *www.shopkateross.com* ⊗ *Closed Mon.*

Le Bel Age Boutique. Owners Valerie Lee and Michala Lawrence design the women's silk hostess pants and jewelry themselves. ⊠ *1607 W. Lewis St., Mission Hills* ☎ *619/297–7080.*

Maeve Riley. Casual wear for men and women is the focus here. Scoop up adorable Paul Frank tees, ultra cool Joe's Jeans, board shorts, dresses and tops from Jinou and Fleur Wood, unique jewelry, and trendy accessories. ⊠ *2328½ 30th St., South Park* ☎ *629/501–3500* ⊕ *www.maeveriley.com* ⊗ *Closed Mon. and Sun.*

Mimi & Red Boutique. Laidback ambience, friendly service, and racks full of moderate to high-end women's fashions have made this shop a favorite with San Diego hipsters. Rebecca Beeson and Betsey Johnson are here along with RVCA, Blank Denim, and Nu Collective. ⊠ *3032 University Ave., North Park* ☎ *619/298–7933* ⊕ *www.mimiandred. com.*

Mint. Affordably priced ballet flats and wild stilettos share space with urban sneakers, retro boots, and colorful espadrilles. ⊠ *525 University Ave., Hillcrest* ☎ *619/291–6468.*

Neighbourhood. Catering to youthful shoppers who like to mix and match vintage finds with current trends, this high-energy boutique has a DJ who spins tunes on Friday and Saturday. ⊠ *4496 Park Blvd., University Heights* ☎ *619/296–2100* ⊕ *www.neighbourhoodboutique. com* ⊗ *Closed Mon.*

NYLA Kensington. Offering upscale quality at affordable prices, this women's boutique features Mandy Moore's Mblem line and hot brands like Kenzie Girl, Mac and Jac, Yank, and Blue Cult Denim. Splurge on sundresses, jeans, jewelry, bags, and shoes. ⊠ *4095 Adams Ave., North*

Park ☎619/280–5300 ⊕www.nylakensington.com ⊘Tue.–Fri. 11–6, Sat. 10–6.

Pure Clothing Boutique. Edgy and affordable clothing for young men and women includes an eclectic selection of jewelry from local and Cambodian artists. ⊠451 University Ave., Hillcrest ☎619/294–7873 ⊕pureclothingboutique.com.

Vivian Rose. Vintage finds share the racks with modern apparel at this upscale boutique where the staff teaches customers how to pair old and new. ⊠3696 5th Ave., North Park ☎619/297–6487 ⊕www.vivian-rose.com ⊘Closed Sun. and Mon.

Wear It Again Sam. Among the trendy men's and women's vintage clothes are 1960s ball gowns, panama hats, and collectible cowboy shirts. ⊠3823 5th Ave., Hillcrest ☎619/299–0185 ⊕ www.wearit-againsamvintage.com.

GOURMET FOOD **Henry's Marketplace.** This market is a San Diego original for fresh produce, bulk grains, nuts, snacks, dried fruits, and health foods. ⊠4175 Park Blvd., North Park ☎619/291–8287.

Original Paw Pleasers. At this bakery for dogs and cats you'll find oatmeal "dogolate" chip cookies, carob brownies, and "itty bitty kitty treats." ⊠2525 University Ave., North Park ☎619/670–7297.

HOME ACCESSORIES & GIFTS **Babette Schwartz.** This zany pop-culture store sells toys, books, T-shirts, and magnets. ⊠421 University Ave., Hillcrest ☎619/220–7048 ⊕ www.babette.com.

California Fleurish. This perfumery has lots of extras: silk scarves, delicate Japanese pottery, and fine vinegars and soaps. ⊠4011 Goldfinch St., Mission Hills ☎619/291–4755 ⊕www.californiafleurish.com.

Cathedral. Voted the "Best Place to Smell" in a local poll, this store is worth a sniff around. It specializes in candles and home and bath goods. You can find creative combinations, such as the cocoa-hazelnut spice candles, coriander-lavender bath foams, and Asian pear–and–ginger body scrubs. ⊠435 University Ave., Hillcrest ☎619/296–4046 ⊕ www.shopcathedral.com.

Champagne Taste. A haven for busy moms who need pampering, this shop specializes in quality baby items, hip maternity clothes, and shower gifts. ⊠2248 30th St., South Park ☎619/234–3585 ⊕www.champagnetaste.com ⊘Closed Mon.

The Grove. Crafters stock up on beads, fabric trims, pattern books, and knitting and crochet supplies at this popular shop, which also offers instruction classes. Find paintings from local artists, organic clothing, and home decor. ⊠3010 Juniper St., South Park ☎619/284–7684 ⊕www.thegrovesandiego.com ⊘Closed Mon.

Ⓒ **The Lily Pad Store.** This delightful children's store features educational toys, organic apparel, games, and books. ⊠3011 Beech St., South Park ☎619/220–8555 ⊕www.thelilypadsd.com ⊘Closed Mon.

6

Maison en Provence. The French proprietors Pascal and Marielle Giai bring sunny fabrics and pottery from the region. There are also fine soaps, antique postcards, and Laguiole cutlery. ⊠*820 Fort Stockton Dr., Mission Hills* ☎*619/298–5318* ⊕*www.everythingprovence. com.*

★ **Mingei International Museum Store.** Featuring an international collection of textiles, jewelry, apparel, and home decor, this museum shop also offers a rotating gallery of artworks and a nice selection of books on crafts and folk art. ⊠*1439 El Prado, Balboa Park* ☎*619/239–0003* ⊕*www.mingei.org* ☉*Closed Mon.*

Pomegranate Home Collection. Housed in one of Hillcrest's oldest buildings, the Pomegranate has gifts, cards, and home accessories along with contemporary furnishings. ⊠*1037 University Ave., Hillcrest* ☎*619/220–0225.*

Taboo Studio. A rotating roster of artists display and sell handcrafted jewelry at this upscale gallery featuring limited-edition pieces designed with precious metals and gemstones. ⊠*1615½ W. Lewis St, Mission Hills* ☎*619/692–0099* ⊕*www.taboostudio.com* ☉*Closed Sun. and Mon.*

Zuzu's Petals. This whimsically decorated cottage brimming with vintage and imported toys, children's clothing, juvenile furniture, and baby accessories is the perfect spot to find a birthday present or shower gift. ⊠*1918 Fort Stockton Dr., Mission Hills* ☎*619/269–5432* ⊕*www. zuzuspetals.info.*

North County & Environs

WITH TIJUANA

WORD OF MOUTH

"I just spent a day in Carlsbad—wandered through all the shops, found a place to do some wine tasting, walked over to the beach, and spent some time there—it was great!"

—sunbum1944

"The drive through the desert and up [Palomar Mountain] is spectacular: orchards and bougainvillea down low, fields of ferns at the top. There are a lot of good picnic areas both en route and at the mountaintop."

—Gary

"Go see the races in Del Mar!"

—jomomma92024

Updated by
Bobbi Zane

A WHOLE WORLD OF SCENIC grandeur, fascinating history, and scientific wonder lies just beyond San Diego's city limits. If you travel north along the coast, you'll encounter the great beaches for which the region is famous, along with some sophisticated towns holding fine restaurants, great galleries, and museums.

Learn about sea creatures and the history of music in Carlsbad, home of LEGOLAND and Sea Life. If you travel east, you'll find fresh art hubs in Escondido, home of the San Diego Wild Animal Park, and Fallbrook,which boasts a pair of world-class destination spas, a selection of challenging golf courses, and nightlife in bucolic settings. Inspiring mountain scenery plus beautiful places to picnic and hike can be found in the Cuyamacas, the historic Gold Rush–era town of Julian (now known far and wide for its apple pies), and Palomar Mountain. The vast wilderness of the Anza-Borrego desert holds a repository of ancient fossils like no other, and is also home to one of the most colorful displays of native spring flowers. Just beyond the county limits in Temecula you can savor Southern California's only developed wine country, where more than two-dozen wineries offer tastings and tours.

Please note, the 760 area code is scheduled to change to 442 between November 2008 and May 2009. Please try the new area code if you are unable to get through with the number listed.

WHAT IT COSTS					
	¢	$	$$	$$$	$$$$
Restaurants	under $10	$10–$18	$19–$26	$27–$35	Over $35
Hotels	under $90	$90–$160	$161–$230	$231–$300	Over $300

Restaurant prices are for a main course at dinner, excluding 7.75% tax. Hotel prices are for a standard double room in high (summer) season, excluding 9% to 10.5% tax.

NORTH COAST: DEL MAR TO OCEANSIDE

If you venture off the freeway and head for the ocean, you'll discover remnants of the old beach culture surviving in the sophisticated towns of Del Mar, Solana Beach, Cardiff-by-the-Sea, Encinitas, Leucadia, Carlsbad, and Oceanside, where the arts, fine dining, and elegant lodgings also now rule. As suburbanization continues, the towns are reinventing themselves—Carlsbad, for instance, is morphing from a farming community into a tourist destination with LEGOLAND California, several museums, an upscale outlet shopping complex, and the Four Seasons Resort Aviara. Oceanside, home of one of the longest wooden piers on the West Coast (its first pier was built in the 1880s), promotes its beach culture with a yacht harbor, and beachside resort hotel construction is underway.

IF YOU LIKE

BEACHES

Locals stake out their favorite sunning, surfing, body boarding, and walking territories at the easily accessible North Coast beaches. Skilled surfers seeking a challenge head for Swami's Point in Encinitas. While dogs are welcome at several San Diego County beaches, many like to climb down to the water at Del Mar's James Scripps Bluff Preserve, where owners and canines can ride the San Dieguito River out to sea.

DESERT ADVENTURES

Anza-Borrego Desert State Park encompasses more than 600,000 acres, most of it wilderness. Springtime, when the wildflowers are in full bloom, is glorious. In the sandstone canyons you can walk in the footsteps of prehistoric camels, zebras, and giant ground sloths.

DINING

Fine dining, once limited to downtown San Diego, now goes beyond the city limits. At the top of foodies' must-do list is Addison, Grand Del Mar Hotel's signature restaurant. Right behind it is the BlueFire Grill at La Costa Resort. Sure, some of the beach dives serving burgers and smoothies remain, as do some of the area's popular Mexican eateries where the fare is homemade. If you're looking for celebrity chefs, check out Pamplemousse, Addison, or Market Restaurant + Bar. Heading north, Temecula offers a variety of dining options ranging from the simple but satisfying Bank of Mexican Food to the artful Vineyard Rose.

FLOWERS

The North County is a prolific flower-growing region. Nurseries, some open to the public, line the hillsides on both sides of I–5 in Encinitas, Leucadia, and Carlsbad. Most of the poinsettias sold in the United States get their start here. Quail Botanical Gardens in Encinitas displays native and exotic plants year-round. The gardens at the San Diego Wild Animal Park attract nearly as many people as the animals do.

LODGING

The North County is home to a growing number of luxury hotels, making it possible to enjoy the great outdoors in many places while pampering yourself indoors. Leading the list is the splendid Four Seasons Aviara Resort, which occupies a storied vantage point overlooking the Pacific. The Casa del Zorro in the Anza-Borrego desert is a storied oasis of class and culture surrounded by glorious desert scenery. For those who want the ultimate pampered vacation, the North County holds two world-class destination spas: Cal-A-Vie and the Golden Door. Bed-and-breakfast lodging rules in Julian, where you can kick back in a cool country cabin or an historic house.

DEL MAR

23 mi north of downtown San Diego on I–5, 9 mi north of La Jolla on Rte. S21.

Del Mar comprises two sections: the small historic village adjacent to the beach west of Interstate 5 and a growing business center surrounded by multimillion-dollar tract housing east of the freeway. Tiny

Del Mar Village, the smallest incorporated city in San Diego County, holds a population of 4,500 tucked into a 2.1-square-mi beachfront. It's known for its quaint half-timbered Tudor-style architecture, 2 mi of accessible beaches, and the Del Mar racetrack and San Diego County Fairgrounds complex. The

> **DID YOU KNOW?**
>
> San Diego County consists of 18 incorporated cities and 17 unincorporated communities, and is about the same size as the state of Connecticut.

village attracted rich and famous visitors from the beginning; they still come for seclusion and to watch the horses run. Its new face is the Del Mar Gateway business complex with high-rise hotels and fast-food outlets east of the interstate at the entrance to Carmel Valley. Both Del Mars, old and new, hold expensive homes belonging to staff and scientists who work in the biotech industry and at UC San Diego in adjacent La Jolla. Access to Del Mar's beaches is from the streets that run east–west off Coast Boulevard; access to the business complex is via Highway 56.

Along with its collection of shops, **Del Mar Plaza** contains outstanding restaurants and landscaped plazas and gardens with Pacific views. The shops and restaurants are pricey, but the view—best enjoyed from the upper level benches and chairs—is free.

Summer evening concerts take place at the west end of **Seagrove Park** (✉ *15th St.*), a small stretch of grass overlooking the ocean.

☾ The Spanish mission–style **Del Mar Fairgrounds** is the home of the **Del Mar Thoroughbred Club** (☎ *858/755–1141* ⊕ *www.dmtc.com*). Crooner Bing Crosby and his Hollywood buddies—Pat O'Brien, Gary Cooper, and Oliver Hardy, among others—organized the club in the 1930s, primarily because Crosby wanted a track near his Rancho Santa Fe home. Even now the racing season here (usually July–September, Wednesday–Monday, post time 2 PM) is one of the most fashionable in California. If you're new to horse racing, stop by the Plaza de Mexico where you'll staff who can explain how to place a bet on a horse. The track also hosts free Four O'Clock Friday concerts following the races. Del Mar Fairgrounds hosts more than 100 different events each year, including the Del Mar Fair (San Diego County), which draws more than a million visitors annually, plus a number of horse shows. ✉ *2260 Jimmy Durante Blvd.* ☎ *858/793–5555* ⊕ *www.sdfair.com.*

☾ **Freeflight,** a small exotic-bird training aviary adjacent to the Del Mar Fairgrounds, is open to the public. You're allowed to handle the birds— a guaranteed child-pleaser. ✉ *2132 Jimmy Durante Blvd.* ☎ *858/481– 3148* 🎟 *$5* ⊙ *Thurs.–Tues. 10–4, Wed. 10–2.*

WHERE TO EAT

$$$$
Fodor's Choice
★

✕**Addison.** Sophisticated and stylish, Addison challenges many ideas about what fine dining is all about. William Bradley, one of San Diego's most acclaimed rising star chefs, serves up explosive flavors in his four course prix-fix dinners, such as Prince Edward Island mussels with Champagne sabayon and lemon verbena jus or foie gras de canard with

Le Puy lentils, port wine, and smoked bacon mousse. Entrées include spring lamb persille with pistachio pâté brisée and caramelized garlic puree or perfectly cooked wild Scottish salmon with sauce vin jaune, roasted eggplant stick, and pine nuts. Acclaimed for its extensive wine collection, Addison challenges vino lovers with a 160-page wine list. ⊠ *5200 Grand Del Mar Way* ☎*858/314–1900* ⚑*Reservations essential* ▤*AE, D, DC, MC, V* ⊗ *Closed Mon. No lunch.*

$$$ ✕ **Arterra Restaurant & Bar.** The name of this hot dining spot, created by celebrity chef Bradley Ogden and tucked inside the San Diego Marriott Del Mar hotel, means "art of the earth." You find just that in gorgeous hors d'oeuvres such as Hawaiian ahi and scallop roulades or Julian apple and pear salad. Entrées include Chino Farms English pea tortelloni, Neiman Ranch flat iron steak, or rainbow trout stuffed with Maine lobster and chorizo. The chef also offers tasting menus with wine pairings. The menu changes daily to reflect what's fresh. A sushi bar is open nightly. The extensive wine list is all-American. ⊠*11966 El Camino Real* ☎ *858/369–6032* ▤ *AE, D, DC, MC, V* ⊗ *No lunch Sat. and Sun.; Sushi bar closed Sun.*

$$$ ✕ **Market Restaurant + Bar.** Carl Schroeder—one of San Diego's hottest young chefs—makes his debut with a restaurant that combines casual mod decor with creative and fun New Califonia fare. The menu changes regularly depending upon what's fresh. The well-heeled foodie crowd digs Schroeder's seasonally inspired dishes that have a playful spirit, whether it's a blue cheese soufflé with seasonal fruit, a Cobb salad with crispy oysters and local avocados, or a bluenose bass paired with Maine scallops and forest mushrooms. A well-edited wine list offers food-friendly wines by the best and brightest young winemakers around the world. Desserts are exquisite, such as the lemon soufflé tart with buttermilk ice cream or the milk chocolate panna cotta with espresso caramel. ⊠*3702 Via de la Valle* ☎*858/523–0007* ▤ *AE, M, V.*

Fodor's Choice ★

$$$ ✕ **Pacifica Del Mar.** The view of the shimmering Pacific from this lovely restaurant perched atop Del Mar Plaza is one of the best along the coast, and compliments the simply prepared, beautifully presented seafood. The highly innovative menu is frequently rewritten to show off such creations as barbecue sugar-spice salmon with mustard sauce and mustard catfish with Yukon Gold potato–corn succotash. The crowd ranges from young hipsters at the bar to well-dressed businesspeople on the terrace, where glass screens block any hint of a chilly breeze. ⊠ *Del Mar Plaza, 1515 Camino del Mar* ☎ *858/792–0476* ▤ *AE, D, DC, MC, V.*

$ ✕**Le Bambou.** Small, carefully decorated, and more elegant than any Vietnamese restaurant in San Diego proper, Le Bambou snuggles into the corner of a neighborhood shopping center and is easy to overlook. Those in the know, however, seek it out for authoritative versions of such classics as ground shrimp grilled on sugarcane; Imperial rolls generously stuffed with shrimp and noodles; and make-your-own meat wraps at the table. ⊠*2634 Del Mar Heights Rd.* ☎*858/259–8138* ▤ *MC, V* ⊗ *Closed Mon. No lunch Sat. and Sun.*

7

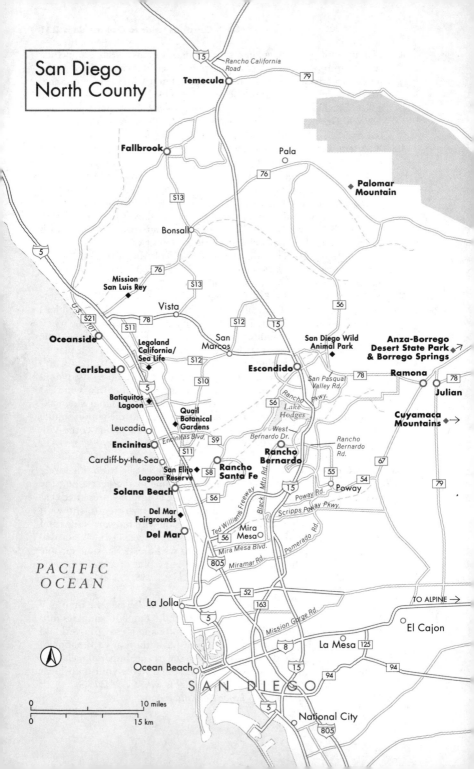

San Diego North County

15 Rancho California Road
Temecula
79

Fallbrook
Pala
76
Palomar Mountain

S13

Bonsall

5
76
Mission San Luis Rey
S13
Vista
S21
S11
78
San Marcos
S12
15
56
S12
Oceanside
Legoland California/ Sea Life
San Diego Wild Animal Park
Anza-Borrego Desert State Park & Borrego Springs

Carlsbad
Escondido
78
Ramona
78

Batiquitos Lagoon
S10
5
San Pasqual Valley Rd.
Julian

Quail Botanical Gardens
S6
Lake Hodges
Cuyamaca Mountains

Leucadia
West Bernardo Dr.
Rancho Bernardo Rd.

Encinitas
S9
Rancho Bernardo
67
79

Cardiff-by-the-Sea
S11
55

San Elijo Lagoon Reserve
S8
Rancho Santa Fe
Poway Rd.
54
Poway

Solana Beach
S6
Scripps Poway Pkwy.

Del Mar Fairgrounds
Pomerado Rd.

Del Mar
56
Mira Mesa
Mira Mesa Blvd.

805
Miramar Rd.

PACIFIC OCEAN

52
TO ALPINE →
La Jolla
5
163
El Cajon

Mission Gorge Rd.

8
La Mesa
125

Ocean Beach
SAN DIEGO
94
15
94

5

0   10 miles
0   15 km

National City
805

WHERE TO STAY

$$$$
Fodor'sChoice
★
⌂**The Grand Del Mar.** The opulent Mediterranean-style resort, set in a secluded canyon surrounded by 4,100-acre Los Penasquitos Canyon Preserve, is just 12 mi north of urban San Diego. The hotel is drop-dead beautiful, done up in marble, crystal, and gold. Large rooms feature brocaded corner love seats, fine European linens, crystal lamps, and marble bathrooms with separate soaking tubs and showers. Every window, deck, patio, balcony, and lawn affords a view of the surrounding mountains, where you can hike tree-lined trails and dip your toes in streams, fish-filled ponds, or waterfalls. Take advantage of the resort's four cabana-flanked pools and the Tom Fazio–designed golf course. Topping the resort's amenities is complimentary limousine service within the area. **Pros:** Ultimate luxury, secluded, on-site golf course. **Cons:** Service can be slow, hotel is not on the beach. ⊠*5300 Grand Del Mar Ct.,* ☎*858/314–2000 or 888/314–2030* ⊕*www.thegranddelmar. com* ⇨*218 rooms, 31 suites* ⌂*In-room: safe, refrigerator, DVD, Ethernet, dial-up, Wi-Fi. In-hotel: 6 restaurants, room service, bars, golf course, tennis courts, pools, gym, spa, bicycles, children's programs (ages 5–12), laundry service, concierge, public Internet, public Wi-Fi, valet parking (fee), some pets allowed (fee), no smoking rooms* ▭*AE, D, DC, MC, V.*

★ $$$$
⌂ **L'Auberge Del Mar Resort and Spa.** A boutique hotel occupying a coveted corner in Del Mar, just steps from restaurants, shopping, and the beach, L'Auberge del Mar completed a major renovation in 2008 that transformed it from a French château to a sophisticated beach estate. The new look is bright and airy with an outdoor feel, even when you're indoors. Pristine white walls throughout public areas and rooms contrast with dark wood floors and furnishings. Ample rooms surround the Waterfall Terrace, where guests gather for informal meals and drinks. Accented by sea grass colored walls and carpeting, rooms have balconies or patios, huge armoires holding flat screen TVs, shell sculptures, and a collection of art and design books. Plantation shutters add to the airy ambience, and spacious marble bathrooms hold step-in showers. L'Auberge is home to one of San Diego's top celebrity chefs, Paul McCabe, who expects to open his signature restaurant in fall 2008. **Pros:** Sunset views from the Waterfall Terrace, excellent service, walk to the beach. **Cons:** Even with good soundproofing the Amtrak train can be heard as it roars through town, adult atmosphere, ground-level rooms surrounding the terrace are very public. ⊠*1540 Camino del Mar* ☎*858/259–1515 or 866/893–4389* ⊕*www.laubergedelmar. com* ⇨*112 rooms, 8 suites* ⌂*In-room: safe, Wi-Fi. In-hotel: 2 restaurants, room service, bars, tennis courts, pools, gym, spa, bicycles, laundry service, concierge, public Internet, public Wi-Fi, airport shuttle, parking (fee), no-smoking* ▭*AE, D, DC, MC, V.*

SHOPPING

The tiered, Mediterranean-style **Del Mar Plaza** (⊠ *1555 Camino Del Mar* ☎ *858/792–1555* ⊕ *www.delmarplaza.com*) has flower-filled courtyards, fountains, a spectacular view of the Pacific, and some fine restaurants. Some businesses validate parking, which is underground. **Georgiou** (☎ *858/481–1964*) specializes in designer women's fashions.

San Diego Beachwear (☎*858/259–0473* ⊕*www.sandiegobeachware.com*) stocks the latest bikini styles in mix and match and multiple sizes. **Shoetique 101** (☎*858/350–7642* ⊕*www.shoetique101.com*) puts you into hand-made sexy high-heeled sandals and boots.

SOLANA BEACH

1 mi north of Del Mar on Rte. S21, 25 mi north of downtown San Diego on I–5 to Lomas Santa Fe Dr. west.

Once-quiet Solana Beach is *the* place to look for antiques, collectibles, and contemporary fashions and artwork. The Cedros Design District, occupying four blocks south of the Amtrak station, contains shops, galleries, designers' studios, restaurants, and a popular jazz and contemporary music venue, the Belly Up Tavern. The town is known for its excellent restaurants, but most area lodging (excluding a Holiday Inn) is in adjacent Del Mar and Encinitas. Solana Beach was the first city in California to ban smoking on its beaches. Now most cities in San Diego have followed suit.

WHERE TO EAT

★ $$$$ ✕ **Pamplemousse Grille.** Justly celebrated as one of North County's best restaurants, the "Grapefruit Grill," across the street from the racetrack, offers casual French-country dining California style. Chef-proprietor Jeffrey Strauss brings a caterer's sensibilities to the details, like a mix-or-match selection of sauces—wild mushroom, grey mustard, or peppercorn—to complement the simple but absolutely top-quality grilled meats and seafood. Appetizers can be very clever, like the Kim Chee Seafood Martini. Whatever you do, save room for dessert; you can watch the pastry chef build it for you at the demonstration area in the dining room. Popular sweet endings include pear tart tatin, almond brown butter tart, and chocolate peanut-butter bombe. The comfortable rooms are painted with murals of bucolic country scenes, and the service is quiet and professional. ✉*514 Via de la Valle* ☎*858/792–9090* ♢ *Reservations essential* ▭ *AE, MC, V* ☉ *No lunch Sat.–Thurs.*

$$ ✕ **Red Tracton's.** Across the street from the Del Mar racetrack, this deluxe old-fashioned steak and seafood house is a high-roller's heaven. Everyone from the bar pianist to the exceptional waitresses is well aware that smiles and prompt service can result in tips as generously sized as the gigantic Australian lobster tails that the menu demurely lists at "market price." Tracton's serves simple but good food, and the menu highlights roasted prime rib in addition to prime New York sirloin and a monstrous 28-ounce porterhouse steak, top-grade pork back ribs, panfried scallops, and such starters as lobster bisque and "jumbo" shrimp on ice. ✉ *550 Via de la Valle* ☎*858/755–6600* ♢ *Reservations essential* ▭ *AE, D, DC, MC, V* ☉ *No lunch Sun.*

$ ✕**Don Chuy.** Family-run and utterly charming, Don Chuy serves authentic Mexican cuisine to Southern Californians who, before dining here, may have tasted only a pale version of the real thing. The flavors are savory and convincing, and the portions sufficient to banish hunger until the following day. For something straight from the soul of Mexican home cooking, try the *nopales con chorizo y huevos,* a scramble of tender cactus leaves, crumbled spicy sausage, and eggs; this is served with piles of rice and beans as well as a warm tortilla and the palate-warming house salsa. ⊠*650 Valley Ave.* ☎*858/794–0535* ⊟*AE, D, MC, V.*

$ ✕ **Pizza Port.** Local families flock to the casual Port for its great pizza and handcrafted brews. Pick a spot at one of the long picnic-type tables, choose traditional or whole-grain beer crust for your pie and any original topping—such as the Monterey, with pepperoni, onions, mushrooms, and artichoke hearts—and tip back a brew from one of the longest boutique lists in San Diego. Even dessert reeks of hops: beer floats with homemade ice cream for the over-21 set, or made with root beer for everyone else. ⊠ *135 N. Hwy. 101* ☎ *858/481–7332* ⌂ *Reservations not accepted* ⊟ *AE, MC, V.*

NIGHTLIFE

Belly Up Tavern (⊠*143 S. Cedros Ave.* ☎ *858/481–9022* ⊕ *www.bel-lyuptavern.com*), a fixture on local papers' "best of" lists, has been drawing crowds of all ages since it opened in the mid-'70s. The BUT's longevity attests to the quality of the eclectic entertainment on its stage. Within converted Quonset huts, critically acclaimed artists play everything from reggae and folk to—well, you name it.

SHOPPING

★ The **Cedros Design District** (⊕ *www.cedrosdesigndistrict.net*) is a collection of more than 85 shops that specialize in interior design and gifts. **Antique Warehouse** (⊠*212 S. Cedros Ave.* ☎ *858/755–5156*) holds more than 100 booths that carry American and European antiquities, art, books, glass, dolls, and jewelry. **Birdcage** (⊠ *143 S. Cedros Ave., Suite J* ☎ *858/793–6262*) specializes in unusual home accessories. At **Frangipani Resort Wear** (⊠*130 S. Cedros Ave.* ☎*858/259–0288*) you can find sarongs and aloha shirts, as well as South Seas fragrances, hats, and shoes. Cool accessories such as designer beds and totes for *haute* dogs and cats are at **Muttropolis** (⊠*227 S. Cedros Ave.* ☎*858/755–3647*).

Trios Gallery (⊠ *404 N. Cedros Ave.* ☎*858/793–6040*) showcases the work of local artists, including James Hubbell, art glass, Judaica, and designer jewelry.

RANCHO SANTA FE

4 mi east of Solana Beach on Rte. S8, Lomas Santa Fe Dr., 29 mi north of downtown San Diego on I–5 to Rte. S8 east.

Groves of huge, drooping eucalyptus trees cover the hills and valleys of this affluent and exclusive town east of I–5. Rancho Santa Fe and the areas surrounding it are primarily residential, where you'll see mansions at every turn in the road. It's also common to see entire families riding horses on the many trails that crisscross the hillsides.

WHERE TO EAT & STAY

★ $$$$ ✕**The Restaurant at Rancho Valencia.** It always feels like spring when dining in the garden room at the Restaurant at Rancho Valencia. Bouquets of fresh flowers are everywhere, potted plants fill nooks and crannies, and rattan furnishings complete the mood. This is a serious restaurant, however, where you're likely to dine on Kobe beef, Royal Cambridge Scottish smoked salmon, Jidori coq au vin, or braised duck legs with cherry espresso sauce. And that's just dinner. The restaurant serves a selection of entrée salads and sandwiches at lunch and a full breakfast. The restaurant is refined without being stuffy; service is beyond attentive. ⊠ *5921 Valencia Circle* ☏*858/756–1123* ⊟*AE, DC, MC, V.*

$$$ ✕ **Mille Fleurs.** Mille Fleurs is a winner, from its location in the heart of wealthy, horsey Rancho Santa Fe to the warm Gallic welcome extended by proprietor Bertrand Hug and the talents of chef Martin Woesle. The quiet dining rooms are decorated like a French villa. Menus are written daily to reflect the market and Woesle's mood, so you'll find some interesting seasonal choices such as duck rillettes and fois gras with Belgian endive or grilled Alaskan halibut with blue potatoes, asparagus, and saffron sauce. ⊠ *Country Squire Courtyard, 6009 Paseo Delicias* ☏*858/756–3085* ⚞ *Reservations essential* ⊟ *AE, MC, V* ⊘ *No lunch weekends.*

★ $$$$ 🛏 **Inn at Rancho Santa Fe.** Understated elegance is the theme of this genteel old resort, designed in 1924 by Lilian Rice. Guest rooms, all completely redone in 2007, are in red-tile cottages spread around the property's 20 lushly landscaped acres. There are now skylights, Saltillo tile or hardwood floors, original paintings, oversize showers, granite countertops in the bathrooms, and private patios with fireplaces. Some decor is modern and some is in keeping with the historic theme of the property. The inn offers many services, the most coveted may be the chance to play golf at the exclusive Rancho California Golf Club just up the road. **Pros:** Historic hotel, excellent service. **Cons:** Cottages spread out around grounds. ⊠*5951 Linea del Cielo,* ☏*858/756–1131 or 800/843–4661* ⊕*www.theinnatrsf.com* ⤙*75 rooms, 12 suites* ⚭ *In-room: safe, kitchen (some), refrigerator, DVD, Ethernet, Wi-Fi. In-hotel: restaurant, room service, bar, tennis court, pool, gym, spa, no elevator, laundry service, public Internet, public Wi-Fi, parking (no fee), no-smoking rooms* ⊟ *AE, D, DC, MC, V.*

$$$$
Fodor's Choice
★
🛏 **Rancho Valencia Resort and Spa.** One of Southern California's hidden treasures has luxurious accommodations in Spanish-style casitas scattered on 40 acres of landscaped grounds. Suites have corner fireplaces, luxurious Berber carpeting, and shuttered French doors leading to private patios. Twelve suites also have steam showers, private outdoor hot tubs, and plasma flat-screen TVs. Rancho Valencia is one of the nation's top tennis resorts, with a highly regarded tennis training program for children and adults. There also are two fitness centers, walking trails throughout the property, a croquet lawn, and a sport court where you can play volleyball, shoot some baskets, or smash a birdie over the badminton net. If you're a hotel guest, you can indulge yourself at the spa all day long without charge—unless that indulgence includes a treatment. **Pros:** Gorgeous surroundings, impeccable ser-

vice, large rooms. **Cons:** Secluded, expensive. ✉*5921 Valencia Circle,* ☎*858/756–1123 or 800/548–3664* ⊕*www.ranchovalencia.com* ➫*49 suites* ⚹ *In-room: safe, refrigerator (some), DVD, Ethernet, Wi-Fi. In-hotel: restaurant, room service, bar, tennis courts, pools, gym, spa, bicycles, no elevator, laundry facilities, laundry service, public Internet, public Wi-Fi, parking (no fee), some pets allowed, no-smoking rooms* ▭*AE, MC, V.*

SHOPPING

Country Friends (✉*6030 El Tordo* ☎*858/756–1192*) is a great place for unusual gifts. Operated by a nonprofit foundation, it carries collectibles, silver, and antiques donated or consigned by the community's residents. The **Vegetable Shop** (✉*6123 Calzada del Bosque* ☎ *858/756–3184*) is the place to buy the same premium (and very expensive) fruits and rare baby vegetables that the Chino Family Farm grows for many of San Diego's upscale restaurants, and for such famed California eateries as Chez Panisse in Berkeley and Spago in Los Angeles.

ENCINITAS

6 mi north of Solana Beach on Rte. S21, 7 mi west of Rancho Santa Fe on Rte. S9, 28 mi north of downtown San Diego on I–5.

Flower breeding and growing has been the major industry in Encinitas since the early part of the 20th century; the town now calls itself the Flower Capital of the World, thanks to the large number of nurseries operating here. The city, which encompasses the coastal towns of Cardiff-by-the-Sea and Leucadia as well as inland Olivenhain, is home to Paul Ecke Poinsettias (open only to the trade), which tamed the wild poinsettia in the 1920s and today is the largest producer and breeder of the Christmas blossom in the world. During the spring blooming season some commercial nurseries east of I–5 are open to the public. The palms and the golden domes of the Self-Realization Fellowship Retreat and Hermitage mark the southern entrance to downtown Encinitas.

7

� **Quail Botanical Gardens** displays more than 4,000 rare, exotic, and endangered plants on 35 landscaped acres. Displays include plants from Central America, Africa, Australia, the Middle East, the Mediterranean, the Himalayas, Madagascar, and more; the most diverse collection of bamboo in North America; California native plants; and subtropical fruits. Kids can roll around in the Seeds of Wonder garden, explore a baby dinosaur forest, discover a secret garden, or play in a playhouse. An Under the Sea Garden is actually a rock garden of succulents that uncannily mimics an underwater environment. ✉ *230 Quail Gardens Dr.* ☎ *760/436–3036* ⊕ *www.qbgardens.com* ▦ *$10, free first Tues. of the month* ☼ *Daily 9–5.*

The **San Elijo Lagoon Conservancy,** between Solana Beach and Encinitas, is the most complex of the estuary systems in San Diego North County. A 7-mi network of trails surrounds the 1,000-acre park, where more than 300 species of plants, many fish, and more than 319 species of birds (106 of them migratory) live. Docents offer free public walks on the second Saturday of the month from 9 to 11 AM. ⊠ *2710 Manchester Ave.* ☎*760/436–3944* ⊕*www.sanelijo.org* ⊑ *Free* ⊙ *Daily dawn–dusk.*

Founded in 1936 as a retreat and place of worship, the **Self-Realization Fellowship Retreat** also offers one of the best views along the Pacific coast, a sweeping seascape extending north and south as far as the eye can see. Paramahansa Yogananda, author of the classic *Autobiography of a Yogi*, created two beautiful meditation gardens that are open to the public. The gardens are planted with flowering shrubs and trees and contain a series of ponds connected by miniature waterfalls populated by tropical fish. Swami's Point at the south end of the gardens is a popular surfer's break. ⊠*215 K St.* ☎*760/753–2888* ⊕*www.encinitastemple.org* ⊑ *Free* ⊙ *Tues.–Sun. 10–5.*

☺ The pros test their skills and make videos at **Magdalena Ecke Family YMCA Skate Park.** The facility holds a 25,000-square-foot street course with quarter pipes, bank ramps, roll-in ramps, pyramids, hips, handrail stations, slider boxes, a 12-foot vertical wall, and a little kids' course. Ask your nearest 13-year-old what these things mean. There are two classic cement pools, one kidney-shaped and the other clover-shaped. A 120-foot-wide ramp was used by the X Games in 2003. Even if you don't skate or ride it's exciting just to sit and watch. ⊠*200 Saxony Rd.* ☎*760/942–9622* ⊑*$10* ⊙ *Hours vary; call for information.*

WHERE TO EAT

$$ ✕**Calypso Café.** Escape to French Polynesia or any other exotic locale at this dinner house and music venue. The atmosphere sizzles with a bustling bar and live blues, rock, or reggae music that starts nightly at 7:30. The dining room has a "Survivor" feel, thanks to thatched walls; fortunately the French cuisine is more sophisticated, with offerings such as coq au vin, tomato basil fettuccine, and whole sea bass stuffed with rosemary and baked in a sea-salt crust. Mussels are a specialty, whether served in a spicy Thai peanut broth or the classic garlic-and-white-wine preparation. Quarters can be a bit tight, but the crowd is friendly. ⊠*576 N. Highway 101* ☎*760/632–8252* ⚖ *Reservations essential* ▤ *AE, MC, V* ⊙ *No lunch.*

$$ ✕**La Bonne Bouffe.** A longtime North County favorite, this tiny storefront restaurant offers expertly prepared classic French fare, including cassoulet, a delicious beef bourguignon, roast duckling in green peppercorn sauce, Dover sole, and frogs' legs. With lace curtains, beige tablecloths, bistro chairs, and patio dining, you can pretend you're eating in France. ⊠*471 Encinitas Blvd.* ☎*760/436–3081* ⊕*www.labonnebboufferestaurant.com* ⚖ *Reservations essential* ▤ *AE, D, DC, MC, V* ⊙ *Closed Mon. No lunch.*

$ ✕ **Ki's Restaurant.** Veggies with a view could be the subtitle for this venerable Cardiff-by-the-Sea restaurant that grew from a simple juice shack. Ki's is well known for healthy, ovo-lacto vegetarian-friendly dishes like huevos rancheros, filling tofu scrambles, egg salad wraps, chopped salads with feta and nuts, watermelon juice, and carrot ice cream smoothies. The menu also includes turkey wraps piled on wheat bread and dinner entrées such as pork chops with apple amaretto glaze and spicy seafood stew, all prepared with minimal fat. Get a table up top for incomparable ocean views, but be prepared for a wait, as service is rather poor. ⊠*2591 S. Coast Highway 101* ☎*760/436–5236* ▭*AE, MC, V.*

¢ ✗**Bubby's Gelato.** A hardworking French couple makes the region's best gelato and sorbets in this unassuming little shop tucked away in the Lumberyard Shopping Center. Each flavor is clear and intense, with a dense creaminess. Sit on the sunny patio whiling away the afternoon as flavors of honey-lavender, green tea, or roasted banana wash over you. The rainbow of flavors ranges from chocolate-hazelnut to vanilla tinged with rose. On the lighter side, try the sunset-colored apricot sorbet or the deep red raspberry. Bubby's also serves an assortment of tasty sandwiches. ⊠*937 S. Coast Highway 101, Encinitas* ☎*760/436–3563* ▭*No credit cards.*

¢ ✗**La Especial Norte.** Casual to the point of funkiness, this Mexican café is a great hit with locals who flock here to slurp up large bowls of delicious homemade soups. Try the chicken, beans, and rice, or the Seven Seas fish soup accompanied by tortillas and a dish of cabbage salad. You can also order renditions of the standard burrito, enchilada, and taco, and premium margaritas. ⊠*644 N. Coast Hwy. 101* ☎*760/942–1040* ▭*AE, D, MC, V.*

WHERE TO STAY

$ ⊞**Moonlight Beach Motel.** This folksy, laid-back motel just steps from the surf looks better on the outside than inside. Well-kept grounds supporting blooming hibiscus, bird of paradise, and sago palms contrast with rooms that have seen better days. But they are spacious and clean, and most have balconies and ocean views. There's a barbecue available for guest use. **Pros:** Within walking distance of the beach, public barbecues. **Cons:** Plain motel, small rooms. ⊠*233 2nd St.,* ☎*760/753–0623 or 800/323–1259* ⊕*www.moonlightbeachmotel.com* ⌨*24 rooms* ⌂*In-room: kitchen. In-hotel: no elevator, parking (no fee), no-smoking rooms* ▭*AE, D, DC, MC, V.*

¢ ⊞**Ocean Inn Hotel.** Across from the train tracks on the main drag through the north end of Leucadia, this basic motel is apt to be somewhat noisy. The simple guest rooms set around a central courtyard are done in soft pink and blue floral fabrics, and some have Jacuzzi tubs. In the afternoon you can share a *cuppa* in the hotel's cheery tearoom. Continental breakfast is included in the price. **Pros:** Basic motel, close to beach. **Cons:** On busy highway, motel is outdated. ⊠*1444 N. Coast Hwy. 101,* ☎*760/436–1988 or 800/546–1598* ⊕*www.oceaninnhotel. com* ⌨*50 rooms* ⌂*In-room: refrigerator, Wi-Fi. In-hotel: no elevator, laundry facilities, public Wi-Fi, parking (no fee), no-smoking rooms* ▭*AE, D, MC, V* ⦿*CP.*

SHOPPING

Souvenir items are sold at shops along U.S. 101 and in the Lumberyard Shopping Center. Encinitas also abounds in commercial plant nurseries where you can pick up a bit of San Diego to take home.

Anderson's La Costa Nursery (✉*400 La Costa Ave.* ☎*760/753–3153* ⊕*www.andersonslacostanursery.com*) offers rare and hard-to-find orchids, bromeliads, cactus, and succulents. **Hansen's** (✉*1105 S. Coast Hwy. 101* ☎*760/753–6595* ⊕*www.hansensurf.com*), one of San Diego's oldest surfboard manufacturers, is owned by Don Hansen, surfboard shaper extraordinaire, who came here from Hawai'i in 1962. The store also stocks a full line of recreational clothing and casual wear. **Weideners' Gardens** (✉*695 Normandy Rd.* ☎*760/436–2194*) carries begonias, fuchsias, and other flowers. It's closed sporadically in fall and winter; call for hours.

CARLSBAD

6 mi from Encinitas on Rte. S21, 36 mi north of downtown San Diego on I–5.

Once-sleepy Carlsbad, lying astride I–5 at the north end of a string of beach towns extending from San Diego to Oceanside, has long been popular with beach goers and sun seekers. On a clear day in this village you can take in sweeping ocean views that stretch from La Jolla to Oceanside by walking the 2-mi-long seawalk running between the Encina power plant and Pine Street. En route, you'll find several stairways leading to the beach and quite a few benches. More recently, however, much of the attention of visitors to the area has shifted inland, east of I–5, to LEGOLAND California and other attractions in its vicinity—two of the San Diego area's most luxurious resort hotels, one of the last remaining wetlands along the Southern California coast, a discount shopping mall, golf courses, the cattle ranch built by movie star Leo Carrillo, and colorful spring-blooming Flower Fields at Carlsbad Ranch. Until the mid-20th century, when suburban development began to sprout on the hillsides, farming was the main industry in Carlsbad, with truckloads of avocados, potatoes, and other vegetables shipped out year-round. Some agriculture remains. Area farmers develop and grow new varieties of flowers, including the ranunculus that transform a hillside into a rainbow each spring, and Carlsbad strawberries are among the sweetest you'll find in Southern California; in spring you can pick them yourself in fields on both sides of I–5.

Carlsbad village owes its name to John Frazier, who dug a well for his farm here in the 1880s. The water bubbling from it was soon found to have the same properties as water from the mineral wells of Karlsbad, Bohemia (now Karlovy Vary, Czech Republic, but then under the sway of the Austro-Hungarian Empire). When Frazier and others went into the business of luring people to the area with talk of the healing powers of the local mineral water, they changed the name of the town to Carlsbad, to emphasize the similarity to the famous Bohemian spa.

Remnants from this era, including the original well and a monument to Frazier, are found at the **Carlsbad Mineral Water Spa** (✉*2802 Carlsbad Blvd.* ☎*760/434–1887* ⊕*www.carlsbadmineralspa.com*), a stone building that houses a small day spa and the Carlsbad Water Company, a 21st-century version of Frazier's waterworks, where the Carlsbad water is still sold.

Development has destroyed many of the lagoons and saltwater marsh wildlife habitats that used to punctuate the North County coastline, but 610-acre **Batiquitos Lagoon,** one of the few remaining tidal wetlands in Southern California, has been restored to support fish and bird populations. A stroll along the 2-mi trail from the Batiquitos Lagoon Foundation Nature Center along the north shore of the lagoon reveals nesting sites of the red-wing blackbird, lagoon birds such as the great blue heron, the great egret, and the snowy egret, and life in the mud flats. This is a quiet spot for contemplation or a picnic. Free docent tours are offered on weekends; visit the Web site for updated schedules. Take the Poinsettia Lane exit off I–5, go east, and turn right onto Batiquitos Drive, then right again onto Gabbiano Lane. ⊠ *7380 Gabbiano La.* ☎ *760/931–0800* ⊕ *www.batiquitosfoundation.org* ⊗ *Mon–Fri. 9–12:30, Sat. and Sun. 9–4.*

LEGOLAND California, the centerpiece of a development that includes resort hotels and a designer discount shopping mall, offers a full day of entertainment with more than 50 rides and attractions for pint-size fun-seekers and their parents. The mostly outdoor experience is best appreciated by kids ages 2 to 10, who often beg to ride the mechanical horses around the Royal Joust again and again or to take just one more turn through the popular Volvo Jr. Driving School. Miniland USA, an animated collection of U.S. cities and other areas constructed entirely of Lego blocks, captures the imaginations of all ages. Kids get a chance to dig for buried fossils on Dino Island, which holds the Dig Those Dinos paleontological play area as well as the Coastersaurus, a junior roller coaster. At the Fun Town Fire Academy, families compete at fire fighting by racing in a model fire truck and hosing down a simulated burning building. Also in Fun Town, besides the driving school, with miniature cars, is the Skipper School, with miniature boats. In Splash Battle, kids cruise through pirate-infested waters past exploding volcanoes; Treasure Falls, a mini-flume log ride with a 12-foot soaking plunge; and Pirate Shores, water-fight headquarters. Lost Kingdom Adventure, LEGOLAND'S first dark ride (meaning indoors) and part of a new four-ride block opened in 2008, features the adventures of popular LEGO mini-figure Johnny Thunder battling the bad guys in an Egyptian temple with the help of riders using laser blasters to accumulate points and ultimately capture Sam Sinister and find the treasure. Also part of the mix are stage shows and restaurants with kid-friendly buffets. ⊠ *1 LEGOLAND Dr.,* ✛ *exit I–5 at Cannon Rd. and follow signs east ¼ mi* ☎ *760/918–5346* ⊕ *www.legolandca.com* 🎫 *$60, additional fees for some ride* ⊗ *Hours vary; call for information.*

FodorsChoice
★

In spring the hillsides are abloom at **Flower Fields at Carlsbad Ranch,** the largest bulb production farm in Southern California. Here, from mid-March through mid-May, you can walk through fields planted with thousands of Giant Tecolote ranunculus—a stunning 50-acre display of color against the backdrop of the blue Pacific Ocean. Also to be seen

7

are the rose gardens—including the miniature rose garden and the Walk of Fame garden, lined with examples of every All-American Rose Selection award-winner since 1940—and demonstration gardens created by artists who normally work with paint and easel. You can walk through a sweet-pea maze and a historical display of Paul Ecke poinsettias that were bred at nearby nurseries. Family activities include an open-air wagon drawn by an antique tractor (fee), Lego Flower Garden, and kids playground. The unusually large and well-stocked Armstrong Garden Center at the exit carries plants, garden accessories, and ranunculus bulbs. ✉ *5704 Paseo del Norte, east of I–5* ☎ *760/431–0352* ⊕ *www.theflowerfields.com* ⌧ *$9* ☉ *Mar.–May, daily 9–6.*

☾ **Sea Life Aquarium,** opened in 2008 right next door to Legoland California, offers an educational and interactive underwater experience. The first of its kind in North America, it features more than 70 Lego models including a huge Lego fish and a submarine. Exhibits focus on creatures found in local waters including California lakes and streams and the cold water marine animals that live along the California coast. Other exhibits include an underwater acrylic tunnel that affords a deep sea (but dry) look at sharks, fish, and invertebrates. There's a seahorse kingdom, interactive tide pools, and a chance for kids to build a Lego coral reef. This park has a separate admission from Leogland, although one- and two-day tickets including both venues are available. ✉ *One Legoland Dr.,* ☎ *760/918–5346* ⊕ *www.legoland.com/sealife* ⌧ *$18.95.*

☾ Take an interactive journey through 100 years of popular music at the **Museum of Making Music,** which displays more than 500 vintage instruments and samples of memorable tunes from the past century. Hands-on activities include playing a digital piano, drums, guitar, and electric violin. ✉ *5790 Armada Dr., east of I–5* ☎ *760/438–5996 or 877/551–9976* ⊕ *www.museumofmakingmusic.org* ⌧ *$5* ☉ *Tues.–Sun. 10–5.*

The **Leo Carrillo Ranch Historic Park** was a real working ranch with 600 head of cattle owned by actor Leo Carrillo, who played Pancho in the Cisco Kid television series in the 1950s. Before Carrillo bought the spread, known as *Rancho de Los Kiotes,* in 1937, the rancho, occupying portions of a Spanish land grant, was the home of a band of Luiseno Indians. Carrillo's hacienda and other buildings have been restored to reflect the life of the star when he hosted his Hollywood friends for long weekends in the country. Four miles of trails take visitors through colorful native gardens to the cantina, wash house, pool and cabana, barn, and stable that Carrillo used. You can see the insides of these buildings on weekends when guided tours are offered. After Carrillo's death in 1961, the ranch remained in the family until 1979, when part of the acreage was acquired by the city for a park. ✉ *6200 Flying LC La.* ☎ *760/476–1042* ⊕ *www.leocarrilloranch.org* ⌧ *Free* ☉ *Tues.–Sat. 9–5, Sun. 11–5.*

WHERE TO EAT

$$$$ ✕ **The Argyle Restaurant and Lounge.** Even if you don't play golf, the Argyle, occupying the Aviara Golf clubhouse, is a good choice for breakfast or lunch on a sunny day. The 18th green, Batiquitos Lagoon, and the Pacific create beautiful vistas from nearly every table, whether you are inside at the clubby bar or outside on the deck. The breakfast menu lists classics like smoked salmon, omelets, and breakfast burrito. Soups, salads, sandwiches, and "lite" entrées fill the bill at lunch. By dinnertime the Argyle becomes a steakhouse purveying dry-aged prime beef from Nebraska, Kobe-style Angus steaks, and Colorado lamb chops. ⊠ *7100 Four Seasons Point* ☎*760/603–6800* ☐*AE, D, DC, MC, V* ⊘*No dinner Sun. or Mon.*

$$$
Fodor's Choice
★
✕ **BlueFire Grill.** Starting with the setting and concluding with a dinner, fire and water drama defines this signature restaurant that's part of the La Costa resort complex. The centerpiece of the resort's entrance plaza, the grill holds an outdoor patio with fire pits, fountains, and a year-round floral display. Inside is a contemporary Mission-style room surrounding a green bottle glass fountain that extends the length of the main dining room. The menu features local seafood and vegetables combined in exciting ways. As a starter, try a tiny red wine braised short rib with wild mushroom and shaved Parmesan, followed by roasted chicken breast tangine with Moroccan-spiced gold raisin couscous or grilled salmon with mango mustard glaze presented on a bed of saffron risotto with wild mushrooms. Tantalizing desserts include luscious Carlsbad strawberries marinated in balsamic and butterscotch white-chocolate mousse bomb. ⊠ *2100 Del Mar Rd.* ☎*760/929–6306* ⚑*Reservations essential* ☐*AE, D, DC, MC, V* ⊘*No lunch.*

$$ ✕ **Bistro West.** This busy spot, part of the West Inn complex, might be called the boisterous bistro, especially if you get there during happy hour when it appears that all of Carlsbad is tipping back a few. The bistro specializes in comfort food; a huge chicken potpie tops the list that also includes meatloaf, several burger variations, pastas, and pizza. You can select from a long wine list of mostly California products at fair prices; many are available by the glass. ⊠ *4960 Avenida Encinas* ☎*760/930–8008* ⚑*reservations essential weekends* ☐*AE, D, DC, MC, V.*

WHERE TO STAY

ⓒ **$$$$**
Fodor's Choice
★
⊞ **Four Seasons Resort Aviara.** This hilltop resort on 30 acres offers one of the most sublime views in Southern California. Stroll out to the pool overlooking Batiquitos Lagoon, where the panorama stretches endlessly from lagoon to the Pacific. If you watch for a while you may catch sight of one of the 130 species of birds that inhabit the wetland. The quietly elegant Aviara is one of the most luxurious hotels in the San Diego area, with gleaming marble corridors, original artwork, crystal chandeliers, and enormous flower arrangements. Rooms have every possible amenity: oversize closets, private balconies or garden patios, and marble bathrooms with double vanities and deep soaking tubs. The resort is exceptionally family-friendly, providing a wide selection of in-room amenities designed for the younger set. Kids also

have their own pool, plus nature walks with wildlife demonstrations. The on-site golf course is considered one of the best in California, and jazz concerts are presented on the lawn on summer Friday evenings. **Pros:** Unbeatable location, fabulous service. **Cons:** A little stiff. ⊠*7100 Four Seasons Point,* ☎*760/603–6800 or 800/332–3442* ⊕*www.fourseasons.com/aviara* ⬦*329 rooms, 44 suites* ☖*In-room: safe, refrigerator, DVD (some), Ethernet, Wi-Fi. In-hotel: 4 restaurants, room service, bars, golf course, tennis courts, pools, gym, spa, children's programs (ages 4–12), laundry service, concierge, public Internet, Wi-Fi, parking (fee), some pets allowed (fee), no-smoking rooms* ▤*AE, D, DC, MC, V.*

☾ **$$$$** ⌖**La Costa Resort and Spa.** A major transformation turned the legendary '50s-style resort into a chic Spanish colonial oasis with dark wood, open-beam ceilings and paneling, crystal chandeliers, and leather and wrought-iron furnishings. Ample guest rooms, in shades of brown and sand with oversize chairs and sofas, fill a collection of two-story buildings surrounding the lobby, Club House, and conference center. There are flower-decked gardens and fairway views throughout the resort's 400 tree-shaded acres—and the best of all fairway views may be from one of the state-of-the-art bikes in the fitness center. The family-friendly resort holds a kids' club, Kidtopia, and has a teen lounge, Vibz, as well as three swimming pools with waterslides and a water play zone.There are two PGA championship golf courses, a large tennis center, and a family entertainment area. **Pros:** Huge glamorous spa, excellent kids' facilities, popular restaurant. **Cons:** Very spread out, making long walks necessary; lots of kids. ⊠*2100 Costa del Mar Rd.,* ☎*760/438–9111 or 800/854–5000* ⊕*www.lacosta.com* ⬦*610 rooms, 120 villas* ☖*In-room: safe, refrigerator (some), DVD, Ethernet, dial-up, Wi-Fi. In-hotel: 6 restaurants, room service, bars, golf courses, tennis courts, pools, gym, spa, bicycles, children's programs (ages 3–12), laundry facilities, laundry service, concierge public Internet, public Wi-Fi, parking (fee), no-smoking rooms* ▤*AE, D, DC, MC, V.*

☾ **$$$** ⌖**Carlsbad Inn Beach Resort.** Gable roofs, half-timber walls, and stone supports are among the noteworthy architectural elements at this sprawling inn and time-share condominium complex with direct access to the beach. Public areas, including a library furnished with overstuffed sofas and chairs, are warmed by big rock fireplaces; and you can hear the soothing sounds of a rock waterfall in the lobby. The entire facility surrounds brilliant seasonal gardens. Rooms, which range from cramped to large, are furnished Queen Anne style, with pencil-post beds and wall sconces. Many have ocean views, balconies, and kitchenettes; some also have fireplaces and hot tubs. With sprawling, landscaped grounds the inn is well equipped to accommodate families. The resort offers a schedule of activities that includes tours to Mexico and Hollywood, a beach cabana fully equipped with toys in summer, crafts classes, and Victorian tea. Pros: Walk to the beach, warm ambience. Cons: lots of kids, on the main drag. ⊠*3075 Carlsbad Blvd.,* ☎*760/434–7020 or 800/235–3939* ⊕*www.carlsbadinn.com* ⬦*61 rooms, 1 suite* ☖*In-room: safe, kitchen (some), DVD, VCR, dial-up,*

Wi-Fi. In-hotel: restaurant, pool, gym, water sports, bicycles, children's programs (ages 5–12), laundry facilities, concierge, public Internet, public Wi-Fi, parking (no fee), no-smoking rooms

$$$ **Grand Pacific Palisades Resort & Hotel.** It's all about the Lego at the Grand Pacific, where primary-colored Lego Snow White and King Arthur preside over the lobby. The hotel has direct access to LEGO-LAND, and in spring a colorful view of the Flowerfields at Carlsbad Ranch and the ocean beyond from the adult pool area. This is a hotel/time-share complex that does a lot of group tour business. Most of the hotel rooms are smallish, with tiny closets, but they have nice ocean or mountain views from step-out balconies. The time-shares, which are available for overnight guests, are the best choice for families. Surrounding a Lego-themed swimming pool, they have one, two, and three bedrooms. An outlet of San Diego's popular Karl Strauss Brewery Restaurant is a short walk from the hotel entrance, and offers room service for hotel guests. **Pros:** Close walk to LEGOLAND, gorgeous adult pool with Pacific view, kid area and pool. **Cons:** Small rooms, tiny closets. ⊠ *5805 Armada Dr. 92008* ☎ *760/827–3231 or 800/725–4723* ⊕ *www.grandpacificpalisades.com* ⊲ *90 rooms, 140 time-share villas* ☆ *In-room: kitchen (some), refrigerator (some), DVD, VCR, Ethernet, dial-up, Wi-Fi. In-hotel: pools, gym, laundry facilities, laundry service, concierge, executive floor, public Internet, public Wi-Fi, parking (fee), no smoking rooms* ▭ *AE, D, MC, V.*

$$$ **Sheraton Carlsbad Resort & Spa.** If location is everything, this brand new Sheraton has it two ways: You can walk right into LEGOLAND's Castle Hill through a private back entrance directly from the hotel, or you can walk to the new Crossings at Carlsbad golf course. The look here is dramatic Arts & Crafts, with floor to ceiling windows in the public areas as well as in the guest rooms. Colorful gardens rim the entire complex. Modern-looking rooms are fairly large and are done in tones of beige, brown, and white. There are ample work desks, expansive bathrooms with soaking tubs, and flat-screen TVs. **Pros:** Private entrance to LEGOLAND, lovely views from many rooms. **Cons:** High noise level in public areas. ⊠ *5480 Grand Pacific Dr.,* ☎ *760/827–2400 or 800/965–6577* ⊕ *www.sheratoncarlsbadresort.com* ⊲ *250 rooms* ☆ *In-room: safe, refrigerator, DVD, Ethernet, dial-up, Wi-Fi. In-hotel: restaurant, room service, bar, tennis court, pool, gym, spa, children's programs (ages 5–12), laundry service, concierge, executive floor, public Internet, public Wi-Fi, parking (fee), some pets allowed, no smoking rooms* ▭ *AE, D, DC, MC, V.*

★ $$ **West Inn and Suites.** Warm and friendly defines this boutique hotel, located on the west side of I–5, closer to the beaches than to LEGO-LAND. A family-run operation, West Inn offers large, well-appointed guest rooms, all furnished with king-size beds and streamlined Arts & Crafts decor with dark hardwood floors and bead-board paneling. There are flat-screen TVs, oversize desks, large walk-in showers, and fresh orchids. The attractive pool area has a stone waterfall at one end. The inviting lobby/sitting room holds a large stone fireplace that can take the chill off a cool day. Staff is exceptionally accommodating and friendly. The inn offers shuttle services for guests within the Carlsbad

Spas

San Diego can claim one of the largest concentrations of spas in the United States. They include destination spas, resort spas, and day spas. At destination spas, a treatment program is developed for each guest, and the stay is usually all-inclusive. The spa is an adjunct to other resort facilities at a resort spa, to be ignored or not, but using it can be the ultimate indulgence whether you're staying at the hotel for business or pleasure. You can design your own luxurious day by selecting treatments à la carte from the spa's menu. Many resorts also have special treatment facilities for couples; they also typically offer elegant lounges, fitness facilities, and locker rooms. Day spas, found throughout the San Diego area, offer skin and body treatments, facials, and makeup and hair care services. Although it's possible to walk into most day spas, it's a good idea to make a reservation to be sure you get the service you want when you want it.

DESTINATION SPAS

Some of the most beautiful women in the world hang out in drab grey sweats while sipping tea in a lounge bulging with 17th-century French antiques at **Cal-a-Vie Spa** (⊠ *29402 Spa Havens Way, Vista* ☎ *760/945–2055 or 866/772–4283* ⊕ *www.cal-a-vie.com*). Owners Terri and John Havens filled every nook and cranny with tapestries, paintings, fireplaces, and furnishings that came straight from old French châteaux. Recently, Julia Roberts, Kathleen Turner, and Sharon Gless made the trek to this intimate destination spa in the hills near Escondido. Oprah Winfrey, a longtime guest, even snagged the chef for herself. Like the celebs, you can spend a few days hiking the hillsides, working your buns, listening to health lectures, and being massaged, rubbed, and wrapped. All the while devouring delicious, nutritionally balanced meals. The chef even teaches you how to cook your healthy gourmet meals at home. The spa caters to a maximum of 24 guests, each ensconced in his or her own elegant European-inspired cottage, appointed with travertine floors, luxury linens, and Wi-Fi. The state-of-the-art fitness center is housed in a light-filled, frescoed Turkish-style bathhouse with travertine marble tile. There are tennis courts and privileges at the adjacent Ted Robinson golf course. All this comes at a price, of course, around $6,500 to $7,000 per week, although less expensive three- and four-day programs are also available.

Considered by many to be the world's best destination spa, the venerable **Golden Door** (⊠ *777 Deer Springs Rd., San Marcos* ☎ *760/744–5777 or 800/424–0777* ⊕ *www.goldendoor. com*) occupies a serene camellia-filled canyon just outside Escondido. Although some say the spa's age is showing, the Golden Door still collects accolades for its beauty, service, and food. From the moment you step through its entrance, you're in a hushed Zen-inspired realm of perfectly manicured gardens surrounding simply furnished guest rooms. Catering to just 40 guests (women-only most of the time) with a guest-to-staff ratio of 1 to 4, the Golden Door pampers luxuriantly, beginning with the schedule for your week's stay printed on a folded fan. Indulge in a daily massage, meditation, beauty and skin-care treatments, and an exercise program, including the chance to explore 25 mi of hiking trails, designed expressly for you. Menus complement the Zen experience with simple preparations such as pan-seared prawns or Parmesan-crusted organic chicken breast served with organic herbs and vegetables grown on the premises. Everything you need is provided, at $7,995 per week, although some discounts are available.

RESORT SPAS

The spa and fitness center at **Four Seasons Resort Aviara** (⊠ *7100 Four Seasons Point, Carlsbad* ☎ *760/603–6800* ⊕ *www.fourseasons.com/aviara*) holds 20 treatment rooms including a Couple's Suite with side-by-side massage tables, a lounge with marble fireplace and double shower, and a private patio with whirlpool. Facilities include a fitness center with machines and free weights, plus an indoor solarium with steam room, sauna, and whirlpools. The spa offers a full menu of massages, scrubs, body wraps, facials, and bath rituals. À la carte treatments range from $145 to $170 for 50 minutes, a 3-hour day of beauty is $570, and the couples' programs are $570 (two hours) to $1,990 (eight hours).

The venerable spa at **La Costa Resort and Spa** (⊠ *2100 Costa Del Mar Rd., Carlsbad* ☎ *800/854–5000* ⊕ *www.lacosta.com*) is an elegant Spanish-colonial sanctuary with 42 treatment rooms, a bright lounge with garden view, a boutique and café, an outdoor courtyard with pool, a shoulder-pounding Roman water massage, sunbathing areas, and an herb garden. The mood here is warm but business-like. Services include massages, mineral baths and water therapies, scrubs and wraps, and facials; rates range from $150 to $165 for 50-minute massages, $155 for body treatments, and $160 for 50-minute facials. Couples' programs using a VIP spa suite with two tables are also available ($475 to $625). The adjacent Chopra Center for Well Being offers seminars, workshops, treatments, and medical consultation based on ayurveda, the ancient Indian healing system.

The subtropical-themed spa at **Rancho Valencia Resort** (⊠ *16199 Rancho Valencia Dr., Rancho Santa Fe* ☎ *858/759–6490* ⊕ *www.ranchovalencia.com*) is a garden of tranquillity. Serenity envelops you the minute you step into the front courtyard/lushly landscaped tropical garden that leads to the hacienda-style spa. There are ten treatment rooms, all filled with flowers and plants, where you can take your treatment indoors or outside in a private garden patio; five have soaking tubs. Couples rooms also have soaking tubs for two and outdoor showers. The extensive treatment menu starts with bountiful baths ($80) and ends with spa fusions (90 to 300 minutes $205 to $700). Bodywork and massages run from 60 to 120 minutes ($140 to $280). Salon services include hand and foot renewal with manicures and pedicures, waxing, and aesthetics. There's a collection of services just for men. Spa guests have access to the fitness facilities and private cabanas in the secluded pool.

DAY SPAS

Just across the street from the San Diego Convention Center, **Spa Tiki** (⊠ *200 Harbor Dr. San Diego* ☎ *619/231–4363* ⊕ *www.spatiki.com*) draws a lot of foot-weary and back-stressed visitors. You can select from South Seas–themed wraps, scrubs (coconut), bath rituals (coco loco), soaks (passion flower), facials, massages, and nail and beauty treatments. Prices are competitive at $50 to $130 for most 50-minute services; facials are $65 to $160. Valet parking is also available for $8.

—Bobbi Zane

7

area. There are two restaurants on-site, both locally popular and busy. A full buffet breakfast is included in the price, and milk and cookies are served in the lobby each night. Kids will enjoy the heated outdoor pool and playing board games in the library. **Pros:** Family- and pet-friendly, full breakfast, organized activities. **Cons:** Adjacent to railroad tracks and freeway. ⊠*4970 Avenida Encinas 92008* ☎*760/448–4500 or 888/431–9378* ⊕*www.westinnandsuites.com* ⤳*86 rooms, 36 suites* ⅋*In-room: safe, refrigerator, DVD, Ethernet, dial-up, Wi-Fi. In-hotel: 2 restaurants, bars, pool, gym, laundry facilities, concierge, public Internet, public Wi-Fi, parking (no fee), some pets allowed, no-smoking rooms* ⊟*AE, D, DC, MC, V* ⦿*BP.*

$ ⌂**Pelican Cove Inn.** Two blocks from the beach and surrounded by palm trees and mature colorful gardens with secluded nooks, this two-story bed-and-breakfast has spacious rooms with gas fireplaces, canopied feather beds, and private entrances. You can walk to the beach just two blocks away. Gracious innkeepers provide beach chairs and towels, and can make arrangements for biplane rides. Breakfast served in the parlor is included in the price. **Pros:** Welcoming host, attractive rooms. **Cons:** Limited facilities, located on a side street away from downtown. ⊠*320 Walnut Ave.,* ☎*760/434–5995 or 888/735–2683* ⊕*www.pelican-cove.com* ⤳*10 rooms* ⅋*In-room: no a/c, refrigerators (some), DVD (some), Ethernet, Wi-Fi. In-hotel: no elevator, parking (no fee), no-smoking rooms* ⊟*AE, MC, V* ⦿*BP.*

SHOPPING

★ **Carlsbad Premium Outlets** (⊠*5620 Paseo Del Norte* ☎*760/804–9000 or 888/790–7467* ⊕*www.premiumoutlets.com/carlsbad*) is the only upscale designer factory outlet in the San Diego area. Within this attractively landscaped complex you can find Wedgwood, Le Creuset, and Polo Ralph Lauren. **Thousand Mile Outdoor Wear** (☎*760/804–1764*) makes the bathing suits used by most lifeguards in Southern California and also has a line of outerwear manufactured from recycled soft-drink bottles. **Barney's New York** (☎*760/929–9600*) carries a large selection of designer women's and men's fashions. You can find home accessories at the **Crate & Barrel Outlet** (☎*760/692–2100*). **Dooney & Bourke** (☎*760/476–1049*) sells their popular handbags and accessories at discounted prices.

OCEANSIDE

8 mi north of Carlsbad on Rte. S21, 37 mi north of downtown San Diego on I–5.

The beach culture is alive and well in Oceanside despite redevelopment activities that are changing the face of the waterfront. Mixed-use hotels and residences are under construction to enhance the beach culture and make it more accessible. The first of several planned hotels opened in 2008; primarily all-suite, it's a great choice for families who want to spend a few days or a week at the beach. Visitors to this part of downtown Oceanside can stay within walking distance of the city's best swimming and surfing beaches: Harbor Beach, brimming with beach activities and fun, and Buccaneer Beach, where you'll find the best surfing in North County. This area is also a short walk from the Oceanside Transportation Center, where Amtrak and Coaster trains stop and depart. Many who have been in the military link Oceanside with Camp Pendleton, the huge Marine base that lies at the north end of the city. Until recently the military was Oceanside's main industry, now being eclipsed by tourism; proximity to the base still has its benefits, as most businesspeople offer discounts to active military personnel and their families. Also home to the largest and one of the best-preserved California missions, Mission San Luis Rey, Oceanside's history extends back to the 1700s, when the Spanish friars walked along the California coast founding missions as they went. Today Oceanside celebrates its historic culture with the regionally exciting Oceanside Museum of Art, displaying the works of San Diego area artists. Residents and visitors gather weekly at the Farmers' Market and Sunset Market, where shopping for fresh-picked produce is a pleasant pastime.

California Welcome Center Oceanside offers complete state travel information, foreign-language assistance, and a concierge service inside a mission-style, white-arched building. You can buy discount tickets to many Southern California attractions. ⊠ *928 N. Coast Hwy.* ☎ *760/721–1101 or 800/350–7873* ⊕ *www.californiawelcomecenter. org* ⊗ *Daily 9–5.*

With 900 slips, **Oceanside Harbor** (☎ *760/435–4000*) is North County's fishing, sailing, and water-sports center. **Helgren's Sportfishing** (⊠ *315 Harbor Dr. S* ☎ *760/722–2133* ⊕ *www.helgrensportfishing.com*) schedules daily ocean fishing trips and whale-watching coastal excursions. South of Oceanside Harbor, **Oceanside Pier**, at 1,942 feet, is one of the longest on the West Coast. The water surrounding it is known for its surf breaks and good fishing. A restaurant, Ruby's Diner, stands at the end of the wooden pier's long promenade. **California Surf Museum** displays a large collection of surfing memorabilia, photos, vintage boards, apparel, and accessories. ⊠ *223 N. Coast Hwy.* ☎ *760/721–6876* ⊕ *www.surfmuseum.org* ⊠ *Free* ⊗ *Daily 10–4.*

Camp Pendleton, the nation's largest amphibious military training complex, encompasses 17 mi of Pacific shoreline. It's not unusual to see herds of tanks and flocks of helicopters maneuvering through the dunes and brush alongside I–5. You may also see herds of sheep keeping the bushland down and fertile fields growing next to the Pacific coastline.

Ⓒ **Mission San Luis,** known as the King of the Missions, was built in 1798
FodorsChoice by Franciscan friars under the direction of Father Fermin Lasuen to
★ help educate and convert local Native Americans. Once a location for filming Disney's *Zorro* TV series, the well-preserved mission, still owned by the Franciscans, was the 18th and largest and most prosperous of California's missions. The *sala* (parlor), the kitchen, a friar's bedroom, a weaving room, and a collection of religious art convey much about early mission life. Retreats are still held here, but a picnic area, a gift shop, and a museum (which has the most extensive collection of old Spanish vestments in the United States) are also on the grounds, as are

7

sunken gardens and the *lavanderia,* the original open-air laundry area. Self-guided and docent-led tours are available. The mission's retreat center has limited, inexpensive dormitory-style overnight accommodations. ✉*4050 Mission Ave.* ☎*760/757–3651* ⊕*www.sanluisrey.org* 🖃*$6* ⊘*Daily 10–4.*

Oceanside Museum of Art is housed in side-by-side buildings designed by two Southern California modernist architects; the old City Hall designed by Irving Gill and the new Central Pavilion designed by Frederick Fisher. The museum showcases works by San Diego area artists including paintings and photography. Exhibits scheduled for 2009 include "Millard Sheets and the Southern California Legacy" and "Quilt Visions," an international juried show of contemporary quilts. ✉*704 Pier View Way* ☎*760/721–2787* ⊕*www.oma-online.org* 🖃*$5* ⊘*Tues.–Sat. 10–4, Sun. 1–4.*

The **Wave Waterpark** is a 3-acre water park run by the City of Vista. It's also one of the few places in the country with a flow-rider, a type of standing wave that allows riders on bodyboards to turn, carve, and slash almost as though they were surfing on a real wave. If you haven't learned how to do that, you can tube down the park's own river or slip down the 35-foot waterslide. ✉*101 Wave Dr., Vista* ☎*760/940–9283* ⊕*www.thewavewaterpark.com* 🖃*$15* ⊘*Memorial Day–Labor Day, daily 10:30–5:30; Labor Day–end Sept., weekends 11–5.*

WHERE TO EAT

$$ ╳**Vigilucci's Osteria.** Part of a growing North San Diego County restaurant chain, the Oceanside branch channels San Francisco's North Beach. The long narrow storefront with brick walls is hung with large paintings and gilt-framed mirrors. The traditional menu includes tagliatelle alla Bolognese, penne vodka con porcini, cotoletta di polla alla Milanese, and spumoni. ✉ *608 Mission Ave.* ☎*760/966–1203* 🖩 *AE, D, DC, MC, V.*

$ ╳**Jolly Roger.** This casual café is a good choice for waterside dining. You can watch traffic move through the harbor while savoring nicely prepared salmon, halibut, ahi, or even teriyaki steak or prime rib. The dining room is a bit old-fashioned, with leather-lined booths and laminate-topped tables. Entertainment is presented on weekends. ✉*1900 N. Harbor Dr.* ☎*760/722–1831* 🖩*AE, D, MC, V.*

¢ ╳**Harbor Fish & Chips.** Pick up a basket of fresh-cooked fish-and-chips at this dive and you're in for a treat. The shop has been serving the combo—and clam chowder, shrimp cocktail, and fish sandwiches—to boaters and visitors for more than 40 years. It looks like it, too, with fish trophies hung on walls and from the ceiling. Outdoor tables offer terrific views of the Oceanside Marina. ✉ *276 S. Harbor Dr. 92054* ☎*760/722–4977* 🖩*AE, D, MC, V.*

¢ ╳**101 Cafe.** A diner dating back to 1928, this is both a local hangout and the headquarters of the historic Highway 101 movement. You'll find all kinds of Highway 101 memorabilia here along with breakfast, lunch, and dinner. The menu lists burgers, sandwiches, and salads for lunch, and biscuits and gravy, chicken-fried steak, spaghetti, and meat loaf for dinner. ⊠*631 S. Coast Hwy.* ☎*760/722–5220* ⚑*Reservations not accepted* ▭*No credit cards.*

WHERE TO STAY

$$$$
★
⌐⌐⌐**Oceanside Marina Suites.** Of all the oceanfront lodgings in North County towns, this hotel occupies the best location—a spit of land surrounded by water and cool ocean breezes on all sides. Depending upon your room selection, you can enjoy the comings and goings of harbor activity, sailors sprucing up their craft, or the waves crashing over the breakwater. The rooms, renovated in 2007 to reflect a Tommy Bahama feel with hardwood floors, floral and leather upholstery, and granite counters in kitchens and bathrooms, are mostly one- and two-bedroom suites. They are unusually large, and have fireplaces and expansive balconies; all have either ocean or harbor views. There are public barbecues for guest use. A free boat shuttles you to the beach in summer. Continental breakfast is included in the price. **Pros:** Best sunsets in Oceanside, spacious rooms, free parking. **Cons:** Marina location apt to be busy on weekends. ⊠*2008 Harbor Dr. N,* ☎*760/722–1561 or 800/252–2033* ⊕*www.omihotel.com* ⌐*6 rooms, 51 suites* ⌂*In-room: no a/c, kitchen, refrigerator, DVD, Ethernet, Wi-Fi. In-hotel: pool, no elevator, laundry facilities, public Internet, public Wi-Fi, parking (no fee), no-smoking rooms* ▭*AE, MC, V* ⏍*CP.*

$$$
⌐⌐**Wyndham Oceanside Pier Resort.** Located just steps from the beach and Oceanside Pier, this family-friendly resort is the first of several set to open along the Oceanside beachfront, featuring a combination of hotel rooms and condo rentals. Long corridors lead to spacious two- and three-bedroom suites that are ideal for families; they have fully equipped kitchens, ocean-view balconies, flat-screen TVs, and whirlpool tubs in the bathrooms. Hotel rooms are smaller, but have the same views and hotel amenities. The decor throughout combines Streamline dark-wood furnishings and beachy mosaic accents. Watching the waves crash against the sand can be a fulltime pastime here. Admire the view while biking in the fitness center or relaxing in the hotel's bright and airy lobby. **Pros:** Beachfront location, family-friendly. **Cons:** No spa, limited hotel rooms. ⊠*333 N. Myers 92054* ☎*760/901–1200* ⊕*www. extraholidays.com* ⌐*24 rooms, 132 suites* ⌂*In-room: safe, kitchen (some), refrigerator (some), DVD, Ethernet, Wi-Fi. In-hotel: 2 restaurants, room service, bar, pool, gym, beachfront, children's programs (ages 2–15), concierge, public Internet, public Wi-Fi, parking (no fee), no-smoking rooms* ▭*AE, D, DC, MC, V.*

SHOPPING

Oceanside Photo & Telescope (⊠*918 Mission Ave.* ☎*760/722–3348 or 800/483–6287* ⊕*www.optcorp.com*) is the place to pick up a telescope or binoculars for viewing San Diego County's dazzling night sky. The Underground Gallery downstairs (☎ *760/231–0103*) displays a collection of photographic works by a dozen local artists featuring astronomical, landscape, and computer images. Call for information about the photo gallery and stargazing parties the store holds regularly in the San Diego area.

NORTH COAST ESSENTIALS

To research prices, get advice from other travelers, and book travel arrangements, visit www.fodors.com.

AIR TRAVEL

McClellan Palomar Airport is run by the county of San Diego. This is the airport of choice for many corporate jet and charter operators. Air taxi service is also available.

Airport Information **McClellan Palomar Airport** (✉ *2192 Palomar Airport Rd., Carlsbad* ☎ *760/431–4646* ⊕ *www.sdcounty.ca.gov*).

BUS TRAVEL

The Metropolitan Transit System covers the city of San Diego up to Del Mar. The North County Transit District serves San Diego County from Del Mar north.

Bus Information **North County Transit District** (☎ *800/266–6883* ⊕ *www.sd-commute.com*). **Metropolitan Transit System** (☎ *619/233–3004 or 800/266–6883* ⊕ *www.sdcommute.com*).

CAR TRAVEL

Interstate 5 is the main freeway artery connecting San Diego to Los Angeles. Running parallel west of I–5 is Route S21, also known and sometimes indicated as Highway 101, Old Highway 101, or Coast Highway 101, which never strays too far from the ocean. An alternate, especially from Orange and Riverside counties is I–15, the inland route through Temecula, Escondido, and eastern San Diego.

TRAIN TRAVEL

Amtrak stops in Solana Beach and Oceanside. Coaster operates commuter rail service between San Diego and Oceanside, stopping in Old Town, Sorrento Valley, Solana Beach, Encinitas, and Carlsbad en route. The last Coaster train leaves San Diego at about 7 each night. The North County Transit District Sprinter runs a commuter service between Oceanside and Escondido.

Train Information **Amtrak** (☎ *760/722–4622 in Oceanside, 800/872–7245* ⊕ *www.amtrakcalifornia.com*). **Coaster and Sprinter** (☎ *800/262–7837* ⊕ *www. sdcommute.com*).

TOUR OPTIONS

Civic Helicopters gives whirlybird tours of the area along the beaches for about $100 per person per half hour. Biplane, Air Combat and War-bird Adventures conducts excursions aboard restored 1920s-vintage open-cockpit biplanes and military-style Top Dog air combat flights on prop-driven Varga VG-21s. Flights are from McClellan Palomar Airport and start at $199 per couple.

Tour Companies **Biplane, Air Combat and Warbird Adventures** (☎ *760/438–7680 or 800/759–5667* ⊕ *www.barnstorming.com*). **Civic Helicopters** (☎ *760/438–8424 or 866/438–4354* ⊕ *www.civichelicopters.com*).

VISITOR INFORMATION

Contacts **Carlsbad Convention and Visitors Bureau** (☎ *760/434–6093 or 800/227–5722* ⊕ *visitcarlsbad.com*). **Del Mar Regional Chamber of Commerce** (☎ *858/755–4844* ⊕ *www.delmarchamber.org*). **Oceanside Welcome Center** (☎ *760/721–1101 or 800/350–7873* ⊕ *www.californiawelcomecenter. org*). **San Diego North Convention and Visitors Bureau** (☎ *760/745–4741 or 800/848–3336* ⊕ *www.sandiegonorth.com*).

INLAND NORTH COUNTY & TEMECULA

Long regarded as San Diego's beautiful backyard, replete with green hills, quiet lakes, and citrus and avocado groves, inland San Diego County and the Temecula wine country are among the fastest-growing areas in Southern California. Subdivisions, many containing palatial homes, now fill the hills and canyons around Escondido and Rancho Bernardo. At the northern edge of this region, Fallbrook (longtime self-proclaimed Avocado Capital of the World) has morphed into an emerging arts community. Beyond Fallbrook is Temecula, the premium winemaking area of southern Riverside County. Growth notwithstanding, inland San Diego County still has such natural settings as the San Diego Wild Animal Park, Rancho Bernardo, and the Welk Resort. The region is also home to a number of San Diego County's Indian casinos, among them Pala, Harrah's Rincon, Valley View, and Pauma. Pachenga lies just over the county line near Temecula. In October 2007, wildfires blew through much of this area, touching on Rancho Bernardo, the Wild Animal Park, and Fallbrook. While all sustained some damage, the effects of the fires are now barely visible in most areas.

Numbers in the margin correspond to points of interest on the San Diego North County map.

RANCHO BERNARDO

23 mi northeast of downtown San Diego on I–15.

Rancho Bernardo straddles a stretch of I–15 between San Diego and Escondido and is technically a neighborhood of San Diego. Originally sheep- and cattle-grazing land, it was transformed in the early 1960s into a planned suburban community, one of the first, and a place where many wealthy retirees settled down. It's now home to a number of high-tech companies, the most notable of which is Sony. If you want to spend some time at the nearby Wild Animal Park, this community makes a convenient and comfortable headquarters for a multi-day visit, with world-class restaurants and resorts.

WHERE TO EAT

$$$$ ✕ **El Bizcocho.** Wealthy locals rate this restaurant at the Rancho Bernardo Inn tops for style and cuisine. The tranquil setting features candlelit tables, plush banquettes, and quiet, live piano music. An ever-changing menu usually features more than one preparation of ahi, prime fillet of beef, difficult to find Arctic char, and duck. A tasting menu ($60–$110 per person, wine pairing additional) offers a succulent selection based on what's fresh. The wine list has more than 1,500 wines, including rare vintages, although the by-the-glass selection is limited. ⊠*Rancho Bernardo Inn, 17550 Bernardo Oaks Pkwy.* ☎*800/267–5662 or 858/675–8500* ⚑*Reservations essential* ☰*AE, D, DC, MC, V* ⊗*No lunch. No dinner Sun.*

$$$ ✗**Bernard'O.** Intimate despite its shopping-center location, Bernard'O is the choice for a romantic dinner. Sit fireside in the small dining room, dine by candlelight, and savor contemporary versions of classic rack of lamb or grilled king salmon with white and green asparagus. An extensive wine list includes rare old vintages from California and France along with well-priced newer bottles. ⊠*12457 Rancho Bernardo Rd.* ☎*858/487–7171* ☰*AE, D, DC, MC, V* ⊗*No lunch Sat.–Tues.*

$$ ✗**French Market Grille.** The Grille's flower-decked dark-wood dining room and patio with twinkling lights will help you forget that you're eating in a shopping center. The French fare changes with the seasons; typical entrées include rack of lamb, oven-roasted halibut and lobster with vermouth, or roasted chicken with fresh herbs. If you love French desserts, save room for one of the classics offered here, apple tarte tatin, crepes Suzette, and crème brûlée. ⊠*15717 Bernardo Heights Pkwy.* ☎*858/485–8055* ☰*AE, D, DC, MC, V.*

$ ✗**Chin's Szechwan Cuisine.** Locals pick Chin's for special occasions. It feels rich, with dark-red walls, blooming orchids everywhere, and heavy wooden furnishings. The extensive menu lists popular items such as Kung Pao chicken, sizzling beef and scallops, and tangerine crispy beef. ⊠*15721 Bernardo Heights Pkwy.* ☎*858/676–0166* ⊕*www.chins.com* ☰*AE, D, MC, V.*

WHERE TO STAY

☾ ★ **$$$** 🏨**Rancho Bernardo Inn.** On 265 oak-shaded acres surrounded by a well-established residential community, the resort's two-story, red-roof adobe buildings are complemented by bougainvillea-decked courtyards adorned with original art. Public areas are a collection of small sitting rooms where Spanish Mission–style sofas and chairs invite you to linger with a good book. There are fireplaces everywhere, overstuffed furniture, and Oriental rugs on tile floors. Ample rooms updated in 2007 hold platform beds tucked into corner upholstered banquettes, all very streamlined. Great golf course or garden views are visible from private patios or balconies. Among the amenities are flat-screen TVs, iPod players bedside, and minibars. Suites also have fireplaces. A spa, opened in 2007, holds the ultimate treatment rooms: shuttered and heated garden casitas where you can relax under the sun to the tune of moving water. The resort also has one of the most popular golf courses in the San Diego area; the oak-studded and hilly Rancho Bernardo Resort Course has hosted both PGA and LPGA tournaments. Seasonal children's activities include science and sports instruction. **Pros:** Gorgeous flower-decked grounds, excellent service, spa. **Cons:** Walking required in spacious grounds, distance from most visitor attractions. ⊠*17550 Bernardo Oaks Dr. 92128* ☎*858/675–8500 or 877/517–9340* ⊕*www.ranchobernardoinn.com* ⇆*272 rooms, 15 suites* ⚑*In-room: safe, refrigerator, DVD, Ethernet, Wi-Fi. In-hotel: 3 restau-*

*rants, room service, bars, golf courses, tennis courts, pools, gym, spa, no
elevator, children's programs (ages 5–13), concierge, no-smoking rooms*
⊟*AE, D, DC, MC, V.*

SHOPPING

A trip to **Bernardo Winery** (⊠*13330 Paseo Del Verano Norte* ☎*858/
487–1866* ⊕*www.bernardowinery.com*) feels like traveling back to
early California days; some of the vines on the former Spanish land-
grant property have been producing grapes for more than 100 years.
The oldest operating winery in Southern California, Bernardo was
founded in 1889, and has been operated by the Rizzo family since
1928. Most of the grapes come from other wine-growing regions.
Besides the wine-tasting room and shop selling cold-pressed olive oil
and other gourmet goodies, restaurant Cafe Merlot serves lunch daily
except Monday. About a dozen shops offer apparel, home-decor items,
and arts and crafts. If you're lucky, the glassblowing artist will be working at the outdoor furnace. The winery is open Monday–Friday 9–5,
weekends 10–5; the shops are open Tuesday–Sunday 10–5.

ESCONDIDO

*8 mi north of Rancho Bernardo on I–15, 31 mi northeast of downtown
San Diego on I–15.*

Escondido and the lovely rolling hills around it were originally a land
grant bestowed by the governor of Mexico on Juan Bautista Alvarado
in 1843. The Battle of San Pasqual, a bloody milestone in California's
march to statehood, took place just east of the city. For a century and
a half, these hills supported citrus and avocado trees, plus large vineyards. The rural character of the area began to change when the San
Diego Zoo established its Wild Animal Park in the San Pasqual Valley
east of town in the 1970s. By the late 1990s suburban development
had begun to transform the hills into housing tracts. The California
Center for the Arts, opened in 1993, now stands as the downtown
centerpiece of a burgeoning arts community that includes a branch of
the Mingei Folk Art Museum and a collection of art galleries along
Grand Avenue. Despite its urbanization, Escondido still supports several pristine open-space preserves that attract nature lovers, hikers, and
mountain bikers.

☾ **San Diego Wild Animal Park** is an extension of the San Diego Zoo, 35
Fodor\$Choice mi to the south. The 1,800-acre preserve in the San Pasqual Valley is
★ designed to protect endangered species from around the world. Exhibit
areas have been carved out of the dry, dusty canyons and mesas to
represent the animals' natural habitats in various parts of Africa, the
Australian rain forest, and Asian swamps and plains.

The best way to see these preserves is to take the 45-minute, 2.5-mi
Journey into Africa bus tour (extra charge with general admission).
As you pass in front of the large, naturally landscaped enclosures, you
can see animals bounding across prairies and mesas as they would in
the wild. More than 3,500 animals of more than 400 species roam or

fly above the expansive grounds. Predators are separated from prey by deep moats, but only the elephants, tigers, lions, and cheetahs are kept in isolation. Photographers with zoom lenses can get spectacular shots of zebras, gazelles, and rhinos. In summer, when the park stays open late, the trip is especially enjoyable in the early evening, when the heat has subsided and the animals are active and feeding. When the bus travels through the park after dark, sodium-vapor lamps illuminate the active animals.

The park is as much a botanical garden as a zoo, serving as a "rescue center" for rare and endangered plants. Unique gardens include cacti and succulents from Baja California, a bonsai collection, a fuchsia display, native plants, protea, and water-wise plantings. The park sponsors a number of garden events throughout the year, including a winter camellia show and a spring orchid show.

> ## SHOOTS AND LEAVES
>
> Not only rare and endangered plants grow at the botanical gardens of the San Diego Wild Animal Park. You might consider them kitchen gardens for some of the San Diego Zoo's rare and endangered animals. For instance, the zoo grows 10.5 tons of bamboo annually to feed its pandas, some of it at the park and some in gardens at the zoo. Because bamboo is low in nutrients, one panda can eat as much as 80 pounds of it a day. Similarly, both the park and the zoo grow eucalyptus to feed the koalas, each of which eats from a pound to a pound and a half of leaves a day.

The **Lion Camp** gives you a close-up view of the king of beasts in a slice of African wilderness complete with sweeping plains and rolling hills. As you walk through this exhibit, you can watch the giant cats lounging around through a 40-foot-long window. The last stop is a research station where you can see them all around you through glass panels.

The 1¼-mi-long **Kilimanjaro Safari Walk** winds through some of the park's hilliest terrain in the East Africa section, with observation decks overlooking the elephants and lions. A 70-foot suspension bridge spans a steep ravine, leading to the final observation point and a panorama of the entire park and the San Pasqual Valley.

The ticket booths at **Nairobi Village**, the park's center, are designed to resemble the tomb of an ancient king of Uganda. Animals in the **Petting Kraal** here affectionately tolerate tugs and pats and are quite adept at posing for pictures with toddlers. At the **Congo River Village** 10,000 gallons of water pour each minute over a huge waterfall into a large lagoon. **Hidden Jungle**, an 8,800-square-foot greenhouse, is a habitat for creatures that creep, flutter, or just hang out in the tropics. Gigantic cockroaches and bird-eating spiders share the turf with colorful butterflies and hummingbirds and oh-so-slow-moving two-toed sloths. **Lorikeet Landing**, simulating the Australian rain forest, holds 75 of the loud and colorful small parrots—you can buy a cup of nectar at the aviary entrance to induce them to land on your hand. Along the trails of 32-acre **Heart of Africa** you can travel in the footsteps of an early explorer through forests and lowlands, across a floating bridge to a research station, where an expert is on hand to answer questions; finally you arrive at Panorama Point for an up-close-and-personal view of cheetahs, a chance to feed the giraffes, and a distant glimpse of the expansive savanna where rhinos, impalas, wildebeest, oryx, and beautiful migrating birds reside. At **Condor Ridge,** the Wild Animal Park, which conducts captive breeding programs to save rare and endangered species, shows off one of its most successful efforts, the California condor. The exhibit, perched like one of the ugly black vultures it features, occupies nearly the highest point in the park, and affords a sweeping view of the surrounding San Pasqual Valley. Also on exhibit here is a herd of rare desert bighorn sheep.

All the park's animal shows are entertainingly educational. The gift shops here offer wonderful merchandise, much of it limited-edition items. Rental camcorders, strollers, and wheelchairs are available. Serious shutterbugs might consider joining one of the special Photo Caravan Safari tours ($90–$150 plus park admission). You can also get a behind-the-scenes look at the new lion and tiger exhibits on the Cats and Carnivores tour ($25, plus park admission), overnight in the park in summer on a Roar and Snore Camp-Over (adults $129–$199, kids 8–11 $119–$139, plus admission), and celebrate the holidays during the annual Festival of Lights. ⊠ *15500 San Pasqual Valley Rd.* ⚓ *Take I–15 north to Via Rancho Pkwy. and follow signs, 6 mi.* ☎ *760/747-8702* ⊕ *www.sandiegozoo.org/wap* ⊠ *$28.50 includes all shows and monorail tour; $60 combination pass grants entry within 5 days of purchase to San Diego Zoo and San Diego Wild Animal Park; parking $8* ☉ *Mid-June–Labor Day, daily 9–8; mid-Sept.–mid-June, daily 9–4* ▭ *D, MC, V.*

☼ The **California Center for the Arts,** an entertainment complex with two theaters, an art museum, and a conference center, presents operas, musicals, plays, dance performances, and symphony and chamber-music concerts. Performers conduct free workshops for children; check the Web site for dates. The museum, which focuses on 20th-century art, occasionally presents blockbuster exhibits such as the glass art of Dale Chihuly or photos by Ansel Adams, making a side trip here worthwhile. ⊠ *340 N. Escondido Blvd.* ☎ *800/988–4253 box office, 760/839–4100* ⊕ *www.artcenter.org* ⊠ *$5* ☉ *Tues.–Sat. 10–4, Sun. noon–4.*

The outdoor **Heritage Walk Museum** is adjacent to the California Center for the Arts, in Grape Day Park. The museum, operated by the Escondido Historical Society, consists of several historic buildings moved here to illustrate local development from the late 1800s, when grape growing and gold mining supported the economy. Exhibits include the 1888 Santa Fe Depot, Escondido's first library, the Bandy Blacksmith shop, a furnished 1890 Victorian house, and other 19th-century buildings. ⊠ *321 N. Broadway* ☎ *760/743–8207* ⊕ *www.escondidohistory. org* ⊠ *$3* ☉ *Tues.–Sat. 1–4.*

The **Escondido Municipal Gallery** showcases works by local artists. The Arts Bazaar gift shop carries locally crafted jewelry, blown glass, and textiles. ✉ *142 W. Grand Ave.* ☎ *760/480–4101* ⏲ *Tues.–Sat. 11–4.*

The **Mingei International Museum North County,** a satellite of the larger facility in San Diego's Balboa Park, occupies a former JCPenney store at the foot of Escondido's emerging arts district. All the Mingei art is classified as folk art; collections include pre-Columbian items, ceramics, textiles, glass, and a variety of Japanese arts of daily life. ✉ *155 W. Grand Ave.* ☎ *760/735–3355* 🌐 *www.mingei.org* 🎟 *$5* ⏲ *Tues.–Sat. 1–5, Sun. noon–4.*

A 3,058-acre conservation area and historic ranch site, **Daley Ranch** holds over 20 mi of multipurpose trails for hikers, mountain bikers, and equestrians. The 2.4-mi Boulder Loop affords sweeping views of Escondido, and the 2.5-mi Ranch House Loop passes two small ponds, the Daley family ranch house built in 1928, and the site of the original log cabin. Private cars are prohibited on the ranch, but a Sunday shuttle service is provided from the parking area to the entrance. Free naturalist-guided hikes are offered on a regular basis; call for schedule. ✉ *3024 La Honda Dr.* ☎ *760/839–4680* 🌐 *www.ci.escondido.ca.us* 🎟 *Free* ⏲ *Daily dawn–dusk.*

OFF THE BEATEN PATH

Lavender Fields. In spring a visit to this organic lavender farm is worth a detour. A self-guided walking tour takes you through 6 acres planted with 28 varieties of lavender and to an area where plants are distilled into essential oils. A gift shop sells lavender products and plants. ✉ *12460 Keys Creek Rd., Valley Center* ☎ *760/742–1489 or 888/407–1489* 🌐 *www.thelavenderfields.com* 🎟 *Free* ⏲ *May and June, weekends 10–5.*

Orfila Vineyards offers tours and tastings of award-winning syrah, sangiovese, and viognier produced from grapes harvested from the 10,000-acre vineyard. The Rose Arbor has a picnic area, and there's a gift shop with wine-related merchandise. ✉ *13455 San Pasqual Rd.* ☎ *760/738–6500* 🌐 *www.orfila.com* ⏲ *Daily 10–6, guided tours at 2.*

The last work by sculptor Niki de Saint Phalle (1930–2002), **Queen Califia's Magical Circle** is a sculpture garden consisting of nine totemic figures up to 21 feet tall. Adorned with stylized monsters, animals, protective deities, geometric symbols, and crests, they evoke ancient tales and legends. Saint Phalle designed the garden for the entertainment of children, who can scramble around and on the giant fanciful figures. ✉ *Kit Carson Park, Bear Valley Pkwy. and Mary La.* ☎ *760/839–4691* 🌐 *www.queencalifia.org* 🎟 *Free* ⏲ *Daily 9–dusk except when raining. Closed Monday.*

San Dieguito River Park maintains several hiking and walking trails in the Escondido area. These are part of an intended 55-mi-long Coast to Crest Trail that will eventually link the San Dieguito Lagoon near Del Mar with the river's source on Volcan Mountain, north of Julian. Among the existing trails are three that circle Lake Hodges: the **North Shore Lake Hodges Trail;** the **Piedras Pintadas Trail,** which informs about native American Kumeyaay lifestyles and uses for native plants; and the **Highland Valley Trail,** the first mile of which is the Ruth Merrill Children's Walk. Three trails in **Clevenger Canyon** lead to sweeping views of the San Pasqual Valley. Visit the Web site for a list of upcoming guided hikes. ✉ *18372 Sycamore Creek Rd.* ☎ *858/674–2270* ⊕ *www. sdrp.org* ✆ *Free* ☉ *Daily dawn–dusk.*

WHERE TO EAT & STAY

With the exception of the Welk Resort, which is now primarily a time-share property, Escondido has little to offer in the way of accommodations.

★ $$ ✕ **150 Grand Cafe.** This pretty storefront restaurant lies a block from the California Center for the Arts. It consists of a collection of individually decorated, gardenlike dining rooms, and a sidewalk dining area. The seasonal menu might feature honey-peppercorn salmon, pan-roasted breast of duck with raspberry-orange glaze, or filet mignon with blue cheese crust. A five-course tasting menu is also available. ✉ *150 W. Grand Ave.* ☎ *760/738–6868* ⚓ *Reservations essential AE, D, MC, V.*

$$ ✕ **Vincent's on Grand.** Here's an excellent choice for dining before attending an event at the nearby California Center for the Arts. Original paintings decorate the walls, and crisp white tablecloths cover the tables, adorned with fresh flowers. The menu changes frequently; offerings might include tournedos Rossini, a grilled portobello mushroom with Parmesan, beef Wellington, or duck à l'orange. The wine list is serious, as are the desserts. The service is friendly and attentive. ✉ *113 W. Grand Ave.* ☎ *760/745–3835* 🗖 *AE, D, MC, V* ☉ *Closed Mon. No lunch weekends.*

☾ $$$ 🏨 **Welk Resort.** Sprawling over 600 acres of rugged, oak-studded hillside, this resort, built by bandleader Lawrence Welk in the 1960s, is now a time-share property. It still makes a good headquarters for families visiting the Wild Animal Park nearby. Fully furnished and appointed one- and two-bedroom villas are rented to nonowners when available. Amenities include fireplaces, hot tubs, original art, and balconies or patios. The resort complex is family-friendly, with abundant children's activities, although parents must supervise. A museum displays Welk memorabilia and the Lawrence Welk Theater presents a popular year-round season of Broadway musicals. ✉ *8860 Lawrence Welk Dr.,* ☎ *760/749–3000 or 800/932–9355* ⊕ *www.welkresort.com/ sandiego* ⇨ *574 suites* ☍ *In-room: kitchen, DVD (some), VCR (some), Ethernet, dial-up. In-hotel: restaurant, room service, bar, golf courses, tennis courts, pools, gym, children's programs, laundry facilities, parking (no fee), no-smoking rooms* 🗖 *AE, D, MC, V.*

$ 🏨 **Holiday Inn Express.** This basic motel, right off I–15, is one of the closest to the Wild Animal Park, about 6 mi away. It caters to park visitors and business travelers working in the area. It's on a busy thoroughfare, but close to the California Center for the Arts and a large strip mall where you can find everything from Target to many fast-food outlets. Simply decorated rooms are vaguely African in theme. Continental breakfast is included in the price. ✉ *1250 W. Valley Pkwy.,*

7

☎760/741–7117 ⊕*www.hiexescondido.com* ⬦60 rooms, 25 suites
⚒*In-room: kitchen (some), refrigerator (some), Wi-Fi. In-hotel: pool,
gym, laundry services, laundry facilities, public Wi-Fi, parking (no fee),
no-smoking rooms* ☰*AE, D, DC, MC, V* ⌾*CP.*

SHOPPING

Although farmland began to give way to suburbs in the 1990s, and
the area's fruit, nut, and vegetable bounty has diminished, you can still
find overflowing farmstands in the San Pasqual Valley and in Valley
Center, just east of the city. These days Escondido has begun to look
to the arts to sustain its economy. The downtown streets surrounding
the California Center for the Arts are getting makeovers, attracting
mid- to high-end art galleries and restaurants to replace the thrift stores
and diners.

♻ **Bates Nut Farm** (⊠*15954 Woods Valley Rd., Valley Center* ☎*760/749–
3333* ⊕*www.batesfarm.com*) is the home of San Diego's largest
pumpkin patch in fall, where you might find 200-pound squash. The
100-acre farm, in the Bates family for five generations, sells locally
grown pecans, macadamia nuts, and almonds. There's a petting zoo
holding farm animals, a picnic area, and gift shop. **Canterbury Gardens**
(⊠*2402 S. Escondido Blvd.* ☎*760/746–1400* ⊕*www.canterburygar-
dens.com*), occupying an old winery, specializes in giftware and seasonal decorative accessories for the home, plus a year-round selection
of Christmas ornaments and collectibles by Christopher Radko, Mark
Robert's Fairies, and Department 56.

FALLBROOK

*19 mi northwest of Escondido on I–15 to Mission Rd., Rte. S13, to
Mission Dr.*

A quick 5-mi detour off I–15 between Temecula and San Diego,
Fallbrook bills itself as the Avocado Capital of the World. Avocado
orchards fill the surrounding hillsides, and guacamole is served in just
about every eatery. You can even pig out on avocado ice cream at
the annual Avocado Festival in April. But this small agricultural town
is also morphing into an interesting arts center. The art and cultural
center showcases the work of local and regional painters, sculptors,
and fiber artists. The National Gourd and Fiber Show in June draws
lovers of this art from all over Southern California. You'll find several
intriguing galleries displaying antiques, jewelry, watercolors, and photography on Main Avenue. Innovative restaurants now supplement the
staple fast food joints, and the Fallbrook Winery is making a name for
itself in the South Coast wine region.

Blue Heron Gallery. You'll find tons of interesting stuff in this storefront
gallery/antiques shop, operated by Robert Sommers, whose own photographic images are quite dramatic. Other images are from Native
American collections by Edward Curtis and George Wharton James.
If you're into antiques, try some of the mid-century or earlier Crafts-

man furnishings or pick up some antique silver. ⊠*113 N. Main Ave.* ☎*760/731–9355* ⊕*www.brandonartfallbrook.com*

Brandon Gallery. A Fallbrook art institution that has been showing works of local emerging and professional artists for more than 30 years is the place to find excellent quality watercolors, ceramics, jewelry, and baskets. It's a cooperative in which all work shown is judged and artists showing are members. ⊠*105 N. Main Ave.* ☎*760/723–1330* ⊕*www. brandonartfallbrook.com*

Art Center at Fallbrook. Housed in a typical mid-century modern building that served as the Rexall Pharmacy for 30 years, the spacious center hosts more than a dozen local and regional art shows yearly. The center now lures a number of national touring art shows as well, among them the National Gourd Fine Art and Fiber Show, National Water Media Fine Art Show, and Reflections of Nature. The Café des Artistes, tucked into a back corner of the center, serves salads and sandwiches, plus grilled items for dinner. ⊠*103 S. Main St.* ☎*760/728–1414 or 800/919–1159* ⊕*www.fallbrookart.org* ⊠*Varies by show* ☺ *Open: Mon.–Sat. 10–4, Sun. 12–3, occasionally closed between shows. Café: No lunch Sun. No dinner Sun.–Thurs.*

Fallbrook Winery. It's worth visiting this small winery, perched on a lovely hillside outside Fallbrook, where winemaker Duncan Williams produces bottles that bring back medals from state and national competitions. He makes wine from grapes grown on 36 hilly acres surrounding the winery and from other areas in California. Try the estate-bottled Rosato Sangiovese Rose, fruity sauvignon blanc reserve, or the big syrah special selection. ⊠*2554 Via Rancheros* ☎*760/728—0156* ⊕*www.FallbrookWinery.com* ⊠*Free* ☺*Open by appointment.*

WHERE TO EAT & STAY

$$ ✗**AquaTerra.** A pleasant room in the Pala Mesa Resort, AquaTerra is locally popular. Most come for the seafood selections on the wide-ranging menu that lists miso salmon with bok choy, pina colada scallops, and Parmesan halibut, or the expertly made items on the sushi bar menu. Tables here offer good golf course views, and in warm weather you can dine outside on the patio. The restaurant serves breakfast, lunch, and dinner. ⊠*2001 Old Hwy. 395* ☎*760/728–5881* ⚓*Reservations recommended* ▭*AE, D, DC, MC, V*

$ ✗**Brothers Bistro.** Everything from sauces to breads is made in-house at this cozy bistro that's tucked into a back corner of the Major Market Shopping Center. Chef Ron Nusser has a New York touch with Italian specialties such as Alla Pasta Diana, an antipasto-like Monterey seafood salad, and roasted halibut. But the most popular item on the menu is homemade lasagna, nearly a pound per serving with house-made marinara and three cheeses. Eat in the small dining room, where huge paintings adorn every wall, or on the tree-shaded patio outdoors. There's an extensive list of California wines, many available by the glass. ⊠*835 S. Main St.* ☎*760/731–9761* ▭*AE, D, DC, MC, V* ☺*No lunch Sat. or Sun.*

$ ✕**La Caseta.** The monster 2000-pound Guinness Book of World Records largest burrito notwithstanding, La Caseta, or little cottage, serves up small surprises. The casual cottage with wraparound widows and colorful murals is bright and cheerful. You can dine indoors or in good weather outside on the patio. Chef Delos Eyer brings traditional Mexican fare up to date with options including grilled chicken wrap with achiote sauce and savory black beans, San Filipe fish tacos, charbroiled shrimp Diablo, and meatless black bean quesadillas. Don't miss the fabulous Xango, a banana caramel cheesecake with vanilla ice cream, and Death by Chocolate, a tower of chocolate ice cream perched on a huge chocolate walnut cookie. ☒ *111 N. Vine St.* ☎*760/728–9737* ▤*AE, D, DC, MC, V* ☉*Closed Sun.*

$–   🏨**Pala Casino Resort Spa.** More than most casino resorts tucked into the San Diego County backcountry, the Pala Resort pampers guests with lovely spacious rooms and suites, a big selection of dining options, a tranquil spa, and an enticing entertainment schedule. Located just 5 mi east of I–15 on Hwy. 76, the complex stands alone on the edge of Pala, the historic home of the Pala Band of Mission Indians, which owns it. Decor everywhere is simple, evoking the work of Frank Lloyd Wright, dark-wood furnishings set off by white accents, Arts & Crafts designs reflected in upholstery and lighting fixtures. Even the smallest room is spacious at more than 500 square feet; all have mountain or pool views. Restaurant choices range from the casual Terrace Buffet to the fine dining Oak Room. **Pros:** Classy ambience, cabanas at pool. **Cons:** Remote location, challenging drive from I–15. ☒*35008 Pala Temecula Rd.* ☎*760/510–5100 or 877/946–7252* ⊕*www.palacasino. com* ⇆*425 rooms, 82 suites* ♿*In-room: safes, refrigerators, Ethernet. In-hotel: 8 restaurants, room service, bars, gym, spa, concierge, parking (no fee), no-smoking rooms* ▤*AE, D, DC, MC, V.*

★ $ 🏨**Pala Mesa Golf Resort.** This friendly two-story resort, tucked into a canyon right off the I–15 midway between Temecula and Escondido, offers excellent value and is popular with convention groups and golf enthusiasts. Built in the 1970s, it still has a vague Hawaiian feel, despite many renovations over the years. Large, simply furnished rooms have floor-to-ceiling windows and open-beam ceilings. Most have balconies, some with great fairway, garden, or mountain views. Mature gardens holding azaleas and agapanthus frame grottos, waterfalls, and colorful banks. The resort offers a free golf clinic throughout the week. Locals flock to the AcquaTerra Restaurant and Sushi Bar for fresh seafood and sushi. **Pros:** Attractive grounds, spacious rooms, dog-friendly. **Cons:** Adjacent to freeway, resort's age is showing. ☒*2001 Old Hwy. 395,* ☎*760/728–5881 or 800/722–4700* ⊕*www.palamesa.com* ⇆*133 rooms* ♿*In-room: refrigerator (some), Ethernet. In-hotel: restaurant, room service, bar, golf course, tennis courts, pool, gym, no elevator, laundry service, concierge, public Wi-Fi, parking (no fee), some pets allowed, no-smoking rooms* ▤*AE, D, DC, MC, V.*

TEMECULA

29 mi from Escondido, 60 mi from San Diego on I–15 north to Rancho California Rd. east.

Once an important stop on the Butterfield Overland Stagecoach route and a market town for the huge cattle ranches surrounding it, Temecula (pronounced teh-*mec*-yoo-la) is now a developed wine region, part of the South Coast region, which also includes some wineries in San Diego County. Known for its gently rolling hills, the region is studded with ancient oak trees and vernal pools, and with premium wineries whose wine makers are experimenting with a number of European varietals such as roussanne, nebbiolo, and viognier with fragrant and flavorful results. Most of the wineries that line both sides of Rancho California Road as it snakes east from downtown offer tours and tastings daily and have creatively-stocked boutiques, picnic facilities, and restaurants on the premises. Lately visitors will also find that the wineries have been joined by luxury boutique lodgings. Meanwhile, local developers have created an Old Town along historic Front Street on the west side of I–15. This section is home to boutique shops, good restaurants, a children's museum, and a theater. In addition to its visitor appeal, Temecula is also a suburban bedroom community for many who work in San Diego North County.

THE GREAT OAK

Standing adjacent to the Resort & Casino Pechanga in Temecula is an oak tree estimated to be 1,500 to 2,000 years old, one of the oldest in the world. It's also the largest natural-growing indigenous live oak tree in the United States. Before California became a state in 1850, the area around the tree belonged to the Pechanga tribe, but when they could not produce a title to satisfy the California legislature, it fell into other hands. When the federal government established the Pechanga reservation in 1882, the tree stood just outside its boundary, even though it had been a gathering place for the tribe for generations and the area around it held tribal interment sites. Eventually it became part of the Great Oak Ranch, which was owned from 1931 until 1970 by famed mystery writer Erle Stanley Gardner. The tribe was able to buy the land back from subsequent owners, but it took an act of Congress and the President's approval in 2003 to add it and the tree to the reservation.

The **Temecula Valley Winegrowers Association** (✉ *34567 Rancho California Rd.* ☎ *951/699–6586 or 800/801–9463* ⊕ *www.temeculawines. org* ⊗ *Weekdays 9–4*), which distributes brochures and sells tickets to special wine events, is a good resource for information on Temecula's 20-some wineries. **Thornton Winery** (✉ *32575 Rancho California Rd.* ☎ *951/699–0099* ⊕ *www.thorntonwine.com*), known for its line of popular sparkling wines, has added still wines made from Rhône- and Mediterranean-type varietals such as roussanne, nebbiolo, and old-vine zinfandels. Tours and structured tastings are offered daily, and jazz concerts are presented weekends April through October (reservations required). **Callaway Vineyard & Winery** (✉ *32720 Rancho California Rd.*

☎951/676–4001 or 800/472–2377 ⊕*www.callawaywinery.com*) produces award-winning roussanne, pinot gris, and dolcetto. Tours and tastings are offered daily; you'll find an excellent gift shop adjacent to the tasting room. **Ponte Family Estate Winery** (✉*35053 Rancho California Rd.* ☎951/694–8855 or 877/314–9463 ⊕*www.pontewinery. com*) produces interesting specialized wines such as dry white Graciela (a blend of chardonnay, viognier, sauvignon blanc, and French colombard) and zinfandel port. The formal gardens and marketplace here are especially appealing. **South Coast Winery, Resort and Spa** (✉*34843 Rancho California Rd.* ☎951/587–9463 or 866/994–6379 ⊕*www. wineresort.com*) has a wine list that features estate-grown and -made viognier, merlot, cabernet sauvignon, and black jack port. The winery also operates an inn, spa, and family restaurant; *see Where to Stay & Eat, below.*

Once a hangout for cowboys, **Old Town Temecula** has been updated and expanded while retaining its Old West appearance. A walking tour put together by the **Temecula Valley Historical Society,** starting at the Temecula Valley Museum, covers some of the old buildings; most are identified with bronze plaques.

♺ **Temecula Valley Museum,** adjacent to Sam Hicks Monument Park, focuses on Temecula Valley history, including early Native American life, Butterfield stage routes, and the ranchero period. A hands-on interactive area for children holds a general store, photographer's studio, and ride-a-pony station. Outside there's a playground and picnic area. ✉*28314 Mercedes St.* ☎951/694–6450 ▱*$2 suggested donation* ☉*Tues.–Sat. 10–5, Sun. 1–5.*

♺ The **Santa Rosa Plateau Ecological Reserve** provides a glimpse of what this countryside was like before the developers took over. Trails wind through oak forests and past vernal pools and rolling grassland. A visitor and operations center has interpretive displays and maps; some of the reserve's hiking trails begin here. No pets allowed. Take I–15 south to Clinton Keith Rd. exit and head west 5 mi. ✉*39400 Clinton Keith Rd., Murrieta* ☎951/677–6951 ⊕*www.santarosaplateau.org* ▱*$2* ☉*Daily dawn–dusk; visitor center Thurs. and Fri. 10–4, Sat. and Sun. 9–5.*

♺ **Imagination Workshop: Temecula Children's Museum** is the imaginary home of Professor Phineas Pennypickle, where kids accompanied by parents enter a time machine that carries them through six rooms of interactive exhibits demonstrating perception and illusion, music-making, flight and aviation, chemistry and physics, plus power and electricity. The shop stocks an array of educational toys, games, and books. ✉*42081 Main St.* ☎951/308–6370 ▱*$4.50* ☉*2-hour sessions Tues.–Thurs. and Sat. at 10, 12:30, and 3, Fri. and Sun. 12:30, 3, 5:30.*

Temecula draws thousands of people to its **Balloon and Wine Festival** held in late spring. Hot-air balloon excursions are a good choice year-round. **A Grape Escape Balloon Adventure** (☎951/699–9987 or 800/965–2122 ⊕*www.hotairtours.com*) has morning lift-offs from Wilson Creek Winery.

California Dreamin' (☎800/373–3359 ⊕*www.californiadreamin.com*) schedules both hot-air and biplane adventures, including flights to Palomar Mountain and opportunities to fly it yourself.

WHERE TO EAT

$$$ ✕**Café Champagne.** The Thornton Winery's airy country restaurant, whose big windows overlook the vineyards, serves serious contemporary cuisine seasoned with the winery's own products. You may find warm Brie en croute with honey-walnut sauce, pan-roasted duck with pomegranate reduction, and smoked filet mignon in a cabernet-merlot demi-glace. ✉*32575 Rancho California Rd.* ☎*951/699–0088* ⚓*Reservations essential* ⊟*AE, D, MC, V.*

☺ $$$ ✕**Vineyard Rose.** Big and barnlike, the Vineyard Rose is a good choice for Mediterranean-style family dining, one that will give the kids a chance to sample some excellent cooking by chef Alessandro Serni. Consider ahi tuna proscuitto or grilled pork chop with bourbon sauce. The restaurant, part of the South Coast Winery complex, serves three meals daily. ✉*34843 Rancho California Rd.* ☎*951/587–9463 or 866/994–6379* ⚓*Reservations essential* ⊟*AE, D, DC, MC, V.*

$$ ✕**Baily's.** A genteel clientele and attentive service mark this fine-dining restaurant on the second floor of Baily's Old Town Dining establishment (downstairs is the Front Street Bar & Grill). Tall windows draped in red frame a town-and-country view. Contemporary cuisine leans heavily on fresh interpretations of classics such as rack of lamb, roasted duck, and veal scaloppini. But the menu changes frequently to take advantage of locally grown produce. There's an impressive wine list. ✉*28699 Old Town Front St.* ☎*951/676–9567* ⚓*Reservations essential* ⊟*AE, D, DC, MC, V.*

$ ✕**Front Street Bar & Grill.** Having fun is the rule here, where you can dine in a big indoor room or outside on a quiet patio. The easy-on-the-budget menu lists gourmet burgers, chipotle-braised barbecued ribs, chili-stuffed chicken, and jambalaya. You can also nosh on smoked duck spring rolls or a hummus platter appetizer. This can be a noisy place as there's entertainment weekend nights. ✉*28699 Old Town Front St.* ☎*951/676–9567* ⚓*Reservations not accepted* ⊟*AE, D, DC, MC, V.*

☺ ¢ ✕**The Bank of Mexican Food.** *Flautas*—shredded beef or chicken rolled in a flour tortilla and deep-fried—crab enchiladas, and other south-of-the-border dishes are served in this building that started out as a bank in 1913. The second-oldest restaurant in Old Temecula, the Bank has been serving traditional Mexican food since the 1970s. For an authentic experience, request the table set in the vault. There's also a ceramic-tile patio if you want to eat outside. Meals come with beans and rice, and there's a kids' menu, too. ✉*28645 Front St.* ☎*951/676–6160* ⊟*AE, D, MC, V.*

WHERE TO STAY

$$$ ☷**South Coast Winery Resort & Spa.** The Temecula wine country's most luxurious resort offers richly appointed rooms surrounded by 38 acres of vineyards. Each room, designed for privacy with no common walls or entrances, offers a sweeping view of mountains and sky from a

private patio. There are hand-painted frescoes, in-room fireplaces, oversize marble bathrooms, and small dining areas. The resort also has a spa with 13 treatment rooms, the Vineyard Rose restaurant, plus shops. The resort offers a number of packages that make it a value choice when staying in the Temecula wine country. **Pros:** Elegantly appointed rooms, full-service resort, good value. **Cons:** Spread out property requires lots of walking, $9.50 resort fee. ⊠*34843 Rancho California Rd.,* ☎*951/587–9463 or 866/994–6379* ⊕*www.wineresort.com* ⇦*82rooms, 2 suites* ⮂*In-room: safe, refrigerator, DVD (some), Wi-Fi. In-hotel: restaurant, room service, bar, pool, spa, laundry service, concierge, parking (fee), no-smoking rooms* ▤*AE, D, DC, MC, V* ¶O¶*CP.*

$$ ▦ **Inn at Churon Winery.** Picture yourself in a French château surrounded by vineyards, brilliantly colored gardens, and softly rolling hills. Rooms at this inn offer that view and more from balconies or patios. There are fireplaces, French-style furnishings, spacious bathrooms with granite counters, and two-person hot tubs. Public areas include a dramatic two-story lobby, a wine-tasting room with gift shop, and a small sushi bar open on Saturdays. Outside you can stroll through manicured formal gardens. A full breakfast served in the room and an afternoon wine reception are included in the price. **Pros:** Very spacious rooms, beautiful landscaping. **Cons:** Service just okay, public areas are noisy. ⊠*33233 Rancho California Rd.,* ☎*951/694–9070* ⊕*www.innatchuronwinery.com* ⇦*20 rooms, 5 suites* ⮂*In-room: Ethernet. In-hotel: restaurant, room service, bar, no elevator, parking (no fee), no-smoking rooms* ▤*AE, D, MC, V* ¶O¶*BP.*

$$ ▦ **Temecula Creek Inn.** This upscale golf resort occupies a hillside adjacent to I–15 a short distance from the wine-touring area. Rooms are in a collection of low-slung buildings (those facing the freeway are apt to be noisy) and are unusually large and bright, nicely appointed with double vanity areas, and with expansive windows offering a tranquil golf-course view (which you also get from a private balcony or patio). Decorated in soft desert colors, rooms contain interesting displays of Native American pottery, basket remnants, and antique tribal weavings. **Pros:** Golf, convenient for wine touring, popular restaurant onsite. **Cons:** Some rooms are noisy. ⊠*44501 Rainbow Canyon Rd.,* ☎*951/694–1000 or 877/517–1823* ⊕*www.temeculacreekinn.com* ⇦*130 rooms, 4 suites* ⮂*In-room: safe, refrigerator, DVD, Ethernet, Wi-Fi. In-hotel: restaurant, room service, bar, golf course, tennis courts, pool, gym, laundry service, concierge, public Internet, public Wi-Fi, parking (fee), no-smoking rooms* ▤*AE, D, DC, MC, V.*

SHOPPING

Tastings of locally-pressed olive oil are offered at the **Temecula Olive Oil Company** (⊠*28653 Old Town Front St.* ☎*951/693–0607* ⊕*www. awesome-oil.com*), where you can find a selection of oils seasoned with garlic, herbs, and citrus. This Old Town shop has dipping and cooking oils, locally crafted oil-based soaps and bath products, and a selection of preserved and stuffed olives.

INLAND NORTH COUNTY & TEMECULA ESSENTIALS

To research prices, get advice from other travelers, and book travel arrangements, visit www.fodors.com

BUS TRAVEL

Buses and trains operated by North County Transit District serve all coastal communities in San Diego County, going as far east as Escondido. Routes are coordinated with other transit agencies serving San Diego County.

Bus Information **North County Transit District** (☎ *800/266–6883* ⊕ *www. transit.511.com*).

CAR TRAVEL

Escondido sits at the intersection of Route 78, which heads east from Oceanside, and I–15, the inland freeway connecting San Diego to Riverside, which is 30 minutes north of Escondido. Del Dios Highway winds from Rancho Santa Fe through the hills past Lake Hodges to Escondido. Route 76, which connects with I–15 north of Escondido, veers east to Palomar Mountain. Interstate 15 continues north to Fallbrook and Temecula.

TOUR OPTIONS

Several companies offer individual and group tours of the Temecula wine country with departures from San Diego and Temecula. Some include lunch or refreshments as part of the package.

Limousine Tours **Destination Temecula** (☎ *951/695–1232 or 800/584–8162* ⊕ *www.destem.com*). **Grapeline Wine Country Shuttle** (☎ *951/693–5755 or 888/894-6379* ⊕ *www.gogrape.com*).

VISITOR INFORMATION

Contacts **Escondido Chamber of Commerce** (☎ *760/745–2125* ⊕ *www.escondidochamber.org*). **Fallbrook Area Visitors Bureau** (☎ *760/541-3282* ⊕ *www. FindFallbrook.com*). **San Diego North Chamber of Commerce** (☎ *858/487–1767* ⊕ *www.sdncc.com*). **San Diego North Convention and Visitors Bureau** (☎ *760/745–4741 or 800/848-3336* ⊕ *www.sandiegonorth.com*). **Temecula Valley Visitor Center Old Town** (☎ *951/506–0056* ⊕ *www.temeculacvb.org*).

THE BACKCOUNTRY & JULIAN

The Cuyamaca and Laguna mountains to the east of Escondido—sometimes referred to as the backcountry by county residents—are favorite weekend destinations for hikers, nature lovers, stargazers, and apple-pie fanatics. Most of the latter group head to Julian, a historic mining town now better known for apple pie than for the gold once extracted from its hills. Nearby Cuyamaca Rancho State Park, once a luscious ancient oak and pine forest, was temporarily closed after it burned in a 2003 fire. While evidence of the fire is still visible in some areas, many of the park's ancient oak trees have come back to life, hiking and horse trails have been repaired, and most campgrounds are open with new facilities.

The **Sunrise National Scenic Byway,** in the Cleveland National Forest, is the most dramatic approach to Julian—its turns and curves reveal amazing views of the desert from the Salton Sea all the way to Mexico. You can spend an entire day roaming these mountains; an early-morning hike to the top of Garnet Peak (mile marker 27.8) is the best way to catch the view. Springtime wildflower displays are spectacular, particularly along Big Laguna Trail from Laguna Campground. There are picnic areas along the highway at Desert View and Pioneer Mail.

On many summer weekends you can view the heavens through a 21-inch telescope in the **Mount Laguna Observatory** (⊠*Morris Ranch Rd., off Sunrise Scenic Byway, Mt. Laguna* ☎*619/594–1415*), which sits on Mount Laguna at an altitude of 6,100 feet. It's operated by San Diego State University and University of Illinois at Urbana-Champaign.

CUYAMACA MOUNTAINS

Cuyamaca Rancho State Park (⊠*12551 Hwy. 79, Descanso* ☎*760/765–0755* ⊕*www.parks.ca.gov*) spreads over more than 25,000 acres of open meadows, oak woodlands, and mountains, rising to 6,512 feet at Cuyamaca Peak. Much of the park, including all of its infrastructure, burned during a wildfire in 2003. Local volunteers are rebuilding the 120 mi of hiking and nature trails, picnic areas, campgrounds, and museum, and much has been completed. However, even five years later a drive through the park will reveal nature's healing processes, as abundant seasonal wildflowers and other native plants emerge from the earth in a breathtaking display. For an inspirational desert view, stop at the lookout about 2 mi south of Julian on Route 79; on a clear day you can see several mountain ranges in hues ranging from pink to amber stepped back behind the Salton Sea.

☺ Behind a dam constructed in 1888 the 110-acre **Lake Cuyamaca** offers fishing, boating, picnicking, nature hikes, and wildlife-watching. Anglers regularly catch trout, smallmouth bass, and sturgeon. A shaded picnic area occupies the lakeshore. Families can rent small motorboats, rowboats, canoes, and paddleboats by the hour. Free fishing classes for adults and kids are held Saturday at 10 AM. Fishing licenses and advice are available at the tackle shop. Two rental condominiums, three sleeping cabins, 40 RV campsites with hookups, and 10 tent sites are available at Chambers Park on a first-come, first-served basis. ⊠*15027 Hwy. 79, Julian* ☎*760/765–0515 or 877/581–9904* ⊕*www.lake-cuyamaca.org* ☺*$6 per vehicle for picnic area* ☉*Daily dawn–dusk.*

WHERE TO EAT

$ ✕**Lake Cuyamaca Restaurant.** This tidy, lace-curtained lakefront café specializes in Austrian fare, highlights of which include a selection of schnitzels and wursts, plus several chicken and steak entrées. Austrian beers are on tap. The restaurant, as well as the adjacent food market, is popular with anglers and locals. ⊠*15027 Rte. 79, Julian* ☎*760/765–0700* ⊟*AE, D, DC, MC, V.*

JULIAN

62 mi from San Diego to Julian, east on I–8 and north on Rte. 79.

Gold was discovered in the Julian area in 1869, and gold-bearing quartz a year later. More than $15 million worth of gold was taken from local mines in the 1870s. Many of the buildings along Julian's Main Street and the side streets today date back to the Gold Rush period; others are reproductions.

When gold and quartz became scarce, the locals turned to growing apples and pears. During the fall harvest season you can buy fruit, sip cider, eat apple pie, and shop for local original art, antiques, and collectibles. But spring is equally enchanting (and less congested), as the hillsides explode with wildflowers—thousands of daffodils, lilacs, and peonies. More than 50 artists have studios tucked away in the hills surrounding Julian; they often show their work in local shops and galleries. The Julian area comprises three small crossroads communities: Santa Ysabel, Wynola, and historic Julian. You can find bits of history, shops, and dining options in each community. Most visitors come to spend a day in town, but the hillsides support many small B&B establishments for those who want to linger longer.

The rundown-looking **Banner Queen Trading Post Gallery** is a remnant of an old gold mine dug into a hillside on Banner Grade, 5 mi east of Julian. A step inside what was the mine superintendent's home reveals a wealth of contemporary art. Five rooms are filled with paintings, photos, sculpture, ceramics, stained glass (even some fire glass), and woven pieces by Julian artists. Prices range from $30 or less for photos and pottery to hundreds for paintings and sculptures by widely recognized artists such as James Hubbell and Bob Verdugo. ✉*36766 Hwy. 78* ☎*760/765–2168* ☉*Fri.–Sun. 1–5.*

★ One of the few places in North America where you can get an up-close view of the gray wolves that once roamed much of the continent lies just outside Julian. The **California Wolf Center,** which is dedicated to the preservation of the endangered North American gray wolf and participates in breeding programs, houses several captive packs, including some rare Mexican grays, a subspecies of the North American gray wolf that came within seven individuals of extinction in the 1970s. The animals are kept secluded from public view in 3-acre pens, but some may be seen by visitors during weekly educational tours. Private tours are by appointment. ✉*Hwy. 79 at KQ Ranch Rd.* ☎*619/234–9653* ⊕*www.californiawolfcenter.org* ✉*$10, reservations required* ☉*Tour Sat. 2 pm.*

At the **Eagle Mining Company,** five blocks east of the center of Julian, you can take an hour-long tour of an authentic Julian gold mine. A small rock shop and gold-mining museum are also on the premises. ✉*C St.* ☎*760/765–0036* ✉*$10* ☉*Daily 10–1, weather permitting.*

When the gold mines in Julian played out, the mobs of gold miners who had invaded it left, leaving behind discarded mining tools and

🔄 empty houses. Today the **Julian Pioneer Museum,** a 19th-century brewery, displays remnants of that time, including pioneer clothing, a collection of old lace, and old photographs of the town's historic buildings and mining structures. ✉️*4th and Washington Sts.* ☎️*760/765–0227* 🏷️*$2* 🕐*Apr.–Nov., Wed.–Sun. 10–4; Dec.–Mar., weekends 10–4.*

One of the best ways to see Julian's star-filled summer sky is by taking a sky-tour at the **Observer's Inn,** where Mike and Caroline Leigh have set up an observatory with research-grade telescopes. The hosts guide you through the star clusters and galaxies, pointing out planets and nebulae. ✉️*3535 Hwy. 79* ☎️*760/765–0088* 🏷️*$20 per person* ⚠️*Reservations required.*

The 1¼-mi trail through **Volcan Mountain Wilderness Preserve** passes through Engleman oak forest, native manzanita, and rolling mountain meadows to a viewpoint where the panorama extends north all the way to Palomar Mountain. On a clear day you can see Point Loma in San Diego. At the entrance you pass through gates designed by James Hubbell, a local artist known for his ironwork, wood carving, and stained glass. ✛*From Julian take Farmer Rd. to Wynola Rd., go east a few yards, and then north on Farmer Rd.* ☎️*760/765–2300* 🌐*www. volcanmt.org* 🏷️*Free* 🕐*Daily dawn–dusk.*

The Santa Ysabel Valley, where three Native American tribes live, looks pretty much the way the backcountry appeared a century ago, with sweeping meadows surrounded by oak-studded hillsides. The tribes operate small farms and run cattle here, although the valley's beautiful pasturelands have been threatened by development in recent years. However, in 2000 the Nature Conservancy acquired large portions of the valley to set aside as a nature preserve. The village of **Santa Ysabel,** 7 mi west of Julian, has several interesting shops. West of Santa Ysabel, tiny **Mission Santa Ysabel** (✉️*23013 Hwy. 79* ☎️*760/765–0810*) is a late-19th-century adobe mission that continues to serve several local Native American communities. A small museum on the premises (open daily 8–3) holds memorabilia from local families, Native Americans, and the parish.

WHERE TO EAT

$$ ✕**Julian Grille.** The menu at this casual restaurant inside one of Julian's historic homes appeals to a variety of tastes, including vegetarian. Chicken dishes are popular, as are steaks and the smoked pork chops served with applesauce. Lunch options include good burgers, whopping sandwiches, and soups. There's a tree-shaded dining area that is heated on cool evenings. Beware, service can be hit or miss. ✉️*2224 Main St.* ☎️*760/765–0173* 💳*AE, D, MC, V* 🕐*No dinner Mon.*

★ $ ✕**Julian Pie Company.** The apple pies that made Julian famous come from the Smothers family bakery in a one-story house on Main Street. In pleasant weather you can sit on the front patio and watch the world go by while savoring a slice of hot pie—from Dutch apple to apple mountain berry crumb—topped with homemade cinnamon ice cream. The Smothers family has been making pies in Julian since 1986; by 1989 they had bought their own orchard, and by 1992 they had built a larger bakery in Santa Ysabel. At lunchtime the Julian location also serves soup and sandwiches. The Santa Ysabel bakery just makes pies. ⊠*2225 Main St.* ☎*760/765–2449* ⊠*21976 Hwy. 79, Santa Ysabel* ☎*760/765–2400* ⊕*www.julianpie.com* ⊟*AE, D, MC, V.*

♻ $ ✗ **Julian Tea and Cottage Arts.** Sample finger sandwiches, scones topped with whipped cream, and lavish sweets during afternoon tea inside the Clarence King House, built by Will Bosnell in 1898. Regular sandwiches, soups, salads, and a children's tea are also available. Owner Edie Seger presents Victorian teas during the holiday season to the delight of little girls. ⊠*2124 3rd St.* ☎*760/765–0832 or 866/765-0832* ⊗*No dinner* ⚭*Reservations essential* ⊟*AE, D, MC, V.*

> ### BLACK GOLD
>
> According to local history and old photos, the Julian area had a large population of African Americans in the years following the Civil War. Indeed, it was a black man, Fred Coleman, who discovered gold in Julian, and the Julian Hotel was founded and operated by Albert and Margaret Robinson, also black. Headstones recognizing the contributions of Julian's black pioneers continue to be placed in the old section of the Pioneer Cemetery.

$ ✗ **Romano's Dodge House.** You can gorge on huge portions of antipasto, pizza, pasta, sausage sandwiches, and seafood in a cozy old house. Specialties include pork Juliana simmered in apple cider, pasta Pacifica, and brasciole. This is a casual, red-checked-tablecloth kind of place, where you can dine outside in good weather. There's usually entertainment on weekends. ⊠*2718 B St.* ☎*760/765–1003* ⊟*D, MC, V* ⊗*Closed Tues.*

$ ✗ **Wynola Pizza Express.** Locals come to this casual indoor–outdoor restaurant for delicious, single-portion pizzas such as pesto pizza, Thai chicken pizza, vegan pizza, and tostada pizza. Other items include chili, lasagna, and a killer fire-roasted artichoke dip served with homemade buffalo crackers. Entertainers usually perform on weekends in the adjacent Red Barn, or in fine weather, outdoors. ⊠*4355 Hwy. 78, Wynola* ☎*760/765–1004* ⊗ *Closed Tues.* ⊟*AE, MC, V.*

WHERE TO STAY

★ $$$ ▦ **Orchard Hill Country Inn.** On a hill above town, this lodge and five Craftsman-style cottages have a sweeping view of the countryside. The luxurious backcountry accommodations are decorated with antiques, original art, and handcrafted quilts. Some of the cottage suites have see-through fireplaces, double whirlpool tubs, and wet bars—even private patios or balconies. Guests gather in the late afternoon for wine and hors d'oeuvres in the Great Room, where a fire blazes in the stone fireplace. Breakfast is included. Dinner is served nightly except Monday and Wednesday to guests only at an extra charge. **Pros:** Most luxurious digs in Julian, good food. **Cons:** Limited amenities. ⊠*2502 Washington St.,* ☎*760/765–1700 or 800/716–7242* ⊕*www.orchardhill.com* ⇥*10 rooms, 12 suites* ⚭*In-room: refrigerator (some), VCR, dial-up. In-hotel: bar, no elevator, laundry service, public Wi-Fi, parking (no fee), no-smoking rooms* ⊟*AE, MC, V* ⓇⓄⅠBP.

$$ 🏨**Butterfield Bed and Breakfast.** Built in the 1930s, this inn on a 3-acre hilltop is cordial and romantic with knotty pine ceilings, Laura Ashley accents, and a gazebo in the backyard. Rooms, ranging from small to ample, may have fireplaces or woodstoves and private entrances. The property is beautifully landscaped with terraced rose gardens. Innkeepers offer nice touches such as a guest pantry with refrigerator. Breakfast and afternoon refreshments are included. **Pros:** Great food, interesting hosts, secluded. **Cons:** Very quiet, no phone. ⊠*2284 Sunset Dr.,* ☎*760/765–2179 or 800/379–4262* ⊕*www.butterfieldbandb.com* ⤳*5 rooms* ◊*In-room: no phone, refrigerator (some), VCR, Wi-Fi. In-hotel: no elevator, Wi-Fi, parking (free), no-smoking rooms* ⊟*AE, D, DC, MC, V* ⦿*BP.*

$$ 🏨**Wikiup Bed and Breakfast.** Best known for its herd of llamas, Wikiup appeals to animal lovers. The inn consists of a main contemporary cedar-and-brick structure with cedar paneling, modern ranch style furnishings, and high, open-beam ceilings holding skylights. Guest rooms in the main house and a pair of cottages have private entrances, fireplaces, and outdoor hot tubs for stargazing. The innkeepers offer full- and half-day llama treks to guests. A full breakfast is included. **Pros:** Private entrances, fireplaces in all rooms. **Cons:** Limited facilities. ⊠*1645 Whispering Pines Dr.,* ☎*760/765–1890 or 800/694–5487* ⊕*www.wikiupbnb.com* ⤳*5 rooms* ◊*In-room: refrigerator, DVD. In-hotel: no elevator, parking (no fee), no-smoking rooms* ⊟*MC, V* ⦿*BP.*

$ 🏨**Julian Gold Rush Hotel.** Built in 1897 by freed slave Albert Robinson and his wife Margaret, this more than 100-year-old hotel is Julian's only designated national landmark. Current owners Steve and Gig Ballanger brought the old place into the 21st century, but it still feels thoroughly Victorian. Smallish rooms have antique furnishings and colorful quilts. Cottage accommodations have private entrances and fireplaces. The innkeepers serve afternoon tea and invite guests to sit on the porch. Full breakfast is included. **Pros:** Genuine historic hotel, convivial atmosphere. **Cons:** Small rooms, no TV. ⊠*2032 Main St.,* ☎*760/765–0201 or 800/734–5854* ⊕*www.julianhotel.com* ⤳*14 rooms, 2 suites* ◊*In-room: no phone, no TV. In-hotel: no elevator, public Wi-Fi* ⊟*AE, MC, V* ⦿*BP.*

$ 🏨**Julian Lodge.** A replica of a late-19th-century Julian hotel, this two-story lodge calls itself a bed-and-breakfast. The rooms and public spaces are furnished with antiques; on chilly days you can warm yourself at the large stove in the small lobby. Buffet-style continental breakfast is included in the price. **Pros:** In town location, free parking. **Cons:** Limited facilities, simple appointments. ⊠*4th and C Sts., Julian 92036* ☎*760/765–1420 or 800/542–1420* ⊕*www.julianlodge. com* ⤳*23 rooms* ◊*In-room: no phone, refrigerator (some). In-hotel: no elevator, parking (no fee), no-smoking rooms* ⊟*AE, D, MC, V* ⦿*CP.*

SHOPPING

The Julian area has a number of unique shops that are open weekends, but midweek hours vary considerably. In autumn locally grown apples, pears, nuts, and cider are available in town and at a few roadside stands. The best apple variety produced here is a Jonagold, a hybrid of Jonathan and Golden Delicious.

The **Birdwatcher** (✉*2775 B St.* ☎*760/765–1817*) offers items for wild-bird lovers, including birdhouses, birdseed, hummingbird feeders, plus bird-theme accessories such as jewelry, apparel, novelties, and guidebooks for serious birders. The **Falcon Gallery** (✉*2015A Main St.* ☎*760/765–1509*), in a replica of one of Julian's original hotels, has works by local artists, books about area history including Native American history, and a small but tantalizing collection of books and art and science kits for kids. **Mountain Gypsy** (✉*2007 Main St.* ☎*760/765–0643*) is popular area-wide for an extensive collection of jewelry and trendy apparel in petite and plus sizes. **Once Upon a Time** (✉*Rte. 78 and Rte. 79, Santa Ysabel* ☎*760/765–1695*) comprises three tiny cottages devoted to antiques, florals, gifts, and Christmas decorations. **Santa Ysabel Art Gallery** (✉*Rte. 78 and Rte. 79, Santa Ysabel* ☎*760/765–1676*) shows watercolors, stained glass, sculptures, and other creations by local artists.

★ ☾ **King Leo Chocolate Factory and Store** (✉*4510 Hwy. 78, Wynola* ☎*760/765–2264*) makes and sells creamy chocolates and fudges, including seasonal items such as apple pie and butterscotch fudge. Factory tours are also available.

RAMONA

7

For many heading into the San Diego mountains or desert, Ramona is the last stop. It's where drivers fill up with gas (sometimes less expensive than in the city), pick up provisions at one of several supermarkets (there are none further east), and have a bite to eat. Increasingly, visitors are spending time in Ramona for a couple of reasons: to play golf at two highly rated courses, and to drop some cash at the Barona casino, located along a country road a few miles south of town. Ramona's history is intertwined with Julian's, the town 22 miles east, where a gold rush drew argonauts in the 1870s. Descendants of those settlers still run cattle on ranches extending from Ramona to Julian. Today Ramona is a fast-growing unincorporated area of about 28,000 residents, most of whom have ranches. There's a budding wine-making industry, although sales are limited to tasting rooms found on Main Street. The main thoroughfare also houses the largest selection of antiques shops in the backcountry. With the exception of the Barona Resort, lodging and dining fall into the simple and comfortable category. Don't come here if you're looking for luxury.

SIGHTS TO SEE

Wildlife Research Institute. The 4,000 acres of grasslands that have been preserved in the Ramona valley are a good place to enjoy seeing wildlife in a natural setting. The grasslands are typical of much of the Southern California landscape before development. A half-century ago grasslands formed the backdrop for Western movies where cowboys rode off into the sunset. This small parcel supports more raptors than any other place in Southern California. It's home to falcons, hawks, owls, and eagles, as well as bobcats, coyotes, and badgers. The institute sponsors hawk watch weekends in January and February. ✉ *18030 Highland Valley Rd.* ☎ *760/789–3992* ⊕ *www.wildlife-research.org* ☒ *Free* ⊗ *Daily 9–5.*

WHERE TO EAT & STAY

$$$$ ✗ **Barona Oaks Steakhouse.** The fine-dining restaurant at Barona Resort caters to high rollers whose culinary choice often involves steak, thus the menu here lists a large selection of prime steaks including dry-aged porterhouse and buffalo rib eye. Surf and turf items including shrimp, crab, or lobster with portions up to a pound are truly high-roller sized and priced. Beyond the turf items, you can get veal Oscar, sautéed shrimp with risotto, or Alaskan halibut. This lovely, intimate restaurant is one of the few fine dining venues east of San Diego, and it's the only restaurant at the Barona Resort that serves alcoholic beverages and wines. ✉ *1932 Wildcat Canyon Rd., Lakeside 92040* ☎ *619/443–2300* ⛛ *reservations essential* ⊟ *AE, D, DC, MC, V* ⊗ *No lunch.*

$ ✗ **D'Carlos.** The parking lot in front of D'Carlos is always full, a sure sign that Ramonans like this casual dinner house. The menu offers something for everyone: burgers, sandwiches, salads, barbecue, and pasta. Daily specials include chicken-fried steak and barbecued chicken. When busy, which is usually, the ambience feels chaotic, but friendly waitresses are surprisingly efficient. There's also patio dining in good weather. ✉ *1347 Main St.* ☎ *760/789–4340* ⊟ *AE, D, DC, MC, V.*

$ ⛺ **Barona Valley Ranch Resort.** Like most of the Indian casino resorts, Barona is a stand-alone complex; it's located on a country road in a valley midway between Lakeside and Ramona. Thus the resort provides accommodations for players who want to spend a couple of days in the casino; about 80 percent of the rooms are available to them. Throughout the resort, the decor style is modified Arts and Crafts, clean and simple. Even if you don't gamble, there's a lot to enjoy here: spacious, beautifully appointed rooms with mountain or golf-course views, a selection of dining options including fine dining, a buffet, food court, and 24-hour café. The golf course is considered to be one of the best in the area. Colorful gardens surround the hotel complex; you can visit the chef's garden or the expansive rose garden. The hotel has a small but appealing day spa for those who want to be pampered. **Pros:** Golf, casino that's separated from hotel, beautiful gardens. **Cons:** Isolated. ✉ *1932 Wildcat Canyon Rd., Lakeside* ☎ *619/443–2300* ⊕ *www.barona.com* ⬆ *400 rooms, 32 suites* ⛊ *In-room: safes, refrigerator, DVD, Wi-Fi. In-hotel: 6 restaurants, room service, bars, golf course, pool, gym, spa, laundry service, concierge, public Wi-Fi, parking (fee), no smoking rooms* ⊟ *AE, D, DC, MC, V.*

$ ⛺ **San Vicente Inn and Golf Course.** This low-key resort dating back to the 1970s is part of a time-share and residential complex. It's long been a popular destination for golfers who want to avoid high green fees and still be challenged by the course. The accommodations in a three-story building are clean, pleasant, and somewhat dated. But there are nice golf course and mountain views from balconies or patios. You can dine in the bright and airy Oaks Grill every day but Monday. The Par Lounge is locally popular for lunch and dinner. **Pros:** Scenic location, jogging and nature trails, golf packages are a great value. **Cons:** Rooms dated, limited amenities. ⊠*24157 San Vicente Rd. 92065* ☎*760/789– 3788 or 800/776–1289* ⊕*www.sanvicenteresort.com* ⇔*28 rooms* ⚹*In-room: refrigerator. In-hotel: restaurant, bar, golf course, tennis courts, pools, no elevator, laundry service, public Internet, parking (no fee), no-smoking rooms.* ▤*MC, V.*

SPORTS & THE OUTDOORS

Mount Woodson Golf Club. Beautiful and unique, this 6,004-yard course is set amid a grove of ancient oak trees and granite boulder-strewn hillsides with spectacular views. A popular local tournament site, the course is rated 68.2/slope 132. The most you'll pay here is $85 for a weekend round of golf. ⊠*16422 N. Woodson Dr.* ☎*760/788–3555.*

Barona Creek Golf Course. Opened in 2001, this 7000-yard course won accolades from day one for its challenging slopes, strategically placed boulders, and native grass landscaping. It's rated 74.5 and 140 slope, and was the site of the 2007 Nationwide Tour Championship. Each hole has two sets of tees to accommodate different skill levels. Green fees run from $64 to $160, with discounts for visitors who have Players cards. ⊠*1932 Wildcat Canyon Rd., Lakeside* ☎*888/722–7662* ⊕*www.barona.com.*

PALOMAR MOUNTAIN

7

35 mi northeast of Escondido on I–15 to Rte. 76 to Rte. S6, 66 mi northeast of downtown San Diego on Rte. 163 to I–15 to Rte. 76 to Rte. S6.8.

Palomar Mountain, at an altitude of 6,140 feet and with an average of 300 clear nights per year, has the distinction of being the home of one of the world's most significant astronomical observation sites, the Hale 200-inch telescope installed at the Palomar Observatory in 1947. Before that, the mountain played a role in San Diego County's rich African American history and culture. One of many who migrated to the area in the mid-19th century was Nathan Harrison, a former slave who owned a large swath of property on the mountain where he farmed and raised cattle, the significance of which is just being revealed through archaeological excavations conducted by local university students. According to local historians, Harrison and other former slaves made up a significant segment of the backcountry population until about 1900. A devastating fire burned most of the lower slopes of Palomar Mountain in 2007, but the top of the mountain (home to the telescope, campgrounds, and a little settlement) remained untouched.

Palomar Observatory, atop Palomar Mountain, is owned and operated by the California Institute of Technology, whose astronomy faculty conducts research here. The observatory houses the Hale Telescope, as well as 60-inch, 48-inch, 24-inch, 18-inch, and Snoop telescopes. Some of the most important astronomical discoveries of the 20th century were made here, and already in this century scientists using the observatory's 48-inch telescope have detected a 10th planet. For the time being, this most distant known object in the solar system, a body larger than fellow dwarf-planet Pluto, has been named Eris. The small museum contains photos of some of these discoveries, as well as photos taken by NASA's Hubble Space Telescope and from recent NASA–European Space Agency missions to Mars and Saturn. A park with picnic areas surrounds the observatory. ☒*Rte. S6, north of Rte. 76, east of I–15, Palomar Mountain* ☎*760/742–2119* ⊕*www.astro.caltech.edu/palomar* ☒*Free* ☉*Observatory for self-guided tours daily 9–4.*

☼ **Mission San Antonio de Pala** is a living remnant of the mission era. Built in 1816 to serve Native American Indians, it still ministers to the Native American community—the only original Spanish mission still serving its initial purpose. The old jail and cemetery are part of the original mission. ☒*Pala Mission Rd. off Rte. 76, 6 mi east of I–15, Pala* ☎*760/742–1600* ☒*$2* ☉*Museum and gift shop Fri.–Sun. 10–4.*

One of the few areas in Southern California with a Sierra-like atmo-
☼ sphere, **Palomar Mountain State Park** holds a forest of pines, cedars, western dogwood, native azalea, and other plants. Wildflower viewing is good in spring. **Boucher Lookout,** on one of several nature/hiking trails, affords a sweeping view to the west. There's trout fishing in Doane Pond. The Doane Valley campground offers 31 sites with tables, fire pits, and flush toilets. ☒*Off Hwy. S6 at Hwy. S7, Palomar Mountain* ☎*760/742–3462 ranger station, 800/444–7275 campsite reservations* ⊕*www.palomarsummit.com/statepark.html* ☒*$6, camping $20.*

WHERE TO EAT
☼ ¢ ✕**Mother's Kitchen.** This popular stop for well-heeled motorcyclists (the road up there is the most popular biker route in Southern California) serves up huge portions of mountain chili, Boca tacos, and lasagna. Sides include steaming-hot soup, nachos, and quesadillas. The atmosphere is mountain casual, with open-beam ceilings, knotty-pine tables, and fresh flowers everywhere. Waitresses are friendly, and local musicians entertain on weekends. ☒*Junction Hwys. S6 and S7, Palomar Mountain* ☎*760/742–4233* ⊕*www.motherskitchenpalomar.com* ▤*MC, V* ☉*No dinner. Closed Tues. and Wed. Labor Day–Memorial Day.*

THE BACKCOUNTRY & JULIAN ESSENTIALS

To research prices, get advice from other travelers, and book travel arrangements, visit www.fodors.com.

CAR TRAVEL
A loop drive beginning and ending in San Diego is a good way to explore this area. You can take the Sunrise National Scenic Byway (sometimes icy in winter) from I–8 to Route 79 and return through Cuyamaca Rancho State Park (also icy in winter). If you're only going to Julian (a 75-minute trip from San Diego in light traffic), take either the Sunrise Byway or Route 79, and return to San Diego via Route 78 past Santa Ysabel to Ramona and Route 67; from here I–8 heads west to downtown.

VISITOR INFORMATION
Contact **Julian Chamber of Commerce** (☎ *760/765–1857* ⊕ *www.julianca. com).*

THE DESERT

In most spring seasons the stark desert landscape east of the Cuyamaca Mountains explodes with colorful wildflowers. The beauty of this spectacle, as well as the natural quiet and blazing climate, lures many tourists and natives each year to Anza-Borrego Desert State Park, less than a two-hour drive from central San Diego.

For hundreds of years the only humans to linger here were Native Americans of the Cahuilla and Kumeyaay tribes, who made their winter homes in the desert. It was not until 1774, when Mexican explorer Captain Juan Bautista de Anza first blazed a trail through the area seeking a shortcut from Sonora, Mexico, to San Francisco, that Europeans had their first glimpse of the oddly enchanting terrain.

The desert is best visited from October through May to avoid the extreme summer temperatures. Winter temperatures are comfortable, but nights (and sometimes days) are cold, so bring a warm jacket.

Numbers in the margin correspond to points of interest on the San Diego North County map.

7

ANZA-BORREGO DESERT STATE PARK

88 mi from downtown San Diego (to park border due west of Borrego Springs), east on I–8, north on Rte. 67, east on Rte. S4 and Rte. 78, north on Rte. 79, and east on Rtes. S2 and S22. Alternatively, take I–8 east to Hwy. 79, follow Hwy. 79 to Julian, where it intersects with Hwy. 78, take Hwy. 78 east to Yaqui Pass Rd., which will take you to Borrego Springs.

Today more than 1,000 square mi of desert and mountain country are included in the Anza-Borrego Desert State Park, one of the few parks in the country where you can follow a trail and pitch a tent wherever you like. No campsite is necessary, although there are two developed campgrounds. Rangers and displays at an excellent **Visitors Information Center** (✉ *200 Palm Canyon Dr., Borrego Springs* ☎ *760/767–4205, 760/767–4684 wildflower hotline* ⊕ *www.parks.ca.gov* ☉ *Oct.–May, daily 9–5; June–Sept., weekends and holidays 9–5*) can point you in the right direction.

Five hundred miles of paved and dirt roads traverse the park, and you are required to stay on them so as not to disturb its ecological balance. There are also 110 mi of hiking and riding trails that allow you to explore canyons, capture scenic vistas, and tiptoe through fields of wildflowers in spring. The park is also home to rare Peninsula Big Horn sheep, mountain lions, coyotes, black-tailed jackrabbit, and roadrunners. State Highway 78, which runs north and south through the park, has been designated the Juan Bautista de Anza National Historic Trail, marking portions of the route of the Anza Colonizing Expedition of 1775–76 that went from northern Mexico to the San Francisco Bay area. In addition, 28,000 acres have been set aside in the eastern part of the desert near Ocotillo Wells for off-road enthusiasts. General George S. Patton conducted field training in the Ocotillo area to prepare for the World War II invasion of North Africa.

Many of the park's sites can be seen from paved roads, but some require driving on dirt roads, where it's easy to sink up to your wheel covers in dry sand. Rangers recommend using four-wheel-drive vehicles on the dirt roads. Carry the appropriate supplies: shovel and other tools, flares, blankets, and plenty of water. Canyons are susceptible to flash flooding; inquire about weather conditions before entering.

> ## UNBURIED TREASURE
>
> The Anza-Borrego Desert is one of the most geologically active spots in North America and a repository of geologic and paleontological treasure. Beneath its surface are fossil-bearing sediments containing the record of 7 million years of climate change, tectonic activity, upthrust, and subsidence—the richest fossil deposits in North America. Reading the fossil record, scientists have revealed that the badlands were once a wonderland of green, the home of saber-toothed tigers, flamingos, zebras, camels, the largest known mammoths, and a flying bird with a 16-foot wingspan.

Wildflowers, which typically begin to bloom in January and are at their peak in mid-March, attract thousands of visitors each spring. A variety of factors including rainfall and winds determine how extensive the bloom will be in a particular year. However, good displays of low-growing sand verbena and white evening primrose can usually be found along Airport Road and DiGeorgio Road. Following wet winters, spectacular displays fill the dry washes in Coyote Canyon and along Henderson Canyon Road. The best light for photography is in early morning or late afternoon. Most of the desert plants can also be seen in the demonstration desert garden at the visitor center.

Narrows Earth Trail, off Route 78 east of Tamarisk Grove, is a short walk that reveals the many geologic processes involved in forming the desert canyons. Water, wind, and faulting created the commanding vistas along **Erosion Road,** a self-guided, 18-mi auto tour along Route S22. The **Southern Emigrant Trail** follows the route of the Butterfield Stage Overland Mail through the desert.

At **Borrego Palm Canyon,** a few minutes west of the Visitors Information Center, a 1½-mi trail leads to a small oasis with a waterfall and palms. The Borrego Palm Canyon campground is one of only two developed campgrounds with flush toilets and showers in the park. (The other is Tamarisk Grove Campground, at the intersection of Route 78 and Yaqui Pass Road; day use at both sites is $6 and camping is $20 in high season, $29 with hookup at Borrego Palm Canyon.)

Geology students from all over the world visit the Fish Creek area of Anza-Borrego to explore a famous canyon known as **Split Mountain** (⊠*Split Mountain Rd., south from Rte. 78 at Ocotillo Wells*), a narrow gorge with 600-foot perpendicular walls that was formed by an ancestral stream. Fossils in this area indicate that a sea covered the desert floor at one time. A 2-mi nature trail west of Split Mountain rewards hikers with a good view of shallow caves created by erosion.

BORREGO SPRINGS

31 mi from Julian, east on Rte. 78 and Yaqui Pass Rd., and north on Rte. S3.

A quiet town with a handful of year-round residents, Borrego Springs is set in the heart of the Anza-Borrego Desert State Park and is emerging as a destination for desert lovers. From September through June, temperatures hover in the 80s and 90s, and you can enjoy activities such as hiking, nature study, golf, tennis, horseback riding, and mountain-bike riding. Even during the busier winter season, Borrego Springs feels quiet. There are five golf resorts, two B&B inns, and a growing community of winter residents, but the laid-back vibe prevails. If winter rains cooperate, Borrego Springs puts on some of the best wildflower displays in the low desert.

WHERE TO EAT

7

$$ ✕ **Krazy Coyote Bar & Grill.** The theme at this café at the Palms Hotel is trendy mid-'50s, with dark red walls adorned with movie posters and other memorabilia. But the menu is strictly contemporary, listing entrées such as Santa Fe crab cakes, beef Wellington, and Australian lobster tail. ⊠*2220 Hoberg Rd.* ☎*760/767–7788* ⚠*Reservations essential* ▤*AE, D, MC, V* ☽*Closed mid-May–Oct., Mon. and Tues. rest of the year. No lunch.*

$ ✕ **Carlee's Bar & Grill.** The local watering hole, Carlee's is the place to go any night of the week. A large, dimly lighted room holds both bar and dining tables. The menu lists pasta and pizza in addition to old-fashioned entrées such as liver and onions and mixed grill. Dinners come with soup or salad. ⊠*660 Palm Canyon Dr.* ☎*760/767–3262* ▤*AE, D, MC, V.*

★ $ ✕ **Red Ocotillo.** The only indication that this Quonset hut on the east side of town is a restaurant is the "Eat" sign out front. Inside, the menu says "Congrats you found us," making it clear that they know their worth, as you will, too, as soon as your food arrives. This casual place serves breakfast (omelets, pancakes, eggs Benedict, breakfast burritos, and so on) all day every day, but it also serves lunch (soups, sandwiches, burgers, and salads) and dinner (appetizers, plus such things as top sirloin, chicken-fried steak, and a three-cheese pasta may be on the menu), and a few desserts. The food is absolutely outstanding. A delightful courtyard out back has tables for dining, and the waitstaff is friendly. ⊠*818 Palm Canyon Dr.* ☎*760/767–7400* ▤*AE, D, DC, MC, V.*

WHERE TO STAY

$$$$ ☷**La Casa del Zorro.** This serene resort pampers guests with spectacular
Fodor'sChoice desert scenery, luxurious accommodations, and gracious and superb
★ service. You only have to walk a few hundred yards from your room
to find yourself in a quiet desert garden surrounded by ocotillo and
cholla or alone under the stars at night. Accommodations range from
ample standard rooms to private casitas with their own pools or private
outdoor hot tubs. Most rooms have original art on the walls and are
appointed with mini bars, fireplaces, and extra large bathrooms. Guests
here have access to the private Montesoro golf course. There's a full
menu of sports activities including archery, table tennis, volleyball, and
croquet. The elegant Butterfield dining room puts on a good Sunday
brunch. La Casa schedules wine weekends throughout the year. **Pros:**
Luxurious, quiet desert setting, many activities onsite. **Cons:** Too quiet
for some. ⊠*3845 Yaqui Pass Rd.,* ☎*760/767–5323 or 800/824–1884*
⊕*www.lacasadelzorro.com* ⤴*44 rooms, 19 1- to 4-bedroom casitas*
♿*In-room: kitchen (some), refrigerator (some), DVD (some), VCR
(some), Ethernet, dial-up, Wi-Fi. In-hotel: 2 restaurants, room service,
tennis courts, pools, gym, spa, bicycles, laundry service, concierge,
public Wi-Fi, airport shuttle, parking (no fee), some pets allowed, no-
smoking rooms* ▭*AE, D, MC, V.*

★ **$$$** ☷**Borrego Valley Inn.** Desert gardens of mesquite, ocotillo, and creo-
sote surround the adobe buildings of this Southwestern-style inn. Spa-
cious rooms with plenty of light are decorated in Indian-design fabrics
and hold original art. Santa Fe–style furnishings include lodgepole
beds with down comforters, double futons facing corner fireplaces,
and walk-in showers with garden views. Every room opens out to its
own enclosed garden with chaises, chairs, and table. Rooms in the east
wing have direct access to a secluded clothing-optional pool. Friendly
innkeepers serve a tasty Continental breakfast and invite guests to
enjoy the courtyard desert garden while dining. **Pros:** Room to move
around inside and out, lovely desert gardens, extremely private. **Cons:**
Very quiet. ⊠*405 Palm Canyon Dr., Borrego Springs* ☎*760/767–
0311 or 800/333–5810* ⊕*www.borregovalleyinn.com* ⤴*15 rooms, 1
suite* ♿*In-room: kitchen (some), refrigerator (some), Wi-Fi. In-hotel:
pools, no elevator, public Wi-Fi, no-smoking rooms* ▭*AE, D, MC, V*
♟❘*CP.*

$$$ ☷**The Palms at Indian Head.** Spectacular desert views can be had from
this small hotel. Large guest rooms are furnished with hand-crafted,
Southwest lodgepole furniture and original art by local artists. Two
poolside rooms have fireplaces. When it was called the Old Hoberg
Resort, Marilyn Monroe, Bing Crosby, and Lon Chaney Jr., among
others, vacationed here. Continental breakfast is included in the price.
Pros: Mid-century modern ambience, star connection, great views.
Cons: Somewhat remote location, simple decor. ⊠*2220 Hoberg Rd.,*
☎*760/767–7788 or 800/519–2624* ⊕*www.thepalmsatindianhead.
com* ⤴*12 rooms* ♿*In-room: no phone, refrigerator. In-hotel: restaurant, bar, pool, no elevator, public Wi-Fi, no kids under 13, no-smoking
rooms* ▭*AE, D, MC, V* ♟❘*CP.*

$ ☷ **Borrego Springs Resort and Country Club.** A popular choice for families who want to have fun, play a little golf, and hang out at the pool, this casual resort has the ambience of a country club (which it is) but none of the snooty trappings. You'll find desert views from most rooms; most also have balconies or patios. Furnishings are simple, functional, and contemporary, but undistinguished. A Continental breakfast, served at the Arches restaurant on the property, is included in the price. **Pros:** Good value, relaxed ambience. **Cons:** Plain Jane as it can be, rooms around pool apt to be noisy, perfunctory service. ✉*1112 Tilting T Dr., Borrego Springs* ☎*760/767–5700 or 888/826–7734* ⊕*www. borregospringsresort.com* ⇆*66 rooms, 34 suites* ☖*In-room: kitchen (some), refrigerator. In-hotel: restaurant, bar, golf course, tennis courts, pools, gym, laundry facilities, parking (no fee), some pets allowed (fee)* ▭*AE, D, MC, V* ⦿|*CP.*

$ ☷ **Palm Canyon Resort.** One of the largest properties around Anza-Borrego Desert State Park includes a hotel, an RV park, a restaurant, and recreational facilities. Rooms are no-frills motel style, some in need of a sprucing up. Decor is Western style, and rooms around the pool have balconies. **Pros:** Low rates, Chinese restaurant on-site, proximity to state park. **Cons:** Maintenance needed, part of an RV park. ✉*221 Palm Canyon Dr., Borrego Springs* ☎*760/767–5341 or 800/222–0044* ⊕*www.pcresort.com* ⇆*60 rooms, 1 suite* ☖*In-room: refrigerator (some), Ethernet, dial-up, Wi-Fi (some). In-hotel: restaurant, room service, bar, pools, gym, no elevator, laundry facilities, public Internet, public Wi-Fi, no-smoking rooms* ▭*AE, D, DC, MC, V.*

SPORTS & THE OUTDOORS

The 27-hole course at **Borrego Springs Resort and Country Club** (☎*769/767–3330*) is open to the public. The green fees range from $40 to $80, including mandatory cart; discounts may be available to foursomes midweek. The **Roadrunner Club** (☎*760/767–5373*) has an 18-hole par-3 golf course. The green fee is $30, cart $14.

Smoketree Arabian Horse Ranch (☎*760/767–5850 or 866/408–1812* ⊕*www.smoketreearabianranch.com*) offers a variety of equine encounters—guided desert rides on Arabian or quarter horses, pony rides for kids, and a nonriding human-to-horse communication experience similar to horse-whispering.

OFF THE BEATEN PATH

Ocotillo Wells State Vehicular Recreation Area. The sand dunes and rock formations at this 80,000-plus acre haven for off-road enthusiasts are fun and challenging. Camping is permitted throughout the area, but water is not available. The only facilities are in the small town (really no more than a corner) of Ocotillo Wells. ✉*Rte. 78, 18 mi east from Borrego Springs Rd., Ocotillo Wells* ☎*760/767–5391.*

7

THE DESERT ESSENTIALS

To research prices, get advice from other travelers, and book travel arrangements, visit www.fodors.com.

CAR TRAVEL

From downtown San Diego, take I–8 east to Route 67 north, to Route 78 east, to Route 79 north, to Routes S2 and S22 east.

TOUR OPTIONS

California Overland Excursions offers day tours and overnight excursions into hard-to-reach scenic desert destinations using old military vehicles. Typical destinations include Font's Point, the Badlands, and 17-Palm Oasis.

Tour Companies California Overland Excursions (✉ *1233 Palm Canyon Dr.* ☎ *760/767–1232 or 866/639–7567* ⊕ *www.californiaoverland.com*).

VISITOR INFORMATION

Contacts Anza-Borrego Desert State Park (☎ *760/767–4205* ⊕ *www. parks.ca.gov*). **Borrego Springs Chamber of Commerce** (☎ *760/767–5555 or 800/559–5524* ⊕ *www.borregospringschamber.com*). **State Park Reservations** (☎ *800/444–7275* ⊕ *www.reserveamerica.com*). **Wildflower Hotline** (☎ *760/767–4684*).

TIJUANA

Updated by
Coco Krumme

18 mi (29 km) south of San Diego.

Over the course of the 20th century, Tijuana grew from a ranch populated by a few hundred Mexicans into a Prohibition retreat for boozing and gambling—then it morphed yet again into an industrial giant infamous for its proliferation of *maquiladoras* (sweat shops). With a documented population of 1.2 million (informal estimates run as high as 2 million), Tijuana has surpassed Ciudad Juárez to become the country's sixth-largest city. Whether the legendary sleazefest is now primary or secondary to Tijuana's economy, the place certainly hasn't shaken its bawdy image; tell someone you're going to Tijuana, and you'll still elicit knowing chuckles all around.

Gone are the glamorous days when Hollywood stars would frequent hot spots like the Agua Caliente Racetrack & Casino, which opened in 1929. When Prohibition was repealed, Tijuana's fortunes began to decline, and, in 1967, when the toll highway to Ensenada was completed, Tijuana ceased to be such a necessary pit stop on the overland route to the rest of Baja. Even the Jai-Alai Palace—which survived into the new millennium as the city's last bastion of gambling—is just a museum now.

That's not to say that the knowing chuckles aren't still deserved, because Tijuana has more recently managed to redefine itself as a hot spot for young Californians in search of the sort of fun not allowed back home, like a lower drinking age, and perhaps some souvenirs,

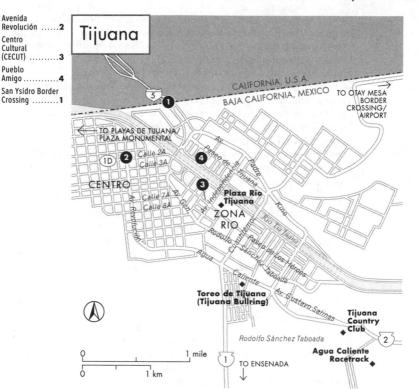

like duty-free tequila, overpriced trinkets, marked-down medicines, and Polaroid photos taken with donkeys painted as zebras (which, we kid you not, are readily available on Avenida Revolución). Even amid the high-profile hotels, casual dining chains, art museums, and Omni movies that have swooped into the city's swankier Zona Río in the last decade, much of Tijuana still represents border culture at its most bleakly opportunistic, from corrupt cops to pharmacies loudly advertising volume discounts on 100mg Viagra tablets (about enough for a horse).

Meanwhile, as the population has mushroomed, driven largely by the *maquiladoras,* the government has struggled to keep up with the growth and demand for services; thousands live without electricity, running water, or adequate housing in villages along the border. And nowhere in Mexico are the realities of commercial sex laid out more starkly. Open prostitution is everywhere: in the Zona Norte, street-walkers accost passersby as they sidestep pools of vomit; strip bars like Casa Adelita and Chicago Club also function as giant, multifloor brothels—every single dancer is for sale. Maybe that's why they sell the Viagra in such ludicrous doses.

Getting to Tijuana from San Diego takes about an hour, all told, and in spite of terrible rush-hour traffic it's easy as border crossings go. You can reach the border at San Ysidro—30 to 45 minutes from San Diego—by car, trolley, or taxi. Once there, you can cross the border on foot or on a shuttle bus that will take you to the center of Tijuana. If you cross on foot, you can walk from the border bridge to the center of Tijuana, which takes less than half an hour; or, you can take a taxi to the center or Zona Río (a better option at night). Alternatively, a Greyhound bus will take you all the way from the San Diego bus terminal to downtown Tijuana, or you can even hop a San Diego taxi for the whole route, crossing the border in the taxi (the priciest, but perhaps most relaxing, option). *For detailed information on the various border-crossing options, see* ⇨ *Crossing the Border in Essentials, below.*

ABOUT THE RESTAURANTS

As a rule, restaurants in Baja California are low-key and casual, though in Tijuana you're as apt to find upscale Continental dining rooms as you are *taquerías* (taco stands). Dress is accordingly informal, and reservations aren't generally required. Moderate prices prevail, though some places add a 15% service charge to the bill.

ABOUT THE HOTELS

You can find great deals at small, one-of-a-kind hostelries. A few out-of-the-way and budget-price hotels accept cash only, no credit cards; some of the more lavish places add a 10%–20% service charge to your bill. Most properties also raise their rates for the December–April high season (and raise them even higher for the days around Christmas). Expect to pay 25% less during the off-season. Many hotels offer mid-week discounts of 30%–50% off the weekend rates.

WHAT IT COSTS					
	¢	$	$$	$$$	$$$$
Restaurants	under $5	$5–$10	$11–$15	$16–$25	over $25
Hotels	under $50	$50–$75	$76–$150	$151–$250	over $250

Restaurant prices are for a main course at dinner excluding tax and tip. Hotel prices are for two people in a standard double room in high season, based on the European Plan (EP, with no meals) and excluding service and 17% tax.

Numbers in the margin correspond to points of interest on the Tijuana map.

EXPLORING

2 **Avenida Revolución.** This infamous strip, lined with shops and restaurants that cater to uninhibited travelers, has long been Tijuana's main tourism zone, even if the classier side of things has moved over to the Zona Río. Shopkeepers call out from doorways, offering low prices for garish souvenirs and genuine folk-art treasures. Many shopping arcades open onto Avenida Revolución; inside their front doors are mazes of stands with low-priced pottery and other crafts.

★ ⟲ ❸ **Centro Cultural (CECUT).** The cultural center's stark, low-slung, tan buildings and globelike Omnimax Theater are beloved landmarks. The center's Museo de las Californias provides an excellent overview of Baja's history and natural profile, while the Omnimax shows films, some in English. The film *Marine Oasis: The Riches of the Sea of Cortez* has fabulous underwater scenes. ⊠ *Paseo de los Héroes and Av. Mina, Zona Río* ☎ *664/687–9600* ⊕ *www.cecut.gob.mx* 🖃 *Museum: $2; museum and Omnimax Theater: $4* ☉ *Tues.–Sun. 10–6; Marine Oasis weekends at 3.*

❹ **Pueblo Amigo.** This entertainment center resembles a colonial village, with stucco facades and tree-lined paths leading to a domed gazebo. The complex includes a hotel, several restaurants and clubs, a huge grocery store, and a large branch of the Caliente Race Book, where gambling on televised sporting events is legal. Things get lively at night. ⊠ *Paseo de Tijuana between Puente Mexico and Calz. Independencia, Zona Río.*

❶ **San Ysidro Border Crossing.** Locals and tourists jostle each other along the pedestrian walkway through the Viva Tijuana dining and shopping center and into the center of town. Artisans' stands line the walkway and adjoining streets, offering a quick overview of the wares to be found all over town.

WHERE TO EAT & STAY

$$-$$$
MEXICAN
✕ **La Diferencia.** "The difference" at this gorgeous restaurant in the Zona Río, which features an indoor patio with elegant, relaxing tables that surround a central fountain, is nouvelle Mexican cuisine that completely transcends past notions of Tijuana cuisine. Chef Juan Carlos Rodriguez's creations include a delicious tamarind duck. He also makes liberal use of *huitlacoche* (corn fungus), which is a real treat. ⊠ *Blvd. Sánchez Taboada 10611A, Zona Río* ☎ *664/634–3346* ⊕ *www.ladiferencia.com.mx* ▭ *AE, DC, MC, V.*

$-$$
MEXICAN
★
✕ **La Especial.** At the foot of the stairs that run down to an underground shopping arcade you'll find the best place in the tourist zone for home-style Mexican cooking. The gruff, efficient waiters shuttle around platters of carne asada, enchiladas, and burritos, all with a distinctive flavor found only at this busy, cavernous basement dining room. ⊠ *Av. Revolución 718, Centro* ☎ *664/685–6654* ▭ *MC, V.*

$-$$
SEAFOOD
✕ **El Faro de Mazatlán.** Fresh fish prepared simply is the hallmark of one of Tijuana's best seafood restaurants. This is the place to try ceviche, abalone, squid, and lobster without spending a fortune, the dining room is a peaceful spot for a long, leisurely lunch. Appetizers and soup are included in the price of the meal. ⊠ *Blvd. Sánchez Taboada 9542, Zona Río* ☎ *664/684–8883* ▭ *AE, MC, V.*

> **WORD OF MOUTH**
>
> "We wound up eating at Especial three times. The prices are wonderful and the food is to die for. There's a great leather goods place on the same side of the street, within a few blocks to the right if you're facing the café."
>
> —Catmomma

7

$$-$$$ ⓘLucerna. Long one of the most charming hotels in Tijuana, the Lucerna has regained its former glory with modern touches like wireless Internet access and a business center. Although the place has American airs, the lovely gardens, large pool surrounded by palms, touches of tile work, and folk art lend the hotel a Mexican character, too. **Pros:** Nicely landscaped. **Cons:** Food so-so, on a busy intersection. ⊠*Paseo de los Héroes 10902, at Av. Rodríguez, Zona Río,* ☎*664/633–3900 or 800/582–3762* ⊕*www.lucerna.com.mx* ⚲*156 rooms, 9 suites* ⌂*In-room: Wi-Fi. In-hotel: Restaurant, room service, pool, gym, laundry service* ▭*AE, MC, V.*

SHOPPING

From the moment you cross the border, people will approach you or call out and insist that you look at their wares. Bargaining is expected in the streets and arcades, but not in the finer shops. If you drive, workers will run out from auto-body shops to place bids on new paint or upholstery for your car.

All along **Avenida Revolución** and its side streets, stores sell everything from tequila to Tiffany-style lamps. This shopping area spreads across Calle 2 to a pedestrian walkway leading from the border. Begin by checking out the stands along this walkway. Beware of fake goods, and above all, beware of higher prices offered to gringos. You may find that the best bargains are closer to the border; you can pick up your piñatas and sarapes on your way out of town. Between Calles 1 and 8, Avenida Revolución is lined with establishments stuffed with crafts and curios.

★ The **Mercado Hidalgo** (⊠*Calz. Independencia at Blvd. Sánchez Taboada, 5 blocks east of Av. Revolución, Zona Río*) is Tijuana's municipal market, with rows of fresh produce, some souvenirs, and Baja's best selection of piñatas.

TIJUANA ESSENTIALS

To research prices, get advice from other travelers, and travel arrangements, visit www.fodors.com.

TRANSPORTATION

CROSSING INTO MEXICO

When you go to Tijuana, it's preferable not to be burdened with a car in the city. In that case, you'll want to either drive to the border at San Ysidro and leave your car in a parking lot on the U.S. side, or take the San Diego Trolley (or a taxi) to San Ysidro, which will leave you at the border. At that point, you'll either walk across the border through the turnstiles (at which point you'll have the option of continuing into downtown Tijuana on foot or catching a Tijuana taxi to your destination in the city), or take a shuttle bus from the trolley station or parking lot to downtown Tijuana.

GETTING TO THE BORDER There are several options for getting to the border at San Ysidro, which is 30 to 45 minutes from San Diego.

By Car: The trip on I–5 takes from a half hour in no traffic to an hour or more in rush hour. Leave your car on the U.S. side at one of the border parking lots, which charge $7–$15 per day, and then cross the border on foot or by bus. Of the various lots, Border Station Parking, a 24-hour guarded lot at San Ysidro's Camino de la Plaza, next to the San Diego Factory Outlet Center, is a reliable choice. To get there, take the last U.S. exit off I–5 (marked "Last US Exit, Camino de la Plaza"), take a right at the stoplight off the ramp, and follow the signs for the lot.

By Taxi: A taxi ride from downtown San Diego to the border at San Ysidro will cost around $50. Expect to pay $60 or more if you want the taxi to take you across the border to downtown Tijuana, which some cabs will do.

By Trolley: The San Diego Trolley travels from the Santa Fe Depot in San Diego, at Kettner Boulevard and Broadway. You'll take the blue line to the last stop, San Ysidro/Tijuana, which is within 100 feet of the border. The blue line runs every 15 minutes from 5 AM to 1 AM. The 45-minute trip costs $2.50.

Information Border Station Parking (✉ *Camino de la Plaza, San Ysidro* ☎ *619/428–1422 in U.S.*). **San Diego Trolley** (☎ *619/233–3004 in U.S.* ⊕ *www.sdcommute.com*).

CROSSING THE BORDER **On Foot:** The most common way to cross the border is on foot, and the experience—going through a metal turnstile from one country to the next amidst the throngs of Americans and Mexicans—is also in many ways a more memorable one than any other. Don't expect much of a hassle when crossing into Mexico, but allow extra time on your way back and expect random inspections. To reach the border from the San Ysidro trolley stop (a 5-minute walk) or any of the border parking garages, just follow the crowds—you can't miss it.

Once you've crossed the border, you'll be inundated with taxi drivers, who will take you to downtown Tijuana for about $7—a good option at night—but many people choose to simply walk to downtown, a ½-mi walk that takes less than half an hour; again, just follow the crowds. Along that route, locals and tourists jostle each other on the pedestrian walkway that leads through the Viva Tijuana dining and shopping center and into the center of town. Artisans' stands line the walkway and adjoining streets, offering a quick overview of the wares to be found all over town.

By Bus: Crossing the border by bus is a way to avoid the mobs going through the turnstiles. Which bus to take depends on how you get to San Ysidro. If you arrive by trolley, you'll take the "Big Blue Bus," run by a company called Border Shuttle, from the San Ysidro trolley terminal to the new Tijuana Tourist Terminal, a modern facility in downtown Tijuana, on Avenida Revolución between 6th and 7th streets. Border Shuttle buses run every 15–20 minutes. If you arrive by car, you can take the Mexicoach shuttle (every 15 minutes between 8 AM and 9 PM, $8 round-trip) from the Border Station parking lot to the Tijuana Tourist Terminal.

Alternatively, you can circumvent it all with Greyhound, which runs regular bus service from San Diego to Tijuana, a trip that takes about an hour; you need only show your passport when the bus stops at the border, and everything else is taken care of. Greyhound buses head between San Diego's downtown bus terminal (120 W. Broadway) and Tijuana's Central Camionera (Calz. Lázaro Cárdenas and Blvd. Arroyo Alamar) 14 times a day; the one-way fare is $8.

Information **Border Shuttle** (⊠ *Tijuana Tourist Terminal, Av. Revolución 1025* ⊕ *www.san-diego-charter-bus.com*). **Greyhound** (☎ *664/686–0697, 664/688–0165 in Tijuana, 01800/710–8819 in Mexico, 800/231–2222 in the U.S.* ⊕ *www.greyhound. com*). **Mexicoach** (⊠ *4570 Camino de la Plaza, San Ysidro* ⊕ *www.mexicoach. com* ☎ *619/428–9517 in U.S.* ⊠ *Tijuana Tourist Terminal, Av. Revolución 1025* ☎ *664/685–1470*).

CONTACTS & RESOURCES

BANKS & MONEY

Because of the ubiquity of U.S. dollars as an accepted currency, the money situation is a bit different in Baja Norte than elsewhere in Mexico. It is possible to spend your entire vacation in Baja Norte without changing your money into pesos, and because the U.S. currency is so universal, you won't usually be shortchanged on the exchange rate if you pay in dollars, as you might farther south. Many, or even most, establishments quote prices in both dollars and pesos. Sometimes, it can be advantageous to pay in dollars as opposed to pesos—be prepared to do a lot of quick arithmetic in your head.

If you do get pesos—and it's always a good idea, regardless, to get some—as elsewhere in Mexico, use ATMs rather than exchange booths. The former tend to have better exchange rates, and they're absolutely everywhere in Tijuana.

CHILDREN IN MEXICO

Mexico has a very strict policy about children entering the country. All children, including infants, must have proof of citizenship for travel to Mexico (⇨ Entry Requirements). All children up to age 18 traveling with a single parent must also have a notarized letter from the other parent stating that the child has his or her permission to leave their home country. If the other parent is deceased or the child has only one legal parent, a notarized statement saying so must be obtained as proof.

EMERGENCIES

In an emergency, dial 066. The operators speak at least a bit of English. For tourist assistance with legal problems, accidents, or other incidents dial the Tourist Information and Assistance hotline at 078. If you need serious hospital treatment, you are well advised to head back to San Diego for treatment.

ENTRY REQUIREMENTS

Under new legislation, all U.S. citizens, including minor children, must show a passport to enter or reenter the United States from Mexico. Minors traveling with one parent need notarized permission from the absent parent (⇨ *Children in Mexico).*

Citizens of the United States, Canada, Australia, and New Zealand do not need visas to visit Mexico. However, if you're going to be staying in Mexico for more than 72 hours or traveling more than 20–30 km (12–19 mi) from the border, make sure you get and keep a tourist card, *tarjeta de turista,* which you may be asked for if, for example, you take a domestic flight in Mexico.

TOUR OPTIONS

Baja California Tours has comfortable, informative bus trips throughout northern Baja. Seasonal day and overnight trips focus on whale-watching, fishing, shopping, wineries, sports, dude ranches, and art and cultural events in Tijuana. Five Star Tours runs a daily Tijuana shuttle. San Diego Scenic Tours offers half- and full-day bus tours of Tijuana, with time allowed for shopping.

Information **Baja California Tours** (☎ *858/454–7166 or 800/336–5454* ⊕ *www. bajaspecials.com).* **Five Star Tours** (☎ *619/232–5049* ⊕ *www.efivestartours.com).* **San Diego Scenic Tours** (☎ *858/273–8687* ⊕ *www.sandiegoscenictours.com).*

VISITOR INFORMATION

Baja tours, Mexican auto insurance, a monthly newsletter, discounts, and lectures are available through Discover Baja, a San Diego–based membership club for Baja travelers. In Baja, tourism offices in the larger cities are usually open weekdays 9–7 (although some may close in early afternoon for lunch) and weekends 9–1. Some of the smaller areas don't have offices. In Tijuana, tourist information offices, which distribute maps and other useful information, are positioned both at the border and downtown on Avenida Revolución; Tijuana also has a Baja California State Secretary of Tourism office, which distributes more information about Baja generally.

Tijuana Information **Tijuana Convention and Visitors Bureau** (✉ *Zona Río* ☎ *664/684–0537* ✉ *Avenida Revelución* ☎ *664/685–2210* ⊕ *www.tijuanaonline. org* ✉ *San Ysidro Pedestrian Border Crossing* ☎ *664/683–1405).*

Baja Information **Baja California State Secretary of Tourism** (☎ *646/686–1103* ⊕ *www.discoverbajacalifornia.com).* **Discover Baja** (☎ *619/275–4225 or 800/727–2252* ⊕ *www.discoverbaja.com).*

7

San Diego Essentials

PLANNING TOOLS, EXPERT INSIGHT, GREAT CONTACTS

There are planners and there are those who, excuse the pun, fly by the seat of their pants. We happily place ourselves among the planners. Our writers and editors try to anticipate all the issues you may face before and during any journey, and then they do their research. This section is the product of their efforts. Use it to get excited about your trip to San Diego, to inform your travel planning, or to guide you on the road should the seat of your pants start to feel threadbare.

GETTING STARTED

We're really proud of our Web site: Fodors.com is a great place to begin any journey. Scan "Travel Wire" for suggested itineraries, travel deals, restaurant and hotel openings, and other up-to-the-minute info. Check out "Booking" to research prices and book plane tickets, hotel rooms, rental cars, and vacation packages. Head to "Talk" for on-the-ground pointers from travelers who frequent our message boards. You can also link to loads of other travel-related resources.

▌RESOURCES

ONLINE TRAVEL TOOLS
All About San Diego For a dining and entertainment guide to San Diego's most popular nightlife district, check out ⊕*www.gaslamp.org.* Visit ⊕*www. hillquest.com,* an urban guide to San Diego's diverse alternative-lifestyle community. For entertainment suggestions in San Diego's most upscale enclave, visit ⊕*www.lajollabythesea.com.*   ⊕*www. littleitalysd.com* offers event and traveler information for Little Italy. For insider tips from a local perspective, visit ⊕*www. localwally.com.* For information on the birthplace of California, search ⊕*www. oldtownsandiego.org.* For a calendar of upcoming events in popular beach community Pacific Beach, visit ⊕*www. pacificbeach.org.* Browse San Diego's premier upscale lifestyle magazine at ⊕*www. ranchandcoast.com.* Stop by ⊕*www. sandiego-online.com* to check out *San Diego Magazine.* Search ⊕*www.sandiegoperforms.com* for half-price tickets to San Diego performances. Find out about special tours and events going on at the San Diego Zoo at ⊕*www.sandiegozoo. org.* For a comprehensive listing of San Diego concerts, performances, and art exhibits, check out the local alternative paper at ⊕*www.sdreader.com.* For the

San Diego Union-Tribune, visit ⊕*www. signonsandiego.com.* The paper's Visitors Guide is a great trip-planning tool.

Safety San Diego Police Department (☎619/531–2000 ⊕www.sandiego.gov/ police). **Transportation Security Administration** (TSA ⊕www.tsa.gov).

Time Zones Timeanddate.com (⊕www.time-anddate.com/worldclock) can help you figure out the correct time anywhere in the world.

INSPIRATION
Check out these books for further San Diego reading. The novel *Drift* by Jim Miller explores San Diego's boom time through the eyes of a college professor in the year 2000. *Leave Only Paw Prints: Dog Hikes in San Diego* offers a myriad of walking spots that are dog-friendly, along with smart travel tips for your furry friend. *San Diego Legends: Events, People and Places That Made History* goes beyond the typical history book material to reveal little-known stories about San Diego.

San Diego has a rich film history, thanks to the city's unique geography and proximity to Los Angeles. Some of the better known films made here include *Top Gun, Traffic,* and *Almost Famous.* The bar scene in *Top Gun* was filmed at a local restaurant, Kansas City BBQ, on the corner of Kettner Boulevard and W. Harbor Drive. And of course, don't forget to take *Anchorman* Ron Burgundy's advice, and "Stay Classy, San Diego."

VISITOR INFORMATION

For general information and brochures before you go, contact the San Diego Convention & Visitors Bureau, which publishes the helpful *San Diego Visitors Planning Guide*. When you arrive, stop by one of the local visitor centers for general information.

Citywide San Diego Convention & Visitors Bureau (☎619/232-3101 ⊕www.sandiego. org). **San Diego Convention & Visitors Bureau International Visitor Information Center** (☎619/236-1212 ⊕www.sandiego. org). **San Diego Visitor Information Center** (☎619/276-8200 for recorded information ⊕www.infosandiego.com).

San Diego County Borrego Springs Chamber of Commerce and Visitor Center (☎760/767-5555 ⊕www.borregosprings-chamber.org). **California Welcome Center Oceanside** (☎760/721-1011 or 800/350-7873 ⊕www.oceansidechamber.com). **Carlsbad Convention & Visitors Bureau** (☎800/227-5722 ⊕www.visitcarlsbad.com). **Chula Vista Convention & Visitors Bureau** (☎619/425-4444 ⊕www.chulavistaconvis. com). **Coronado Visitor Center** (☎619/437-8788 ⊕www.coronadovisitorcenter.com). **Del Mar Regional Chamber of Commerce** (☎858/793-5292 ⊕www.delmarchamber. org). **Encinitas Chamber of Commerce** (☎760/753-6041 ⊕www.encinitaschamber. com). **Julian Chamber of Commerce** (☎760/765-1857 ⊕www.julianca.com). **Promote La Jolla, Inc.** (☎858/454-5718 ⊕www.lajollabythesea.com). **San Diego East Visitors Bureau** (☎800/463-0668 ⊕www. visitsandiegoeast.com). **San Diego North Convention & Visitors Bureau** (☎800/848-3336 ⊕www.sandiegonorth.com).

Statewide California Travel and Tourism Commission (☎916/444-4429 or 800/862-2543 ⊕www.visitcalifornia.com).

▌ THINGS TO CONSIDER

PASSPORTS & VISAS

PASSPORTS

When traveling to Mexico by air, you must have a valid passport. Starting June 1, 2009, everyone traveling between the United States and Mexico by land or sea (including ferries) will be required to present a passport as well. Until then, you may present two documents verifying citizenship and identity, such as a valid driver's license and a birth certificate. When traveling to Mexico, passports must be valid for a minimum of six months from date of departure, regardless of how long you intend to stay in the country. Check with the Department of Homeland Security for updates before planning a trip in to Mexico from San Diego at *www.dhs.gov*.

U.S. passports are valid for 10 years. You must apply in person if you're getting a passport for the first time; if your previous passport was lost, stolen, or damaged; or if your previous passport has expired and was issued more than 15 years ago or when you were under 16. All children under 18 must appear in person to apply for or renew a passport. Both parents must accompany any child under 14 (or send a notarized statement with their permission) and provide proof of their relationship to the child.

▐**TIP→** Before your trip, make two copies of your passport's data page (one for someone at home and another for you to carry separately). Or scan the page and e-mail it to someone at home and/or yourself.

There are 13 regional passport offices, as well as 7,000 passport acceptance facilities in post offices, public libraries, and other governmental offices. If you're renewing a passport, you can do so by mail. Forms are available at passport acceptance facilities and online.

The cost to apply for a new passport is $97 for adults, $82 for children under 16; renewals are $67. Allow six weeks for processing, both for first-time passports and renewals. For an expediting fee of $60 you can reduce this time to about two weeks. If your trip is less than two weeks away, you can get a passport even more rapidly by going to a passport office with the necessary documentation. Private expediters can get things done in as little as 48 hours, but charge hefty fees for their services.

Take special note if you're traveling with a child: it's no longer necessary for single parents, unaccompanied minors, widows–widowers, or parents with estranged partners to produce notarized letters or other supporting documentation for minors entering Mexico. Instead, each child must have his or her own passport. As with adults, the passport must be valid for at least six months from the date of departure.

When a minor child is traveling alone, without a parent or legal guardian, all parents and guardians named on the child's birth certificate, adoption papers, or court documents must give signed and notarized authorization for the child to travel without them. It's advised that they also travel with a clear copy of the authorizing parent or guardian's driver's license.

VISAS

A visa is not required for U.S. tourists visiting Mexico for up to 90 days. However, tourists traveling beyond the border zone or entering Mexico by air must pay a $23 fee to obtain a tourist card, also known as an FM-T, available from Mexican consulates, Mexican border crossing points, Mexican tourism offices, airports within the border zone, and most airlines serving Mexico. The fee for the tourist card is generally included in the price of a plane ticket for travelers arriving by air.

The tourist card is issued upon presentation of proof of citizenship, such as a U.S. passport or a U.S. birth certificate, plus photo ID, such as a driver's license. Tourist cards are issued for up to 90 days with a single entry, or if you present proof of sufficient funds, for 180 days with multiple entries.

Upon entering Mexico, retain and safeguard the traveler's copy of your tourist card so you may surrender it to Mexican immigration when you depart. You must leave Mexico before your tourist card expires or you will be subject to a fine.

U.S. Passport Information U.S. Department of State (☎877/487–2778 ⊕http://travel.state.gov/passport).

U.S. Passport & Visa Expediters A. Briggs Passport & Visa Expeditors (☎800/806–0581 or 202/464–3000 ⊕www.abriggs.com). **American Passport Express** (☎800/455–5166 or 603/559–9888 ⊕www.americanpassport.com). **Passport Express** (☎800/362–8196 or 401/272–4612 ⊕www.passportexpress.com). **Travel Document Systems** (☎800/874–5100 or 202/638–3800 ⊕www.traveldocs.com). **Travel the World Visas** (☎866/886–8472 or 202/223–8822 ⊕www.world-visa.com).

GENERAL REQUIREMENTS FOR ENTRY TO MEXICO FROM SAN DIEGO	
Passport	Must be valid for 6 months after date of arrival.
Visa	Americans do not need a visa. Instead, they must buy a $23 tourist card.
Vaccinations	Not required, but Hepatitis A, Hepatitis B, Measels, and Typhoid are recommended.
Driving	Driver's license required; be sure to buy Mexican car insurance if you're bringing your own car into Mexico or if you're renting a car there.
Departure Tax	US$20, payable in cash only.

BOOKING YOUR TRIP

Unless your cousin is a travel agent, you're probably among the millions of people who make most of their travel arrangements online. But have you ever wondered just what the differences are between an online travel agent (a Web site through which you make reservations instead of going directly to the airline, hotel, or car-rental company), a discounter (a firm that does a high volume of business with a hotel chain or airline and accordingly gets good prices), a wholesaler (one that makes cheap reservations in bulk and then resells them to people like you), and an aggregator (one that compares all the offerings so you don't have to)? Is it truly better to book directly on an airline or hotel Web site? And when does a real live travel agent come in handy?

ONLINE

You really have to shop around. A travel wholesaler such as Hotels.com or Hotel-Club.net can be a source of good rates, as can discounters such as Hotwire or Priceline, particularly if you can bid for your hotel room or airfare. Indeed, such sites sometimes have deals that are unavailable elsewhere. They do, however, tend to work only with hotel chains (which makes them just plain useless for getting hotel reservations outside of major cities) or big airlines (so that often leaves out upstarts like jetBlue and some foreign carriers like Air India). Also, with discounters and wholesalers you must generally prepay, and everything is nonrefundable. And before you fork over the dough, be sure to check the terms and conditions, so you know what a given company will do for you if there's a problem and what you'll have to deal with on your own.

■ TIP→ **To be absolutely sure everything was processed correctly, confirm reservations made through online travel agents, discounters, and wholesalers directly with your hotel before leaving home.**

Booking engines like Expedia, Travelocity, and Orbitz are actually travel agents, albeit high-volume, online ones. And airline travel packagers like American Airlines Vacations and Virgin Vacations—well, they're travel agents, too. But they may still not work with all the world's hotels.

An aggregator site will search many sites and pull the best prices for airfares, hotels, and rental cars from them. Most aggregators compare the major travel-booking sites such as Expedia, Travelocity, and Orbitz; some also look at airline Web sites, though rarely the sites of smaller budget airlines. Some aggregators also compare other travel products, including complex packages—a good thing, as you can sometimes get the best overall deal by booking an air-and-hotel package.

Online Accommodations Hotelbook.com (⊕www.hotelbook.com) focuses on independent hotels worldwide. **Hotel Club** (⊕www.hotelclub.net) is good for major cities worldwide. **Hotels.com** (⊕www.hotels.com) is a big Expedia-owned wholesaler that offers rooms in hotels all over the world. **Quikbook** (⊕www.quikbook.com) offers "pay when you stay" reservations that allow you to settle your bill when you check out, not when you book.

Other Resources Bidding For Travel (⊕www.biddingfortravel.com) is a good place to figure out what you can get and for how much before you start bidding on, say, Priceline.

WITH A TRAVEL AGENT

If you use an agent—brick-and-mortar or virtual—you'll pay a fee for the service. And know that the service you get from some online agents isn't comprehensive. For example Expedia and Travelocity don't search for prices on budget airlines like jetBlue, Southwest, or small foreign carriers. That said, some agents (online or not) *do* have access to fares that are difficult to find otherwise, and the savings can more than make up for any surcharge.

A knowledgeable brick-and-mortar travel agent can be a godsend if you're booking a cruise, a package trip that's not available to you directly, an air pass, or a complicated itinerary including several overseas flights. What's more, travel agents that specialize in a destination may have exclusive access to certain deals and insider information on things such as charter flights. Agents who specialize in types of travelers (senior citizens, gays and lesbians, naturists) or types of trips (cruises, luxury travel, safaris) can also be invaluable.

■ TIP→ Remember that Expedia, Travelocity, and Orbitz are travel agents, not just booking engines. To resolve any problems with a reservation made through these companies, contact them first.

A top-notch agent planning your trip to Russia will make sure you get the correct visa application and complete it on time; the one booking your cruise may get you a cabin upgrade or arrange to have a bottle of champagne chilling in your cabin when you embark. And complain about the surcharges all you like, but when things don't work out the way you'd hoped, it's nice to have an agent to put things right.

Agent Resources **American Society of Travel Agents** (☎703/739–2782 ⊕www.travelsense.org).

San Diego Travel Agents **Kahala Travel** (☎619/282–8300 ⊕www.kahalatravel.com). **Paradise Cruises and Travel** (☎760/735–2800 or 800/707–0062 ⊕www.paradisecruisesandtravel.com). **World View Travel** (☎858/459–0681or 800/869–0674 ⊕www.worldviewtravel.com).

■ ACCOMMODATIONS

Most hotels and other lodgings require you to give your credit-card details before they will confirm your reservation. If you don't feel comfortable e-mailing this information, ask if you can fax it (some places even prefer faxes). However you book, get confirmation in writing and have a copy of it handy when you check in.

Be sure you understand the hotel's cancellation policy. Some places allow you to cancel without any kind of penalty— even if you prepaid to secure a discounted rate—if you cancel at least 24 hours in advance. Others require you to cancel a week in advance or penalize you the cost of one night. Small inns and B&Bs are most likely to require you to cancel far in advance. Most hotels allow children under a certain age to stay in their parents' room at no extra charge, but others charge for them as extra adults; find out the cutoff age for discounts.

■ TIP→ Assume that hotels operate on the European Plan (EP, no meals) unless we specify that they use the Breakfast Plan (BP, with full breakfast), Continental Plan (CP, Continental breakfast), Full American Plan (FAP, all meals), Modified American Plan (MAP, breakfast and dinner), or are all-inclusive (AI, all meals and most activities).

For price categories, consult the price chart found in the "Where to Stay" chapter.

APARTMENT & HOUSE RENTALS

If you plan to stay a week or more in San Diego, or have a larger group traveling with you, it's often more cost-effective to rent a condominium or house in the neighborhood that interests you. Many inexpensive options can be found on Craigslist on short notice (www.craigslist.com); however, there are several rental and real estate companies specializing in locating rentals based on your personal preferences. Apartment or condo options downtown will keep you close to attractions like the Gaslamp, Balboa Park, PETCO Park, and the Harbor. Rentals in Pacific Beach and Ocean Beach will get you that much closer to that coveted surf.

Contacts Craigslist San Diego (⊕www. sandiego.craigslist.org). **Gaslamp Vacations** (☎619/446–6329 ⊕www.gaslampvacations. com). **San Diego Sunset Vacation Rentals** (☎858/488–5204 ⊕www.sandiegosunset-vacationrentals.com). **San Diego Vacation Rentals** (☎800/222–8281 ⊕www.sdvr.com). **Vamoose, Inc.** (⊕www.vamoose.com). **Vacation Home Rentals Worldwide** (☎201/767–9393 or 800/633–3284 ⊕www.vhrww.com). **Villas International** (☎415/499–9490 or 800/221–2260 ⊕www.villasintl.com).

BED & BREAKFASTS

If you're looking for romantic and relaxing vacation accommodations, San Diego offers a multitude of B&B options. You can find them throughout the county and most are within a short drive of all the major attractions. Staying at a B&B is also a great way to gain more intimate knowledge of a specific neighborhood, such as the affluent and offbeat Hillcrest area, historic Mission Hills with its Victorian, Craftsman, and mid-century modern architecture, and upscale La Jolla with all its great shopping. The beach communities also have a few good B&Bs within walking distance of the sand.

Contacts Bed & Breakfast.com (☎512/322–2710 or 800/462–2632 ⊕www.bedandbreak-fast.com), also sends out an online newsletter. **Bed & Breakfast Inns Online** (☎310/280–4363 or 800/215–7365 ⊕www.bbonline. com). **BnB Finder.com** (☎212/432–7693 or 888/547–8226 ⊕www.bnbfinder.com). **Pamela Lanier's Bed and Breakfasts, Inns and Guesthouses International** (⊕www. lanierbb.com). **San Diego Bed & Breakfast Guild** (⊕www.bandbguildsandiego.org).

HOME EXCHANGES

With a direct home exchange you stay in someone else's home while they stay in yours. Some outfits also deal with vaca-

tion homes, so you're not actually staying in someone's full-time residence, just their vacant weekend place.

Exchange Clubs Digsville Home Exchange Club (☎877/795–1019 ⊕www.digsville.com); $44.95 for a one-year membership. **Home Exchange.com** (☎800/877–8723 ⊕www. homeexchange.com); $59.95 for a one-year online listing. **HomeLink International** (☎800/638–3841 ⊕www.homelink.org); $90 yearly for Web-only membership; $140 includes Web access and two catalogs. **Intervac U.S.** (☎800/756–4663 ⊕www.intervacus. com); $78.88 for Web-only membership; $126 includes Web access and a catalog.

HOSTELS

Hostels offer bare-bones lodging at low, low prices—often in shared dorm rooms with shared baths—to people of all ages, though the primary market is young travelers, especially students. Most hostels serve breakfast; dinner and/or shared cooking facilities may also be available. In some hostels you aren't allowed to be in your room during the day, and there may be a curfew at night. Nevertheless, hostels provide a sense of community, with public rooms where travelers often gather to share stories. Many hostels are affiliated with Hostelling International (HI), an umbrella group of hostel associations with some 4,500 member properties in more than 70 countries. Other hostels are completely independent and may be nothing more than a really cheap hotel.

Membership in any HI association, open to travelers of all ages, allows you to stay in HI-affiliated hostels at member rates. One-year membership is about $28 for adults; hostels charge about $10–$30 per night. Members have priority if the hostel is full; they're also eligible for discounts around the world, even on rail and bus travel in some countries.

Whether you're on the beach or downtown, the San Diego hostel scene offers something for everyone traveling on a budget. All feature large dormitory-style sleeping quarters that are enthralling for international party animals, but most also offer private rooms suitable for couples or families. Each has varying levels of service and cleanliness, so do some research to avoid surprises.

Information Hostelling International—USA (☎301/495–1240 ⊕www.hiusa.org).

▮ AIRLINE TICKETS

Most domestic airline tickets are electronic; international tickets may be either electronic or paper. With an e-ticket the only thing you receive is an e-mailed receipt citing your itinerary and reservation and ticket numbers. The greatest advantage of an e-ticket is that if you lose your receipt, you can simply print out another copy or ask the airline to do it for you at check-in. You usually pay a surcharge (up to $50) to get a paper ticket, if you can get one at all. The sole advantage of a paper ticket is that it may be easier to endorse over to another airline if your flight is canceled and the airline with which you booked can't accommodate you on another flight.

▮TIP→ Discount air passes that let you travel economically in a country or region must often be purchased before you leave home. In some cases you can only get them through a travel agent.

▮ RENTAL CARS

When you reserve a car, ask about cancellation penalties, taxes, drop-off charges (if you're planning to pick up the car in one city and leave it in another), and surcharges (for being under or over a certain age, for additional drivers, or for driving across state or country borders or beyond a specific distance from your point of rental). All these things can add substantially to your costs. Request car seats and extras such as GPS when you book.

Rates are sometimes—but not always—better if you book in advance or reserve through a rental agency's Web site. There are other reasons to book ahead, though: for popular destinations, during busy times of the year, or to ensure that you get certain types of cars (vans, SUVs, exotic sports cars).

▮TIP→ Make sure that a confirmed reservation guarantees you a car. Agencies sometimes overbook, particularly for busy weekends and holiday periods.

A car is essential for San Diego's sprawling freeway system and comes in handy for touring Baja California (though the trolley serves the border at Tijuana). Rates in San Diego fluctuate with seasons and demand, but generally begin at $39 a day and $250 a week for an economy car with air-conditioning, automatic transmission, and unlimited mileage. This does not include tax on car rentals, which is 7.75%.

In California you must be 21 to rent a car, and rates may be higher if you're under 25. Some agencies will not rent to those under 25; check when you book. Children up to age six or 60 pounds must be placed in safety or booster seats. Non-U.S. residents must have a license whose text is in the Roman alphabet, though it need not be in English. An international license is recommended but not required.

In most cases, you will be unable to rent a car in the United States and drive it into

Mexico; most American car rental companies prohibit drivers from taking rentals south of the border. If you do take a rental to Mexico, you must get permission from the car rental company and you should always carry your rental agreement with you.

Automobile Associations American Automobile Association (AAA) (☎315/797–5000 ⊕www.aaa.com); most contact with the organization is through state and regional members. **National Automobile Club** (☎650/294–7000 ⊕www.thenac.com); membership is open to California residents only.

Local Agencies Fox Rent A Car (☎619/692–0300 or 800/225–4369 ⊕www.foxrentacar.com) and **Rent 4 Less Car Rental** (⊕www.rentfourless.com) are reliable, local rental agencies. **Autorent Car Rental** (☎619/692–3006) and **Enterprise** (☎858/483–3800) pick up at area hotels.

Major Agencies Alamo (☎800/462–5266 ⊕www.alamo.com). **Avis** (☎800/331–1212 ⊕www.avis.com). **Budget** (☎800/527–0700 ⊕www.budget.com). **Hertz** (☎800/654–3131 ⊕www.hertz.com). **National Car Rental** (☎800/227–7368 ⊕www.nationalcar.com).

CAR-RENTAL INSURANCE

Everyone who rents a car wonders whether the insurance that the rental companies offer is worth the expense. No one—including us—has a simple answer. It all depends on how much regular insurance you have, how comfortable you are with risk, and whether or not money is an issue.

If you own a car and carry comprehensive car insurance for both collision and liability, your personal auto insurance will probably cover a rental, but read your policy's fine print to be sure. If you don't have auto insurance, then you should probably buy the collision- or loss-damage waiver (CDW or LDW) from the rental company. This eliminates your liability for damage to the car. Some credit cards offer CDW coverage, but it's usually supplemental to your own insurance

and rarely covers SUVs, minivans, luxury models, and the like. If your coverage is secondary, you may still be liable for loss-of-use costs from the car-rental company (again, read the fine print). But no credit-card insurance is valid unless you use that card for *all* transactions, from reserving to paying the final bill.

■TIP➜ Diners Club offers primary CDW coverage on all rentals reserved and paid for with the card. This means that Diners Club's company—not your own car insurance—pays in case of an accident. It *doesn't* mean that your car-insurance company won't raise your rates once it discovers you had an accident.

You may also be offered supplemental liability coverage; the car-rental company is required to carry a minimal level of liability coverage insuring all renters, but it's rarely enough to cover claims in a really serious accident if you're at fault. Your own auto-insurance policy will protect you if you own a car; if you don't, you have to decide whether you are willing to take the risk.

U.S. rental companies sell CDWs and LDWs for about $15 to $25 a day; supplemental liability is usually more than $10 a day. The car-rental company may offer you all sorts of other policies, but they're rarely worth the cost. Personal accident insurance, which is basic hospitalization coverage, is an especially egregious rip-off if you already have health insurance.

■TIP➜ You can decline the insurance from the rental company and purchase it through a third-party provider such as Travel Guard (www.travelguard.com)—$9 per day for $35,000 of coverage. That's sometimes just under half the price of the CDW offered by some car-rental companies.

Some states, including California, have capped the price of the CDW and LDW.

If you're bringing a rental to Mexico, it's important to purchase Mexican car insurance to protect yourself from theft and liability to third parties for property damage or bodily injury as a result of an accident. If you're involved in an accident in Mexico and don't have car insurance, you could be detained by the authorities until they can determine fault. They mean business. If you're at fault, you would be required to demonstrate financial responsibility to post bond and cover the estimated costs of the damage.

■ GUIDED TOURS

Guided tours are a good option when you don't want to do it all yourself. You travel along with a group (sometimes large, sometimes small), stay in prebooked hotels, eat with your fellow travelers (the cost of meals sometimes included in the price of your tour, sometimes not), and follow a schedule. But not all guided tours are an if-it's-Tuesday-this-must-be-Belgium experience. A knowledgeable guide can take you places that you might never discover on your own, and you may be pushed to see more than you would have otherwise. Tours aren't for everyone, but they can be just the thing for trips to places where making travel arrangements is difficult or time-consuming (particularly when you don't speak the language). Whenever you book a guided tour, find out what's included and what isn't. A "land-only" tour includes all your travel (by bus, in most cases) in the destination, but not necessarily your flights to and from or even within it. Also, in most cases prices in tour brochures don't include fees and taxes. And remember that you'll be expected to tip your guide (in cash) at the end of the tour.

In San Diego, guided tours will show you the city's highlights efficiently without having to navigate the winding streets and busy freeways. The downside to guided tours is that you'll be left with little time to explore the nuances of this sunny Southern California destination. For a city that's known for its laid-back attitude, such scheduling can find you scoping out the city's surface instead of exploring the city's lesser-known treasures and relaxing at the beach.

Recommended Companies San Diego Tours (☎800/303-7197 ⊕www.sandiegotours.us).

■ CRUISES

Several cruise lines make San Diego a port of call. Holland America and Royal Caribbean use San Diego as a regular point of embarkation for seasonal cruises to Alaska, the Mexican Riviera, and the Panama Canal. Other lines, including Princess and Celebrity, originate repositioning cruises in San Diego throughout the year. The San Diego cruise-ship terminal is on the downtown waterfront just steps from the San Diego Maritime Museum and Midway Museum. The terminal is a short taxi ride from Balboa Park, Little Italy, and the Gaslamp Quarter.

Cruise Lines Carnival (☎888/227-6482 ⊕www.carnival.com). **Celebrity** (☎800/647-2251 ⊕www.celebrity.com). **Crystal** (☎310/785-9300 ⊕www.crystalcruises.com). **Holland America** (☎800/426-0327 ⊕www.hollandamerica.com). **Norwegian Cruise Line** (☎800/327-7030 ⊕www.ncl.com). **Princess** (☎800/774-6237 ⊕www.princess.com). **Regent Seven Seas Cruises** (☎800/477-7500 ⊕www.rssc.com). **Royal Caribbean International** (☎800/398-9819 ⊕www.royalcaribbean.com). **Silversea** (☎800/722-9955 ⊕www.silversea.com).

TRANSPORTATION

Getting around San Diego County is pretty simple if you have a car—most major attractions are within a few miles of the Pacific Ocean. The neighborhoods are connected via highways, limited light-rail trolley, and the bus system.

Downtown San Diego is comprised of several smaller communities that you can easily get to by walking, driving, riding the bus, or hailing a taxi. If you drive, be prepared to navigate some one-way streets. You can often find metered street parking during the week or park your car in any number of public parking lots and garages. In the heart of the city, numbered streets run west to east and lettered streets run north to south. The business district around the Civic Center at 1st Avenue and C Street is dedicated to local government and commerce.

■TIP➔ Ask the local tourist board about hotel and local transportation packages that include tickets to major museum exhibits or other special events.

■ BY AIR

Flying time to San Diego is 5 hours from New York, 3½ hours from Chicago, 3½ hours from Dallas, and 45 minutes from Los Angeles.

Coastal fog at San Diego International Airport can delay landings and takeoffs, and a delayed flight or two can jam the small boarding areas. During inclement weather call your airline or visit www.san.org to see if there are delays.

■TIP➔ If you travel frequently, look into the TSA's Registered Traveler program. The program, which is still being tested in several U.S. airports, is designed to cut down on gridlock at security checkpoints by allowing prescreened travelers to pass quickly through kiosks that scan an iris and/or a fingerprint. How sci-fi is that?

Airlines & Airports Airline and Airport Links.com (⊕www.airlineandairportlinks.com) has links to many of the world's airlines and airports.

Airline Security Issues Transportation Security Administration (⊕www.tsa.gov) has answers for almost every question that might come up.

Air Travel Resources in San Diego San Diego International Airport (⊕www.san.org) has flight status updates, airport terminal maps, and driving directions.

AIRPORTS

The major airport is San Diego International Airport, called Lindbergh Field locally. The airport's three-letter code is SAN. Major airlines depart and arrive at Terminal 1 (east) and Terminal 2 (west); commuter flights identified on your ticket with a 3000-sequence flight number depart from a third terminal, the commuter terminal. A red shuttle bus provides free transportation between terminals.

With only one runway serving two main terminals, San Diego's airport is too small to accommodate the heavy traffic of busy travel periods. Small problems including fog and rain can cause congested terminals and flight delays. Delays of 20–30 minutes in baggage claim are not unusual.

If you need travel assistance at the airport, note that there are two Travelers Aid information booths, one in Terminal 1 and one in Terminal 2, open daily 8 AM–11 PM.

Most international flights depart from and arrive at the Los Angeles International Airport (LAX); both American Eagle and United Express have frequent flights between LAX and San Diego. Ground shuttle service is available between LAX and San Diego.

Flight delays at San Diego International Airport don't necessarily mean hours of boredom. The airport's Cultural Exhibits Program in Terminal 2 showcases a variety of stimulating and educational exhibits that highlight the city's cultural history and diversity. Exhibits change several times per year. Terminal 2 also features jazz performances between 7 PM and 9:15 PM on the second Friday of each month.

If you have several hours of flight delay, consider catching a 10-minute cab ride downtown to go shopping or take one last stroll around the city.

■ TIP→ Long layovers don't have to be only about sitting around or shopping. These days they can be about burning off vacation calories. Check out www.airportgyms.com for lists of health clubs that are in or near many U.S. and Canadian airports.

Airport Information San Diego International Airport (☎619/400-2400 ⊕www. san.org).

GROUND TRANSPORTATION

San Diego International Airport is 3 mi from downtown. Ground transportation services include shuttle vans, buses, and taxis. All services operate from the Transportation Plaza, reached via the skybridges from Terminals 1 and 2. The cheapest and sometimes most convenient shuttle is the Metropolitan Transit System's Flyer Route 992, red-and-blue-stripe buses that serve the terminals at 10- to 15-minute intervals between 5 AM and 1 AM. These buses have luggage racks and make a loop from the airport to downtown along Broadway to 9th Avenue and back, stopping frequently within walking distance of many hotels; they also connect with the San Diego Trolley, Amtrak, and the Coaster. The fare is $2.25, including transfer to local transit buses and the trolley, and you should have exact fare handy. If you're heading to North County, the Flyer can drop you off at the Santa Fe Depot, where you can take the Coaster commuter train as far north as Oceanside

for $4.00–$5.50. Of the various airport shuttles, only Cloud 9 has tie-downs for wheelchairs; however, Access Shuttle can provide curbside service if requested in advance.

Limousine rates vary and are per hour, per mile, or both, with some minimums established.

Taxi fare is $10 plus tip to most downtown hotels. Fare to Coronado runs about $16 plus tip.

Major car-rental agencies have outlets near the airport; use the courtesy phones in the baggage claim areas of Terminals 1 and 2. Agency shuttles cruise the airport continuously and pick you up at the islands outside the terminals to take you to their rental locations. If you rent a car at the airport, take Harbor Drive east to reach downtown, or west to reach Shelter Island and Point Loma. To access I–5 and I–8 to go north or east, take Harbor Drive east to Laurel, follow signs to northbound freeway entrance; follow I–5 North to I–8 East. You can reach La Jolla and North County via I–5 North. Interstate 8 East leads to Hotel Circle, Fashion Valley, Mission Valley, and Qualcomm Stadium. To reach Mission Bay, continue on Nimitz Boulevard, which intersects with Sunset Cliffs Boulevard. To get to Coronado, take Harbor Drive east and turn left on Grape Street to reach I–5 South. Take the Highway 75 exit to cross the San Diego–Coronado Bridge.

Contacts Cloud 9 Shuttle (☎800/974-8885 ⊕www.cloud9shuttle.com). **Coronado Livery** (☎619/435-6310). **Five Star** (☎619/294-3300 or 866/281-4288 ⊕www.fivestarshuttle. com). **San Diego Transit** (☎619/233-3004, 619/234-5005 TTY and TDD ⊕www.sdcommute.com).

FLIGHTS

All major and some regional U.S. carriers serve San Diego International Airport. Aero Mexico and Air Canada are the only international carriers to San Diego. All others require a connecting flight, usually

San Diego by Boat

BOAT/FERRY LINE	Coronado Ferry	San Diego Bay Ferry	Water Taxi
FREQUENCY	Every hour 9 AM to 9 PM	Every hour from 10 AM to 10 PM	On call daily from 3 PM to 10 PM
TRAVEL TIME	15 minutes	15 minutes	10 minutes
COST	$2 each way; 50 cents more for bikes	$6 round trip; $7 with a bike	$7 each way
PHONE	619/234-4111	800/442-7847	619/235-8294
WEB	www.coronado.ca.us/sd_ferry.asp	www.sdhe.com/san-diego-bay-ferry.html	www.sdhe.com/san-diego-water-taxi.html

in Los Angeles. Other connection points are Chicago, Dallas, and San Francisco.

Airline Contacts AeroMexico (☎800/237-6639 ⊕www.aeromexico.com). **Air Canada** (☎888/247-2262 ⊕www.aircanada.com). **Alaska Airlines** (☎800/252-7522 ⊕www.alaskaair.com). **American Airlines** (☎800/433-7300 ⊕www.aa.com). **ATA** (☎800/435-9282 or 317/282-8308 ⊕www.ata.com). **Continental Airlines** (☎800/523-3273 for U.S. and Mexico reservations, 800/231-0856 for international reservations ⊕www.continental.com). **Delta Airlines** (☎800/221-1212 for U.S. reservations, 800/241-4141 for international reservations ⊕www.delta.com). **jetBlue** (☎800/538-2583 ⊕www.jetblue.com). **Northwest Airlines** (☎800/225-2525 ⊕www.nwa.com). **Southwest Airlines** (☎800/435-9792 ⊕www.southwest.com). **United Airlines** (☎800/864-8331 for U.S. reservations, 800/538-2929 for international reservations ⊕www.united.com). **USAirways** (☎800/428-4322 for U.S. and Canada reservations, 800/622-1015 for international reservations ⊕www.usairways.com).

Regional & Smaller Airlines Frontier Airlines (☎800/432-1359 ⊕www.frontierairlines.com). **Hawaiian Airlines** (☎800/367-5320 ⊕www.hawaiianair.com). **Midwest Airlines** (☎800/452-2022 ⊕www.midwestairlines.com). **Sun Country Airlines** (☎800/359-6786 ⊕www.suncountry.com). **WestJet** (☎888/937-8538 ⊕www.westjet.com).

❚ BY BOAT

If you're arriving in San Diego by private boat, keep in mind that many hotels, marinas, and yacht clubs rent slips short-term. Call ahead, because available space is limited. The San Diego and Southwestern yacht clubs have reciprocal arrangements with other yacht clubs.

The small Coronado ferry is a reminder of the pre-San Diego–Coronado Bridge days when ferries provided regular transportation between Coronado and downtown. Now it's a small excursion service that is fun to ride, but not often used as a practical transportation method. The San Diego Bay Ferry also takes you between downtown and Coronado in a nostalgic, old-school ferry, and the Water Taxi is a great alternative for nighttime transit.

Marinas Best Western Island Palms Hotel & Marina (☎619/223-0301). **The Dana on Mission Bay** (☎619/222-6440). **Kona Kai Resort** (☎619/224-7547). **San Diego Marriott Hotel and Marina** (☎619/230-8955). **San Diego Yacht Club** (☎619/221-8400). **Southwestern Yacht Club** (☎619/222-0438).

❚ BY BUS

Almost all Greyhound service to San Diego is via Los Angeles, an approximately 2½-hour ride; there are about two dozen round-trips daily between the two cities. There are also a few buses a day direct from Phoenix and Las Vegas, not routed through Los Angeles. The Grey-hound terminal is downtown at Broadway and 1st Avenue, a block from the Civic Center trolley station.

One-way fare to Los Angeles is $16.50 (weekday) or $17.50 (weekend), round-trip is $28 or $29. You can buy Greyhound tickets in advance by phone or at the terminal.

San Diego County is served by a coordinated, efficient network of bus and rail routes that includes service to Oceanside in the north, the Mexican border at San Ysidro, and points east to the Anza-Borrego Desert. Under the umbrella of the Metropolitan Transit System, there are two major transit agencies: San Diego Transit and North County Transit District (NCTD). The staff at the downtown Transit Store sells passes and can help plan your travel.

Almost all stops on the San Diego Trolley light-rail system connect with a San Diego Transit bus route. NCTD routes connect with Coaster commuter train routes between Oceanside and the Santa Fe Depot in San Diego. They serve points from Del Mar North to San Clemente, inland to Fallbrook, Pauma Valley, Valley Center, Ramona, and Escondido, with transfer points within the city of San Diego. NCTD also offers special express-bus service to Qualcomm Stadium for select major sporting events.

San Diego Transit fares range from $1 to $4; North County Transit District fares are $1.75. Discounted fares are available for seniors and for people with disabilities. The Transit Store sells packets of discounted universal tokens that can be used interchangeably on buses and the trolley. Most transfers are free; request one when boarding. Schedules are posted at each stop, and the buses usually are on time.

You must have exact change in coins and/or bills. Pay upon boarding.

Also see ⇨ By Trolley.

Bus Information Greyhound (☎619/515–1100 ⊕www.greyhound.com). **North County Transit District** (☎800/266–6883 ⊕www.sdcommute.com). **San Diego Transit** (☎619/233–3004, 619/234–5005 TTY and TDD ⊕www.sdcommute.com). **Transit Store** (☎619/234–1060).

▌BY CAR

When traveling in the San Diego area, it pays to consider the big picture to avoid getting lost. Water lies to the west of the city. To the east and north, mountains separate the urban areas from the desert. Interstate 5, which stretches from Canada to the Mexican border, bisects San Diego. Interstate 8 provides access from Yuma, Arizona, and points east. Drivers coming from Nevada and the mountain regions beyond can reach San Diego on I–15. During rush hour there are jams on I–5 and on I–15 between I–805 and Escondido.

There are Border Inspection stations along the major highways in San Diego County. For this reason, it's best to travel with your driver's license, or passport if you're an international traveler, in case you're asked to pull into one.

GASOLINE

The cost of gas varies widely depending on location, oil company, and whether you use the full-serve or self-serve aisle. Prices on the West Coast tend to be higher than those in the rest of the country, and in San Diego prices run about 15% higher than in many other California cities.

PARKING

Balboa Park and Mission Bay have huge free parking lots and it's rare not to find a space, though it may seem as if you've parked miles from your destination. The once-plentiful lots downtown have disappeared as a result of the opening of PETCO Park in 2004 and the construction of hotels surrounding the ball field. On game day, expect to pay $17 or more for a short walk to the stadium, less for a longer one. Other downtown lots cost $5–$35 per day. The Web site of the Gaslamp Quarter Association maps currently open lots and shares parking secrets (www.gaslamp.org). Old Town has large lots surrounding the Transit Center. Parking is more of a problem in La Jolla and Coronado, where you generally need to rely on hard-to-find street spots or expensive by-the-hour parking lots.

Parking at meters costs $2 an hour; enforcement is 8 AM–6 PM except Sunday. Be extra careful around rush hour, when certain street-parking areas become tow-away zones. In the evenings and during events it can be difficult to locate parking spaces downtown. Parking violations in congested areas can cost you $25 or more. Car renters are liable for any parking tickets and towing charges they incur.

ROAD CONDITIONS
Highways are generally in good condition in the San Diego area. Traffic is particularly heavy on I–5, I–8, I–805, and I–15 during morning and afternoon rush hours, 6–8:30 AM and 3:30–6 PM. Before venturing into the mountains, check on road conditions; mountain driving can be dangerous. Listen to radio traffic reports for information on the length of lines waiting to cross the border into Mexico. For roadside assistance, dial 511 from a mobile phone.

▌BY TAXI

Taxis departing from the airport are subject to regulated fares—all companies charge the same rate ($1.90 for the first mile, $2.30 for each additional mile). Fares on other routes, including the ride back to the airport, vary among companies. If you call ahead and ask for the flat rate ($8), you'll get it; otherwise you'll be charged by the mile (which works out to $9 or so). Taxi stands are at shopping centers and hotels; otherwise you must call and reserve a cab. The companies listed below do not serve all areas of San Diego County. If you're going someplace other than downtown, ask if the company serves that area.

Taxi Companies Orange Cab (☎619/291–3333 ⊕www.orangecabsandiego.com). **Silver Cabs** (☎619/280–5555). **Yellow Cab** (☎619/234–6161 ⊕www.driveu.com).

▌BY TRAIN

Amtrak serves downtown San Diego's Santa Fe Depot with daily trains to and from Los Angeles, Santa Barbara, and San Luis Obispo. Connecting service to Oakland, Seattle, Chicago, Texas, Florida, and points beyond is available in Los Angeles. Amtrak trains stop in San Diego North County at Solana Beach and Oceanside. You can obtain Amtrak timetables at any Amtrak station, or by visiting the Amtrak Web site.

Coaster commuter trains, which run between Oceanside and San Diego Monday–Saturday, stop at the same stations as Amtrak plus others. Frequency is about every half hour during the weekday rush hour, with four trains on Saturday (and occasional Friday evening northbound service from downtown). One-way fares are $4.00 to $5.50, depending on the distance traveled. The Oceanside, Carlsbad, and Solana Beach stations have beach access. You can pick up Coaster flyers or brochures with detailed itineraries for each stop, including walking directions and connections to local bus service. Trains are typically on time.

Metrolink operates high-speed rail service between the Oceanside Transit Center and Union Station in Los Angeles.

Amtrak and the Coaster vending machines accept all major credit cards. Metrolink requires cash.

Many Amtrak trains require advance reservations, especially for long-distance transcontinental routes. Reservations, which you can make online, are suggested for trains running on weekends between San Diego and Santa Barbara. For security reasons, Amtrak requires ticket purchasers to appear in person with photo ID.

Information Amtrak (☎800/872-7245 ⊕www.amtrak.com). **Coaster** (☎800/266-6883 ⊕www.sdcommute.com). **Metrolink** (☎800/371-5465 ⊕www.metrolinktrains. com). **Oceanside Train Station** (☎760/722-4622 ⊕www.sdcommute.com). **Santa Fe Depot** (☎619/239-9021). **Solana Beach Amtrak Station** (☎858/259-2697).

∎ BY TROLLEY

The bright-orange trolleys of the San Diego Trolley light-rail system serve downtown San Diego, Mission Valley, Old Town, South Bay, the U.S. border, and East County. The trolleys operate seven days a week from about 5 AM to midnight, depending on the station, at intervals of about 15 minutes. The trolley system connects with San Diego Transit bus routes—bus connections are posted at each trolley station. Bicycle lockers are available at most. Trolleys can get crowded during morning and evening rush hours. On-time performance is excellent.

San Diego Trolley tickets are priced according to the number of stations traveled, beginning at $1.25 for travel within the downtown area and rising to $1.50 for one station, $1.75 for two stations, and up to $3 for 20 stations. Within the downtown area, tickets are good for two hours of unlimited travel in any direction from the time of purchase. Beyond the downtown area they are good for two hours, but for one-way travel only. Round-trip tickets are double the one-way fare. Tickets are dispensed from self-service ticket machines at each stop; exact fare in coins is recommended, although some machines accept bills in $1, $5, $10, and $20 denominations. Transfers between buses and/or the trolley are free or require an upgrade if the second fare is higher.

Day Tripper passes, available for one, two, three, or four days ($5, $9, $12, and $15, respectively), give unlimited rides on regional buses and the San Diego Trolley. They may be purchased from most trolley vending machines, at the Transit Store, and at some hotels.

Trolley Information San Diego Transit (☎619/233-3004, 619/234-5005 TTY and TDD ⊕www.sdcommute.com) for city transit and San Diego Trolley.

ON THE GROUND

▮ CUSTOMS & DUTIES

You're always allowed to bring goods of a certain value back home without having to pay any duty or import tax. But there's a limit on the amount of tobacco and liquor you can bring back duty-free, and some countries have separate limits for perfumes; for exact figures, check with your customs department. The values of so-called duty-free goods are included in these amounts. When you shop abroad, save all your receipts, as customs inspectors may ask to see them as well as the items you purchased. If the total value of your goods is more than the duty-free limit, you'll have to pay a tax (most often a flat percentage) on the value of everything beyond that limit.

If you make a shopping trip to Mexico, keep receipts for all purchases. Upon reentering the country, be ready to show customs officials what you've bought. Pack purchases together in an easily accessible place. If you think a duty is incorrect, appeal the assessment. If you object to the way your clearance was handled, note the inspector's badge number. In either case, first ask to see a supervisor. If the problem isn't resolved, write to the appropriate authorities, beginning with the port director at your point of entry.

Customs officers operate at the San Ysidro border crossing, at San Diego International Airport, and in the bay at Shelter Island.

U.S. Information U.S. Customs and Border Protection (⊕www.cbp.gov).

▮ DAY TOURS & GUIDES

Pedal your way around San Diego with Bike Tours San Diego. Daytripper and Five Star Tours are motor-coach companies that do one-day or multiple-day excursions to attractions in Southern California and Baja Mexico. San Diego Scenic Tours does narrated tours of San Diego and Tijuana, Mexico. Secret San Diego, by Where Tours, offers tours of places off the beaten path.

Recommended Tours/Guides Bike Tours San Diego (☎619/238–2444 ⊕www.bike-tours.com). **Daytripper** (☎619/299–5777 or 800/679–8747 ⊕www.daytripper.com). **Five Star Tours** (☎619/232–5040 or 800/553–8687 ⊕www.efivestartours.com). **San Diego Scenic Tours** (☎858/273–8687 ⊕www.sandiegoscenictours.com). **Secret San Diego** (☎619/917–6037 ⊕www.wheretours.com).

BOAT TOURS

San Diego Harbor Excursion and Hornblower Cruises & Events both operate one- and two-hour harbor cruises departing from the Broadway Pier. No reservations are necessary for the tours, which cost $16–$23; both companies also do dinner cruises ($65–$85) and brunch cruises. Classic Sailing Adventures, at Shelter Island Marina, has afternoon and evening cruises of the harbor and San Diego Bay aboard six-passenger sailing ships ($65 per person). These companies also operate during whale-watching season, from mid-December to mid-March. Other fishing boats that do whale watches in season include H&M Landing and Seaforth Boat Rentals.

Information Classic Sailing Adventures (☎800/659–0141 ⊕www.classicsailingadventures.com). **H&M Landing** (☎619/222–1144 ⊕www.hmlanding.com). **Hornblower Cruises & Events** (☎619/234–8687 or 800/668–4322 ⊕www.hornblower.com). **San Diego Harbor Excursion** (☎619/234–4111 or 800/442–7847 ⊕www.sdhe.com). **Seaforth Sportfishing** (☎619/223–1681 ⊕www.seaforthboatrental.com).

BUS & TROLLEY TOURS

Free two-hour bus tours of the downtown redevelopment area, including the Gaslamp Quarter, are conducted by the

Centre City Development Corporation, the agency in charge of redevelopment. Tours take place on the first and third Saturday of the month at 10 AM and noon and leave from the agency's Downtown Information Center. Advance reservations are necessary, as the tour may be canceled if there aren't enough passengers.

Gray Line San Diego provides narrated sightseeing tours, picking up passengers at many hotels; the selection includes daily morning and afternoon city tours ($32 for adults, plus a possible fuel surcharge), tours to the San Diego Zoo, Wild Animal Park, SeaWorld, and Legoland California, and trips to Tijuana, Rosarito, and Ensenada. Old Town Trolley Tours takes you to ten sites including Old Town, Seaport Village, Horton Plaza and the Gaslamp Quarter, Coronado, the San Diego Zoo, and El Prado in Balboa Park. The tour is narrated, and for the price of the ticket ($30 for adults and $15 for children 4–12; under 4, free) you can get on and off as you please at any stop. The trolley leaves every 30 minutes, operates daily, and takes two hours to make a full loop. The Old Town Trolley Tour is included in the price of the San Diego Passport, along with one Hornblower cruise, admission to the San Diego Zoo, the Maritime Museum, the San Diego Museum of Art, and other goodies for a total package price of $79. The passport is available at visitor centers and is good for one year.

Information Centre City Development Corporation Downtown Information Center (☎619/235–2222 ⊕www.ccdc.com). **Gray Line San Diego** (☎800/331–5077 ⊕www. sandiegograyline.com). **Old Town Trolley Tours** (☎619/298–8687 ⊕www.trolleytours. com).

WALKING TOURS

Several fine walking tours are available on weekdays or weekends; upcoming walks are usually listed in the Thursday "Night and Day" section of the *San Diego Union-Tribune*. Coronado Walk-

ing Tours offers an easy 90-minute stroll ($12, Tuesday, Thursday, Saturday at 11 AM) through Coronado's historic district with departures from the Glorietta Bay Inn. Make reservations. On Saturday at 10 AM and 11:30 AM, Offshoot Tours conducts free, hour-long walks through Balboa Park that focus on history, palm trees, and desert vegetation. Urban Safaris, led by long-time San Diego resident Patty Fares, are two-hour-long Saturday walks ($10) through interesting neighborhoods such as Hillcrest, Ocean Beach, and Point Loma. The tours, which always depart from a neighborhood coffeehouse, focus on art, history, and ethnic eateries. Reservations are required. The Gaslamp Quarter Historical Foundation leads two-hour historical walking tours of the downtown historic district on Saturday at 11 AM ($10).

Information Coronado Walking Tours (☎619/435–5993). **Gaslamp Quarter Historical Foundation** (☎619/233–4692 ⊕www.gaslampquarter.org). **Offshoot Tours** (☎619/239–0512 ⊕www.balboapark.org). **Urban Safaris** (☎619/944–9255 ⊕www. walkingtoursofsandiego.com).

▌ MONEY

With its mild climate and proximity to the ocean and mountains, it's no wonder that San Diego is a relatively expensive place to visit. Three-star rooms average between $200 and $280 per night in high season, but there is also a good variety of modest accommodations available. Meal prices compare to those in other large cities, and you can usually find excellent values by dining in smaller, family-run establishments. Admission to local attractions can cost anywhere from $10 to $60. Thankfully, relaxing on one of the public beaches or meandering through the parks and neighborhoods is free—and fun.

Prices throughout this guide are given for adults. Substantially reduced fees are almost always available for children, students, and senior citizens.

CREDIT CARDS

Throughout this guide, the following abbreviations are used: **AE,** American Express; **D,** Discover; **DC,** Diners Club; **MC,** MasterCard; and **V,** Visa.

It's a good idea to inform your credit-card company before you travel. Otherwise, the credit-card company might put a hold on your card owing to unusual activity—not a good thing halfway through your trip. Record all your credit-card numbers—as well as the phone numbers to call if your cards are lost or stolen—in a safe place, so you're prepared should something go wrong. Both MasterCard and Visa have general numbers you can call if your card is lost, but you're better off calling the number of your issuing bank, since MasterCard and Visa usually just transfer you to your bank; your bank's number is usually printed on your card.

Reporting Lost Cards American Express (☎800/528–4800 ⊕www.americanexpress. com). **Diners Club** (☎800/234–6377 ⊕www. dinersclub.com). **Discover** (☎800/347–2683 ⊕www.discovercard.com). **MasterCard** (☎800/622–7747 ⊕www.mastercard.com). **Visa** (☎800/847–2911 ⊕www.visa.com).

TRAVELER'S CHECKS & CARDS

Some consider this the currency of the caveman, and it's true that fewer establishments accept traveler's checks these days. Nevertheless, they're a cheap and secure way to carry extra money, particularly on trips to urban areas. Both Citibank (under the Visa brand) and American Express issue traveler's checks in the United States, but Amex is better known and more widely accepted; you can also avoid hefty surcharges by cashing Amex checks at Amex offices. Whatever you do, keep track of all the serial numbers in case the checks are lost or stolen.

Contacts American Express (☎888/412–6945 ⊕www.americanexpress.com).

∎ SAFETY

San Diego is generally a safe place for travelers who observe all normal precautions. Dress inconspicuously, remove badges when leaving convention areas, know the routes to your destination before you set out. At the beach, check with lifeguards about any unsafe conditions such as dangerous rip tides or water pollution. The San Diego Convention & Visitors Bureau publishes a Visitor Safety Tips brochure listing normal precautions for many situations. It's available at the International Visitor Information Center.

∎TIP➜ **Distribute your cash, credit cards, IDs, and other valuables between a deep front pocket, an inside jacket or vest pocket, and a hidden money pouch. Don't reach for the money pouch once you're in public.**

∎ TAXES

In San Diego County a sales tax of 7.75% is added to the price of all goods, except food purchased at a grocery store or as takeout from a restaurant. Hotel taxes are 9%–13%.

INDEX

Photo Credits:. 6 and 7 (left), Richard Cummins/viestiphoto.com. 7 (right), Jeff Greenberg/age fotostock. 8, Johnny Stockshooter/age fotostock. 9 (left), Corbis. 9 (right) and 12, Richard Cummins/viestiphoto. com. 13, Jeff Greenberg/age fotostock. 15 (left and right), Corbis. 17 (left), Richard Cummins/viestiphoto.com. 17 (right) John W. Warden/age fotostock.18, Joe Viesti/viestiphoto.com. 19 (left), Doug Scott/age fotostock. 19 (right), Werner Bollmann/age fotostock. 21 (left and right), Corbis. **Chapter 1: Exploring San Diego:** 28, Artifan/Shutterstock. 39, Joanne DiBona.

NOTES

ABOUT OUR WRITERS

A Chicago native, Maria C. Hunt could only name one favorite restaurant when she moved to San Diego 14 years ago; now her list spans pages. Maria was the restaurant critic and food writer for the *San Diego Union Tribune* for 10 years and her freelance work has appeared in *Cooking Light, Saveur, The New York Times,* and *Riviera* magazine. Her first book: *The Bubbly Bar: 57 Champagne and Sparkling Wine Cocktails for Every Occasion* will be released in Summer 2009. Maria also updated our hotel coverage.

As a freelance journalist and author, Marlise Elizabeth Kast has contributed to more than 50 publications including *Forbes, Surfer, San Diego Magazine,* and the *New York Post.* Her passion for traveling has taken her to 60 countries and short-term residency in Switzerland, Dominican Republic, Spain, and Costa Rica. Now based in San Diego, Marlise is currently working on her fourth book. For this book, she updated our Exploring chapter.

Tanja Kern delights in diving into Southern California culture: from its breezy beaches and boardwalks to trend-setting restaurants and rich historical districts. She lived in "America's Finest City" for several years before relocating to Southwestern Missouri, but her heart still calls San Diego home. Along with our Essentials chapter, Tanja also writes travel and lifestyle pieces for *American Airlines, Better Homes & Gardens,* and *Woman's Day.*

Amanda Knoles has explored many cities in her 15 years as a travel writer, but San Diego tops her list for favorite weekend getaway. As a contributing writer for Citysearch.com, she has explored all the city's major malls and boutiques, making her the perfect writer to update our shopping chapter. She's also written *Las Vegas Shop: Great Shopping Wherever You Are.*

A native of "Alta" California, Coco Krumme has traveled extensively in Mexico and Latin America, so updating our Tijuana coverage was no problem for her at all. She lived in Argentina while working as a journalist for the *Buenos Aires Herald,* and recently co-authored the *Fearless Critic* restaurant guide to Washington, D.C.

Raised in the OC and gratefully relocated to San Diego as a teen, Jane Onstott has had 30-plus years to become an expert on her adopted county's beaches, from Oceanside to Imperial Beach. An editor and translator as well as freelance writer, Jane's written several books, including *National Geographic Traveler Mexico* and *Fodor's Puerto Vallarta.*

College lured L.A.-born AnnaMaria Stephens south to San Diego some 15 years ago. The weather and laidback lifestyle made it impossible for her to leave. AnnaMaria writes about all the things she loves—music, art, and nightlife—for *San Diego CityBeat* and *Riviera* magazine. It was a no-brainer that she write about what's hot with San Diego's party people and culturati in the nightlife and arts chapter. She also mapped out the perfect San Diego vacation in our front of book section.

Longtime Southern Californian Bobbi Zane lives in the mountain hamlet of Julian, making her the perfect person to update our North County chapter. Bobbi's byline has appeared in the *Los Angeles Times,* the *Los Angeles Daily News, Westways* magazine, and the *Orange County Register.*